**Formal Approaches to Computing and
Information Technology**

T0137820

Springer
*London
Berlin
Heidelberg
New York
Barcelona
Hong Kong
Milan
Paris
Singapore
Tokyo*

Hung Dang Van, Chris George,
Tomasz Janowski and Richard Moore (Eds)

Specification Case Studies in RAISE

Springer

Hung Dang Van, PhD
Chris George, MA
Tomasz Janowski, MSc, PhD
The United Nations University International Institute for Software Technology
(UNU/IIST), PO Box 3058, Macau, China

Richard Moore, MA, PhD
IFAD A/S, Forskerparken 10, 5230 Odense M, Denmark

Series Editor
Professor S.A. Schuman, BSc, DEA, CEng

British Library Cataloguing in Publication Data
Specification case studies in RAISE. – (Formal approaches
   to computing and information technology)
   1. Software engineering
   I. Dang Van, Hung
   005.1
ISBN 1852333596

Library of Congress Cataloging-in-Publication Data
A catalog record for this book is available from the Library of Congress

FACIT series ISSN 1431-9683
ISBN 1-85233-359-6 Springer-Verlag London Berlin Heidelberg
a member of BertelsmannSpringer Science+Business Media GmbH
http://www.springer.co.uk

Typesetting: Camera ready by editors
Printed and bound at the Athenæum Press Ltd., Gateshead, Tyne & Wear
34/3830-543210 Printed on acid-free paper SPIN 10776873

Foreword

Before software can be designed one must have a fair understanding of its requirements. Before requirements can be formulated one must have a reasonable understanding of the domain of application into which the required software is to be inserted. In order to have any trust in software it must be possible to prove (perhaps abstractions of) properties of that software. Such proofs are then with respect to the requirements and the assumptions expressed in the domain descriptions.

The present book illustrates that understanding of the domain, formulations of the requirements, and the architectural design of the software can be expressed as a sequence of mathematically (possibly proof) related indicative, putative, respectively imperative specifications.

What is new in this book is the insistence on both informally and formally describing the domain, and the insistence that functional requirements be strongly (possibly proof) related to, including somehow rigorously "derived" from the domain description.

This book has been produced by the staff and fellows of the United Nations University's (UNU's) International Institute for Software Technology, UNU/IIST, located in Macau, near Hong Kong, and its publication coincides with UNU/IIST's 10th anniversary in 2002. UNU/IIST has, in its software engineering research and post-graduate training group, practised the above dogma: (i) researched possible method principles, techniques and tools, (ii) propagated these through courses around the world, on four continents: Africa, South America, Asia and Eastern Europe, and (iii) applied the dogmas in around 50 explorative software development projects of various sizes and durations with over 100 post-graduate Fellows from around 30 countries from these continents and regions. This book offers you a sample of parts of these projects. But the chapters of this book illustrate far more than just the domain/requirements/software design spectrum: As carefully surveyed in the Thematic Introduction, the case studies detail uses of formal techniques that go beyond the software development triptych spectrum.

Thus the United Nations has offered something quite unique. I believe it is fair to say that UNU/IIST, given its modest size, has had a rather significant impact in these approximately 30 countries. I believe it is fair to say that few research and training institutes anywhere in the world, sizewise, can offer a track record as successful as that of UNU/IIST. But then, of course, I am not exactly the most trustworthy person to say so. I was, after all, the founding and first UN Director of UNU/IIST: Designated in May 1991, and active in Macau 2 July 1992–1 July 1997. So, obviously I am biased. But try me out. And I believe you will come to agree.

UNU/IIST is more than its software engineering research, courses and explorative projects. UNU/IIST also has a similar sized computer science research and post-graduate training group. It was and is the close collaboration between and co-existence of these two groups that really explains the success of UNU/IIST. Altogether more than 170 between three and twelve month post-graduate Fellows have been trained at UNU/IIST since 1992. Many now are senior professors at their home universities in most of these 30 or so countries. Again, I believe that no other university computing science and software engineering department, sizewise, can register such an impact as can UNU/IIST. We are many who are grateful to the three donors, Macau, Portugal and China, and to the UN University, to have made this possible. But we are equally positively amazed at the kind, open-minded reception that UNU/IIST always received, in each of these approximately 30 countries.

Most ordinary university computer science and software engineering departments are, by necessity, obliged to cover a full curriculum spectrum of computer science and software engineering topics in order believably to furnish comprehensive Masters' degrees. UNU/IIST was and is in the enviable position to have been able to focus on what its staff, its always forthcoming Board, as well as the UNU Council, judged important focal points.

These were, as you can now gather, twofold: first, formal programming methodological techniques: specification and verification of software in the light of the triptych dogma of domain engineering, requirements engineering and software design – as are amply illustrated in this book; and second, computer science research into specification and verification techniques and tools for the development of real-time, safety critical embedded systems, notably around the paradigm of Duration Calculi, a set of calculi based on interval temporal logics for reasoning about functions of time. It was and is this focus that has enabled, and enables, UNU/IIST to have an enviable track record, in addition to what has already been mentioned, in publications at international conferences and in international journals.

You will be truly amazed to study this collection of widely different applications of formal software engineering techniques. You may even be surprised to observe that it has been done by young Fellows from developing countries, including countries in transition. I tell you, there is no end to the talent, the eagerness and the hard work that these Fellows and their countries can muster. To me it was and is a constant source of joy to have served as the head of UNU/IIST from 1991 to 1997. That satisfaction is multiplied severalfold when now, more than four years after my return to Denmark, I witness that my successor, my dear friend Professor Zhou Chaochen, has continued, refined and thus further strengthened the line of research and training he and I set out in 1991–1992. We set out to prove that a first rank research and post-graduate training centre could indeed be established in less than five years in an unlikely place such as Macau. This book bears strong, positive witness to our effort.

Without dear scientific colleagues and visitors, without our Fellows, and without a dear and wonderfully dedicated administrative staff this would not have been possible. I am especially indebted to the editors (and co-authors) of this book: Not only for their work in co-authoring and editing this book, but for years of unselfish collaboration.

Dines Bjørner
Holte, Denmark, October 2001

This foreword is dedicated to the late António Rodrigues Júnior

Contents

1. Thematic Introduction

Formal methods have grown out of their infancy: firm foundations are established, a variety of languages are available to describe specifications at different levels of abstraction, and methods and calculi exist to guide development of specifications into correct programs, supported by a wide range of tools. There is also a growing number of well-documented experience reports and case studies which present stories and analyses of both successful and less successful applications. A further evidence for maturing of formal methods is their increasing presence in industrial, large-scale software development. Faced with realistic expectations, they become integrated into the industrial software development process in such a way as to complement, not replace, traditional methods of software design and analysis.

The purpose of this book is to present our experience in developing and applying formal specifications. The book describes 12 case studies which use RAISE – Rigorous Approach to Industrial Software Engineering – to construct, analyse, develop and apply formal specifications. The case studies present a wide range of application areas: authentication of communications protocols, error detection in programs, geographic information systems, library management, multi-lingual documents, production planning, run-time verification, software design patterns, software reuse, taxation management, telephony, and travel planning. Most have little or nothing to do with safety-critical systems, traditionally considered as the area in which formal methods are most applicable, and many of them do not involve verification. The cases studies illustrate diverse uses of formal specifications: to capture requirements for new software, to carry out software development from requirements, to formalise algorithms in order to prove their correctness, to check if software behaves correctly at run-time, to build models of application domains, to relate descriptive and prescriptive models, to formalise notations for software development, and various other uses. They also try to put the task of creating formal specifications into perspective, asking questions about the purpose, scope and use of the formal models before the models are built.

The case study chapters have each been written by one of this book's editors. Each case study describes work done at the United Nations University's International Institute for Software Technology (UNU/IIST) in Macau by that editor in collaboration with "fellows" – lecturers or post-graduate students – from developing countries. Each case study chapter concludes with information about the fellows involved, the relevant UNU/IIST technical report(s), and other related work.

This introduction consists of six sections. Section 1.1 describes some factors promoting the application of formal specifications in industry. Section 1.2 presents some paradigms for software development which require the use of formal or semi-formal specifications. Section 1.3 gives a high-level overview of specification languages, development methods and tools. It concludes with a summary description of RAISE. Sections 1.4 and 1.5 contain respectively an overview of the case studies in the book and a discussion of several themes recurring throughout these case studies. Finally, Section 1.6 describes the lessons learned from the case studies. A more detailed technical introduction to the RAISE language and method is given in Chapter 2.

1.1 Specifications in Industry

There is growing evidence that formal specifications are affecting, directly or indirectly, the practice of industrial software development. Many concepts that arose from work on program semantics and logic, and on formal specification and verification, can now be found in textbooks on software engineering and program development, and even implemented in higher-order programming languages and program generators. Such concepts include abstract data-types, pre- and post-conditions, symbolic evaluation, invariants, run-time assertions, state-space analysis, and many others.

There are several factors that may explain this trend:

- First and foremost, there is a growing number of applications with minimal or zero tolerance for failures due to software design errors. These include avionics, industrial process control, medical monitoring and diagnosis, space exploration, banking and finance, security, and so on.
- Second, there are well-publicised social, environmental and economic consequences of design errors in electronic products, including hardware and software. This in turn is causing growing social awareness and concern and hence pressure on governments and organisations to take corrective action.
- Third, regulatory and standards organisations have consequently taken a more active stance on setting and enforcing quality standards for software and hardware vendors. Indeed, a number of these standards specifically advocate mathematical modelling, including the use of formal specifications and specification-based proofs.

These factors constitute the traditional arguments used to justify the development and use of formal specifications for safety critical systems. However, safety-critical systems constitute just a fraction of all applications.

Moreover, even though formal specifications make proofs of correctness possible, such proofs are typically very expensive in terms of the time, the expertise, and the tools required, and are very often infeasible to carry out in full. Model checking has developed as an alternative to proof, but there is still a problem in showing the models that can be checked to be correct abstractions of systems.

There are other practical applications of formal specifications where reliability is not of paramount importance or has to be considered along with other goals (e.g. productivity). Formal specifications can be used to generate test cases to gain some, albeit incomplete confidence in the correctness of unverified components or the satisfaction of unverified properties. Experience also shows that specifications can play a uniquely positive role in organizing the whole software process, especially when development involves collaboration within and between large teams. They can help people to decompose design problems, to propose, discuss and justify solutions, to allocate responsibility for carrying out development, to review and monitor progress, to integrate solutions to sub-problems, and so on. In addition, and by no means least important, a specification can act as a precise "contract" between software customers and software designers, to be used in discussions and negotiations.

This "lightweight" use of formal methods applies as much to the design of software systems in general as to the design of safety critical systems, as we hope the case studies in this book illustrate.

1.2 Specification-Based Development

The rapidly growing demand for software in general makes the economy of software production an issue of primary importance. This promotes new paradigms for software development and integration which have to employ formal or at least semi-formal specifications in some way. Some examples are:

Reuse In order to carry out software development from pre-existing components one has to describe what kind of functionality is needed in the new software and also to determine whether or not an existing component actually offers this functionality. To achieve this we need to associate some form of specifications with existing software components and to have a precise way of formulating queries which can use these specifications as the basis of the search process. Formality is needed to decide, with as high a level of confidence as possible and preferably automatically, whether a given component satisfies a query.

Interoperability This makes it possible for heterogeneous components, written in different programming languages, to interact with each other. We need specifications to describe such components in a way which is independent of their actual implementation language in order that they can be selected at design-time (static invocation) or retrieved at run-time (dynamic invocation). Formal specifications make full semantic integration possible, with the components sharing a common understanding of every concept they exchange.

Synthesis Software synthesis employs specifications to describe particular computational problems, for instance programming of an interactive user interface, control of an industrial robot, parsing of a context-free language, and presentation of lecture materials on-line. Specifications are used to formulate input to the synthesiser which generates software to solve the corresponding problem. Using formal specifications makes it possible to formalise the working of the generator itself, to describe its intended purpose and perhaps to verify its correctness with respect to this purpose, thus gaining confidence in its outputs.

Fault-tolerance Fault-tolerance is about building reliable systems from unreliable components. The system has to monitor the behaviour of its components in order to detect possible errors and respond accordingly by masking, recovery, reconfiguration or some other means. Specifications are needed to define what constitutes an error, to partition errors according to their severity, as well as to guide decisions about error recovery. They can also define the assumptions under which a system remains fault-tolerant. In order to carry out automatic error detection we need a formal definition of errors which can be used by error detection software.

This is not an all-inclusive list but it shows how different paradigms employ specifications and how they all need formal specifications in order to fully realise their potential to facilitate and improve software production.

1.3 Overview of Formal Methods

Another factor contributing to the growing interest in formal specifications is the existence of a large and growing number of languages, methods and tools that promote their application. This section presents a brief overview of the important features that distinguish different specification languages (Section 1.3.1), and development methods and tools (Section 1.3.2). It concludes with a summary description of RAISE (Section 1.3.3).

1.3.1 Specification Languages

Specification languages were traditionally divided into model-oriented or property-oriented languages. Model-oriented languages are based on concrete mathematical domains such as numbers, functions, sets and lists, and are generally considered to be more concrete, while property-oriented languages are based on axiomatic definitions and are more abstract.

Depending on the class of properties one would like to formulate and verify about specifications, semantics of specification languages can be defined in one of three styles: operational, denotational or axiomatic. In general, operational semantics is the most concrete and least suitable for carrying out proofs directly; denotational semantics is both abstract and well suited to proving various kinds of properties; axiomatic semantics is the most abstract but often limits the properties to conditional or unconditional equations.

Different specification languages also adopt different approaches to the use of variables. Applicative specifications prohibit the use of variables entirely because that makes the specification more abstract, therefore easier to validate, develop and verify. The use of variables is central to imperative specifications, as they try to be closer to an implementation. Some languages support both applicative and imperative specifications.

A further distinction is between state-based and action-based specifications. The former are generally used for specifying data-intensive systems, that is systems which possess a state (contents of all variables) and offer a range of operations for inspecting and modifying that state. The latter are particularly important for concurrent and distributed systems, which consist of a collection of essentially independent components which continuously interact with each other and with their environment. Rather than formalising a state explicitly, action-based specifications formalise state-changes which explicitly capture observable behaviour.

Action-based specifications can be based on linear or branching time, which represent system executions respectively as sequences or trees of actions. Branching time captures not just the ability of a system to carry out an action but also its refusal to perform an action, which in turn allows both deterministic and non-deterministic behaviours to be represented.

When several actions are performed concurrently, a specification may regard these as happening synchronously, as if driven by a global clock, or asynchronously, each action happening at its own time (according to local clocks). The former is more common for non-distributed systems, the latter for distributed systems. Similarly, non-distributed systems are more likely to communicate by shared-memory, that is by writing to and reading from shared variables, while distributed systems typically communicate by message-passing, that is by sending and receiving messages. A further distinction for message-passing is that synchronous communication requires the sender and receiver to participate simultaneously while asynchronous communication allows them to proceed independently using some kind of buffering.

Such semantic properties of a specification language crucially affect its use in software development. They determine its scope, focus, and the extent of automation and proof support. However, the selection of a particular language also has a lot to do with its visual appearance. Some languages employ graphical notation which many feel is more intuitive and facilitates communication with non-experts, some use textual notation which is well-suited for machine support, and some use a mixture of text and drawings in order to get the benefits of both. In particular, graphical notations generally hide the fact that they represent formal specifications and that design transformations are carried out according to formally-defined rules – the mathematics involved does not become apparent except when carrying out proofs.

1.3.2 Methods and Tools

A specification language defines what kind of expressions can be written in the language and what these expressions mean. It does not explain how to construct and validate specifications to capture customer requirements, how to develop abstract specifications to more concrete specifications and eventually to an implementation, or how to verify if the properties of the specification are preserved during such a development. This is the responsibility of a development method.

A development method typically defines a refinement relation which can be used to decide if one (concrete) specification is a correct refinement of another (abstract) one. Two common forms of refinement relation are based on sub-classing of models and preservation of properties. Other development methods support refinement through the application of verified transformation rules to the specification. Such rules ensure that all the properties of the original specification are preserved. A development method should ideally be (and usually is) compositional on the structure of the specification so that different components of the system can be refined independently of each other while still preserving the properties of the system as a whole.

Most formal methods are supported by tools which facilitate the construction of specifications. Many also offer support for other aspects of the design and development process, for example checking the consistency of a specification, animating a specification, proving properties about a specification, refining a specification, documenting a specification, and automatically generating code from a specification. In fact the ability to use a particular formal method in an industrial context depends critically on how well it is supported by tools, in particular on how much of the design, analysis and development process can be automated.

1.3.3 RAISE

The formal method used in all the case studies in this book is RAISE – Rigorous Approach to Industrial Software Engineering – which comprises a specification language (called RSL), a method for software development based on RSL, and a set of supporting tools.

RSL is a formal, wide-spectrum specification language. It permits both model-oriented and property-oriented forms of specification, supports both explicit (algorithmic) and implicit (based on pre- and post-conditions) function definitions, as well as abstract and concrete types. It thus allows specifications to be written at different levels of abstraction. RSL includes three specification styles: applicative, imperative and concurrent. Concurrency is based on message-passing with synchronous communications and with executions carried out asynchronously. The semantics of RSL is defined in operational [12], denotational [96] and axiomatic [117] styles and is based on the branching-time model.

The RAISE method includes a refinement relation which is defined such that all properties of an abstract specification remain the properties of a concrete specification. Refinement is compositional on the structure of specifications. The method recommends that most of the development is carried out with purely applicative specifications, since reasoning about such specifications is much easier than reasoning about imperative or concurrent specifications. Transformation rules defined in the method can then be used to transform the specification from applicative to imperative and from imperative to concurrent. These are systematic so the resulting specifications are guaranteed to be correct by construction.

The RAISE tools offer support for the construction, checking, verification and refinement of specifications. They also support automatic translation of a concrete specification to programs in several programming languages.

A more detailed introduction to the RAISE language and method can be found in Chapter 2 and in two books: [116] describing the language and [117] describing the method.

1.4 Specification Case Studies in RAISE

The aim of this section is to briefly describe each of the 12 case studies in the book: their application/problem domains, the purpose of the specifications, how the specifications are constructed, and how they are applied. The order of presentation follows the ordering of the chapters. For each case study we also introduce a short name which we use to refer to it later.

1. A University Library Management System, called the library case study. This case study describes the development of a management system for a university library. It highlights the typical issues involved when building a data-intensive information system. Specifications are embedded into a more general discussion of user requirements, which are given informally, and possible design decisions for implementing them. The specifications pay particular attention to the definition of the data structures and their associated consistency conditions so as to facilitate the effective implementation of the most commonly used operations and to make sure that the specifications are both reasonable and reflect user requirements. The preservation of consistency by state-changing operations, for instance the operation representing the borrowing of an item by a user, is also discussed and formalised. The specifications combine the definition of types with an intensive use of modularity.

2. Development of a Distributed Telephone Switch, called the `telephony` case study. This chapter describes the development of a distributed telephone switch which integrates radio communication with a public telephone network. The case study uses specifications to document and formalise the whole development process. In order to gain confidence in the initial abstract specification, it is validated against the general properties we expect of a telephone system irrespective of the technology used for its connections. It is then refined several times to take more implementation details into account such as allocating radio frequencies, establishing connections between subscribers, and the protocols used. The correctness of each refinement step is addressed and some steps are verified. Refinement not only makes the specifications more concrete but also decomposes them into independent, interconnected modules. Such modules are developed separately and the results integrated at the end.

3. Developing a National Financial Information System, called the `taxation` case study. The topic is the development of a national financial information system, with special focus on the collection of taxes. Specifications are used to formalise various kinds of information needed to calculate tax amounts. This is done at a sufficiently abstract level to allow different tax payers to be treated similarly. At this level, the specifications essentially describe an information system which is defined in terms of a hierarchy of modules. The specifications are used to build a prototype in order to carry out testing and explore opportunities for optimisation. The chapter also describes the organisation of tax-collection offices, from the district and provincial to the national level. Then it addresses the problem of systematically transforming a hierarchical specification which supports only "vertical" lines of communication between offices into a distributed one which also supports "horizontal" communication between offices at the same level. Another problem addressed is the transformation of specifications from synchronous to asynchronous.

4. Multi-lingual Document Processing, called the `multi-script` case study. This chapter considers the problem of creating and editing documents written in several languages, in particular languages with different directionalities, e.g. English, written horizontally left to right with lines proceeding top to bottom, combined with Japanese, written vertically downwards with columns proceeding right to left. The chapter describes the design of a processing system which supports all four directionalities which exist today and also allows them to be arbitrarily intermixed. Specifications are presented which formalise multi-lingual documents using concrete types to define and consistency conditions to constrain their structures. They also formalise typical operations for editing multi-lingual documents, both on their own and in the context of a user environment comprising many documents, a clipboard, and other features of general editing systems.

5. Formalising Production Processes, called the **production** case study. A production process organises activities of one or more manufacturing enterprises in order to fulfil a given production goal. The purpose of this chapter is to formalise what it means for such a process to be feasible (possible to carry out given the resources delegated for its execution) and for a feasible process to be correct (satisfying a given production goal). Specifications are used to formalise what is a production process and what results the process should achieve, with a possibility to justify formally if a given process actually achieves a given goal. Processes are developed gradually, taking into account sequential production, concurrency, distribution, and real-time constraints. Along with formal specifications, a tabular notation is developed to illustrate the definitions by examples.

6. Model-Based Travel Planning, called the **travel** case study. The internet provides travellers with a great deal of information in support of travel planning, in fact so much that finding the optimum solution to one's travel requirements can be quite a challenge. This chapter presents a model-based approach to support the process of systematic travel planning. The approach is: (1) minimal: the models represent travel plans using the minimum number of concepts; (2) formal: the concepts have their meaning expressed in mathematical terms; (3) wide-spectrum: the travel plans capture abstract travel requirements and concrete itineraries; (4) incremental: the travel plans are made more concrete during development; and (5) sound: development applies the rules that guarantee correctness. Specifications are used to formalise the approach: to provide definitions of travel plans; to decide when a concrete plan implements an abstract one; and to formulate correctness of transformation rules.

7. Proving Safety of Authentication Protocols, called the **authentication** case study. The topic of this chapter is verification of the security of authentication protocols. Such protocols are used to establish the identities of two communicating parties (i.e. if they are who they claim to be), which is very important in particular for e-commerce. The chapter considers two well-known protocols, the Needham-Schroeder protocol and the Secure Sockets Layer (SSL) protocol, both of which involve exchange of encrypted information using pairs of public and private keys. The protocols are formalised and security properties are defined and formally verified under given well-defined assumptions. The approach is to include in the state of protocols the minimum information which is required to carry out the proof since adding more information is likely to complicate the proof and introduce unwarranted assumptions.

8. Formalisation of Realm-Based Spatial Data Types, called the **realm** case study. This chapter considers the problem of topological errors caused by approximate representation of spatial data, such as data related to two-dimensional maps, and approximate calculations when manipulating such data. The problem occurs when accumulation of errors causes

distortions to geometric properties of objects on maps, such as overlapping of apparently disjoint regions, intersection of parallel lines, or two non-parallel lines lacking an intersection point. The chapter constructs specifications to formalise a "realm", a planar graph over a finite resolution grid, together with some operations like addition of nodes or edges. Then it formally proves that this data structure avoids the problem of topological errors and demonstrates how to build the definitions of various geometric objects based on it. Here specifications are used to formalise an existing data structure so as to capture and verify some critical properties.

9. Object-Oriented Design Patterns, called the **patterns** case study. Object-oriented design patterns enable systematic reuse of proven solutions to recurring problems in software development. The aim of this chapter is to formalise such patterns, as expressed in an extension of the graphical notation of the Object Modelling Technology (OMT). The chapter first formalises what is an object oriented design, considering individual classes with their methods and state variables as well as how classes are related to each other in various ways (inheritance, association, aggregation and instantiation). Then it shows how to relate designs to patterns, either a single pattern or several of them, by renaming their entities. Finally, it discusses how to specify the properties of specific patterns and how to check if a given design satisfies such properties. With RSL specifications, object-oriented designs, patterns and their properties can be captured, presented and discussed precisely. This is impossible with the graphical notation which is normally used to describe patterns though the graphical notation is of course more intuitive.

10. Automated Result Verification with AWK, called the **awk** case study. The goal of result verification is to prove that an execution run of a program satisfies its specification. Result verification is easier to carry out in practice than program verification, gives more opportunities for automation, and is particularly suitable for complex systems because it is based on the execution record rather than the implementation. This chapter proposes a technical framework for applying this technique in practice. It shows how to write result-based specifications, how to generate a verifier program to check a given specification, and how to carry out result verification according to such programs. The execution record is written as a text file, the verifier is written in AWK (a special-purpose language for text processing), and verification is done by the AWK interpreter given the verifier and the execution record as inputs. RSL specifications are used to formalise what is a program and what is its execution record, and to explore how result verification can be carried out.

11. Fail-Stop Components by Pattern Matching, called the **fail-stop** case study. A fail-stop component is a software component which is required to detect and report immediately any violation of its specification at run-

time. Such components are the main building blocks of fault-tolerant systems. The aim of this chapter is to present formal specifications to make such run-time behaviour checking possible, and to formalise what such checking is supposed to achieve and how it can be carried out. The specifications, called patterns, are regular expressions built from the logical properties of possible observations of the component's behaviour. They are verified at run-time against the component's execution history. RSL is used along with plain mathematics to define the syntax and semantics of the pattern language and to formalise a wrapper generator to carry out verification (called pattern-matching).

12. An Infrastructure for Software Reuse, called the **reuse** case study. The chapter considers the requirements for making software reuse more efficient in practice and proposes an infrastructure for achieving this. This infrastructure assumes a possibly distributed collection of repositories in which reusable components of different types (code, specification, design, test cases, etc.) are stored. It then constructs an interface on top of these which offers abstract and uniform descriptions of the available components. This so-called "component meta-library" is then used as the basis for the specification of a retrieval process which supports different search strategies in a uniform format, and also a lexicon allowing fuzziness in the search to further increase its flexibility. RSL specifications are used to formalise the components of the infrastructure (repositories, meta-library, and lexicon) as well as the formulation of and the processing of queries. The purpose is mainly clarification by formalisation, with an intention to generate a prototype system from the specification by translation.

1.5 Exemplified Themes

This section classifies the case studies according to several themes. The themes explain in part why a formal approach was applied to each case study. The themes are: development from requirements; requirements elicitation; domain modelling; software verification; and support for software design and analysis. Each is elaborated in the following sections.

1.5.1 Development from Requirements

The primary reason for applying formal specifications is to facilitate the process of rigorous and systematic software development. This includes a whole range of issues. First, specifications are used to capture customer requirements in order to understand, review and take care of them during development. Second, specifications document the results of design decisions as they gradually lead from initial requirements towards implementation. Third, specifications make it possible to verify if design decisions were correct –

properties of the abstract specification remain properties of the concrete one. Fourth, when requirements change, specifications can express such changes and establish to what extent the existing design satisfies them. And so on.

Most case studies relate in one way or another to software development, but only two of them start with an explicit statement of customer/user requirements and then go on to consider development:

library From given requirements, the case study carries out an analysis to identify the entities that must exist in the system, how those entities must be related, and what operations the system should support. The analysis is informal, but it directly affects decisions about writing the first specification (we could call it validation by construction). This specification is quite concrete already and is not developed further.

telephony This case study also starts with an informal statement of system requirements. Then it presents the first specification and validates it formally against the properties of a "plain old telephone system". From that moment, the case study carries out a sequence of development steps with informal discussion and formal justification of correctness. Finally, it integrates all the system components. Development has to take into account particular problems caused by having to rely on radio communication, for instance sharing of radio frequencies.

It is not surprising that library and telephony follow the RAISE method more closely than the other case studies since the method gives guidelines for carrying out software development from requirements. The case studies also employ different sets of language constructs and discuss how suitable they are for information modelling as compared to behaviour modelling.

None of the other case studies starts with an explicit statement of requirements for a concrete system. Some instead develop such requirements in an exploratory manner, aiming to clarify, understand and review what is expected from the software during the process. This theme of requirements elicitation is the subject of Section 1.5.2.

1.5.2 Requirements Elicitation

Unclear, imprecise, possibly ambiguous or even contradictory requirements are the cause of great delays and mounting costs in software projects and often also of their failure. Experience has shown that formal specifications can play a highly positive role in overcoming such problems. Attempting to formalise requirements is likely to expose many of these problems because the analysis raises questions about the system which require precise answers before they can be formalised properly. Once a specification exists, we can try to check whether it captures the requirements faithfully. We could either formulate various properties we expect it should possess and then verify formally that it does indeed satisfy those properties, or develop a rough working prototype from the specification and test how this prototype behaves. Of course, this does not preclude that the requirements change at some point during the development, but even if they do the specification can help us to deal with and limit the effects of changes.

Two more case studies focus explicitly on system development: taxation and multi-script. Unlike library and telephony they do not take the system requirements as given, but instead explore/develop them internally:

taxation The more complex a system, the more important it is to understand and account for all its requirements. This is certainly the case for a national financial information system. The specifications are based on data-flow diagrams representing the information flow in the finance ministry as well as the management of taxpayers by its tax offices. As a result, they describe at an abstract level and mostly without reference to software support how the ministry actually works. On the other hand, the specifications help to clarify what software is needed to perform various operations efficiently, reliably, and in a timely fashion. Such operations include: calculating tax liabilities for different categories of taxpayers, recording and maintaining the information about tax payers, exchanging data between tax offices, etc. The specifications are thus used as a basis for description, analysis and implementation.

multi-script This case study starts with a broad domain analysis of documents written in several languages. The analysis identifies four basic directions of writing that exist in the languages used today and investigates the problems involved in allowing them to be intermixed within the same document. This inspires a discussion of how the structure of such documents could be modelled in terms of "frames", and a formal specification of multi-lingual documents is developed from this. There is no given set of requirements that a system for editing such documents should support. Rather, the requirements are clarified and formulated in the process of writing the specification. This specification has been used as the basis of an actual implementation.

1.5.3 Domain Modelling

What is common to the two themes discussed in Sections 1.5.1 and 1.5.2 and the case studies that exemplify them is their focus on a concrete system in various, usually initial stages of its development. Requirements are either given or developed, but in the end they do exist in some form.

Two other case studies carry out modelling of application domains which do not relate to particular systems and which do not contain software as an intrinsic part. Instead, they begin by identifying an area of human activity where there is a need for formalisation:

production The case study is about modelling of industrial processes that organise activities of one or more manufacturing enterprises in order to satisfy certain production goals. The purpose is to formalise such processes on two levels – descriptive (how the process is carried out given the resources allocated for its execution) and prescriptive (what is the goal of the process) – thus allowing the correctness of a process to be established. One result of this is the definition of languages expressing descriptive and prescriptive models with syntax and semantics in RSL.

travel The case study is about travel planning. It presents a formal approach to capture travel requirements abstractly and then refine them gradually towards a concrete itinerary. Specifications define a wide-spectrum language, with syntax and semantics in RSL, which can describe travel plans at various levels of abstraction, a formal notion of refinement from abstract to less abstract travel plans, and a set of transformation rules which respect this refinement and which can be used to implement design decisions. Requirements for a formally-based travel assistant are also drawn up based on the specification.

Such formalisation brings about a better understanding of the domain by identifying the entities involved as well as their purposes, activities and constraints. The domain models create a larger context (organisational for production, personal productivity for travel) within which the need for software can be considered before deciding whether such software should be built, with a host of technical questions following from these considerations.

Another advantage of domain models is that they can support reuse: one domain model may result in various kinds of software being identified and developed. They can also support software integration: specifications which are based on a single domain model, hence also the software developed from them are likely to share the understanding of every domain concept. Consequently, when software components are put to work together and communicate with each other, they will share the understanding of every concept they exchange.

1.5.4 Software Verification

One good reason for formalising software development is the possibility it offers for formally proving that software satisfies its specification. Notwithstanding the difficulty of carrying out such proofs in practice, being able to ensure that software behaves "correctly" for all possible executions certainly provides a strong motivation for using formalisation in the first place. This possibility is very much part of, although not enforced by the RAISE development method as illustrated by the telephony case study.

However, this shows only one aspect of formal verification in RAISE: systematic software construction with development steps verified according to the RAISE refinement relation. Another aspect, more general than refinement, is the possibility to formulate and prove individual properties about specifications. Two case studies, authentication and realm, carry out such verification. Both take existing software (protocol, algorithm) as their starting point, formalise it into a specification (which is a sort of re-engineering task), formalise the property defining what this software should achieve, and then verify that the software indeed satisfies this property. The objective is not to develop software – software already exists – but to ensure its correctness. Requirements elicitation, however, does play an important role here since in order to formalise criteria for correctness they must be first re-engineered from often ambiguous informal descriptions or even from implementations.

authentication This case study considers two well-known authentication protocols: protocols for establishing the identity of two communicating parties, i.e. for establishing that they are who they claim to be. It creates a specification to represent formally the behaviour of each protocol (the minimum that is needed to carry out verification), formulates a property describing what each protocol should achieve, and formally proves that this property is met under precisely stated assumptions. Here software already exists, its correctness criteria are known, and proofs have also been done to verify the correctness, though not in RAISE. The case study presents a new way of proving correctness which is suitable for these and other authentication protocols.

realm This case study considers an existing data structure called a "realm" (a planar graph over a finite resolution grid) which is used to represent spatial data in Geographic Information Systems (GIS). It formalises this data structure by re-engineering its implementation. It also formalises in what sense the realm would be able to avoid problems of topological errors, as claimed in the literature, caused by too low resolution of the grid. The case study then goes on to formally prove that the realm does indeed maintain the required properties under various operations, in particular the insertion of segments, and therefore avoids topological errors.

1.5.5 Support for Software Design and Analysis

The remaining four case studies provide a further demonstration of the range of applications of RAISE. Despite individual differences, a common theme is the support for software design and analysis, not of particular applications which satisfy concrete requirements but generally. The case studies discussed so far involve application-specific concepts like reservations, loans, borrowing, connections, trunks, frames, clipboards, orientation, taxes, accounts, reports, products, workstations, orders, visits, duration, and arrival. These four use technical, software-related concepts like class, method, inheritance, monitor, verifier, observation, interface, invariant, wrapper, query, match, and signature. Specifications in these case studies formalise development, verification, transformation and reuse of software. The case studies are:

patterns Provides a formalisation of object-oriented design and object-oriented design patterns, which are proven solutions to recurring design problems. The specification describes the properties of the elements of the graphical notation which is generally used to represent the classes in the design/pattern and the relationships between these classes, and also formalises the correspondence between designs and patterns. The goal is to help a software designer decide conclusively whether a given problem or design matches a particular pattern or collection of patterns.

awk Considers the problem of verifying software based on the record of its executions. For many kinds of software, because of their complexity, binary format or limited access, this is the only verification method possible. The case study defines a formal language for writing specifications in terms of execution histories and considers how to verify execution in practice using specification-generated programs in AWK (verification is carried out as a text processing task). RSL specifications help us decide how to carry out verification, and thus how to design the verifier generator.

fail-stop Considers how to ensure that unverified software components do not fail in arbitrary, perhaps malicious ways which cause havoc in the systems they are part of, but instead in a fail-stop manner where failures are immediately detected and reported to the larger system. The case study proposes a formal language for specifying such components and at the same time allowing specifications to be checked effectively at run-time. Expressions are called patterns and their checking resembles pattern-matching, carried out by a pattern-generated component wrapper. RSL specifications are used to formalise the wrapper generator.

reuse The topic of this case study is reuse-based software development and the infrastructure to make this technique more practical. This infrastructure comprises software for storing abstract descriptions of components, software for accepting and interpreting queries, and software for retrieving components from remote repositories according to various reuse strategies. All are formalised using the specifications. In particular, the specifications define and formalise a query language.

1.6 Lessons Learned

This book comprises a collection of case studies in areas as diverse as library management, telephony, taxation, document-editing, manufacturing, travel, authentication, geographic information systems, design patterns, result verification, error detection, and software reuse. Applications in many other areas are also possible as demonstrated by the many technical reports published by UNU/IIST (http://www.iist.unu.edu).

Some applications may need to address issues like mobility, broadcasting, real-time, scheduling, or shared-memory concurrency which are not directly represented in RSL. Overcoming such limitations is possible by:

- extensions of RSL itself; an example is the extension of RSL to include real-time features [59, 89, 88];
- building transformations between RSL and other languages; examples are translators from RSL to SML [98, 148] and to C++ [2]; or
- modelling within RSL.

There are several examples of modelling in the book which use features which are not intrinsic to RSL. The telephony case study considers explicitly the problem of allocation of shared resources, here of the radio frequencies for communication between the central station and remote stations, which is not directly supported (neither are limited resources or scheduling) by RSL. The production case study shows how to represent concurrency in production systems, with product stocks being shared between concurrent processes. This form of concurrency (shared memory concurrency) is not supported directly in RSL. The travel case study defines its own concept of refinement which is problem-specific (related only to travel plans) and very different from the refinement defined by the RAISE method.

In the end, decisions about the application of a general-purpose framework like RAISE will certainly depend on individual problems – how easy it is to address such problems with RAISE – as well as availability of domain-specific languages and frameworks to tackle the problems more directly.

2. Introduction to RAISE

RAISE (Rigorous Approach to Industrial Software Engineering) was originally developed during 1985–90 by a European collaborative project in the ESPRIT-I programme involving four companies, two in Denmark and two in the UK. A second project, LaCoS (Large-scale Correct Systems using Formal Methods) was a continuation ESPRIT-II project (1990–95) involving nine companies in seven European countries. LaCoS further developed the RAISE technology, particularly the method and tools [58], and tested RAISE on a wide range of software development projects [22].

The RAISE Specification Language (RSL) is a formal specification language, i.e. a language with a formal, mathematical basis [96, 13, 117] intended to support the precise definition of software requirements and reliable development from such definitions to executable implementations. Particular aims of the language were to support large, modular specifications, to provide a range of specification styles (axiomatic and model-based; applicative and imperative; sequential and concurrent), and to support specifications ranging from abstract (close to requirements) to concrete (close to implementations).

In this chapter we provide an introduction to the RAISE Specification Language and to the RAISE method. Complete information can be found in the books on RSL [116] and the method [117].

There were a few minor changes made to RSL between the RSL book and the method book, and we follow the latter. We also include a few extensions to RSL that have been introduced since the method book was published, and that are supported by the tools available at this book's web site (see page 395).

2.1 The RAISE Specification Language

The RAISE Specification Language (RSL) is a modular language. Specifications are in general collections of (related) modules. There are two kinds of modules: *schemes* and *objects*. Schemes are (possibly parameterised) *class expressions*, and objects are instances of classes. We return to schemes and objects later in Sections 2.1.10, 2.1.11, and 2.1.12. For now, if you have an intuition about classes and objects in object-oriented programming languages, then this intuition largely carries over into RSL.

2.1.1 Basic Class Expressions

There are several ways of making class expressions, but the most common is the *basic class expression* that consists of the keywords **class** and **end** around some *declarations* of various kinds. Each declaration is a keyword followed by one or more *definitions* of the appropriate kind (Table 2.1).

Table 2.1. Declarations and their definitions.

Declaration	Kind of definition
object	Embedded modules
type	Types
value	Values: constants and functions
variable	Variables that may store values
channel	Channels for input and output
axiom	Axioms: logical properties that must always hold
test_case	Test cases: expressions to be evaluated by a translator or interpreter

No declarations are compulsory: many classes just contain type and value declarations. The order in the table is a common one to use, but any order is allowed, and there may be more than one occurrence of a kind of declaration.

2.1.2 Types

RSL, like most specification and also programming languages, is a *typed* language. That is, it must be possible to associate each occurrence of an identifier representing a value, variable or channel with a unique type, and to check that the occurrence of the identifier is consistent with a collection of typing rules. Such rules, such as that typically prohibiting expressions like "1 + **true**", are well known from programming languages and we will not describe them further here.

Built-in types. In order to be able to define the types of values etc. we need a collection of types to use. RSL has seven built-in types (Table 2.2), and a number of ways of constructing other types from these.

Equality = and inequality $\neq$ are also defined for all types.

Technically, the operators for **Bool** are properly referred to as *connectives*. They differ from operators in that a "lazy" or "conditional" evaluation is used for them: see Section 2.1.4. $\sim$ is negation. There is no need for $\Leftrightarrow$ as it would be the same as =.

Nat is a *subtype* of **Int**: all **Nat** values are also **Int** values. The operators are mostly conventional: / for **Int** is *integer division*, and \ is *remainder*. $\uparrow$ for both **Int** and **Real** is exponentiation; **abs** for both **Int** and **Real** gives

Table 2.2. Built-in types.

Type	Example values	Operators
Bool	**true, false**	$\wedge$, $\vee$, $\Rightarrow$ $\sim$
Int	..., -1, 0, 1, ...	$+$, $-$, $*$, $/$, $\backslash$, $\uparrow$, $<$, $\leq$, $>$, $\geq$, **abs**, **real**
Nat	0, 1, ...	Same as for **Int**
Real	..., -4.3, ..., 0.0, ...	$+$, $-$, $*$, $/$, $\uparrow$, $<$, $\leq$, $>$, $\geq$, **abs**, **int**
Char	$'a'$, ...	
Text	$''''$, $''Alice''$, ...	As for lists of **Char**
Unit	()	

the absolute value. **Int** is not a subtype of **Real**: the operator **real** converts from **Int** to **Real**, and the operator **int** from **Real** to **Int**, truncating towards zero.

Unit is a type with just one value "()", also written as **skip**. It is used mainly in imperative and concurrent specifications to provide a parameter type for functions that do not need parameters, and to provide a return type for functions that do not return values.

The operators and other symbols used to construct value expressions (which we will see later in this chapter) are listed in Table 2.3. They are listed in increasing order of precedence (P), so the prefix operators bind most tightly. The column headed A indicates those that are associative, either right (R) or left (L).

Table 2.3. Value expression precedences.

P	Symbols	A
14	λ $\forall$ $\exists$ $\exists!$	R
13	$\equiv$ **post**	
12	⃞ ⃞ ‖	R
11	;	R
10	:=	
9	$\Rightarrow$	R
8	$\vee$	R
7	$\wedge$	R
6	$=$ $\neq$ $>$ $<$ $\geq$ $\leq$ $\subset$ $\subseteq$ $\supset$ $\supseteq$ $\in$ $\notin$	
5	$+$ $-$ $\backslash$ $\widehat{}$ $\cup$ $\dagger$	L
4	$*$ $/$ $\circ$ $\cap$	L
3	$\uparrow$	
2	:	
1	$\sim$ prefix operators	

Type Constructors. There are a number of type constructors for creating types from other types, illustrated in Table 2.4.

Table 2.4. Type constructors.

Ctr	P	A	Example expressions	Operators
×	2		(1,true,'a')	hd, ∈, ∉, ∪, ∩, ⊂, ⊆, ⊃, ⊇, card, \
-set	1		{}, {1,2}	
*	1		⟨⟩, ⟨1,2⟩	hd, tl, ∈, ∉, ^, len, elems, inds
$\overrightarrow{m}$	3	R	[], ['a' ↦ true, 'b' ↦ false]	dom, rng, ∈, ∉, ∪, †, \, /, °
→	3	R	λ x : Int • x + 1	°
$\overset{\sim}{\rightarrow}$	3	R	λ (x,y) : Int × Int • x / y	°

The column headed P indicates the binding precedence of the type constructors, where 1 is the highest. The column headed A indicates the constructors that are right (R) associative; the others do not associate. So, for example:

Int × Real-set → Real* → Bool
means
(Int × (Real-set)) → ((Real*) → Bool)

The product constructor × is used to form tuples. These may be pairs, triples, ... of any types. This constructor is not associative. For example, **Int × Text × Char** and **Int × (Text × Char)** are different types: the first is a triple, the second a pair containing a singleton and a pair.

-set, * and $\overrightarrow{m}$ create finite sets, list and maps respectively. There are also the potentially infinite set (-infset), infinite list ($^\omega$) and infinite map ($\overset{\sim}{\overrightarrow{m}}$) constructors, but they are rarely used.

card gives the number of elements in a (finite) set; **len** gives the length of a (finite) list. For example:

card {} = 0
len ⟨'a', 'b', 'a'⟩ = 3

The operator ^ is the concatenation operator for lists. For example:

⟨1, 2⟩ ^ ⟨2, 3⟩ = ⟨1, 2, 2, 3⟩

Maps are relations, or associations, between pairs of values. Values on the left of the pairs forming the association are said to form the *domain*, and those on the right are said to form the *range*. Finite maps ($\overrightarrow{m}$) are required to be one-one or many-one, not one-many or many-many. In other words, a value in the domain must not be associated with more than one value in the range. For example, the type **Int $\overrightarrow{m}$ Int** contains the value [1 ↦ 2, 2 ↦ 4] but not the value $[1 \mapsto 2, 1 \mapsto 4]$. The **dom** operator returns the domain (a set) and **rng** returns the range (also a set). For example:

dom $[\,] = \{\}$
dom $['a' \mapsto$ **true**, $'b' \mapsto$ **true**$] = \{'a', 'b'\}$
rng $['a' \mapsto$ **true**, $'b' \mapsto$ **true**$] = \{$**true**$\}$

The union ($\cup$) of two maps is formed as if the maps were two sets of pairs and the union of the two sets were the result. But it only gives a finite, many-one map if the domains are disjoint: see below. The override operator $\dagger$ forms a map by taking the union of the two domains, and associating each domain value with the appropriate range value from the second map, if any, otherwise that from the first map. So the second takes precedence over, or "overrides", the first. For example:

$['a' \mapsto$ **true**, $'b' \mapsto$ **true**$] \cup ['a' \mapsto$ **false**, $'c' \mapsto$ **false**$] =$
  $['a' \mapsto$ **true**, $'a' \mapsto$ **false**, $'b' \mapsto$ **true**, $'c' \mapsto$ **false**$]$
$['a' \mapsto$ **true**, $'b' \mapsto$ **true**$] \dagger ['a' \mapsto$ **false**, $'c' \mapsto$ **false**$] =$
  $['a' \mapsto$ **false**, $'b' \mapsto$ **true**, $'c' \mapsto$ **false**$]$

We see that the union of two deterministic maps can be non-deterministic (and hence in the type of possibly infinite maps constructed by $\overrightarrow{m}$), unless their domains are disjoint, while override preserves determinacy. So it is good practice either to never use union, or to only use it when the domains are disjoint.

There are two ways of reducing, or restricting a map. \ (the operator also used for set difference) subtracts a set of elements from the domain. / restricts the domain to values in its second argument. For example:

$[1 \mapsto$ **true**, $2 \mapsto$ **false**$] \setminus \{2,3\} = [1 \mapsto$ **true**$]$
$[1 \mapsto$ **true**, $2 \mapsto$ **false**$] / \{2,3\} = [2 \mapsto$ **false**$]$

$\rightarrow$ is the constructor for forming *total* functions. A total function is one that always returns a value when it is applied and always returns the same value for the same argument. If a function returns some value, we say it *terminates*, and if a function always returns the same value for the same argument we say it is *deterministic*. So a total function is one that terminates and is deterministic for all arguments. Consider tossing coins on a low-gravity planet as a function, with the coin as an argument. It is non-deterministic, because each coin sometimes lands one way up, sometimes the other. If gravity is so low that very light coins are tossed into orbit, then the function does not terminate for some arguments, as we wait for ever for the coin to land. A function that is not known to be total for all arguments is called *partial*, and $\overset{\sim}{\rightarrow}$ is the constructor for partial functions.

We can define functions using "lambda-expressions" as shown in Figure 2.4, though these are not often used. The first, total function is the "add one" function for integers. The second, partial function, is the integer division function. This is partial because it is not defined for division by zero.

The operator **hd** applied to a non-empty set returns an arbitrary value from the set. For a non-empty list, **hd** returns the first element. For a non-empty map, **hd** returns an arbitrary element from the domain of the map. **hd** is not defined when its argument is empty, so it is a partial operator. The definition of **hd** for sets and maps was added to RSL after the publication of the two books on RAISE [116, 117].

For non-empty lists, **tl** returns the list obtained by removing the first element. Note that **hd** returns an element, **tl** a list. For example:

hd $\langle 1, 2 \rangle = 1$
tl $\langle 1, 2 \rangle = \langle 2 \rangle$

$\in$ and $\notin$ for sets are conventional. For a list they refer to the element set; for a map they refer to the domain. For example:

$(1 \in \{\}) = $ **false**
$(1 \in \langle 0, 2 \rangle) = $ **false**
$(1 \notin [1 \mapsto 'a', 2 \mapsto 'b']) = $ **false**

The definition of $\in$ and $\notin$ for lists and maps was added to RSL after the publication of the two books on RAISE [116, 117].

Lists and maps may be applied like functions. For lists, the argument is an integer in the range one to the length of the list inclusive. So an empty list cannot be applied, a list of length one can be applied only to one, a list of length two to one or two, etc. When the argument can be applied, the result is the corresponding element of the list. For example:

$\langle 'a', 'b' \rangle(1) = 'a'.$

The **elems** of a list is the set of elements of it, and the **inds** (the indexes) of a list is the set of possible integer arguments that it can be applied to. For example:

elems $\langle 'a', 'a' \rangle = \{'a'\}$
inds $\langle 'a', 'a' \rangle = \{1, 2\}$

For maps, the possible arguments that it can be applied to are the values in the domain, and the result is the corresponding value in the range. Since we insist that finite maps are many-one, finite map application to values in the domain is deterministic.

The operator $\circ$ is available for maps and functions, with the basic property that, for two maps or two functions **f** and **g**:

$(f \circ g)(x) = f(g(x))$

Type Expressions. Type expressions are defined as one of the following:

- a built-in type
- a user-defined type
- a type formed from type expression(s) using a type constructor
- a *subtype* of another type expression

Subtypes are types that contain only some of the values of another type, the ones that satisfy a predicate. For example, the type **Nat** is defined as the subtype

$$\{| \ i : \textbf{Int} \cdot i \geq 0 \ |\}$$

That is, it is a subtype of **Int**, and is the type containing those integers that are at least zero.

Subtypes are commonly defined using functions, which makes them easier to read. For example, suppose we wanted to define dates as triples of the form (day, month, year), then we might use the subtype

$$\{| \ (d, m, y) : \textbf{Nat} \times \textbf{Nat} \times \textbf{Nat} \cdot \text{is\_date}(d, m, y) \ |\}$$

where the predicate (boolean function) is_date is defined elsewhere, to constrain m to the range one to twelve, and to constrain d according to m and whether y is a leap year.

Type Definitions. Users can define their own types, and there are two kinds of type definitions. *Abbreviation* definitions just define identifiers that one can use instead of the defining expression. For example, here is a type declaration containing two type abbreviation definitions:

type
    Date_base = **Nat** × **Nat** × **Nat**,
    Date = {| (d, m, y) : Date_base · is_date(d, m, y) |}

Type abbreviation definitions take the form "identifier = type expression" and, like all kinds of definitions, are separated by commas.

The second kind of type definition introduces an identifier for a new type. This kind comes in four forms:

- abstract types, or *sorts*
- record types
- variant types
- union types

Abstract types. These are just type identifiers. An abstract type is a type
we need but whose definition we haven't decided on yet. They are commonly
used for two purposes:

- There are many simple types, like identifiers for people, bank accounts,
books in a library, departments of an organisation, etc., that we expect
to implement very easily in the final program, perhaps as numbers, or
characters, or strings. All we need is to use = to compare them, and =
is defined for all types, even abstract ones. There is a standard piece of
advice in specification that you don't choose a design until you have to, so
we typically leave such types abstract. We may later discover during design
that it is useful to distinguish between identifiers for reference books and
those for books that may be borrowed, and we can then design a type with
a suitable structure. An added bonus is that different abstract types are
regarded as different by the type checker, so we avoid the danger of using
a person's identifier for a book: the type checker will report an error.
- Sometimes we want to delay the design of a type not because it is simple,
but for the opposite reason: because it is complicated and we don't yet
know what the design should be. There is more on this when we discuss
the RAISE method, especially in Section 2.2.2.

Records. Records in RSL are very much like those common in programming
languages. Here is an example that might be found in a system for a bookshop:

type
  Book ::
    title : **Text**
    author : **Text**
    price : **Real** ↔ new_price

This defines a new type Book as a record with three components. Each
component has an identifier, called a *destructor*, and a type expression. Optionally a record component can have a *reconstructor*. In our example the
third component has a reconstructor new_price.

Destructors are total functions from the record type to their component's
type expression. For example, the type of price is

Book → **Real**

So we can apply price to a value of type Book to get its price. For a book
value b, we write price(b), as price is a function, rather than b.price as
would be found in some languages.

Reconstructors are total functions that take their component's type expression and a record to generate a new record. The type of new_price is

Real × Book → Book

When we write, say, new_price(17.95, b) we get a new book value with the same title and author as b, but with the price component set to 17.95.

A record type definition also provides, implicitly, a *constructor* function for creating a record value from its component values. The identifier of the constructor is formed by putting mk_ on the front of the identifier of the type, so in our case we have a constructor mk_Book of type

Text × **Text** × **Real** → **Book**

and we can write, say, mk_Book("Oliver Twist", "Charles Dickens", 9.95) as a book value.

Variants. Variant types allow us to define types with a choice of values, perhaps with different structures. The simplest case is rather like the enumeration type found in some programming languages, such as:

type
  Colour == red | green | yellow

This defines a new type called Colour and three (different) constants (red, green, and yellow) of type Colour.

But variant types allow richer structures. For example, the following type defines binary trees holding values of some type Val:

type
  Tree == nil | node(left : Tree, val : Val, right : Tree)

This defines a new type Tree, a constant nil of type Tree, a constructor node of type

Tree × Val × Tree → Tree

and destructors left, val and right. The type of left, for example, is

Tree $\overset{\sim}{\rightarrow}$ Tree

The destructors are partial because they are not defined for nil trees.

Records are in fact special cases of variants: single ones. We could have defined the same type Book that we used as an example of a record:

type
  Book == mk_Book(title : **Text**, author : **Text**, price : **Real** ↔ new_price)

This illustrates the fact that variants, like records, can optionally include reconstructors.

The type Tree is recursive: trees are defined in terms of trees. Variants are the only type definitions that allow recursion.

Unions. Union type definitions allow us to make new types like variants out of existing types. Suppose types B and C are defined somewhere. Then we can define a type A as their union:

type
  A = B | C

This is in fact a shorthand for a variant, in which the identifier A, and the type names B, and C are used to generate constructor and destructor identifiers:

type
  A == A_from_B(A_to_B : B) | A_from_C(A_to_C : C)

In order for these constructor and destructor identifiers to be generated, the constituents of a union must be names of user-defined types, and not general type expressions.

With union types, implicit (unwritten) *coercions* are allowed from union components to the union type. Suppose, for example, a function f has A as its parameter type. Then we can apply f to a value c of type C, simply by writing f(c). This is short for f(A_from_C(c)). We could similarly apply f to values from B.

2.1.3 Values

Having introduced types, we can consider the values that populate the types. We first see how to define values. We define values within value declarations, where a value declaration consists of the keyword **value** followed by one or more value definitions separated by commas.

The simplest value definition takes the form "identifier : type expression", and is called a *typing*, for example:

value
  x : Int

This may look like a variable declaration in a language like C (though the order of identifier and type is reversed in C) but it is really a constant declaration. x is the identifier of a value, not of a variable: a variable is a location where values can be stored, and the stored value can be changed. There is a possible confusion between the way programmers use the term variable (which is the way we use it) and the way a mathematician uses the term. The mathematician means by a variable something whose value is not known, or does not matter, not something whose value may change. The constant x defined above is more like a variable in the mathematical sense: it is a constant but we don't know, without more information, what its value is. Such constants are not allowed in programming languages, because there is not enough information about them. They are useful in specification when, for example, we want to describe a lift (elevator) system without saying how many floors the building has: the lift system can be described for an arbitrary building.

Continuing with the same example, we might want to assume that the number of floors is at least two. It is hard to imagine what a lift would do in a one storey building, or what a building with zero or a negative number of floors would look like. So we might use an *implicit value definition*:

value
  floors : **Int** • floors ≥ 2

(The type **Int** here could be replaced by **Nat** without changing the meaning.) floors is a constant, but it must satisfy the *predicate* (logical expression) that follows the bullet •. The definition is implicit in that we still don't know what the actual value of floors is.

Sometimes we know the value of a constant: the constant identifier is just a convenient shorthand (and, as in a program, makes things easier to maintain). We can use an *explicit value definition*:

value
  floors : **Int** $= 20$

All three forms of value definition start with a typing, an identifier and a type separated by a colon. The same applies if we want to define functions. First, a function definition may just be a typing, as in:

value
  name : Person $\rightarrow$ **Text**

This definition says that there is a total function from the type Person to the type **Text**, i.e. "every person has name". It is used typically when we haven't yet decided how to represent a person, i.e. Person is still an abstract type. Implicitly, it says there must be enough information in the type Person for a name to be extracted.

We can also define functions implicitly, with a *postcondition*:

value
  square_root : **Real** $\xrightarrow{\sim}$ **Real**
  square_root(x) **as** r **post** $r \geq 0.0 \wedge r*r = x$
  pre $x \geq 0.0$

This defines a function to produce square roots, but without specifying how they should be calculated. It requires that the result r should satisfy the predicate following **post**: it should not be negative and its square must equal the parameter x. Since **Real** numbers only have **Real** square roots when they are not negative, it is a partial function and we give it a *precondition*.

This function illustrates the fact that the type **Real** in RSL contains the mathematical real numbers. This function is in practice not *implementable* in a programming language using limited precision arithmetic, and we might prefer a specification requiring the result r to be within some machine-dependent tolerance of the mathematical square root.

The types **Int** and **Nat** are similarly not implementable in normal computer arithmetic, because their values are unbounded. In practice this is usually not a problem because we can be sure that the values used or generated will not be so large as to cause over- or underflow. If it is a problem we would have to write a specification of how arithmetic in the actual implementation behaves.

The final kind of value definition is the *explicit function definition*. Here is an example:

value
    factorial : **Int** $\overset{\sim}{\to}$ **Int**
    factorial(n) ≡ **if** n = 1 **then** 1 **else** n * factorial(n−1) **end**
    pre n > 0

We need a precondition here since our version of `factorial` is non-terminating for 0 or negative numbers. The definition of `factorial` illustrates a *recursive* function, one that is defined in terms of itself. It also illustrates the **if** expression in RSL.

Overloading and Distinguishable Types. Value identifiers in definitions may be *overloaded*, i.e. the same identifier may be used to define different values, provided their types are *distinguishable* by the type checker. Types are distinguishable unless they are subtypes of the same type. For example, **Nat** is not distinguishable from **Int** (or any subtype of **Int**) because they are both subtypes of **Int**. (Any type is a subtype of itself.) Similarly → is not distinguishable from $\overset{\sim}{\to}$, nor $\overset{}{\twoheadrightarrow}$ from $\overset{\sim}{\twoheadrightarrow}$, nor -**set** from -**infset**, nor * from $^\omega$. **Int** and **Real** are distinguishable.

Built-in operators may be overloaded. For example, we might define a new version of "+" as follows:

value
    + : **Real** × **Int** → **Real**
    x + y ≡ x + **real** y

This is possible as the type of "+" is distinguishable from both possible types of the built-in infix operator "+", which are

Int × **Int** → **Int**
Real × **Real** → **Real**

2.1.4 Logic

We have seen several examples of predicates, expressions that (we hope) evaluate to **true** or **false**. But we have to clarify several issues in order to define our *logic*. In particular, we will need to define:

- what happens when expressions do not terminate, and
- what we mean by equality.

We know it is (unfortunately) easy enough to write programs that do not terminate. The problem is present in specification as well, but we need to be very clear about what it means. We could, for example, have written a poor definition of factorial, forgetting the precondition:

value
    poor_factorial : **Int** → **Int**
    poor_factorial(i) ≡ **if** i = 1 **then** 1 **else** i * factorial(i−1) **end**

and then ask what the expression `poor_factorial(0)` means. The technical answer is **chaos**, a special expression in RSL that represents an expression whose evaluation does not terminate. We need to distinguish in general between *expressions* and *values*. Constants like **true** and 0 are expressions that evaluate to themselves. "1 + 1" is an expression that evaluates to the value 2. **chaos** is an expression that does not evaluate: it does not terminate. So what about an expression like "**chaos** + 1"? The general rule in RSL is "left-to-right" evaluation, which means in this case we evaluate the left argument of +, and if this terminates with a value, we evaluate the right argument. If this also terminates with a value, we add the two values to get the value of the whole expression. If either argument does not terminate, neither does the whole expression. So "**chaos** + 1" is equivalent to **chaos**. So is "0 * **chaos**" that arises when we evaluate `poor_factorial(0)`, that you might have thought should be 0. All infix operators are evaluated the same way.

Equality, =, is an infix operator. So if we try to express the equivalence between "0 * **chaos**" and **chaos** we should not write

(0 * **chaos**) = **chaos**

because this expression would evaluate to **chaos**, not to **true**. We write instead

(0 * **chaos**) ≡ **chaos**

where the symbol ≡ is read as "is equivalent to". Technically, two expressions are equivalent when their semantics, their meanings, are equivalent. For values, and more generally for any expressions that are deterministic, terminating, and read-only (do not write to variables or do input or output on channels) equivalence and equality are the same.

We use the equivalence symbol in explicit function definitions, and we can now explain what a function definition means, namely "when the precondition is true, the function application is equivalent to the defining expression". This definition does not say anything about the situation when the precondition is not true. So, for example, we cannot say what factorial(0) is. The definition tells us nothing: it may be **chaos**, or it may be some integer. We say it is *underspecified*. This does not make it a bad specification. Rather, it tells us to be careful only to use factorial when we are sure the argument is positive. We will see later in Section 2.3.8 that there is a tool, called the confidence condition generator, to help us check this.

It seems sensible to be able to assert as true that

$$n > 1 \Rightarrow (\text{factorial}(n) = n * \text{factorial}(n-1))$$

for any integer n. This should be true for 0, so we want

$$0 > 1 \Rightarrow (\text{factorial}(0) = 0 * \text{factorial}(0-1))$$

to be true. That is, we want

false ⇒ chaos

to be true. This means that ⇒ should not behave like an infix operator, and in RSL it does not. We call the symbols ⇒, ∧, ∨ and ~ *connectives* and define them according to the rules, for any expressions e_1, e_2, e:

$e_1 \Rightarrow e_2 \equiv$ **if** e_1 **then** e_2 **else true end**
$e_1 \wedge e_2 \equiv$ **if** e_1 **then** e_2 **else false end**
$e_1 \vee e_2 \equiv$ **if** e_1 **then true else** e_2 **end**
$\sim e \equiv$ **if** e **then false else true end**

To understand these, we need the evaluation rule for **if** expressions. This is:

1. Evaluate the expression following **if**.
2. If this does not terminate, the **if** expression does not terminate.
3. If it evaluates to true, evaluate the expression following **then**.
4. If it evaluates to false, evaluate the expression following **else**.

You can check that the definitions of the connectives and the evaluation rules for **if** expressions give the same results as "classical" logic, which is only concerned with the values **true** and **false**. For example:

false ⇒ false
  ≡ **if false then false else true end**   definition of ⇒
  ≡ **true**   evaluation rule for **if** expression

But now we also know what will happen when some expressions do not terminate. For example, the following all evaluate to true:

false ⇒ chaos
~(false ∧ chaos)
true ∨ chaos

The reason for including **chaos** in RSL is not that it is needed in specifications: you normally do not want your programs to loop forever! It is a useful convenience in expressing the proof theory of RSL, which is what we mean by the logic. (And even if **chaos** were not included, you could write a variety of equivalent expressions, such as "**while true do skip end**".)

The logic in RSL is called a *conditional* logic as it is based on conditionals (if expressions). There are other approaches to the problems of non-terminating expressions, such as the "logic of partial functions" (LPF) [77, 24] which is used by the specification language VDM [76]. Without going into the argument as to which is better, we note two things:

- ∨ and ∧ in RSL are only commutative if their arguments terminate. For example:

  (true ∨ chaos) ≡ true
  (chaos ∨ true) ≡ chaos

- The connectives in RSL are implementable, because they can be translated using if expressions in programming languages, which evaluate just like RSL if expressions.

For LPF the opposite holds: ∨ and ∧ are always commutative, but the connectives are in general only implementable when their arguments terminate.

Quantifiers. RSL includes the *quantifiers* ∀ (for all), ∃ (there exists) and ∃! (there exists exactly one). For example, the following are all true expressions:

∀ i : **Int** • (i ∗ 2) / 2 = i
∀ i : **Nat** • ∃ j : **Nat** • j = i + 1
∃! i : **Int** • i ≤ 0 ∧ i ≥ 0

The quantification is over *values* in the type. It does not include expressions like 1/0 or **chaos**.

Typings. What follows the quantifier is always a typing, just like the start of every kind of value definition. But we can have more general forms of typing than just an "identifier : type expression": the identifier can be a *binding*.

Bindings. A binding is commonly just an identifier, but it can be parentheses enclosing two or more bindings separated by commas. So the following are all bindings:

x
(x,y)
(x,(y,z))

The identifiers in a binding must all be different.

In a typing, the structure of a binding must match the structure of the type: if the binding is for a product, so must the type be. For example, if Pair is defined as an abbreviation for **Int** × **Int**, the possible typings include the following:

x : Pair
(x,y) : Pair
((p,q),(x,y)) : Pair × Pair

but "(x,y) : **Int**", for example, is not possible.

Bindings also occur as the *formal parameters* of implicit and explicit function definitions (like the n in factorial(n) ≡ ...). What about a function f with type

A × B → ...

Does this have two parameters or one? In RSL you can take either view: the formal application can be written f(a,b) or f((a,b)), or even f(p) (where p is a binding for a pair).

2.1.5 Value Expressions

We have already seen the literals, infix and prefix operators for various types in Section 2.1.2, the boolean connectives, if expressions and quantified expressions in Section 2.1.4. There are some other value expressions that we describe in this section.

Set Expressions. Sets may be formed in three ways:

1. *enumerated* sets like {} (the empty set), or {1,3,2}.
2. *ranged* sets (for integers only) like {1..3}, which is equal to the second enumerated set example. If the second number in the range is less than the first, the ranged set is empty.
3. *comprehended* sets like { i/2 | i : **Int** • i ∈ {2..7} }, which is again equal to the second enumerated set example. The predicate following • (called a *restriction*) may be omitted, in which case it is as if it were **true**.

Other expressions may of course also represent sets. For example, a function may return a set and then an application of the function will be a set expression, an expression whose type is T-**set** for some type T. Similar remarks apply for lists and maps.

List Expressions. Lists may be formed in three ways:

1. *enumerated* lists like ⟨⟩ (the empty list), or ⟨2,1,2,3⟩.
2. *ranged lists* (for integers only) like ⟨1..3⟩, which is equal to the tail of the second enumerated list example. If the second number in the range is less than the first, the ranged list is empty.

3. *comprehended* lists like ⟨ i/2 | i **in** ⟨2..10⟩ • i < 8 ⟩ which is again equal to the tail of the second enumerated list example. As with enumerated sets, the restriction may be omitted. A comprehended list takes its elements from another list expression, rather than a typing as with a set, and, see below, a map.

Map Expressions. Maps may be formed in two ways:

1. *enumerated* maps like [] (the empty map), or [1 ↦ **true**, 3 ↦ **true**, 2 ↦ **false**].
2. *comprehended* maps like [i ↦ is_odd(i) | i : **Int** • i > 0 ∧ i < 4], which is again equal to the second enumerated map example (assuming an appropriate definition of is_odd). The restriction may be omitted, in which case it is as if it were **true**.

Let Expressions. Let expressions are used in two main ways:

1. to destruct a product. For example:

   let (x,y) = (1,2) **in** x + y **end**

   will evaluate to 3. First we evaluate the expression following the =. Then we bind x to the first part, and y to the second. Finally we evaluate the expression following the **in**.
2. to organise an evaluation into several steps. For example, a function to sum a list of integers might be defined as:

   value
      sum : **Int*** → **Int**
      sum(s) ≡
        if s = ⟨⟩ **then** 0
        else
          let h = **hd** s, t = **tl** s, x = sum(t) **in** h + x **end**
        end

   This is particularly useful when the sub-expression like **hd** s would, without the **let**, occur more than once. But even when this would not occur, **let** expressions often improve readability.

Case Expressions. Case expressions are commonly used to express functions over lists and over variant structures. For example, the **sum** function could be written:

value
   sum : **Int*** → **Int**
   sum(s) ≡
     case s **of**
       ⟨⟩ → 0,
       ⟨h⟩^t → h + sum(t)
     end

A **case** expression consists of a series of *patterns* plus associated expressions. The case patterns are tried in order, the first pattern that matches is taken, and the associated expression evaluated. The pattern $\langle\rangle$ matches the empty list. The pattern $(h)\hat{\ }t$ matches a non-empty list, and at the same time binds h to the head and t to the tail.

An example of a **case** expression for a variant type is the body of a function to calculate the depth-first traversal of a tree (Section 2.1.2), returning a list of the values in the nodes of the tree:

value
   traverse : Tree $\rightarrow$ Val*
   traverse(t) $\equiv$
     case t **of**
       nil $\rightarrow \langle\rangle$,
       node(l, v, r) $\rightarrow$ traverse(l) $\hat{\ }$ $\langle v\rangle$ $\hat{\ }$ traverse(r)
     end

The bindings in patterns may be replaced by "wildcards", underscores, when their values are not needed. For example, a function to calculate the depth of a tree (assuming **max** is defined somewhere):

value
   depth : Tree $\rightarrow$ Val*
   depth(t) $\equiv$
     case t **of**
       nil $\rightarrow$ 0,
       node(l, _, r) $\rightarrow$ 1 + max(depth(l), depth(r))
     end

The most commonly used case patterns are for lists and variants, but literals are also possible, and there is a "wildcard" pattern _ that matches anything. For example, a strange definition of is_odd:

value
   is_odd : **Nat** $\rightarrow$ **Bool**
   is_odd(n) $\equiv$
     case n **of**
       0 $\rightarrow$ **false**,
       1 $\rightarrow$ **true**,
       _ $\rightarrow$ is_odd(n$-$2)
     end

2.1.6 Axioms

So far we have seen type and value declarations. There are also axiom declarations, introduced by the keyword **axiom** and consisting of axiom definitions separated by commas. Each axiom definition is a predicate, optionally preceded by an identifier in square brackets. For example, instead of defining:

value
    floors : **Int** • floors $\geq$ 2

we could write:

value
    floors : **Int**
axiom
    [floors_constraint] floors $\geq$ 2

In fact all value definitions, functions as well as constants, can be written in this style, a typing plus an axiom. There are "axiomatic" or "algebraic" specification languages, like Larch [62] and CASL [101], that use only this style, and are also restricted to abstract types. This style can be used within RAISE, but we choose also to have available the pre-defined sets, lists, maps, and products that are characteristic of the "model-based" specification languages like Z [131], B [1], and VDM [76].

2.1.7 Test Cases

Test cases have no semantic meaning: they are like comments directed at an interpreter or translator meaning "please provide code to evaluate these expressions and report the results".

The syntax of test cases is much like axioms, except that the test case expressions can be of any type. For example, if we wanted to test the function to sum a list of integers we might define

test_case
    [sum$_0$] sum($\langle\rangle$),
    [sum$_1$] sum($\langle$1,2,2,3$\rangle$)

and expect to see the results

    [sum0] 0
    [sum1] 8

But a perhaps more useful style of test case is to include the expected result in the test case, i.e. to write

test_case
    [sum$_0$] sum($\langle\rangle$) = 0,
    [sum$_1$] sum($\langle$1,2,2,3$\rangle$) = 8

so that the output for every test case should be **true**.

Test cases are always evaluated in order of definition. This is useful for imperative specifications, introduced below in Section 2.1.8, when there are variables storing information. Information stored as a result of one test case is available for the next one, so we can, for example, test use-cases step-by-step as a sequence of test cases, outputting intermediate observations as the result of each.

Test cases were added to RSL after the publication of the two books on RAISE [116, 117].

2.1.8 Imperative Constructs

Much of the specification in RSL is done with the language described so far in this chapter, which we call *applicative*. This comes from the fact that this style of writing specifications (or programs in languages like Lisp, SML, and Haskell) is mainly done in terms of definitions and applications of functions. It is advantageous in that it is close to mathematics, and so supports reasoning in the way mathematics does.

Perhaps the most common style of programming is the *imperative* style of languages like Pascal and C. These depend on the use of *variables*, essentially locations in a store that allow values to be stored and retrieved. RSL allows specifications to use this style, but the RAISE method suggests (Section 2.3.1) that it only be used in later stages of development, as a step towards an implementation in a programming language.

To support the imperative style, RSL includes **variable** declarations, assignment expressions, and sequences of expressions. For example:

variable
  counter : **Nat** := 0
value
  increment : **Unit** → **write** counter **Nat**
  increment() ≡ counter := counter + 1 ; counter

Here we have a variable declaration with one variable definition, consisting of an identifier, a type, and, optionally, an initial value. There is also a function increment which will add 1 to the counter. increment needs no parameters, so we give it none and use **Unit** as its argument type. It returns a **Nat**, so this appears as its result type. But we also include an *access* clause in its type, that says it may write, and so change, the contents of the variable counter. (**read** is the other kind of access; **write** includes **read**.) Accesses are normally written using one or more names of variables, but we may also use the *universal access* **any** to allow access to any variable defined in the same module.

The body of increment consists of two expressions combined by ";", the *sequential combinator*. The assignment is an expression rather than, as in many languages, a statement: there are no statements in RSL, only expressions. This avoids the need for keywords like "return" that just convert an expression to a statement in languages like C. Since an assignment is an expression it must have a type, and this is **Unit**. There is a rule that, for two expressions combined by ";", the first must have type **Unit** and the type of the whole expression is the type of the second.

For an indication of why imperative features cause problems with reasoning, consider the two predicates:

increment() = increment()
increment() ≡ increment()

Is either of these true? Consider the first, and recall the rule for evaluating infix operators like equality: evaluate the left expression; if it terminates evaluate the right; if that also terminates compare the results. It should be clear that the result will be false. In addition, the evaluation of the equality has had the *effect* (commonly called a "side effect" as if it didn't matter too much) of adding 2 to the counter. Yet the equality looks as if it should be true, certainly to any mathematician!

Now consider the second predicate. Is `increment()` equivalent to itself? It seems natural that we should say yes, and indeed it is so: any expression (even one that does not terminate) is equivalent to itself. We defined equivalence as semantic equivalence, and with imperative constructs we can say that expressions are equivalent if (given the same initial state, i.e. the same initial values in all variables) they are either both non-terminating, or they have the same effect on the state and return the same result. The evaluation of the equivalence, unlike the evaluation of the equality, does not change any variables. It simply returns true if the hypothetical questions "Would these two expressions have the same effect?" and "Would these two expressions return the same result?" are both answered with "Yes".

If Expressions. We have seen **if** expressions before, but there are two features we have not described:

1. When there are several alternatives we can include one or more **elsif** clauses. For example:

   type
     Compare == greater | equal | less
   value
     compare : **Int** × **Int** → Compare
     compare(x, y) ≡
       if x > y **then** greater
       elsif x = y **then** equal
       else less **end**

   elsif clauses are equivalent to nested **if** expressions in the obvious way.

2. For **if** expressions of type **Unit** the **else** clause may be omitted, as in:

> **value**
> decrement : **Unit** → **write** counter **Unit**
> decrement() ≡ **if** counter > 0 **then** counter := counter − 1 **end**

The missing else clause is equivalent to **"else skip"**, where **skip** is the "do nothing" expression (of type **Unit**).

Iterative Expressions. There are **while**, **until** and **for** loops in RSL. Consider the following examples:

variable
  counter : **Nat**,
  result : **Real**
value
  sum_1 : **Nat** $\overset{\sim}{\to}$ **write** counter, result **Real**
  $sum_1(n) \equiv$
    counter := n;
    result := 0.0;
    while counter > 0 **do**
      result := result + 1.0/(**real** counter);
      counter := counter − 1
    end;
    result
  pre n > 0,

  sum_2 : **Nat** $\overset{\sim}{\to}$ **write** counter, result **Real**
  $sum_2(n) \equiv$
    counter := n;
    result := 0.0;
    do
      result := result + 1.0/(**real** counter);
      counter := counter − 1
    until counter = 0 **end**;
    result
  pre n > 0,

  sum_3 : **Nat** $\overset{\sim}{\to}$ **write** result **Real**
  $sum_3(n) \equiv$
    result := 0.0;
    for counter **in** ⟨1..n⟩ **do**
      result := result + 1.0/(**real** counter)
    end;
    result
  pre n > 0

It should be apparent that the three functions sum_1, sum_2 and sum_3 all compute the same value, namely

$$1 + 1/2 + ... + 1/n \qquad\qquad (1)$$

Are the preconditions necessary? There are two possible reasons for them:

1. We don't know what the expression (1) would mean if n is zero.
2. We don't want to divide by zero.

It is clear that only sum_2 needs the precondition for the second reason, to avoid dividing by zero. (For the **for** loop, remember that a ranged list is empty when the second number is less than the first. A **for** loop is equivalent to **skip** when the list is empty.)

Local Expressions. It is clear in the examples of loops that it would be better if the variables **counter** and **result** had a smaller scope: they should be inside the functions that use them, when their purpose is clearer. There is a *local expression* in RSL that allows variable declarations, or any other kind of declarations, to be local to an expression. Here is another version of sum_1 using a **local** expression:

```
value
  sum₁ : Nat ⥲ Real
  sum₁(n) ≡
    local
      variable
        counter : Nat := n,
        result : Real := 0.0
    in
      while counter > 0 do
      result := result + 1.0/(real counter);
      counter := counter − 1
      end;
      result
    end
  pre n > 0
```

2.1.9 Concurrency

Concurrency in RSL is based on synchronisation between concurrently executing expressions (commonly called processes) using channels. Channels are declared with the keyword **channel** followed by one or more channel definitions separated by commas. A channel definition is one or more channel identifiers plus a type, the type of data that may be transmitted on the channel(s). For example:

type
  Data
channel
  left, right : Data

Functions that use channels for input and output need **in** and **out** access to channels, similar to access rights for variables. Consider the following definition:

value
  one_place_buffer : **Unit** → **in** left **out** right **Unit**
  one_place_buffer() ≡
    while true do
      let x = left? **in** right!x **end**
    end

left? is an *input expression* which returns the value made available on the channel left. (Hence left? has type Data.) right!x is an *output expression* that puts a value onto the channel right. (right!x has **Unit** type.) So one_place_buffer repeatedly accepts values on the left channel and outputs them on the right channel.

Channel communication in RSL is point-to-point and synchronised: in order for an input like left? or an output like right!x to execute it is necessary for another concurrent process to be executing a corresponding output or input, i.e. in the opposite direction on the same channel. So executing on its own, one_place_buffer can do nothing: it will wait for ever on the input expression left?. This situation, an expression waiting for ever for input or output, is termed *deadlock*, and there is an expression for it in RSL: **stop**. In practice we will want to avoid it occurring.

one_place_buffer is a kind of *server*, and is supposed to run forever. But we earlier characterised a non-terminating process as **chaos**. To resolve this, we redefine non-terminating as meaning a process which either runs forever without doing input or output (**chaos**) or deadlocks (**stop**). We might think that stop means terminate, but termination includes the idea of allowing the next expression in sequence to execute, while deadlocking means that no further progress is possible.

If there are two or more other concurrent processes waiting to output on left then an arbitrary choice of communication is made between them: one will pass its value to one_place_buffer, the other(s) will continue to wait. Then, if there are two or more processes waiting for input on the right channel, one_place_buffer will synchronise with just one of them, passing its value, and leaving the other(s) waiting. Such behaviour, with arbitrary choices between possible behaviours, is usually undesirable, and we often try to avoid it by making sure that there is only one process inputting and one outputting on each channel. Buffers typically serve just one process putting values in and one process taking them out. But some servers, like databases, for example, are intended to support many concurrent users.

Buffers are common components used to allow processes to run at different speeds. If a process A wants to send data to another process B, and we use a channel between them, then A can only send a data item when B is ready. If instead we place a one_place_buffer between them, A can place a value, v, in the buffer by executing left!v and continuing. The expression that represents A and B running in parallel with the one_place_buffer is

A ‖ B ‖ one_place_buffer()

"‖" is the *concurrent composition* combinator. It requires that all its arguments have type **Unit**, and the result is type **Unit**. It is associative and commutative, so its arguments may be written in any order.

With a one place buffer the solution to the problem of processes of different speeds is limited: A cannot get more than one item ahead of B. If A wants to do a second output on left, before B has done an input on right, then one_place_buffer will be waiting on the output right!v and A will have to wait.

A better solution is to have a buffer that can contain many values. Here is a buffer with maximum capacity of max items:

value
  max : **Nat**
variable
  buff : Data* := ⟨⟩
channel
  put, get : Data
  empty : **Unit**
value
  buffer : **Unit** → **write** buff **in** put, empty **out** get **Unit**
  buffer() ≡
    while true do
      empty? ; buff := ⟨⟩
      ⫿
      if len buff < max
      then let x = put? **in** buff := buff ⌢ ⟨x⟩ **end**
      else stop end
      ⫿
      if buff ≠ ⟨⟩
      then get!hd buff ; buff := tl buff
      else stop end
    end

The expression for **buffer** uses *external choice* "⫿" to offer, in general, three choices to its clients:

1. An output on the **empty** channel causes the buffer to be emptied.
2. Provided the buffer is not full, an output of a value **v** on the **put** channel causes **v** to be appended to the buffer.
3. Provided the buffer is not empty, an input on the **get** channel will remove a value from the buffer and return it.

The choice is called "external" because it is the client processes that decide which choice is taken: the server **buffer** will cooperate with whatever is asked of it.

If we have two clients trying to interact with **buffer** at the same time, perhaps one doing a **put** and the other a **get**, an *internal* (arbitrary) choice will be made between them, to choose which interacts first. Such internal choices are common in the execution of concurrent systems. But we always design servers using external choice "[]", as if we used internal choice "⊓" their behaviour would seem very erratic to their clients. The reason for this is that if a client wanted to do a **put**, say, (and the buffer was not full), the nondeterministic version of **buffer** could (even in the absence of any other clients) internally choose, say, the first choice of waiting for a communication on **empty**, resulting in deadlock.

What happens when the buffer is full or empty? We would like in these cases for the **put** or **get** choice respectively to not be available, forcing clients wanting to use these channels to wait. One might expect to see **skip** in the relevant **else** clauses of **buffer**, but in fact **stop** is what we need. The reason for this is that **stop** turns out to be the unit for external choice (like 0 is the unit for addition, and 1 for multiplication): it satisfies, for any expression **e**, the equivalence

e [] **stop** ≡ e

We now consider another example. Suppose we have a database, initially specified as a map from **Key** to **Data**, and we need a **lookup** function. This would be partial, as the key might not be in the database. Part of our applicative specification might be:

type
  Db = Key $\overrightarrow{m}$ Data
value
  lookup : Key × Db $\overset{\sim}{\to}$ Data
  lookup(k, db) ≡ db(k)
  pre defined(k, db),

  defined : Key × Db → **Bool**
  defined(k, db) ≡ k ∈ db

Now suppose we want to make a concurrent database server, to allow multiple concurrent users. The standard approach says that there will be one choice in the server for each function in the applicative version. Functions like lookup and defined will need a channel to pass the input (in each case of type Key) and also a channel to pass back the result (of type Data and Bool respectively).

But this approach is inadequate with partial functions like lookup. In the concurrent case with multiple clients we can get patterns like:

1. A asks if key k is defined, and gets the result **true**
2. B deletes key k
3. A tries to lookup key **k**

We need to combine A's interactions into a single transaction that is atomic in the sense that, once started, no other interaction with the database is possible until it is completed. The way to do this is to create a total version of lookup, that can return a Data value or a "not found" value. We need a new type:

type
    Result == not_found | res(data : Data)

and then the relevant choice in the server process, assuming a variable **db** holding the database, is:

let k = lookup? **in**
    if defined(k, db) **then** lookup_res!res(lookup(k, db))
    else lookup_res!not_found
    end
end

A further improvement is to also define an "interface process" lookup to be used by clients:

value
    lookup : Key → **out** lookup **in** lookup_res Result
    lookup(k) ≡ lookup!k ; lookup_res?

This has two advantages over allowing clients access to the channels directly:

1. The channels can all be hidden, allowing tighter control over access to them. We will see how to hide things in Section 2.1.10.
2. The interface processes enforce the right protocol. In our case we see that the interface process lookup does an output on the channel lookup and then an input on lookup_res. We need to check that there is a choice in the server that offers the dual of this: an input on lookup followed by an output on lookup_res. Provided this is the case, no deadlocks are possible if clients can only call the interface processes. With direct access

to the channels a client could contain an error like an output on lookup without the input that should follow it, which could cause the database to deadlock, waiting to do an output on lookup_res.

Comprehended Expressions. The combinators [], ∏, and ‖ may be applied to comprehended sets of expressions of type **Unit**. For example:

‖ { A[i].init() | i : Index }

is a comprehended expression representing the parallel execution of the init functions of all the objects in A, which is an object array (see Section 2.1.12) indexed by the type **Index**. As with comprehended sets, lists, and maps (Section 2.1.5), the comprehended expression may include a restriction. For example:

[] { A[i].put(d) | i : Index • ok(i) }

is a comprehended expression representing an external choice between invoking the put functions from objects in the array A whose indexes satisfy the condition ok. If there are no such indexes, the comprehended expression will deadlock.

2.1.10 Modules

As we mentioned earlier, there are two kinds of module in RSL, schemes and objects. Schemes are essentially classes, and objects are instances of classes, so the basic thing is the class expression. These come in six forms: basic, extending, renaming, hiding, with, and instantiation.

Basic Class Expressions. These were introduced in Section 2.1.1. They consist of the keywords **class** and **end** with any number of declarations between them. The declarations (and their constituent definitions) may come in any order. There is no "define before use" rule in RSL. All the entities defined in the class expression are exported (visible outside it) by default: there is nothing like an "export" clause in RSL.

Extending Class Expressions. If C_1 and C_2 are class expressions:

extend C_1 **with** C_2

is an extending class expression. The declarations of C_2 are added to those of C_1. The declarations of C_2 can refer to entities defined in C_1, but not vice versa. The declarations of C_1 and C_2 must be *compatible*, which simply means that duplicate definitions are not allowed, any more than they would be in a single class expression.

Renaming Class Expressions. If C is a class expression:

use id_1' **for** id_1, ..., id_n' **for** id_n **in** C $(n \geq 1)$

is a renaming class expression in which the entities id_1, ..., id_n are exported with identifiers id_1', ..., id_n': they are renamed. The entities may be types, values, variables, channels or objects.

Hiding Class Expressions. If C is a class expression:

hide id_1, ..., id_n **in** C $(n \geq 1)$

is a hiding class expression from which the identifiers id_1, ..., id_n are not exported. Hiding is most commonly used to hide objects, variables, channels and *auxiliary* functions (functions only intended for use within the original class to define other functions). Hiding is used to prevent access from outside the class, and also used to hide auxiliary functions or other entities that we don't expect to use in later developments, because hidden entities do not need to be implemented.

With Class Expressions. If C is a class expression:

with O_1, ..., O_n **in** C $(n \geq 1)$

is a with class expression. O_1, ..., O_n are object expressions (see Section 2.1.12). The meaning of **with X in C** is that an applied occurrence of a name N in C can mean either N or X.N, so that, in particular, we can write just N instead of X.N. (It is similar to "using namespace" in C++.)

The with class expression was added to RSL after the publication of the two books on RAISE [116, 117].

Scheme Instantiations. If we define a scheme called S, say:

scheme S = C

then we can use S to mean the class expression C, for example in "**extend S with ...**": the occurrence of S here just means the same as C. The occurrence of S is called an *instantiation* of S.

But it is also possible to *parameterise* a scheme, and we discuss this in the following section.

2.1.11 Parameterised Schemes

The most common use of parameterised schemes is to make *generic* schemes. For example, we considered earlier the type of binary trees. We may want more than one kind of binary tree: one to hold integers, another to hold names, etc. But we would like to define the type **Tree** and its associated functions only once. We can proceed as follows:

- We define a class to act as the scheme parameter. Commonly we use a scheme to define this class:

scheme ELEM = class type Elem end

This is a very simple, as well as a very common scheme to define a parameter. But there are no restrictions on what we can put into a parameter's class expression. This makes the parameterisation mechanism in RSL much more powerful than, for example, templates in C++.

- We define a generic scheme TREE using ELEM as a parameter:

scheme TREE(E : ELEM) =
class
  type
    Val = E.Elem,
    Tree == nil | node(left : Tree, val : Val, right : Tree)
  ...
end

The abbreviation definition of Val is just a commonly used convenience. We could omit it, replacing all other occurrences of Val with E.Elem. Technically the parameter "E : ELEM" is like an object definition (see Section 2.1.12). E is the identifier of an object, so E.Elem means the type Elem defined in the object E.

So how do we make trees of integers, say? We need to make an instantiation of TREE, and the actual parameter we need is an object, just as the formal parameter is an object. So we define an object I, say:

object I : class type Elem = Int end

and now the scheme instantiation TREE(I) is what we want. The formal definition of TREE(I) says that it is the class expression of TREE with every occurrence of the object identifier E replaced by I. So, in particular, the defining type expression of the type Val will be I.Elem, which we can see from the definition of I is just an abbreviation for **Int**.

For type checking, there is a condition between the class of the formal parameter E and the class of the actual parameter I. This is that the latter must be a *static implementation* of the former. This means that for every entity in the formal parameter there must be an entity in the actual parameter of the same kind (type, object, value, variable or channel) with the same identifier and:

- for types, if the formal type definition is an abbreviation, the actual type definition must be an abbreviation for a type that is maximally the same
- for objects, the defining class in the actual parameter must statically implement the defining class in the formal parameter

- for values, variables and channels, the types in the actual and formal parameters must be maximally the same.

  Here "maximally the same" means the types must not be distinguishable (see Section 2.1.3).

  The actual class expression may contain more entities than the formal.

  Schemes can have several parameters. For example, we might define a generic database:

scheme DATABASE(D : ELEM, R : ELEM) =
class
  type
    Domain = D.Elem,
    Range = R.Elem,
    Database = Domain $\overrightarrow{m}$ Range
  ...
end

and we can instantiate **DATABASE** with two different objects, or the same object twice.

Sometimes we find we have an object that defines the things we need for the actual parameters, but with the wrong identifiers. For example, the RAISE method (Section 2.2) suggests defining a number of simple types that will be used throughout the specification in a scheme TYPES, and making an object T from this. Now suppose TYPES defines types Id and Name, and we want to instantiate the DATABASE with Id as the domain type and Name as the range type.

We can instantiate DATABASE as

DATABASE(T{Id **for** Elem}, T{Name **for** Elem})

The construct $\{id_1'$ **for** $id_1, ..., id_n'$ **for** $id_n\}$ is called a *fitting*. It acts as if the fitting had been applied to the formal parameter class as a renaming.

It is possible to have parameters which depend on each other. For example we could define:

scheme S(E : ELEM, T : TREE(E)) = ...

Then if we define objects by, say:

object
  I : **class type** Elem = **Int end**,
  TR : TREE(I)

then S could be instantiated as S(I, TR).

2.1.12 Object Declarations

Technically class expressions denote, or mean, classes (collections) of possible implementations of them. We get different possible implementations with abstract types (since any type can be used as an implementation) and with underspecified values. The possible implementations are called *objects*. Object declarations consist of the keyword **object** followed by one or more object definitions separated by commas.

If C is a class expression, we can define an object O by:

object
    O : C

and O denotes some object in the class C.

If x is an entity in C (and not hidden or renamed in C), then, in the scope of this object definition, x can be referred to by the *name* O.x. This is sometimes called a *qualified name*, and the prefix O the *qualifier*.

The universal access **any** can also be qualified. For example, the access clause **read** O.**any** in a function signature allows the function to read any variable defined in the object O (including variables defined in any objects defined in C). This is often needed to write the signatures of functions that invoke functions in imperative modules, since variable and channel names are commonly hidden.

It is also possible to define *object arrays* in RSL. The object name is given a formal parameter in the form of a (list of) typings. For example, a collection of buffers indexed by a type Index could be defined by

object
    B[i : Index] : BUFFER

and the expression B[e].put(d), where e is an expression of type Index, and put a function defined in BUFFER, would be used to put data value d in the buffer indexed by the value of e.

2.1.13 Comments

There are two kinds of comment supported in RSL. *Block comments* are opened by /* and closed by */. They may be nested. *Line comments* are opened by -- and closed by the end of a line (or file). Both kinds of comment are allowed anywhere where white space would be allowed.

Line comments were introduced, and the original restriction on the use of block comments to only certain syntactic constructs was removed, after the publication of the two books on RAISE [116, 117].

2.2 The RAISE Method: Writing Initial Specifications

As long as you conform to the syntax and type rules of RSL, you can describe and develop software in any way that you choose. But there are a number of ideas for using RSL that have been found useful in practice, and that collectively we describe as "the" RAISE method.

There are two main activities involved in the method: writing an initial specification, and developing it towards something that can be implemented in a programming language, and we describe these separately in this Section 2.2 and the following Section 2.3.

Writing the initial specification is the most critical task in software development. If it is wrong, i.e. it fails to meet the requirements, then following work will be largely wasted. It is well known that mistakes made early in the life-cycle are considerably more expensive to fix than those made later, precisely because they cause so much time and effort to be expended going in the wrong direction. But we should clarify this to say that it is mistakes made *and not quickly found* that are expensive. We can't guarantee that we won't make mistakes, but if we can discover them quickly then not too much harm is done.

What kind of errors are made at the start? The main problem is that we may not understand the requirements. They are set in some domain in which we are usually not experts, while the people who wrote them, to whom the domain is familiar, tend to forget to explain what to them is obvious.

In addition, requirements are written in a natural language, like English or Chinese, and as a result are likely to be ambiguous. They are often large documents developed by several people over a period of time. As a result they are often contradictory: what they say on one page may differ from what they say on another.

The aim of the initial specification is to capture the requirements in a formal, precise manner. Formality means that our specification has just one meaning, it is unambiguous. By *capturing* the requirements we mean re-writing them in our terms, creating our model of what the system will do. So how can we check that the model we create accurately models what the writer of the requirements has in mind?

Be Abstract. The specification should be *abstract*, it should leave out as much detail as possible. The requirements may demand that identifiers have a certain format, or that dates should be presented in a particular style, or that calculations should be done to a certain degree of accuracy, or that a user screen should have a certain appearance, but we try to extract the essential information: that there are identifiers, presumably different for each different entity they identify, that we need dates, that certain calculations need to be done, that users may be requested for certain information and as a consequence they may be presented with other information, or the system's state may be changed in certain ways. We know that we can fill in the details later: we can design screens provided the information to be presented is available or can be calculated, and provided we know what input to demand.

Use Users' Concepts. The concepts in the specification should be the same as the user's concepts. If the requirements say that each customer has an account, and an account is a record of all the customer's transactions, then that is what the specification should say. It should not refer to concepts like databases, tables, and records: these are computer concepts that describe ways of solving the problem, while what we want to do first is *describe the problem, not its solution.*

Make it Readable. Specifications are intended to be read by others: by those who are to check that they correspond to requirements, by those who are to implement them, by those who are to write test plans, by those who later want to maintain the system, etc. So we want to make them as readable as possible. The guidelines here are very much like those for programming languages: meaningful identifiers, comments, simple functions, modules that are coherent and loosely coupled, etc.

Look for Problems. We recall that what we want to do is avoid mistakes, or find them quickly. So we concentrate on the things that appear difficult, strange, or novel, and we ignore or defer things that are straightforward. We might be mistaken as to what is hard, of course, but we hope that with some experience we have a feeling for such things. In capturing requirements we are also trying to find out if the system we intend to develop is feasible, at least within our budget constraints, and so we want to be assured as early as possible that we have appropriate solutions to all the problems. If we don't, we may need to do some experimentation or research before we commit ourselves further.

Minimise the State. State information should be *minimal.* This means in particular that we try hard not to include in the state *dependent* information: information that can be calculated from other information in the state. If C can be calculated from A and B, then we should not model C as part of the state. If C is stored as part of the state, together with A and B, then we will need a *consistency* condition that what is stored for C is the same as would be calculated from the stored A and B. There is a general notion that the simpler the set of consistency conditions needed, the better the state is designed. It may be that later we decide we need to store C, to achieve sufficient speed, but this should be done as a later stage of development.

When we refer to the *state* of a system we mean the information that is stored, that persists between interactions with it. We also speak of the state of a module, where we mean the part of the state associated conceptually with that module, which will typically provide functions to change it and report on it. We use the term *global state* where necessary to refer to the state of the whole system, as opposed to that of a module, or of a group of modules that we see as a subsystem.

Identify Consistency Conditions. While we try to make the state minimal, it is still usually the case that we need *consistency* conditions and *policy* conditions. Consistency conditions are needed if some possible state values cannot correspond to reality: two users of a library borrowing the same copy of a book simultaneously, perhaps. Policy conditions are ones that might perhaps arise in reality, but we intend that they should not happen: a user borrowing too many books at one time, perhaps.

If our system's state cannot correspond to reality then it becomes essentially useless: it cannot tell us who really has the book, and we probably cannot trust any information it might give us. Preserving consistency conditions is more critical for the healthiness of our system than keeping within policy.

We identify the consistency requirements first because sometimes we can think of a state design that will reduce the need for consistency conditions. For example, if we record a borrower against a copy of a book, only one such borrower can be recorded and the inconsistency of two simultaneous borrowers cannot occur. We need to bear the consistency conditions in mind during development, as we will want our functions to maintain consistency, and our initial state to establish it.

Sometimes consistency is dealt with by a subtype: we can record the number of books someone can borrow as a **Nat**, for example, to prevent it being negative. But often consistency requirements will involve more than one module, and then it is generally better to define a function expressing it, but not try to impose it as a subtype. When there are several modules involved it may not always be true during processing: we will merely want to establish that, starting from a consistent state, every top-level function will generate another one.

There are several common sources of possible inconsistency that arise in many domains, because they relate to common data structures:

- Much data is modelled as maps, allowing us to use identifiers as references. These identifiers may then be used elsewhere, and we need to ensure that every reference is to data that exists. For example, the borrower of a copy of a book should be a registered user.
- Sometimes we have relations that relate values of some type to itself, like "child" or "part of" relations. Then we typically need to ensure that there are no cycles in the relation, or else functions using the relation are likely not to terminate.
- It may be possible to access information in two ways (which is an indication that our state is not minimal, but may be done for efficiency reasons, especially in refinements of the initial specification). Then we need to check that the two ways to access information give the same result. If we can find out borrowers from information about copies of books, and find out copies borrowed from information about borrowers, then we can state as a consistency conditions (a) that the recorded borrower of a book (if any)

has a borrow record for that copy for that book, and (b) that each copy in the set of copies borrowed by a borrower has the borrower recorded.

Consistency conditions help us write functions, or at least they help us avoid mistakes in functions that would occur if we overlooked consistency. They also have a relation to preconditions. Preconditions serve two main purposes:

1. They allow us to avoid unsafe or unpredictable situations, like dividing by zero, or in general applying a function or operator when its result would be undefined or non-terminating.
2. They allow us to avoid situations where we would otherwise break consistency. So a function **borrow**, for example, might include in its precondition that the user involved is registered.

It is not usually a good idea to include consistency as part of preconditions. The reason for this is that functions at the top level, accessible by our users (people or other software), will generally need to have preconditions checked when they are invoked. Checking consistency typically involves searches through all the state and this would be too inefficient. (At the same time, including a simple check even though it is implied by consistency is sensible as part of "safety-first" style.) We instead, as we mentioned above, take steps during development to ensure that our functions all preserve consistency, and that our initial state establishes it, so we can then assume it to be true.

Policy conditions are generally separated from consistency. States that violate policy requirements are possible in the real world, and if our system is to be a faithful model of the real world it must also allow them. Such states are often used to generate warning messages, raise alarms, or instigate corrective actions, so we still need to define precisely what the policy conditions are so that we can specify how to check them.

2.2.1 Kinds of Module

We identify two kinds of module that we find most commonly used: *global objects* and *state components*.

Global Objects. Global objects are objects declared at the top level, in a separate file. In general, they are not advised, because they have too wide a scope. But there are typically a collection of, in particular, types that we need in many places, such as identifiers for various kinds of entity, and it is convenient to collect these in one global object. Dates and a few functions or operators like $\leq$ to compare them, and perhaps also periods modelled as pairs of dates, or a date and a duration, are other common candidates. Global objects should not include any part of the state.

Another guide to when types should be in a global object is that types visible to users, i.e. types that occur as parameters to user functions or in the results of user functions, should generally be defined in one.

State Components. Most modules will contain a type modelling (a part of) the state, together with functions to *observe* it and *generate* values of it, and we term these state components. Generators usually include functions to change state values, and perhaps also to create them. The type is often called the *type of interest* of the module. Such modules are usually defined as schemes, and typically instantiated within others, as we will see in Section 2.2.3. Modules should have only one type of interest.

We write separate modules for each state component because we can then enforce a discipline that the part of the state within the module is only accessed through the functions defined for it. This enables us, for example, to change the way that part is modelled without affecting anything else, so long as we maintain the original properties. Such a technique is known as *encapsulation* through *information hiding*.

Object oriented approaches to program design follow the same ideas: they typically call the observers and generators *methods*.

The discussion in the following sections is almost entirely concerned with state component modules, and we will in particular talk of the type of interest, the observers and the generators of a module.

2.2.2 Abstract and Concrete Modules

There are various ways of writing modules, according to way in which the type of interest is defined. We will illustrate these with the idea of a bank account, seen as a record of transactions. We will keep the example very simple, as our purpose here is not to describe banking in detail but to show approaches to modelling. We assume that transactions have a date (the type Date defined in a global object T), an Amount (similarly defined globally, with + also defined for it), and some other information as yet undetermined. We will need functions open, to create a new account, add to add a transaction, and balance to calculate the current balance.

We start with the easiest specification to write, which is concrete as it uses a concrete model of the type of interest Account: an account is an ordered list of transactions:

```
scheme CONC_ACCOUNT =
with T in class
  type
    Account = {| trl : Transaction* • is_ordered(trl) |},
    Transaction ::
      date : Date
      amount : Amount
      info : Info,
```

Info
value
  open : Account = $\langle\rangle$,

  add : Transaction $\times$ Account $\xrightarrow{\sim}$ Account
  add(tr, ac) $\equiv$ $\langle$tr$\rangle$^ac
  pre can_add(tr, ac),

  can_add : Transaction $\times$ Account $\rightarrow$ **Bool**
  can_add(tr, ac) $\equiv$
    case ac **of**
      $\langle\rangle$ $\rightarrow$ **true**,
      $\langle$h$\rangle$^t $\rightarrow$ date(h) $\leq$ date(tr)
    end,

  balance : Account $\rightarrow$ Amount
  balance(ac) $\equiv$
    case ac **of**
      $\langle\rangle$ $\rightarrow$ 0,
      $\langle$h$\rangle$^t $\rightarrow$ amount(h) + balance(t)
    end,

  is_ordered : Transaction* $\rightarrow$ **Bool**
  is_ordered(ac) $\equiv$
    case ac **of**
      $\langle\rangle$ $\rightarrow$ **true**,
      $\langle\_\rangle$ $\rightarrow$ **true**,
      $\langle$h$_1$, h$_2\rangle$^t $\rightarrow$ date(h$_2$) $\leq$ date(h$_1$) $\wedge$ is_ordered($\langle$h$_2\rangle$^t)
    end
end

We realised that **add** needs to be partial, since we should not be able to add a transaction older than the latest one in the account. We adopt a useful convention to define a function can_f to express the precondition of a function f. This allows writers of functions elsewhere to check the precondition using can_f, and to be somewhat insulated from changes to can_f that might be made later.

This very simple specification raises some immediate questions, such as whether **open** should be a function with some parameters, such as the date of opening, or information about the account holder? This is at least in part a question about the requirements, and is typical of the questions that naturally arise from the specification that can indicate missing requirements (either missing from the requirements or missed by us in reading them). We might similarly wonder, since there is a function to add a transaction, if there should also be one to delete or change an existing transaction. And if so, should transactions have identifiers? Similarly, if an account can be opened, can it also be closed, and if so, do its records disappear?

There is also a question about the type Transaction: Should it be in a module of its own? We might consider this not necessary, because it is so simple: the functions needed to generate and observe it are already embodied in its definition and the module would have nothing more to define. But in fact the appropriate conclusion here is that Transaction should probably be defined in the global object T, because it is visible to users, who will have available some function to display or print their account. In the following versions we will assume that Transaction is defined in T. We also realise another missing or missed requirement: that we need another function to report on transactions:

value

    transactions_since : Date × Account → Transaction*

    transactions_since(d, ac) ≡ ⟨ tr | tr **in** ac • d ≤ date(tr) ⟩

The concrete module CONC_ACCOUNT says that an account is precisely its sequence of transactions. But this may not be an adequate model. It might in the final implementation be an archive of previous years' transactions plus this year's stored separately and more immediately available. And balances are in practice not calculated from the beginning each time, but perhaps stored and updated with each transaction. Such a balance would be an example of dependent information not included in the initial specification.

Here is an abstract version of the account module:

scheme ABS_ACCOUNT =
with T in class
  type
    Account
  value
    /* generators */
    open : Account,
    add : Transaction × Account $\overset{\sim}{\to}$ Account,
    /* observers */
    can_add : Transaction × Account → **Bool**,
    balance : Account → Amount,
    transactions_since : Date × Account → Transaction*
  axiom
    [can_add_open] ∀ tr : Transaction • can_add(tr, open) ≡ **true**,

    [can_add_add]
      ∀ tr_0, tr_1 : Transaction, ac : Account •
        can_add(tr_1, add(tr_0, ac)) ≡ date(tr_0) ≤ date(tr_1)
        pre can_add(tr_0, ac),

[balance_open] balance(open) ≡ 0,

[balance_add]
    ∀ tr : Transaction, ac : Account •
      balance(add(tr, ac)) ≡ amount(tr) + balance(ac)
      pre can_add(tr, ac),

[transactions_since_open] ∀ d : Date • transactions_since(d, open) ≡ ⟨⟩,

[transactions_since_add]
    ∀ d : Date, tr : Transaction, ac : Account •
      transactions_since(d, add(tr, ac)) ≡
        if d ≤ date(tr) **then** ⟨tr⟩^transactions_since(d, ac)
        else ⟨⟩ **end**
      pre can_add(tr, ac)
end

Abstract specifications in this style define the type of interest Account as an abstract type, and the constants and functions as signatures only. Axioms then relate observers to generators.

Most people do not find such specifications easy to write. There is an alternative style that gives a specification that is also abstract, in that it allows the same room for the type Account to be developed further, but is easier to write – which means less likely to contain errors!

We define the type Account abstractly, and then define one or more *main observers* that return precisely the type we used in the concrete version CONC_ACCOUNT. (We would use more than one observer if the concrete type had been a product or record.)

scheme ACCOUNT =
with T **in hide** transactions, balance₁ **in class**
  type
    Account,
    Transactions = {| trl : Transaction* • is_ordered(trl) |}
  value
    transactions : Account → Transactions,

    open : Account • transactions(open) = ⟨⟩,

    add : Transaction × Account →̃ Account
    add(tr, ac) **as** ac′ **post** transactions(ac′) = ⟨tr⟩^transactions(ac)
    pre can_add(tr, ac),

    can_add : Transaction × Account → **Bool**
    can_add(tr, ac)

as b **post**
  b $\Rightarrow$
    case transactions(ac) **of**
      $\langle\rangle \rightarrow$ **true**,
      $\langle h\rangle\hat{\ }t \rightarrow$ date(h) $\leq$ date(tr)
    end,

balance : Account $\rightarrow$ Amount
balance(ac) $\equiv$ balance$_1$(transactions(ac)),

balance$_1$: Transaction* $\rightarrow$ Amount
balance$_1$(trl) $\equiv$
case trl **of**
  $\langle\rangle \rightarrow 0$,
  $\langle h\rangle\hat{\ }t \rightarrow$ amount(h) + balance$_1$(t)
end,

transactions_since : Date $\times$ Account $\rightarrow$ Transaction*
transactions_since(d, ac) $\equiv$ $\langle$ tr | tr **in** transactions(ac) • d $\leq$ date(tr) $\rangle$,

is_ordered : Transaction* $\rightarrow$ **Bool**
is_ordered(ac) $\equiv$
case ac **of**
  $\langle\rangle \rightarrow$ **true**,
  $\langle\_\rangle \rightarrow$ **true**,
  $\langle h_1, h_2\rangle\hat{\ }t \rightarrow$ date(h$_2$) $\leq$ date(h$_1$) $\wedge$ is_ordered($\langle h_2\rangle\hat{\ }t$)
end
end

Here the type **Transactions** is just a convenience, and the main observer is **transactions**. Constants are defined by implicit value definitions, and functions by post conditions. The specification of **can_add** says that the new transaction date being no earlier than the last transaction in the account is a necessary, but not a sufficient condition for **add**: we envisage the possibility of adding some means of closing an account, perhaps, or insisting that the balance must always be non-negative. But we are sufficiently sure to define balance and **transactions_since** in terms of **transactions**. The main observer **transactions** is not defined: we can only do so when we decide exactly what the type Account will be. It is usually hidden, and we have also hidden the extra function balance$_1$ we used to define **balance**.

The concrete version CONC_ACCOUNT can easily be obtained as a refinement of ACCOUNT by implementing the main observer **transactions** as the identity function. But there are many other possible refinements with a richer state with more information, such as adding the possibility for accounts to be opened and closed, or including the current balance.

2.2.3 Module Hierarchies

There are several suggested principles in creating a collection of modules to model a system:

- Each module should have only one type of interest, defining functions to create, modify and observe values of the type.
- The modules should as far as possible form a *hierarchy*: each module below the top one should be instantiated in only one other, its *parent*, as an embedded object, and its functions should only be called from its parent.

This leads naturally to a top-down style of specification and development. As we decide on the concrete type for a module, perhaps involving several components, then as long as these component types are non-trivial we define new modules for them as children of the original.

The restriction to a hierarchy sometimes seems more complicated than, say, a collection of global objects each defining one part of the state, with objects able to call functions in any others. But such designs have definite disadvantages:

- The many interdependencies mean that changes to a module may affect many others, so maintenance is more difficult.
- They are harder to test individually. With a hierarchy there is natural testing order that tests children before parents.
- In a concurrent system it is hard to ensure that the system will not deadlock. Following the guidelines for developing concurrent systems from sequential ones in Section 2.3.2 means that freedom from deadlock is guaranteed by a simple syntactic check.

It may not be clear why we suggested using embedded objects to link child modules to their parents. There are three possibilities to use one module (the child) in another (the parent), which we consider in turn:

1. Merging the specifications textually into a single module. This is clearly not very sensible. Apart from breaking the suggestion that there only be one type of interest per module, the resulting large module is hard to read, the child cannot be reused elsewhere, it is tedious to hide the child components (as they must be hidden individually), and there may be name clashes between the two parts.
2. Writing the parent as an extension (**extend S with** ... where S is the scheme defining the child). This gives two separate modules, and so is readable, and the child module S can be reused, but it still suffers from the disadvantages that it is hard to hide the child components, and there may be name clashes between the two parts. (We typically use **extend** to add definitions to an existing type of interest, or perhaps to make a subtype of it, such as defining an interest-bearing deposit account by extending a basic account specification.)

3. Instantiating the child as an object within the parent. The separate modules are small and readable, the child is reusable, the child can be hidden merely by hiding its object identifier, and name clashes cannot occur because within the parent specification all the entities from the child have an object identifier qualifier. Hence this is normally the best solution.

2.2.4 Sharing Child Modules

Consider the proposed module structure in Figure 2.1.

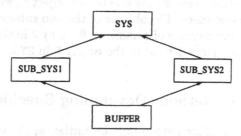

Fig. 2.1. Sharing a child module.

If we take the advice about instantiating children as objects in parents, then in SYS we get two objects, called S_1 and S_2 perhaps, and in each of SUB_SYS$_1$ and SUB_SYS$_2$ we get an object B, say, instantiating BUFFER. How many buffers are there? There are two. We can see this because in SYS they have names S_1.B and S_2.B, and RSL is constructed so that different names imply different objects: there is no possibility of "aliasing", of having different names for the same variable, channel or object. Different objects will have different variables, different channels, and different embedded objects, even if they are instantiations of the same scheme.

If the buffers are intended to be different, this is fine. But what if the two sub-systems want to share one buffer, perhaps for passing information between them? This will break the normal idea of hierarchical design that child modules are independent, since a call in SYS of a function in S_1, say, can result in a change in state of both B and S_2. But sometimes it is necessary. We then have to be more careful than usual how we call child functions from SYS.

If we need such a design, there are two ways to achieve it. The first is to make a global object B, say, from BUFFER, and use this in both SUB_SYS$_1$ and SUB_SYS$_2$. Now there is one buffer (because there is only one name for it) and so the two sub-systems must be sharing it. But other modules can also access it. What we probably want is for the buffer to be shared between the sub-systems, but be hidden within SYS.

The second solution us to use parameterisation. We make BUFFER a parameter of both SUB_SYS$_1$ and SUB_SYS$_2$:

scheme SUB_SYS$_1$(B : BUFFER) = ...
scheme SUB_SYS$_2$(B : BUFFER) = ...

and in SYS we define the following objects:

object
    B : BUFFER,
    S$_1$: SUB_SYS$_1$(B),
    S$_2$: SUB_SYS$_2$(B)

Now we can see that there is only one buffer object B, which is defined in SYS and can be hidden there. The objects of the two sub-systems now share this buffer because any mention of a name prefixed by B in their specifications is now bound to that name defined in the object B in SYS.

2.3 The RAISE Method: Developing Specifications

In this section we consider developing the initial, applicative specification into a program. We will see that there is a standard "development route" that we often use, that develops from an applicative to an imperative style, and possibly on to a concurrent style. We will also discuss what it means for a development to be "correct", and how we can ensure correctness.

2.3.1 Imperative Modules

Our experience is that applicative modules, ones without any variables, following a "functional programming" style, are the easiest to write. This may seem surprising to people used to writing in imperative languages like C++ or Java, but dependence on variables also seems to encourage a style that is programming rather than specification. The idea of specification is, ideally, to write as little as possible, to model the data structures in a minimal way, trying to avoid making premature design decisions about data structures and algorithms. Above all, the aim is to meet the requirements, and the less you write the less there is to validate against the requirements.

If you want to do proof, then proofs are certainly much simpler based on applicative specifications.

But the intended implementation style is likely to be imperative. The comparative run-time efficiency of imperative programs over applicative ones is often exaggerated, but there can be definite advantages in, for example, using iteration instead of recursion if the depth of recursion is deep.

Fortunately, it is very simple to transform an applicative specification into an imperative one. This is normally only done when the design has reached the point where the type of interest is concrete, so we take the previous concrete specification CONC_ACCOUNT as an example. Here is the imperative version:

scheme IMP_ACCOUNT =
with T **in hide** Account, ac **in class**
  type
    Account = {| trl : Transaction* • is_ordered(trl) |}
  variable
    ac : Account := $\langle\rangle$
  value
    open : **Unit** → **write ac Unit**
    open() ≡ ac := $\langle\rangle$,

    add : Transaction $\overset{\sim}{\to}$ **write ac Unit**
    add(tr) ≡ ac := $\langle tr\rangle\hat{\ }$ac
    pre can_add(tr),

    can_add : Transaction → **read ac Bool**
    can_add(tr) ≡
      case ac **of**
        $\langle\rangle$ → **true**,
        $\langle h\rangle\hat{\ }t$ → date(h) ≤ date(tr)
      end,

    balance : **Unit** → **read ac Amount**
    balance() ≡ balance(ac),

    balance : Account → Amount
    balance(ac) ≡
      case ac **of**
        $\langle\rangle$ → 0,
        $\langle h\rangle\hat{\ }t$ → amount(h) + balance(t)
      end,

    transactions_since : Date → **read ac Transaction***
    transactions_since(d) ≡ $\langle$ tr | tr **in** ac • d ≤ date(tr) $\rangle$,

    is_ordered : Transaction* → **Bool**
    is_ordered(ac) ≡
      case ac **of**
        $\langle\rangle$ → **true**,
        $\langle\_\rangle$ → **true**,
        $\langle h_1, h_2\rangle\hat{\ }t$ → date(h_2) ≤ date(h_1) ∧ is_ordered($\langle h_2\rangle\hat{\ }t$)
      end
end

(The type Transaction is omitted because, following the discussion earlier, it is now assumed to be defined in the global object T.)

The changes from CONC_ACCOUNT are quite straightforward:

- A variable is defined to hold values of the type of interest. This is usually initialised if there is an obvious value to use. If the type of interest is a record or product, several variables may be used, one for each component.
- The type of interest is removed from the parameter and result types of functions, and if this leaves nothing as a parameter or result type, **Unit** is inserted.
- Generators are given write access to the variable(s); observers are given read access.
- Formal parameters of the type of interest are removed. References to them in the bodies of functions are replaced with reference to the variable(s).
- Generators include assignment(s) to the variable(s) of the new value generated.
- Constants like open are defined as functions in the way illustrated.
- The type of interest and the variable(s) are hidden.

Sometimes, especially with recursive functions, we define the imperative function in terms of the corresponding applicative one, as with **balance**.

The transformation is very straightforward and easily checked. There is a theorem (explained in detail in the RAISE method book [117]) that the resulting imperative module has the same properties as the applicative one. To be more precise, there is a way of rewriting the properties of the applicative one into corresponding imperative ones that are guaranteed to hold for the imperative version. Intuitively, the applicative and imperative versions "behave in the same way". For example, starting with empty accounts and adding the same transactions to both will give the same observed values for **balance** and **transactions_since**.

This transformation is often applied to leaf modules in the hierarchy, i.e. to modules with no children, but can, as we shall see, be applied at any level in the hierarchy, with the children left applicative.

Parent modules normally have no variables: their state is the state of their children. For parent modules with imperative children the type of interest disappears altogether, and the changes to signatures also involve the removal of this type. Bodies change by calling the new imperative functions of the children, which is just a matter of removing the formal parameters corresponding to the type of interest. Since there are no such parameters needed for the children's functions this is simple.

To illustrate, suppose for simplicity that there is only one account per account-holder, and there are separate modules for storing information about account-holders and their accounts. Then the applicative parent module of CONC_ACCOUNT, ACCOUNT_AND_HOLDER, might have contained:

object
    A : CONC_ACCOUNT,
    H : HOLDER

type
  Account_and_holder ::
    account : A.Account
    holder : H.Holder   -- type of interest of HOLDER
value
  open : Holder_info → Account_and_holder
  open(i) ≡ mk_Account_and_holder(A.open, H.new(i))

The imperative version will contain:

object
  A : IMP_ACCOUNT,
  H : IMP_HOLDER
value
  open : Holder_info → **write A.any, H.any Unit**
  open(i) ≡ A.open() ; H.new(i)

We see that in the imperative version applicative modules are replaced by their imperative versions, and the type of interest disappears entirely.

We know that **open** is a generator, so it may change variables in the child modules. But we don't know what the variables are: they are hidden, the state of these modules is encapsulated. So we use universal accesses to indicate that the generator **open** may change any variables in the two child modules.

Since we know from the rules of hierarchical design that child modules cannot call each others' functions, their states are *independent*: a change in one cannot in itself affect the other. So it doesn't matter in which order we call the functions A.open and H.new: we could even invoke them in parallel.

This method of making leaf modules imperative encounters a difficulty when there is a collection of data at lower levels. If we replace each applicative object with one imperative one, how can we hold data about many accounts, for example? We illustrate by considering the same example at the level above. An applicative module ACCOUNTS, say, might have contained:

object
  AH : ACCOUNT_AND_HOLDER
type
  Accounts = Ac_no $\overrightarrow{m}$ AH.Account_and_holder
value
  open : Ac_no × Holder_info × Accounts $\overset{\sim}{\to}$ Accounts
  open(no, i, acs) ≡ acs † [no ↦ AH.open(i)]
  pre ∼ exist(no, acs),

  exist : Ac_no × Accounts → **Bool**
  exist(no, acs) ≡ no ∈ acs

The simplest solution is to make this module imperative, and keep its children applicative. Their functions are simply those used to create, modify, and observe components of the values held in the variable(s) of the parent. So instead of making ACCOUNT_AND_HOLDER and its children imperative, we would change ACCOUNTS to:

object
    AH : ACCOUNT_AND_HOLDER   -- still applicative
type
    Accounts = Ac_no $\overrightarrow{m}$ AH.Account_and_holder
variable
    acs : Accounts := [ ]
value
    open : Ac_no × Holder_info $\overset{\sim}{\rightarrow}$ **write** acs **Unit**
    open(no, i) ≡ acs := acs † [no ↦ AH.open(i)]
    pre ~ exist(no),

    exist : Ac_no → **read** acs **Bool**
    exist(no) ≡ no ∈ acs

The variable acs holds all the accounts in a map. This is a natural style to use if the variable acs is to be implemented as a database. The applicative child modules are a specification of the database design.

It is also possible to specify ACCOUNTS with imperative child modules, when the object declaration in ACCOUNTS would be replaced by an object array. This is the way to specify ACCOUNTS if we want to program each account as a separate object, rather than, as above, using a single database for all the accounts. It is complicated by the fact that object arrays in RSL are static, so that all accounts potentially exist from the start, and we have to include information about which account numbers are currently "live". Then our imperative version of ACCOUNTS would look something like:

object
    AH[no : Ac_no] : IMP_ACCOUNT_AND_HOLDER   -- imperative
variable
    live : Ac_no-**set** := {}
value
    open : Ac_no × Holder_info $\overset{\sim}{\rightarrow}$ **write** AH.**any**, live **Unit**
    open(no, i) ≡ AH[no].open(i) ; live := live ∪ {no}
    pre ~ exist(no),

    exist : Ac_no → **read** live **Bool**
    exist(no) ≡ no ∈ live

2.3.2 Concurrent Modules

If a concurrent system is required, for example if the system is to have multiple users at the same time, or is to be distributed, concurrent modules can be developed from the imperative ones. (It is also possible to go directly from applicative to concurrent if the specification is simple.) Each imperative module with variables is transformed into a *server*. A server has a main process that is normally a **while true** loop. The purpose of the server is to ensure that the interactions with the imperative module, which is embedded in the concurrent one, are atomic. When one user starts an interaction others are forced to wait until the interaction is complete. The concurrent module is like a wrapper of the imperative one, to mediate interactions with it. To illustrate, we show a concurrent version of ACCOUNT:

```
scheme C_ACCOUNT =
with T in hide I, C, server in class
  object
    I : IMP_ACCOUNT,
    C :
      class
        channel
          open : Unit, add : Transaction, add_res : Add_result,
          balance : Amount, since : Date, since_res : Transaction*
      end
  value
    init : Unit → in C.any out C.any write I.any Unit
    init() ≡ I.open() ; server(),

    server : Unit → in C.any out C.any write I.any Unit
    server() ≡
      while true do
        C.open? ; I.open()
        []
        let tr = C.add? in
          if I.can_add(tr) then I.add(tr) ; C.add_res!ok
          else C.add_res!fail end
        end
        []
        C.balance!I.balance()
        []
        let d = C.since? in C.since_res!I.transactions_since(d) end
      end,

    open : Unit → out C.open Unit
    open() ≡ C.open!(),
```

add : Transaction → **out** C.add **in** C.add_res Add_result
add(tr) ≡ C.add!tr ; C.add_res?,

balance : **Unit** → **in** C.balance Amount
balance() ≡ C.balance?,

transactions_since : Date → **out** C.since **in** C.since_res Transaction*
transactions_since(d) ≡ C.since!d ; C.since_res?
end

We see that the imperative module IMP_ACCOUNT is used to define an embedded object I that is hidden. A number of channels are defined for communicating the parameters and results of the functions. These can be defined in an object, here C, which is just a convenience for hiding them collectively. An **init** process is defined to initialise the object I and then start the **server**. The **server** is a loop containing an external choice, one choice for each function. It simply inputs parameters (if any) on a channel, calls the appropriate function from I, and outputs results (if any) on another channel. Finally there is a set of *interface processes* which are the functions that may be called to access the module. There must be one for each choice in **server**, and it must do the converse of the inputs and outputs in that choice.

If this design approach is followed and checked then it is impossible for the module to deadlock, and concurrent calls of the interface processes will be atomic, i.e. they will be executed sequentially in some arbitrary order.

As we discussed earlier in Section 2.1.9, we need to change partial functions like add into total ones. So we added an Add_result type, defined as a variant with two values ok and fail to the global object T and return an appropriate value of this type. Since can_add was previously only included for the parent module to check the precondition of add, it may now be redundant and is not included in the concurrent version: it could easily be included if still required.

It should be apparent that the concurrent version of ACCOUNT behaves just like the imperative one. All we have done is protect the imperative module against concurrent accesses to it interfering with each other. This theorem is formalised in the RAISE method book [117].

In the transformation to a concurrent system, children of the imperative one with variables remain applicative. Parent modules are changed in minor ways as follows:

- Instantiations of imperative modules are replaced by instantiations of the concurrent ones.
- An **init** process is added that calls the **init** processes of all its children in parallel. This means there will be an **init** process in the top level module

that will, when invoked, initialise and start the servers of all its children running in parallel.

- Calls of previously partial functions need to be changed because they will have new result types.
- Sequential invocations of two or more functions in different children are normally replaced by concurrent invocations. This is safe, because we know that hierarchical design ensures that there can be no interference between the state changes of different children. So different evaluation orders will make the same changes and return the same results.

2.3.3 Development Route

The overall suggested development route is illustrated in Figure 2.2. The initial vertical line indicates development of data structures and algorithms from an initial, abstract specification. The development is done using an "invent and verify" strategy. That is, design decisions are made and reflected in a new specification. This can then be verified, shown to be correct, perhaps by proof, according to the rules discussed later in Section 2.3.6. The transformations to imperative and then concurrent versions may be done if needed, and are applied to concrete modules (modules with concrete type of interest). Some further refinement may be done to particular functions in the imperative and concurrent versions if needed. For example, expressions involving quantifiers might be developed into loops. Techniques for doing this are described in the RAISE method book [117].

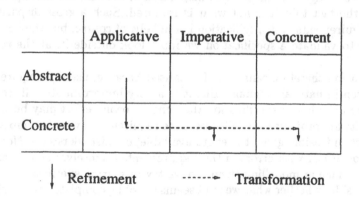

Fig. 2.2. The RAISE development route.

2.3.4 Asynchronous Systems

Some systems, particularly distributed ones, will need further development into asynchronous systems, typically by introducing buffers between components instead of the "remote procedure call" design implied by the concurrent specification described in the previous Section 2.3.2. In outline, to make a system asynchronous, we:

- Define a collection of buffers to carry request and result messages.
- Replace calls of functions in child modules with functions that send request messages and then wait for replies to appear in the appropriate buffers.
- In modules with servers, "wrap" the interface processes with ones that wait for messages in appropriate buffers, call the interface processes to obtain results, and then send replies containing those results. These wrappers are defined as **while true** loops, so that they continually wait for request messages.

Apart from delays, and provided the buffers are fault-free, the asynchronous system will behave just like the synchronous one. Fault tolerance can be introduced by, for example, having a policy that every request is answered by an acknowledgement, and by, in the final implementation, including time-outs on the waits for replies. Section 5.4 of Chapter 5 describes such a distributed development.

2.3.5 Validation and Verification

Validation is the check that we have written the right specification, i.e. that we have met the requirements. It has nothing to do with internal properties: one can have a perfectly satisfactory description of a tunnel when what is wanted is a bridge, and no detailed inspection of the tunnel's description can uncover the fact that it is not what is required. Such a gross disparity between requirements and specification is unlikely, of course, but the basic fact remains: to validate a specification we must look outside it, at the requirements

Validation therefore cannot be formalised because, usually, requirements are written in natural language. But it is a very important step: if we make mistakes in the initial specification then the following effort may be wasted! Many software projects have failed because requirements were incomplete, inconsistent, infeasible given the effort available, or misunderstood. Note that we are concerned with errors in the requirements themselves as well as with errors we make in modelling them. So we try in writing specifications to actively consider whether what we read seems sensible, complete and consistent. In creating a formal model we tend to come up with many questions, and generating these questions to ask of the people responsible for the requirements (the *customers*) has proved to be extremely beneficial in detecting problems at the start of the project. We try to be abstract, but that is not the same thing as being vague!

The main technique in validation is to check that each requirement is met. When we have written the initial specification we go back to the requirements and for each issue that we can find, we should conclude one of the following:

- It is met.
- It is not met, and we need to change the specification.
- It is not met because we think it is not a good idea (because of infeasibility, or for consistency with other parts, perhaps) and we need to discuss with the customers.
- It will be deferred to later in the development. This applies to "nonfunctional requirements" like the intended programming language or operating system, or performance requirements, but also to things that we have not yet designed, like aspects of the user interface or particular algorithms to be used. In this case we add it to a list of the requirements against which later development steps will be validated. We need, of course, to have in mind a development strategy that will allow such requirements to be met eventually.

There are also other validation techniques we can use:

- With experience, we can read the specification to look for properties that it will have that are not mentioned in the requirements. To take a trivial example, when we specify data storage, we naturally ask if it may become full, and if so what should happen. It may be that the user has not considered the possibility. Another example is whether a data structure should be initialised, and if so to what? This is typical of the kind of issue that may seem so obvious to the customers, who know the domain well, that they omitted to mention it. Scenarios, or use-cases, often lack essential but, to the customer, "obvious" steps. We should set up a formal procedure of queries to customers and their answers being documented.
- We should develop system tests (test cases and expected results) along with the specification. Doing this often helps to clarify the requirements, and these can also be shown to the customers, who will usually find them easier to read than the formal specification [3, 68].
- It is possible to rewrite the requirements from the specification. This is an expensive task, but generally produces requirements documents that are clearer, better structured, more concise, and more complete than the originals.
- We can prototype all or part of the system, perhaps by doing a quick and simplified refinement of the abstract types in it, and using the translators to SML or C++ (see Section 2.3.9) in the RAISE tools to run some test cases. We can also let the customers use it to get more feedback from them.

Providing early feedback to the customers in the form of queries, test cases, rewritten requirements, or prototypes has the added advantage of committing them to what has been done so far, and helps demonstrate to them the added cost and danger of later requirement changes, the bane of every software project manager's life! We try to make the initial specification a *contract* between us and the customers.

Verification is the check that we are developing the system correctly, so that the final implementation conforms to the initial specification. It must come after validation, since it assumes the correctness of the initial specification. We discuss it as part of the next section on refinement.

2.3.6 Refinement

We mentioned earlier that we develop by "invent and verify": we invent a more concrete version of a module and then verify that it is correct with respect to previous one. The formal relation that must exist between the two is the *refinement relation*, sometimes also called the *implementation relation*.

The refinement relation needs to be transitive: we want to develop, say, from A_0 to A_1 and then from A_1 to A_2, checking refinement at each step, and be assured that A_2 must refine A_0. Additionally, refinement needs to be monotonic with respect to building modules from other modules. Suppose module A is developed through version A_0 to the final A_2 as above, and module B has first version B_0 that instantiates A_0 and is developed (perhaps by other people) to B_1, say, that still instantiates A_0. Now we want to integrate the final versions. We write module B_2 that differs from B_1 only in substituting the identifier A_2 for the identifier A_0: see Figure 2.3. We want, provided A_2 refines A_0 and B_1 refines B_0, that B_2 should be guaranteed to refine B_1 and hence B_0. Monotonicity is what gives this guarantee. If this were not true we could not conveniently develop modules separately. Effectively A_0 is a *contract* between the developers of B and the developers of A: it says to the developers of B what A will provide, and to the developers of A what they must provide. Just how the latter group does this should be of no concern to the former.

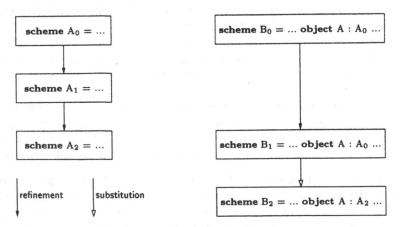

Fig. 2.3. Separate development.

The refinement relation should also hold in instantiations of parameterised of schemes: the class of each actual parameter should be a refinement of the class of the corresponding formal parameter.

The formal definition of refinement can be found in the RAISE method book [117]. Here we give an intuition. It has two components. For A_1 to refine A_0 we require:

- The signature of A_1 must include the signature of A_0. That is, A_1 must contain all the entities (types, values, variables, channels, and objects) with the same names and the same maximal types or, for objects, with classes that are in the same relation. This relation, termed *static implementation*, was introduced earlier in Section 2.1.11. The relation is necessary for the monotonicity property: we need to be able to replace references to A_0 with references to A_1 in other modules without causing type or scope errors. The signature we are concerned with does not include hidden entities: these do not need to be included in refinements. The relation is also one of inclusion: A_1 may have more entities than A_0.
- All the *properties* of A_0 must hold in A_1. Properties may be expressed as axioms, but also include definitions of constants and functions, initial values of variables, and the restrictions in subtypes. Property preservation is clearly transitive.

The first of these conditions can be checked statically, and the RAISE tools do this as part of type checking. The second is not statically checkable, and in general requires proof for full verification. But the "R" in RAISE stands for "rigorous": the method allows for the conditions to be checked informally, by hand. The amount of proof we do will depend on how critical the system is, and how much budget we have. Proof is expensive because it involves considerable time and also skilled, experienced people to do it. It is unfortunately the case that the kinds of proofs that arise in software development are generally beyond the capabilities of automated proof tools. The RAISE tools available at this book's web site (see page 395) do not currently include a proof tool, but there is one in the original RAISE tools [58].

2.3.7 Lightweight Formal Methods

Most of the case studies included in this book do not involve proof. In fact most do not even involve refinement: only one specification is written. Such use of a formal method is sometimes called "lightweight". It is found that most of the benefit of a formal method is in analysing and capturing requirements, in identifying and resolving requirements issues at the start of development, and in providing a sound basis for implementation. If the specification is not too complicated, implementation may be done directly from it.

Not all specifications are written to be developed. For example, in this book there are two chapters, 9 on authentication protocols and 10 on the

Realm structure used in cartography, that are specifications of existing implementations. The purpose here is to formalise and clarify a theory, and perhaps (as in the protocol chapter) to prove properties of it.

There are some formal techniques that we can employ, that may or may not employ proof, that we can adopt to increase confidence in specifications: confidence conditions and theorems. We consider these in turn.

2.3.8 Confidence Conditions

Confidence conditions are conditions that should probably be true if the module is not to be inconsistent, but that cannot in general be determined as true or false by an automatic tool. The following conditions are generated by the RAISE tools:

1. Arguments of invocations of functions and operators are in subtypes, and, for partial functions and operators, preconditions are satisfied.
2. Values supposed to be in subtypes are in the subtypes. These are generated for
   - values in explicit value definitions;
   - values of explicit function definitions (for parameters in appropriate subtypes and satisfying any given preconditions);
   - initial values of variables;
   - values assigned to variables;
   - values output on channels.
3. Subtypes are not empty.
4. Values satisfying the restrictions exist for implicit value and function definitions.
5. The classes of actual scheme parameters implement the classes of the formal parameters.
6. For an implementation relation, the implementing class implements the implemented class. This gives a means of expanding such a relation or expression, by asserting the relation in a theory and then generating the confidence conditions for the theory.
7. A definition of a partial function without a precondition (which generates the confidence condition **false**).
8. A definition of a total function with a precondition (which generates the confidence condition **false**).

Examples of all the first 4 kinds of confidence conditions listed above are generated from the following intentionally peculiar scheme (in which line numbers have been inserted so that readers can relate the following confidence conditions to their source):

```
1 scheme CC =
2 class
3   value
```

```
4     x1 : Int = hd <..>,
5     x2 : Int = f1(-1),
6     x3 : Nat = -1,
7     f1 : Nat -~-> Nat
8     f1(x) is -x
9     pre x > 0
10    variable
11      v : Nat := -1
12    channel
13      c : Nat
14    value
15      g : Unit -> write v out c Unit
16      g() is v := -1 ; c!-1
17    type
18      None = {| i : Nat :- i < 0 |}
19    value
20      x4 : Nat :- x4 < 0,
21      f2 : Nat -> Nat
22      f2(n) as r post n + r = 0
23 end
```

This produces the following confidence conditions (which are all provably false). The first part of each condition is a reference to its source in the form file:line:column:

```
CC.rsl:4:19: CC:
-- application arguments and/or precondition
let x = <..> in x ~= <..> end

CC.rsl:5:18: CC:
-- application arguments and/or precondition
-1 >= 0 /\ let x = -1 in x > 0 end

CC.rsl:6:14: CC:
-- value in subtype
-1 >= 0

CC.rsl:8:5: CC:
-- function result in subtype
all x : Nat :- (x > 0 is true) => -x >= 0

CC.rsl:11:13: CC:
-- initial value in subtype
-1 >= 0

CC.rsl:16:17: CC:
```

```
-- assigned value in subtype
-1 >= 0

CC.rsl:16:24: CC:
-- output value in subtype
-1 >= 0

CC.rsl:18:26: CC:
-- subtype not empty
exists i : Nat :- i < 0

CC.rsl:20:8: CC:
-- possible value in subtype
exists x4 : Nat :- x4 < 0

CC.rsl:22:5: CC:
-- possible function result in subtype
all n : Nat :- exists r : Nat :- n + r = 0
```

It is usually sufficient to carefully *inspect* confidence conditions rather than trying to prove them. Most of the time it is easy to see that the conditions are OK, but they are a good way to find errors, particularly in the first category where we apply a function forgetting its precondition.

There is a danger when proving confidence conditions, since they can indicate an inconsistency in the module. For example, scheme CC above asserts through the definition of x3 that −1 is in the type **Nat**. This is false, and so this definition implies the property **false**. CC is therefore inconsistent and anything can be proved about it. In particular, all the provably false confidence conditions above can also be proved true! So if we try to prove confidence conditions we must proceed with care.

Theorems. Theorems are formal statements about specifications that we state separately: they are intended to be consequences of the specifications, not part of their definitions. They can be proved, formally or by hand, or just examined carefully. Even when not proved they can be useful as part of the documentation.

Theorems can be stated in RAISE by means of a **theory** module. A theory takes the form:

theory name :
axiom

...

end

where ... is one or more axiom definitions. To support theories there are two extensions to the RAISE syntax that are useful:

- The *implementation relation* ⊢ $C_1 \preceq C_0$, where C_1 and C_0 are class expressions. The implementation (or refinement) relation was described in Section 2.3.6.
- The *class scope expression* in C ⊢ expr, where C is a class expression and expr is a boolean expression which may reference entities defined in C.

Generating confidence conditions for an implementation relation will expand it into its constituent properties, allowing us to examine them without necessarily proving them, or perhaps only proving some.

Typically if we want to do proof we will concentrate on critical properties. For example, if there are system consistency properties that should always be maintained, we can formulate as theorems the property that they are maintained by our generators (provided any preconditions hold). For example, suppose in scheme A, **gen** is a generator with a parameter of type U, T is the type of interest, and **can_gen** is a function expressing the precondition of **gen**, so the definition of **gen** looks like:

value
    gen : U × T $\overset{\sim}{\to}$ T
    gen(u, t) ≡ ...
    pre can_gen(u, t)

Then the theorem we would write is:

in A ⊢ ∀ u : U, t : T •
    consistent(t) ∧ can_gen(u, t) ⇒ consistent(gen(u, t))

Consistency conditions are a good choice for doing proofs. Generating the wrong result values of functions often shows up in testing, but creating inconsistencies in the system may not show up until some time after the inconsistency was created, and so it may be be hard to find them in testing and hard to identify when and how an inconsistency was originally generated.

Inclusion of checking consistency is also a good thing to include in test cases. But only with a proof can one be sure that a generator will never cause an inconsistency.

Finally, one should not forget the value of code reading by peers. This is a comparatively cheap and very effective means of discovering errors, and can be applied to specifications as much as to code. In fact it is generally easier to read specifications than programming language code. They are more abstract, and are intended to be read by people rather than machines.

2.3.9 Generating the Executable Program

The traditional development route is from RAISE to a programming language like C++ or Java. The RAISE tools available from this book's web site (see page 395) include a translators from a subset of RSL to C++ and

SML (though the latter is intended mainly for prototyping and testing). Parts of specifications may need to be translated to SQL, say, if part of the specification is intended to specify a database. The original RAISE tools [58] also include a translator to Ada. There is advice on translation by hand, including translation of concurrency, in the RAISE method book [117].

But there are many other possibilities. Chapter 12, for example, uses AWK as the implementation language.

2.4 When Not to Use RAISE

We do not mean to give the impression that RAISE or a similar software specification language should be used to define all software systems. There are exceptions, and we give some examples in this section.

2.4.1 There is a Special-Purpose Formalism

There are many special-purpose formalisms (sometimes with associated tools) that can sometimes be used in preference to a general purpose language like RSL. For example, BNF is a standard notation for defining grammars, and has associated tools like flex and bison for generating parsers and building abstract syntax trees. BNF is well defined, and provides a well-known, convenient, and compact notation. Copying this in RSL could be done, but the result would be less concise and still require the equivalent of flex and bison to be developed.

Real-time systems, ones which depend heavily on precise timing, such as real-time schedulers and process control systems, are often better analysed using a special-purpose formalism like Duration Calculus (DC) [23]. (There is some ongoing work to add real-time features to RSL [59, 89, 88].)

Another example is defining semantics of languages. There are notations like Structured Operational Semantics [115] that have their own compact notations that would be much less readable in RSL.

There is a similar example in this book, in Section 12.5 of Chapter 12. There a grammar of logical expressions is defined using BNF, and its semantics is defined in a traditional mathematical style. This could have been done in RSL, but for a small example the BNF and mathematics provide a more compact presentation, with special symbols well known to many people, and the advantages of using RSL (tools with type checking, for example) are perhaps outweighed.

Another example is Chapter 13 which includes two descriptions of a pattern definition language. The first (Section 13.4) is mathematical in style, and the second (Section 13.6) is in RSL. The mathematical presentation has again the advantage of brevity. The RSL presentation is used to specify both the pattern language and how wrappers are generated from patterns, so the RSL provides a basis for development.

2.4.2 The Effort is Not Worth the Gain

Sometimes there is a language adapted to a particular kind of application that allows the implementation to be written at a level that is very close to how one would specify it. An example is the RAISE tools at this book's web site. These were written in a language Gentle [129] that is a high level language intended for use by compiler constructors. The RAISE tools were written in this language without writing a specification of them. The reason is that for the type checker, for example (the first tool written and a basis for all the others) it was felt that the scope and type rules could not have been written at a much more abstract level: the actual error messages, and some details about input and output to files, which were largely copied from another system, would have been almost the only things left more abstract. So in this case the executable program (Gentle is executable in that it translates to C) is also the specification. (Interested readers can find the source of the tools at this book's web site.) There is, of course, a definition of the semantics of RSL (using a special-purpose formalism) that includes the static semantics (the scope and type rules) but the tools were not developed with close reference to this (and RSL has also been extended): the tool developer had a very good working knowledge of RSL having worked on its original design.

Another, rather different, example is graphical user interfaces. The top level RAISE specification of a system defines the functions that may be accessed by users, which may be people or other software. In the case of people, graphical user interfaces are common, and there are many languages and tools to aid their construction. A main feature of such interfaces is that they are functionally simple. They help users select the function they want to invoke (often with menus or buttons), they ask for the necessary inputs to be provided (by selection or on forms) and they display or output results. The top level specification describes what functions are available, shows through their signatures what inputs are needed and what results will be returned, and defines what preconditions need to be checked. All that needs to be done is the design of the graphical part, the definition of helpful messages when preconditions are violated, and perhaps the design of convenient output formats for extensive result values. There seems in practice little point in trying to specify these aspects, especially the graphical, visual ones.

3. A University Library Management System

3.1 Introduction

This chapter describes the formal development of an information system: a management system for a university library. This is a fairly straightforward example, intended to illustrate how data intensive systems may be designed using RAISE.

3.2 Requirements

The outline requirements for a university library are as follows:

- The library has various *resources* that may be consulted (in a "reading room") or borrowed, including books, (issues of) journals, and resources on other media (audio tapes or disks, audio-visual tapes or disks, CD-ROMs, etc.). Resource items may have multiple copies. Each (copy of an item) will have a unique identifier.
- The library has *users*, people who may consult or borrow resource items.
- The library has a collection of *policies* that may restrict who may borrow or consult resource items, what items may be borrowed or consulted, for how long, and in what quantities. These policies may distinguish between categories of users, and categories of items.
- The library has a *reservation* system by which resource items currently on loan may be reserved by other users so that they become available to them upon return. If several users wish to reserve an item the reservations will form a queue. Some categories of users may have priority over others.
- The library has a *search* facility that may be used to discover if an item is in the stock of the library, and its current status (such as *available, being consulted, on loan, being repaired, lost*). The search facility will support searching by matching words such as author names, names in titles, and item classification as well as identifier.
- The library supports a number of related functions:
  - adding, deleting, and updating items and copies of items
  - adding, deleting, and updating users

   – recording the activities of borrowing, consulting, returning, repairing, losing, and reserving copies of items.

3.3 Domain Analysis

3.3.1 Domain Modelling

A common way to start the analysis of requirements is to try to identify the entities that will exist in the system, (some of) their attributes, and the relations between them. This is commonly termed "domain analysis". For example, we might draw a UML "class diagram" like Figure 3.1.

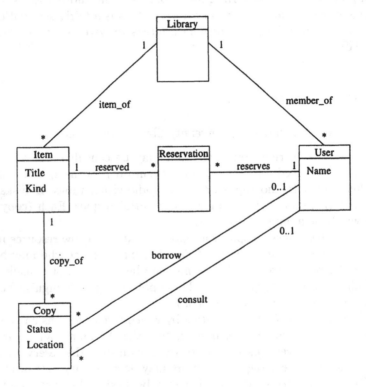

Fig. 3.1. Library class diagram.

   (UML imposes the default that associations that have no arrows, like all those in Figure 3.1, really have two arrows, implying navigability in both directions. In the discussion below this issue is considered open, so you should interpret this class diagram as one in preparation, to which arrows might be added.)

This is by no means the only possible such diagram for our system, and raises some questions:

- Why include the class **Library**?
- It is likely that the **borrow** relation needs to include the date of borrowing, or the return date. Where does this go? Do we need a **Borrow** class like the **Reservation** class?

  There is, incidentally, a good reason for the **Reservation** class that does not apply to a possible **Borrow** class: without it the reservation relation between users and items would be many-many, and such relations are best avoided.
- How can we record that the reservations for an item are supposed to be in a queue?
- Do we need a relation between **Reservation** and **Library**?
- A copy cannot both be being consulted and borrowed at the same time. Would a single relation **access**, say, between user and copy be better?
- What about library policies? Where do they go?

There are no universal answers to such questions, but there are some generally good ideas, at least when we want to make a specification from such a diagram:

1. It is a good idea to include the "top level", "system" class (here **Library**). It will correspond to the top level class in the RSL specification.
2. Many-many relations are often conveniently transformed into pairs of many-one relations using intermediate classes. But needing to record information against a relation does not in general justify creating another class.
3. For each class there needs to be a "main access path" from the top node to it that is composed of one or more relations (typically **X_of** or, in the other direction, **has**). These relation(s) need to be adequate to find all instances of the class. For example, it would be inadequate as well as strange to access **User** from **Library** via **Item** and **Copy**, because a user who currently has no copies borrowed would be inaccessible. There should only be one such path. One-many access paths, the most common form, are typically modelled as RSL maps in the class at the "1" end, and require that each instance of the class at the other end have some unique identifier: unique, that is, within the class containing the map. For example, copy numbers need only be unique within each item. The relations in such paths are referred to in UML as *aggregations*.
4. If two relations are mutually exclusive, a single relation encompassing both is probably better. So we will merge **borrow** and **consult** into a single **access** relation.
5. Other relations can be modelled in a variety of ways. Typically they will involve adding an attribute to the class at one end that mentions identifier(s) of the instances of the class at the other end. So, for **access**,

we could either include as an attribute of a copy who is accessing it, or we could include as an attribute of a user the copies that are currently accessing. Or we could do both. There are a number of issues to bear in mind as we make the choice:

a) An attribute recording one, or at most one, is generally simpler than one recording an arbitrary number.

b) While we try to avoid thinking about efficiency too much, notions of the most common access path in use may affect our decision. If we record accesses against copies, and not against users, we can easily answer "Who has this copy?" but it will require a search to answer "What copies does this user have?". Recording accesses only against users gives the reverse situation.

c) If we feel we want to record both, there is the immediate necessity of ensuring that the two ways of computing answers to questions like "Who has this copy?" give the same answer. We have identified a need for a *consistency* condition. We will also need to ensure that any functions that change the data change it so as to maintain consistency. It is generally the case that the fewer consistency conditions a design needs the better it is. Designers often worry too much about efficiency and not enough about consistency.

d) Even if we decide we need both, it is often a good idea to add the extra information as refinement step later in design, so that we keep our initial model as simple as possible, with the minimum of data and the minimum of consistency conditions. We might even prototype the simpler model in order to determine if the information really needs to be recorded, rather than calculated as needed.

In this example, we decide to record access information against both copies and users, and to do it in the initial specification. We feel that questions like "Who has this copy?" and "What copies does this user have?" are both very common (the first as a natural part of a search, and the second to check borrowing rights). We need to record status against copies, because it will take values like "lost" or "being repaired" that cannot be recorded as user accesses. This means that questions of the form "What copies does this user have?" would, unless we also record loan information against users, require searches of the database of items in the library, which will be fairly large.

6. There is a similar question about Reservations. We could:

a) Store reservations for an item as an attribute of the item.

b) Store reservations made by a user as an attribute of a user.

c) Do both.

We immediately see that the first allows us to store them as a queue for each item, thus meeting the requirement, and there seems no pressing reason to do both and having more data and another consistency condition.

We are now in a position to sketch the structure of the specification in terms of its main modules. There will typically be:

- a module for the top class (here **Library**)
- a module for each main access relation, which effectively models a collection of objects, like items, copies and users
- a module for each class that we have not decided to record as an attribute of something else.

There may well be more modules later, but this gives us a starting point. The structure is illustrated in Figure 3.2.

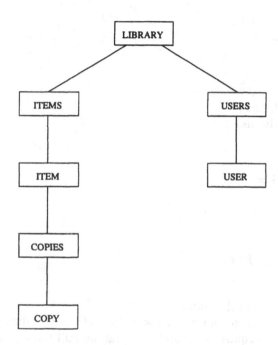

Fig. 3.2. Initial module structure.

Before writing these modules, we start by defining in a scheme TYPES some basic types that we have identified already, for identifying items, copies of items, and users. We also expect to find a globally unique identifier for a copy useful:

scheme TYPES =
class
  type
    Id, No, Uid,

```
    Copy_id ::
       id : Id
       copy : No
end
```

We make a global object T of this scheme.

Modules that arose from relations, like ITEMS, will typically have RSL maps as their main types. Other modules will typically have records as their main types, including components from the types of the modules below them in the hierarchy. So we can start to construct

```
scheme LIBRARY =
class
   object
      US : USERS,
      IS : ITEMS
   type
      Library ::
         users : US.Users
         items : IS.Items
end
```

```
scheme ITEMS =
class
   object
      I : ITEM
   type
      Items = Id ⇾ I.Item
end
```

and similarly for the other modules.

We have a sketch of the module structure of the specification. We need to go back to the requirements and see what we still have to do, and check that it can be fitted in. We start with reservations.

3.3.2 Reservations

In making reservations, the requirements state that some users might have higher priority. Perhaps professors, for example, will be able to overtake students. So we need a priority queue.

There is a problem here in that information about users, in the USERS module, is remote from where we want to maintain these queues, in the ITEMS module (see Figure 3.2). The RAISE method suggests hierarchical designs because they are clearer, easier to maintain, and easier to turn into concurrent systems than designs in which arbitrary connections can be made between modules. So we will not be able to call a function in USERS from ITEMS: we need the information to be given in the parameters of functions like **reserve**, say, defined in ITEMS to be called from LIBRARY.

A common technique is to assume the relative priority of users is encoded in their identifiers, but this short cut is not in general a good idea. If a user changes status their identifier would have to change, and this would be a tedious process because of·the various references that might exist. So, instead, we record the level of a user as part of the User type in USER, and pass this down to functions like **reserve**.

The type User_level is defined in TYPES as an abstract type (we will design it later) together with a means of comparing them:

type
  User_level
value
  $>$: User_level $\times$ User_level $\rightarrow$ **Bool**

We make a separate module for reservations: this is not necessary, but aids clarity. We store the level as well as the identifier of a Reservee so that we can keep the queue ordered by levels:

scheme RESERVATIONS =
with T **in class**
  type
    Reservee :: user : Uid   level : User_level,
    Reservations = {| rs : Reservee* • is_ordered(rs) |}
  value
    is_ordered : Reservee* $\rightarrow$ **Bool**
    is_ordered(rs) $\equiv$
      case rs **of**
        $\langle\rangle \rightarrow$ **true**,
        $\langle\_\rangle \rightarrow$ **true**,
        $\langle r_1, r_2 \rangle \,\hat{}\, t \rightarrow$
          $\sim$(level(r_2) $>$ level(r_1)) $\wedge$ user(r_1) $\neq$ user(r_2) $\wedge$
          user(r_1) $\notin$ reservees(t) $\wedge$ is_ordered($\langle r_2 \rangle \,\hat{}\, t$)
      end,

  reserve : Uid $\times$ User_level $\times$ Reservations $\rightarrow$ Reservations
  reserve(uid, l, rs) $\equiv$
    let rs_1 = cancel_reserve(uid, rs) **in**
      case rs_1 **of**
        $\langle\rangle \rightarrow \langle$mk_Reservee(uid, l)$\rangle$,
        $\langle h \rangle \,\hat{}\, t \rightarrow$
          if l $>$ level(h)
          then $\langle$mk_Reservee(uid, l)$\rangle \,\hat{}\, rs_1$
          else $\langle h \rangle \,\hat{}\,$ reserve(uid, l, t) **end end end**,

      cancel_reserve : Uid × Reservations → Reservations
      cancel_reserve(uid, rs) ≡
        case rs **of**
          ⟨⟩ → ⟨⟩,
          ⟨h⟩ ⌢ t →
            if uid = user(h) **then** t
            else ⟨h⟩ ⌢ cancel_reserve(uid, t)
            end
        end,

      next : Reservations $\xrightarrow{\sim}$ Uid
      next(rs) ≡ user(**hd** rs)
      pre ∼is_empty(rs),

      cancel_next : Reservations $\xrightarrow{\sim}$ Reservations
      cancel_next(rs) ≡ **tl** rs
      pre ∼is_empty(rs),

      is_empty : Reservations → **Bool**
      is_empty(rs) ≡ rs = ⟨⟩,

      reservees : Reservations → Uid-**set**
      reservees(rs) ≡ {user(r) | r : Reservee • r ∈ rs}
end

We keep the list ordered and also without duplicates. Duplication is calculated only using the user identifier, not the level. The latter is regarded as essentially redundant information that should be ignored whenever possible. Then, for example, a user's level changing would not allow the same user to reserve an item twice.

We now have the following for ITEM:

```
scheme ITEM =
class
  object
   CS : COPIES,
   RS : RESERVATIONS
  type
    Item ::
      info : Item_info
      kind : Item_kind
      level : Item_level
      copies : CS.Copies ↔ chg_copies
      reservations : RS.Reservations ↔ chg_reservations
end
```

The abstract type **Item_info** (defined in **TYPES**) will eventually define all the relatively static information about an item like author and title.

3.3.3 Loans

As an attribute of the type **Copy** we will need to define a status:

type
  Status ==
    available | repair | loan(luid : Uid, due : Date) |
    consult(cuid : Uid) | collect(uid : Uid) | lost

consult means the copy is in the reading room with a user. **collect** means the copy is awaiting collection by a user who had reserved it (having just been returned).

Loans need dates, and we add the following to **TYPES** to allow us to deal with dates and periods of time:

type
  Date,
  Period

value
  $>$: Date $\times$ Date $\to$ **Bool**,
  $+$: Date $\times$ Period $\to$ Date,
  $-$: Date $\times$ Date $\overset{\sim}{\to}$ Period,

  get_end_date : Date $\times$ Period $\to$ Date
  get_end_date(d, p) $\equiv$ d + p,

  get_period : Date $\times$ Date $\overset{\sim}{\to}$ Period
  get_period(d_1, d_2) $\equiv$ d_2 − d_1 **pre** d_2 > d_1

The definitions of these types are to be done later. We might just leave these to the implementor: they will typically be easy to define but the details will depend on how dates are defined in the programming language to be used.

3.3.4 Policy

There are many ways of dealing with a policy, ranging from hard-coding limits into the specification to devising a special language for expressing policies together with an interpreter for it. The first is always bad in specification, just as it is in a program.

We would need a language to define policy if it seemed likely that new kinds of rule were to be introduced (and even then we might find our language was not general enough). In our case the parameters for the policy seem to be item and user category, and the things determined by the policy seem to be rights to consult and to borrow, including the time for which something may be borrowed, and the number of items that may be consulted or borrowed. We define the policy as a table defining these things. First we add to TYPES:

type
  Limit ::
    consults : **Nat** $\leftrightarrow$ chg_consults
    loans : **Nat** $\leftrightarrow$ chg_loans
    period : Period,
  User_limit = Item_level $\overrightarrow{m}$ Limit
value
  $>$: Item_level $\times$ Item_level $\rightarrow$ **Bool**,

  max_item_level : Item_level,

  up_item_level : Item_level $\overset{\sim}{\rightarrow}$ Item_level
  up_item_level(il) **as** il$'$ **post** il$'$ $>$ il
  pre max_item_level $>$ il

The scheme POLICY contains

type
  Policy_base =
    Item_kind $\overrightarrow{m}$ User_level $\overrightarrow{m}$ Item_level $\overrightarrow{m}$ Limit,
  Policy = {| p : Policy_base • is_complete(p) |}

value
  is_complete : Policy_base $\rightarrow$ **Bool**
  is_complete(p) $\equiv$
    ($\forall$ k : Item_kind •
      k $\in$ p $\wedge$
      ($\forall$ ul : User_level •
        ul $\in$ p(k) $\wedge$
        ($\forall$ il : Item_level • il $\in$ p(k)(ul)))),

The nested map structure of the type Policy means that for each kind of item we have a limit for each level of user for each level of item.

It seems natural to consider limits as cumulative. That is, if a level of users has, say, a limit of n_a items at level a, and n_b items at level b, where a is one level higher than b, then if such a user has no items at level a, up to $n_a + n_b$ items at level b may be borrowed. So the limit at each item level really means "at this level or below". This is specified as follows for borrowing, and similarly for consulting. can_borrow takes as parameters the user's level, the kind and level of the item to be borrowed, the current loans of the user, and the current policy. subtract_borrow gives the user's limit remaining after considering the current loans, and has_borrow_capacity then checks if the new item can also be borrowed within this remaining limit.

value
can_borrow :
    User_level × Item_kind × Item_level × Loan-set × Policy → **Bool**
can_borrow(ul, k, il, cps, p) ≡
    let
        lim = p(k)(ul),
        lim_1 = subtract_borrow(lim, k, cps)
    in has_borrow_capacity(il, lim_1) **end**,

/* reduce limit by current loans of the right kind */
subtract_borrow : User_limit × Item_kind × Loan-set → User_limit
subtract_borrow(lim, k, loans) ≡
    if loans = {} **then** lim
    else
        let
            l = **hd** loans,
            lim_1 =
                if k = kind(l)
                then subtract_borrow$_1$(lim, level(l))
                else lim **end**
        in subtract_borrow(lim_1, k, loans \ {l}) **end**
    end,

/* reduce limit by one loan if possible; else return empty */
subtract_borrow$_1$: User_limit × Item_level → User_limit
subtract_borrow$_1$(lim, il) ≡
    if il ∈ lim ∧ loans(lim(il)) > 0
    then
        lim †
        [il ↦ chg_loans(loans(lim(il)) − 1, lim(il))]
    elsif max_item_level > il
        then subtract_borrow$_1$(lim, up_item_level(il))
    else [] **end**,

has_borrow_capacity : Item_level × User_limit → **Bool**
has_borrow_capacity(il, lim) ≡
    il ∈ lim ∧ loans(lim(il)) > 0 ∨
    max_item_level > il ∧
    has_borrow_capacity(up_item_level(il), lim)

To check borrowing capacity for a user we need to store for each user their loans and consults, and we need to include in these the kind and level of each copy as well as the copy identifier. So the type Loan is defined (in TYPES) as

type
  Loan ::
    kind : Item_kind   level : Item_level   copy : Copy_id

The POLICY module is placed just below LIBRARY in the module structure, by making it another embedded object in LIBRARY and adding its type to the Library record.

This seems the natural place to put POLICY. Since we have recorded the loans and consults in both COPY and USER, it is clear that checking for existing loans and the current status of copies when we do a borrow, for example, will need to be done in the top level LIBRARY module (see Figure 3.2). So checking for policy limits can be done in LIBRARY as well.

3.3.5 Searching

Until we make some more decisions about the form of information about items, and especially about what information is searchable, we are abstract about how searching is done. We include in TYPES:

type
  Search_info
value
  matches : Search_info × Item_info → **Bool**

This is sufficient for us to specify functions that will return (identifiers of) all items matching some search criteria. We put in ITEMS:

value
  search : Search_info × Items → Id-**set**
  search(info, its) ≡
    {id |
     id : Id •
       item_exists(id, its) ∧
       matches(info, I.info(its(id)))}

3.4 Consistency

Once we have identified the data structures we need to meet the requirements, but before we define most of the functions to change the data, we should think about consistency. Recall from Chapter 2 that inconsistency arises from three main sources:

1. Domain values of maps used as references.
2. Potentially circular relations.
3. More than one access path to the same information.

In category 1 we have user identifiers stored in reservations, and in the statuses of copies. We also have copies referenced in the loans and consults of users. We have no possibly circular relations, but we do have, in category 3, loans and consults accessed via copies and via users. This allows us to define the function **consistent** for the type Library:

value
  consistent : Library → **Bool**
  consistent(lib) ≡
    -- all reserving users exist
    (∀ uid : Uid, id : Id •
      IS.item_exists(id, items(lib)) ∧
      uid ∈ IS.reservees(id, items(lib)) ⇒
        US.user_exists(uid, users(lib))) ∧
    -- all users referred to in copy statuses exist
    (∀ c : Copy_id •
      IS.copy_exists(c, items(lib)) ⇒
        case
          user_in_status(IS.copy_status(c, items(lib)))
        of
          user(uid) → US.user_exists(uid, users(lib)),
          nil → **true**
        end) ∧
    -- all copies in user loans and consults exist
    (∀ uid : Uid, l : Loan •
      US.user_exists(uid, users(lib)) ∧
      (l ∈ US.loans(uid, users(lib)) ∨
      l ∈ US.consults(uid, users(lib))) ⇒
        IS.copy_exists(copy(l), items(lib))) ∧
    -- loans consistent
    (∀ uid : Uid •
      (∀ c : Copy_id •
        IS.on_loan_to(uid, c, items(lib)) ⇒
          (US.user_exists(uid, users(lib)) ∧
          let (k, il) = IS.kind_level(id(c), items(lib))
          in mk_Loan(k, il, c) ∈ US.loans(uid, users(lib))
          end)) ∧
      (∀ l : Loan •
        US.user_exists(uid, users(lib)) ∧
        l ∈ US.loans(uid, users(lib)) ⇒
          IS.on_loan_to(uid, copy(l), items(lib))))) ∧

```
-- consults consistent
(∀ uid : Uid •
   (∀ c : Copy_id •
      IS.on_consult_to(uid, c, items(lib)) ⇒
         (US.user_exists(uid, users(lib)) ∧
           let (k, il) = IS.kind_level(id(c), items(lib))
           in mk_Loan(k, il, c) ∈ US.consults(uid, users(lib))
           end)) ∧
   (∀ l : Loan •
      US.user_exists(uid, users(lib)) ∧
      l ∈ US.consults(uid, users(lib)) ⇒
         IS.on_consult_to(uid, copy(l), items(lib)))))
```

Following the method guidelines of Chapter 2, we do not choose to express as a consistency condition that loans and consults are consistent with policy. We note in particular that violations of policy may occur, since if policy is changed to reduce limits, there may be a temporary violation of policy as we wait for items to be returned.

3.5 Functions

We have still to specify most of the functions needed: for adding and deleting users, adding and deleting items and copies of them, for borrowing and consulting items, for returning them, etc.

To illustrate, consider the requirement for users to borrow copies of items. The borrow function will be in the top module LIBRARY. We realise we need to change the status of the copy, so we will need borrow functions in ITEMS, ITEM, COPIES and COPY. (Remember that the method suggests that functions call functions at most one level down the hierarchy of modules.) We also need to change the borrow information for the user, so we will need similar functions in USERS and USER. This may seem like a lot of functions to define for one requirement, but we will find that each of these functions deals with one aspect of the transaction, and writing them separately helps us deal with one problem at a time.

Borrowing involves storing (in COPY) the due date by which the copy should be returned. To calculate this we need the date today and the borrow period from the POLICY module. The calculation of the due date must be done in the LIBRARY module, since POLICY is not visible in ITEMS or below.

Today's date is conveniently defined as a parameter to borrow. In practice it will be obtained from the operating system, but by making it a parameter to borrow we avoid the need to specify the operating system function.

borrow in LIBRARY is defined as follows:

value
  borrow : Uid × Copy_id × Date × Library $\xrightarrow{\sim}$ Library
  borrow(uid, c, today, lib) ≡
    let
      ul = US.level(uid, users(lib)),
      (k, il) = IS.kind_level(id(c), items(lib)),
      l = IS.make_loan(c, items(lib)),
      d = today + P.period(ul, k, il, policy(lib)),
      lib_1 = chg_users(US.borrow(uid, l, users(lib)), lib)
    in
      chg_items(IS.borrow(uid, d, c, items(lib_1)), lib_1)
    end
  pre
    US.user_exists(uid, users(lib)) ∧
    IS.copy_exists(c, items(lib)) ∧
    let
      ul = US.level(uid, users(lib)),
      (k, il) = IS.kind_level(id(c), items(lib)),
      l = IS.make_loan(c, items(lib))
    in
      US.can_borrow(uid, l, users(lib)) ∧
      let d = today + P.period(ul, k, il, policy(lib)) **in**
        IS.can_borrow(uid, d, c, items(lib))
      end ∧
      let
        loans = US.loans(uid, users(lib)),
        ul = US.level(uid, users(lib))
      in
        P.can_borrow(ul, k, il, loans, policy(lib))
      end
    end

The body of the function is immediately apparent, and we can probably write it before we write the corresponding functions in ITEMS (instantiated in LIBRARY as the object IS) and and USERS (instantiated as US).

As remarked in Chapter 2, a good style is to associate with every partial function f in lower-level modules a function can_f that expresses the precondition for f. This tells us that we will need to check the can_borrow in USERS and in ITEMS because we are using their two borrow functions in the body of borrow in LIBRARY. We realise from the requirements that we also need to check that borrowing is allowed by policy, and for this we will need the current loans for the user. This generates requirements for a can_borrow function in POLICY, and for a loans function in USERS.

borrow in LIBRARY is a top level function, so its precondition will need to be checked as part of the user interface.

The `borrow` function in `ITEMS` needs merely to call the `borrow` function in `ITEM` (instantiated in `ITEMS` as object I) for the relevant item, identified by the `id` component of the `Copy_id`, and update the `Items` map:

value

borrow : Uid × Date × Copy_id × Items $\overset{\sim}{\to}$ Items
borrow(uid, d, c, its) ≡
  its † [id(c) ↦ I.borrow(uid, d, copy(c), its(id(c)))]
pre can_borrow(uid, d, c, its),

can_borrow : Uid × Date × Copy_id × Items → **Bool**
can_borrow(uid, d, c, its) ≡
  item_exists(id(c), its) ∧
  I.can_borrow(uid, d, copy(c), its(id(c)))

`can_borrow` needs the `item_exists` clause to check that the expression `its(id(c))` in `borrow` is well-formed, i.e. that the item `id(c)` is in the domain of the map `its`. In addition, we need to check that we can apply `borrow` in `ITEM`, by using the `can_borrow` from there.

The `borrow` function in `ITEM` is:

value

borrow : Uid × Date × No × Item $\overset{\sim}{\to}$ Item
borrow(uid, d, n, i) ≡
  chg_copies(CS.borrow(uid, d, n, copies(i)), i)
pre can_borrow(uid, d, n, i),

can_borrow : Uid × Date × No × Item → **Bool**
can_borrow(uid, d, n, i) ≡
  CS.can_borrow(uid, d, n, copies(i))

`borrow` just changes the `copies` component of the record type `Item`. `CS` is the object instantiating `COPIES`.

In `COPIES` we have a map `Copies` from copy number `No` to `Copy`, and the pattern is rather like `ITEMS`:

value

borrow : Uid × Date × No × Copies $\overset{\sim}{\to}$ Copies
borrow(uid, d, n, cs) ≡
  cs † [n ↦ C.borrow(uid, d, cs(n))]
pre can_borrow(uid, d, n, cs),

can_borrow : Uid × Date × No × Copies → **Bool**
can_borrow(uid, d, n, cs) ≡
  copy_exists(n, cs) ∧ C.can_borrow(uid, d, cs(n))

Finally, in COPY, borrow just changes the status to a loan. More interesting is the precondition function can_borrow, which says the copy can be borrowed if it is available or already waiting for collection by this user. It would be tempting to allow a borrow if it was renewal of a loan, or being returned from a consult by this user, but it might have been reserved by someone else, in which case the borrow by this user should not be allowed. So it has to be returned first, and then borrowed if still available. It is the specification of return (not included here) that results in a copy being either made available, or saved for collection by someone who reserved it:

value
    borrow : Uid × Date × Copy $\overset{\sim}{\to}$ Copy
    borrow(uid, d, c) ≡ chg_status(loan(uid, d), c)
    pre can_borrow(uid, d, c),

    can_borrow : Uid × Date × Copy → **Bool**
    can_borrow(uid, d, c) ≡
      case status(c) **of**
        available → **true**,
        collect(uid_1) → uid_1 = uid,
        _ → **false**
      end

3.6 Conclusions

This chapter shows how an information system can be specified in RSL. It illustrates in particular how the requirements analysis can lead directly to a module structure with the main type definitions, how to deal with relations between data, how to deal with consistency, and how to derive the functions needed.

The specification is still applicative. It can easily be transformed into an imperative one, and into a concurrent one for a system with multiple users (which it would probably have) using the standard transformations described in Chapter 2.

The information about borrowers could be connected with a personnel database of a university, if it was desired to integrate them.

Background Information

This chapter is based on work done by Pak Jong Ok and Ri Hyon Sul of the Central Information Agency for Science and Technology, DPR of Korea, together with Chris George [108]. That work was carried out as part of a cooperative project during 1999–2000 between UNU/IIST, UNESCO Beijing office and UNESCO Centre of Macau, partly funded by UNESCO/Japanese Funds-in-Trust. The project developed a number of specifications of university administration functions, and is described in a number of UNU/IIST reports [105, 153, 156].

The library specification was translated to C++ using the original RAISE tools [58], and a front-end written using Visual C++. A small Access database was used to replace the Items map (with items specialised to books). This work is described in detail in [109].

This demonstrated a rapid and reliable way to produce a running system with a minimum amount of hand coding.

4. Development of a Distributed Telephone Switch

4.1 Introduction

This chapter describes the development of a distributed telephone switch, where the connections between the parts of the switch are microwave radio links [36]. We consider only a simple telephone system, commonly called *POTS*, "Plain Old Telephone System".

We can look at a telephone system at many levels of detail, and our specification also has several levels of detail.

An abstract view of a telephone system is of a set of phones dynamically connected in some way. In this "monolithic" view there is apparently just one component, a *switch* (or *exchange*) in which there is complete knowledge of which phones are connected to which, and where the switching of connections between phones is managed.

The monolithic view can be used to describe some basic features of phones. For example: if a is connected to b, then b is connected to a, and neither is connected to any other phone. If a dials b and hears a ringing tone, then phone b is indeed ringing.

The monolithic view does not hold if we look a little closer. Now we see that there is not just one switch but many, connected to each other by connections that have no phones on them, called **trunks**. We can model such a "network" (Figure 4.1) as an undirected weighted graph, where the weights represent the capacity of trunks (the number of connections they can carry). Phones are leaf nodes, with single connections to switches.

The network view introduces a number of issues hidden in the monolithic view. There is no global data recording which phone is connected to which (unless they happen to share the same switch). There is only distributed data in the switches about which phone is connected to which trunk, and which trunk is connected to which other trunk. There are new problems to solve, such as how a switch routes a dialled connection to get to the switch serving the target phone, and how trunk resources are allocated to make connections and deallocated when connections are terminated. We also realise that the network only has a certain capacity, so that dialled connections may fail even when the target phone is in the right state to receive a call.

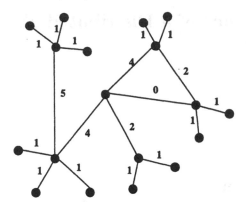

Fig. 4.1. A Telephone Network.

Now we look closer again at a particular switch serving a number of users and find, in our particular case, that it itself has a complex internal structure (Figure 4.2).

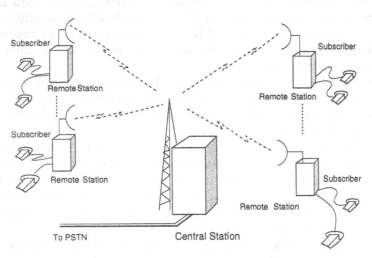

Fig. 4.2. The DiMulT System.

The switch is composed of a *central* station connected to the rest of the public switched telephone network (PSTN) by some trunks, plus a number of *remote* stations connected to it not by wires but by radio (microwave) connections. This kind of switch is intended for use in areas with scattered populations separated by rugged terrain where it would be expensive to lay telephone cables.

There are only two microwave frequencies, one for transmission by the central station, and one for transmissions by the remotes. Multiplexing must be used to support a number of telephone connections at once. Since the system also uses digital rather than analogue signals it is described as Digital Multiplexed (DiMult). Connections from the central station to the remotes are handled by Time Division Multiplexing (TDM) [63]. The central station sends a continual sequence of *frames* of information, receivable by all the remotes. Each frame takes a certain amount of time to send and receive. The frames are conceptually divided into a number of *time slots*, and each time slot corresponds to a single trunk. So, for example, if a remote is allocated trunk numbered 1, say, it will accept the information arriving during the period corresponding to time slot 1 in each frame, and ignore others which are not currently allocated to it.

Information from remotes to central is handled similarly, by a scheme called Time Division Multiple Access (TDMA). Our remote will transmit during the time slot 1 and not during time slots which it is not allocated. Provided all the clocks are synchronised, and provided the trunk management is handled correctly so that each trunk is allocated to at most one remote, all the incoming information will be received by the central station: no two remote stations will transmit simultaneously. A detailed view of the timing requirements involves also knowing what the transmission time delay is between each remote and central. TDM/TDMA is also used for communications between communications satellites and ground stations. Then it becomes more complicated, because the satellites move relative to ground stations and the time delays vary. For our system the delays are constant.

Both TDM and TDMA have portions of the frames reserved for management information, and these portions are used for trunk request, allocation, and return.

The DiMult switch has a new feature compared with the network view. The trunks are allocated in a dynamic fashion to remotes that need them, and relinquished when they are no longer needed. The central station needs to manage these trunks carefully. If two remotes are allocated the same trunk they will transmit at the same time (in the same time slot) and the central station will receive only garbage.

Our task is to specify the software for the DiMult switch. But we can only show that the DiMult switch operates successfully relative to the rest of the network. We need to specify the whole network, then decompose it into our switch and the rest. In the decomposed specification, one part, the DiMult switch, is our requirement. The other part is the assumptions we may make about the rest of the network.

This outline has included two views of the telephone system, the monolithic and the network views. Then we had a third view by looking more closely into one switch in the network. The development of the specification in this chapter follows a similar route.

4.1.1 Chapter Structure

Section 4.2 provides the monolithic view as if the system were just one switch serving a collection of phones. The switch is modelled as dynamic collection of connections between phones. Section 4.3 provides an even more abstract view by describing some properties of a *Plain Old Telephone Service* (POTS) and using these properties to validate the first specification.

Instead of proceeding directly to the network view, we first in Section 4.4 refine the monolithic specification by decomposing a phone into a more simple phone plus a line card, while leaving the monolithic view of the connections. This allows us from then on to ignore the phones: it is only connections that we are interested in, and the leaf nodes in the network will be *line-cards*, which are simpler than phones. Line-cards are identified by the same number as the phones they are attached to.

Instead of decomposing into a network of switches, we next make a more simple decomposition into one switch and the rest of the network. We can view the rest of the network as if it were monolithic. We first, in Section 4.5, partition numbers, and hence line-cards, between our switch (which means they belong to a remote station) and the rest of the network. We also allow for there being only a limited number of connections within the switch (*trunks*). A further refinement in Section 4.6 decomposes the specification of our switch into central, remote and transmission components and defines the protocol for allocating and deallocating trunks. Section 4.7 describes the integration of the modules.

4.1.2 Development Approach

Before proceeding, we might ask why we specify things in this manner, going through several levels of description at different levels of abstraction. Why not just start straight off with the details of the Dimult switch and save a lot of work? There are a number of issues to consider:

- We first observe that the answer depends on the complexity of the system. If it is simple enough then using several levels of abstraction is not worth it. Telephone systems are complicated as we shall see – although we are only considering the basic properties of a simple telephone system.
- When we are only concerned with part of a complex system, there is typically no way to show that the specification of that part is correct without considering the whole system. So a standard technique is to specify the system abstractly and monolithically, so we know the global properties the system must have. Then we decompose into the part we are interested in and "the rest". The rest can usually be specified quite abstractly. The standard rules for showing correctness (refinement rules) are used to show that the combination of our part and the rest still has the correct global properties. Now the specification of the rest is the assumptions we can make as we further develop our part.

- We have seen above how different levels of abstraction allow us to consider particular properties. The monolithic view allows us to specify the connection relation between phones as commutative and one-one. Having established this property, if we check that we do refinement properly at each later stage, we know that this property will be maintained, and we can forget about it. If we tried to specify this property at the network level it would be much more complicated, involving trunks and switches as well as the phones.

  Similarly, the network view allows us to consider the limited connection resources (trunks) that were invisible at the monolithic level. And if we were interested in how connections were made between switches, then the network view would also allow us to consider routing protocols. This is not our purpose here, though another UNU/IIST report considers it [84]. Finding the most abstract level at which a problem can be formulated helps greatly in dealing with complexity. The basic rule is to capture each property at the most abstract level at which it is expressible.

4.2 The Monolithic View

This section introduces some of the notations, constructs and facilities that we use to formulate the abstract view of a telephone system as a collection of phones apparently connected by a single, monolithic switch.

A phone is a component that is at a certain state in an interval of time. By referring to an interval as a state, we abstract from the notion of time. We identify the states of a phone in such a way that a phone is in at most one state at any time. At an abstract level we are concerned mainly with identifying a phone, its current state, and its state of connection without regard to implementation details.

4.2.1 Phone States

Consider a telephone unit that is uniquely identified by a telephone number of type No. Since a telephone number is only a subset of the possible digits that a user can dial, No is a subtype of sort **Digits**. The condition is_no that a **Digits** value is a number of a phone is left unspecified: we just assume we can check it.

type
  Digits,
  No = {| d : Digits • is_no(d) |}
value
  is_no : Digits → **Bool**

The states of a phone are represented as a variant type, **Phone_state**, which includes the constants **on_hook**, **dial_tone**, **busy** and the constructors **connected** and **ringing**. A phone available for connection is in an **on_hook** state, while a phone that is ready to accept a dialing from a user is in a **dial_tone** state. We distinguish the states **ringing(no)** and **on_hook** since a ringing phone is already involved in a connection with a caller **no**. A phone in the state **connected(no')** can either be ringing the phone **no'** or connected to **no'**. An off-hook phone is in a **busy** state as a result of a disconnection from another phone, or an unsuccessful connection. Modelling a phone that is connected as **connected(no)** captures the requirement in a POTS that at most one connection can be established between any two phones.

type
  Phone_state ==
    on_hook |
    dial_tone |
    connected(connected_no : No) |
    ringing(ringing_no : No) |
    busy

To model the states of all phones in the system, we define a total map **Phone_map** from **No** to **Phone_state**. **Phone_map** is a subtype and its predicate **is_phone_map** describes the property that the map is complete (defined for all numbers) and that a phone connected to some other phone implies that the other phone can either be ringing or connected. Conversely, a ringing phone implies that the caller is connected.

type
  Phone_map = {| m : No $\overrightarrow{m}$ Phone_state • is_phone_map(m) |}
value
  is_phone_map : (No $\overrightarrow{m}$ Phone_state) → **Bool**
  is_phone_map(pm) ≡
    (∀ no : No • no ∈ **dom** pm) ∧
    (∀ no : No •
      case pm(no) **of**
        on_hook → **true**,
        dial_tone → **true**,
        connected(no') → pm(no') ∈ {connected(no), ringing(no)},
        ringing(no') → pm(no') = connected(no),
        busy → **true**
      end)

The types and values defined so far are collected in a scheme TYPES, from which a global object T is made.

The global state of a system constitutes the collection of variables and objects upon which the system operates. In the first, abstract specification of the monolithic POTS, PHONE_0, the state of the telephone system is initially defined as a sort State.

We do not want to define State yet: it will finally be some combination of the states of several system components. But whatever this final structure is, it must contain the information that allows us to compute a Phone_map value, so we are able to specify now that we can observe such a value, using an observer phones. So we might specify

type
    State
value
    phones : State → Phone_map

But this turns out to be inadequate. When a phone is involved in a connection, and is replaced on-hook, the state of the other phone must be changed from connected to busy. But this might not happen immediately, as part of the action of replacing the first phone: it needs to be an internal action of the system rather than an action of a user. So we expect there to be states which do not conform to is_phone_map. We deal with this by having a state type State′ that represents more general, inconsistent states, where corrective actions have yet to be completed. Only from a subtype State of State′ can we obtain a Phone_map (which needs to satisfy its subtype condition is_phone_map). So we specify instead in PHONE_0:

type
    State′,
    State = {| s : State′• consistent(s) |}
value
    consistent : State′ → **Bool**,
    phones : State → Phone_map

4.2.2 Phone Actions

Considering a telephone unit in a POTS, one can perform three basic actions: pick up, put down, and dial. These actions change the state of the system and we represent them formally as generator functions pick_up, put_down and dial. However, as one can only pick up a phone when it is on-hook, and dial and put-down when it is off-hook, these functions are partial. We add to PHONE_0:

value
    pick_up : No × State $\overset{\sim}{\to}$ State,
    dial : No × Digits × State $\overset{\sim}{\to}$ State,
    put_down : No × State $\overset{\sim}{\to}$ State′

We have used **State'** as the result state of **put_down** for the reasons explained above: until the system corrects the state of the other phone possibly involved, we will not be in a state satisfying **consistent**. We declare a function **next** to make the correction:

value
next : State' → State

The declaration of **next** as just a signature looks very weak, but it implies quite a strong condition: from any state in **State'**, it is always (since **next** is total) possible to get into a consistent state, i.e. one from which a **Phone_map** value can be constructed.

We define the predicate **on_cradle**, which is used as a precondition for the partial functions **pick_up** and **put_down**: a phone is **on_cradle** if it is either **on_hook** or **ringing**:

value
on_cradle : No × State → **Bool**
on_cradle(no, s) ≡
   phones(s)(no) = on_hook ∨ (∃ no' : No • phones(s)(no) = ringing(no'))

A subscriber trying to connect to the phone of another subscriber will succeed and cause it to ring if the other phone is currently on-hook and resources are available. We express this by introducing a predicate **can_connect**. As part of the network specification, in Section 4.5, we provide a more explicit definition of this constraint in terms of network resources. Until we have the network view, in which we can define resources, we can give some necessary conditions for connection but not sufficient ones:

value
can_connect: No × Digits × State → **Bool**
axiom
[can_connect_ax]
  ∀ no : No, dig : Digits, s : State •
   can_connect(no, dig, s) ⇒
     is_no(dig) ∧ phones(s)(dig) = on_hook ∧ no ≠ dig

With the necessary pre-conditions, we provide definitions for the generators in an algebraic style. We can't give direct definitions of the generators because we have no concrete state type yet. We can only specify what we can observe about a new state using the observer **phones**. The axiom [phones_pick_up_ax] states that picking up an **on_hook** phone will change its state into **dial_tone**. For the other case that a phone is **ringing**, to pick it up will change its state into **connected**:

axiom
[phones_pick_up_ax]

∀ no : No, s : State •
  on_cradle(no, s) ⇒
  (phones(pick_up(no, s)) ≡
    case phones(s)(no) **of**
      on_hook → phones(s) † [no ↦ dial_tone],
      ringing(no′) → phones(s) † [no ↦ connected(no′)]
    end)

There are similar axioms [**phones_put_down_ax**] and [**phones_dial_ax**]. This completes PHONE_0.

With the use of partial functions to define the generators, the specification is silent about operations performed when some assumptions are not met, like when a user attempts to dial in an on_hook state. This leaves open to the developer the choice to either implement exception handling or ignore such actions. Furthermore, by defining the state of the system initially as an abstract type we are able to define the architecture later. A more detailed architecture is introduced later in Section 4.6.

4.3 Validation

Validation is a check of the abstract specification against what is required of the system. Performing a validation will initially ensure that we build the right system, as opposed to verification – that we build the system right [85]. This is an initial step at ensuring correctness of the specification. It is a critical step, because if we get it wrong we are hereafter wasting our time building the wrong system. It is also difficult, because requirements are generally expressed largely in informal, natural language (such as English or Chinese). Natural language requirements suffer notoriously from being ambiguous, incomplete and even contradictory.

In our case the main requirement is for the specification to describe a POTS, a Plain Old Telephone System, and we find we can formalise POTS in terms of some basic properties, some of which we list below. Note we supply natural language descriptions as well, to help our customers check that what we think they want is also what they think they want.

The syntax "**in** C ⊢ **expr**" is a *class scope expression* in RSL, a boolean expression evaluated by evaluating **expr** in the context of class expression C.

- A subscriber dialing a number which is available will, when resources are available, cause the called subscriber's phone to ring and itself to be connected:

[dial_waiting]
in PHONE_0 ⊢
  ∀ no : No, s, s′ : State, dig : Digits •

phones(s)(no) = dial_tone ∧
can_connect(no, dig, s) ∧ s' = dial(no, dig, s) ⇒
phones(s')(dig) = ringing(no) ∧ phones(s')(no) = connected(dig)

- A subscriber picking up a ringing phone will result in a **connected** state for both phones involved:

[pick_up_connected]
in PHONE_0 ⊢
    ∀ no, no' : No, s, s' : State •
    phones(s)(no) = connected(no') ∧
    phones(s)(no') = ringing(no) ∧ s' = pick_up(no', s) ⇒
    phones(s')(no') = connected(no) ∧ phones(s')(no) = connected(no')

- A subscriber replacing the phone involved in a connection, will cause the other phone (eventually, when **next** has been applied) to go into a busy state, and itself into an on-hook state:

[put_down_busy]
in PHONE_0 ⊢
    ∀ no, no' : No, s, s' : State •
    no ≠ no' ∧ phones(s)(no) = connected(no') ∧
    phones(s)(no') = connected(no) ∧ s' = next(put_down(no, s)) ⇒
    phones(s')(no) = on_hook ∧ phones(s')(no') = busy

These and four other similar properties were all defined in a theory and then proved (using the original RAISE tools [58]) to be properties of PHONE_0. This gives us confidence that PHONE_0 has the basic properties required of a POTS.

An alternative and equivalent approach would be to define the properties as axioms in a scheme POTS, say, and then asserting and proving that PHONE_0 implements POTS.

4.4 Decomposition into Phones and Network

Section 4.2 specifies the end-to-end requirements of the telephone service. The specification, however, gives no mention of how this service is to be implemented and what components will be involved. In this section, we introduce a scheme PHONE_1 that refines PHONE_0 by introducing as separate components phones and the telephone network. The telephone network (in a separate module CONNECT_0) provides the connection handling services for the phones.

4.4.1 Connections

In contrast to a subscriber's view of the system, we view a telephone unit as
being attached to a hardware device in the network. We refer to this device as
a line-card. The telephone serves as a user interface to its line-card. Assuming
an instantaneous connection, a line-card can be in two states. It can either
be free or connected to another line-card through some connection resources.

We introduce the notion of a connection resource as a sort **Connection**,
the availability of which determines a successful call. We can now represent
the state of a line-card as a variant type **Line_state** with a constant **free**
and constructor **connected**. It is possible, however, for this device to be in
an intermediate state **connecting** while a connection through the network is
being attempted. We add to TYPES:

type
    Connection,
    Line_state ==
      free |
      connected(connected_conn: Connection) |
      connecting(connecting_conn: Connection)

Why isn't a **Connection** just a **No**? For a connection to another phone
belonging to the same local switch in the network, a **Connection** can be just
the other phone's number, but in general a line card can be connected by the
local switch to a trunk connected perhaps to another switch, and so on. In
this case the **Connection** value is the trunk leading from the local switch. If
the connection is currently complete, i.e. leads all the way to another phone,
we can calculate from the global state the other phone's number:

value
    no_of : Connection × State $\xrightarrow{\sim}$ No

We model a view of the telephone network as a set of line-cards associated
one-one with phones, by associating each line-card with the same number as
its phone. We define **Line_map** to be a total mapping from **No** to **Line_state**.
We add to TYPES:

type
    Line_map = {| m : No $\xrightarrow{m}$ Line_state • is_complete(m) |}
value
    is_complete : (No $\xrightarrow{m}$ Line_state) → **Bool**
    is_complete(m) ≡
      ($\forall$ no : No • no $\in$ **dom** m)

The scheme CONNECT_0 models the telephone network that implements
connection handling. The type of interest **State** in this scheme represents

the state of all components that comprise this network (We note here that State of CONNECT_0 differs from the State of PHONE_0.)

scheme CONNECT_0 =
  with T **in class**
    type State

  ...
end

Among these components are the line-cards. To observe the Line_state of these line-cards, we use an observer function lines:

value
  lines : State → Line_map

The network provides connection handling services to connect and disconnect line-cards. We represent these formally as generator functions **connect** and disconnect:

value
  connect : No × No × State → State,
  disconnect : No × State → State

We are still being abstract about the network: we do not yet model switches and trunks. So we cannot model the resources (trunks) needed to make connections. We can foresee, however, that some connections will need more trunks than others, according to how many switches are involved. So we declare a function has_connect_resources that depends on the two numbers involved as well as the state of the network:

value
  has_connect_resources : No × No × State → **Bool**

There are some states of a phone, namely busy and dial_tone, when the phone is not available to others, but is also not connected to any others. We make the corresponding state of the line-card a connection to itself. This is just a technique to avoid needing an extra variant in Line_state. So a line card can be connected to another when it is connected to itself, the other is free, and there are resources:

axiom
  [can_connect_ax]
    ∀ no, no' : No, s : State •
    can_connect(no, no', s) ⇒
      no ≠ no' ∧
      (∃ cn : Connection •
        lines(s)(no) = connected(cn) ∧ no_of(cn, s) = no) ∧
      lines(s)(no') = free ∧ has_connect_resources(no, no', s)

There are several axioms for connect and disconnect which we do not include here. connect is defined as a total function: if the connection is possible (can_connect is true) then the connection is made. Otherwise the line-card is left connected to itself.

The scheme CONNECT_0 just describes line-cards and their connections. We need an implementation of the previous PHONE_0, which describes connections between phones. The relation between phones and their line-cards is defined in PHONE_1, which we intend to be a refinement of PHONE_0. PHONE_1 is introduced in the next section.

4.4.2 Phones

We need to add to the line-cards and their connections, defined in CONNECT_0, the definition of phones and their connections in a new scheme PHONE_1. PHONE_1 will include an object instantiating CONNECT_0, so we can define the connections between phones in terms of the connections between their line-cards. We start to define PHONE_1:

scheme PHONE_1 =
  with T **in class**
    object
      C : CONNECT_0
    ...
  end

The notion of a phone can now be simpler than that in PHONE_0. A phone is now just a device that can interact with its line-card. When we focus on line cards and their connections, a phone is just a user interface to its line card. A phone can either be on-hook or off-hook. When off-hook, it receives signals that could be heard as tones from its receiver: a dial-tone, a busy-tone, or voice (or fax or modem data) which we refer to as data. A ring-back tone (what you hear when you successfully dial another phone) is not considered separately, since this signal is sent as part of data. The variant type Ph_state captures this notion. We add to CONNECT_0:

type
  Ph_state == off_hk(tone : Tone) | on_hk,
  Tone == busy | dial | data

A total map Ph_map models the system composed of a set of phones each in a certain Ph_state. We add to CONNECT_0:

type
  Ph_map = {| m : No $\overrightarrow{m}$ Ph_state • is_ph_map(m) |}
value
  is_ph_map : (No $\overrightarrow{m}$ Ph_state) → **Bool**
  is_ph_map(m) ≡ (∀ no : No • no ∈ **dom** m)

We want to model Phone_state, since this was the type of phones in PHONE_0 (Section 4.2.1), as a combination of Line_state and Ph_state. Considering a line-card identified by no and possibly connected to another line-card no′, Table 4.1 shows the relation of Line_state and Ph_state:

Table 4.1. Possible combinations of Line_state and Ph_state.

	off_hk(busy)	off_hk(dial)	off_hk(data)	on_hk
free				on_hook
connected(cn)	busy	dial_tone	connected(no′)	ringing(no′)
connecting(cn)			connected(no′)	

The entries left blank represent disallowed combinations of Line_state and Ph_state. We will avoid these combinations by using a subtype predicate inv.

We are now ready to decompose the state of the system, to define a concrete State′ in PHONE_1 in terms of the state of the object C and a Ph_map. State′ will be the combinations of these states that satisfy inv. We add to PHONE_1:

type
    State_base ::
        system : C.State ↔ change_system
        phones_mp : Ph_map ↔ change_phones_mp,
    State′ = {| s : State_base • inv(s) |}
value
    inv : State_base → **Bool**
    inv(s) ≡ ...

We can now also define the function consistent relating State′ to State. Recall that a state could be inconsistent if one phone in a connection was put down and the other was still either connected (if it was off-hook) or still ringing (if it was on-hook).

type
    State = {| s : State′ • consistent(s) |}

If a phone previously connected (on-hook and ringing, or off-hook and with data tone) loses that connection its line card becomes connected to itself. In the first case the line-card must be changed to free, and in the second the phone's tone must be changed to busy. So a state satisfies consistent when a line-card connected to itself does not have a phone that is off-hook with data tone or on-hook. We define consistent (not included here), and also give axioms (not included here) for next to make a State′ consistent.

We also make explicit the definitions of the functions pick_up, dial and put_down. For example:

value
  pick_up : No × State $\xrightarrow{\sim}$ State
  pick_up(no, s) ≡
    let m = phones_mp(s), ls = C.lines(system(s))(no) **in**
      case ls **of**
        connected(cn) →
          change_phones_mp(m † [no ↦ off_hk(data)], s),
        free →
          change_system
            (C.connect(no, no, system(s)),
              change_phones_mp(m † [no ↦ off_hk(dial)], s))
      end
    end
    pre on_cradle(no, s)

When the line-card is connected (i.e. the phone was ringing) the phone's state is changed to off-hook with data tone. When the line-card was free, it is connected to itself using the **connect** function from CONNECT_0, and the phone's state is changed to off-hook with dial tone.

We also provide a definition of **can_connect** in terms of the number dialed being a number, and the resources being available:

value
  can_connect : No × Digits × State → **Bool**
  can_connect(no, dig, s) ≡ is_no(dig) ∧ C.can_connect(no, dig, system(s))

4.4.3 Verification

The abstract specification PHONE_0 captured the monolithic connection requirements of the telephone service. This abstract specification is used as a basis for verifying subsequent refinements. Verification involves determining whether the development step is correct, i.e. the new specification includes all signatures and maintains the properties of the previous step. This is done by proving that PHONE_1 implements PHONE_0.

4.5 Refining the Network

The decomposition has revealed an architecture of the system as a set of phones and a set of line-cards with their connections. From now on we are interested only in the connections, i.e. we just refine CONNECT_0, which represents the network and its line-cards.

We don't need to refine the whole network. We can concentrate on the distributed DiMult switch and regard the rest of the network as monolithic. In fact we can even initially regard the rest of the network as part of the central station of our switch, and decompose it later!

To decompose the network in this way we start by partitioning the telephone numbers. If a number belongs to our switch it belongs to precisely one of the remote stations. Otherwise it belongs to somewhere else in the network: it is a PSTN number.

We also consider the resources (trunks) within the distributed switch, that connect the central station with the remotes. Each internal trunk is effectively a pair of wireless channels, one in each direction, between the central station and a remote station: there are no connections between remotes. The internal trunks needed will depend on the relative locations of numbers. Connections between numbers belonging to the same remote do not involve the central station and need no trunks. Connections between numbers belonging to different remotes need two trunks, one between each remote and the central. Connections between a remote and a PSTN number need one trunk. Finally, connections between PSTN numbers (remember we are still specifying a complete system, so we need to include these) need no trunks within our switch.

4.5.1 Partitioning of Numbers

The system consists of a set of remotes, each uniquely identified by a remote identifier of sort Rid and each managing a set of line cards. We introduce an underspecified partial function remote_of that returns the Rid of a given No. This function is defined only for a No that is associated with some remote as expressed by the predicate is_remote. Numbers for which is_remote is false are PSTN numbers. We add to TYPES:

type
  Rid
value
  remote_of : No $\overset{\sim}{\to}$ Rid,
  is_remote : No $\to$ **Bool**
axiom
  [remote_of_conv]
    $\forall$ no : No • is_remote(no) $\Rightarrow$ (remote_of(no) **post true**)

The function is_remote introduces a partitioning of numbers into numbers connected to the main public network (PSTN) and numbers connected to remotes. The remote_of function further introduces a sub-partitioning of these remote numbers into those belonging to each remote station.

4.5.2 Trunks

From now on we use the term "trunk", modelled as the sort **Trunk**, to mean an internal trunk of the DiMult switch. Each trunk is a pair of wireless channels: the pair is always allocated and deallocated as one. The central station dynamically allocates these trunks. For connections involving a PSTN number and a remote number, we introduce a sort **Pstn_connection** which is used together with one trunk.

The central station functions as a switch for routing and setting up connections. A switch is modelled as a map that models pairs of connected resources. We define a variant type **Pstn_or_trunk** to denote either a **Pstn_connection** or a **Trunk**. We add to TYPES:

type
  Trunk,
  Pstn_connection,
  Pstn_or_trunk ==
    pstn_alloc(pconn : Pstn_connection) |
    trunk_alloc(trunk : Trunk)

For the map modelling the state of connections in the switch we need a subtype that asserts the connections are irreflexive and commutative: if a is connected to b then b is different from a and also connected to a. We add to TYPES:

type
  Trunk_alloc =
    {| m : Pstn_or_trunk $\overrightarrow{m}$ Pstn_or_trunk • is_trunk_alloc(m) |}
value
  is_trunk_alloc: (Pstn_or_trunk $\overrightarrow{m}$ Pstn_or_trunk) → **Bool**

plus an axiom stating the irreflexive and commutative property.

Trunk_alloc is not a total map: it only records the resources that are allocated. Therefore, a **Trunk** in the domain of this map is currently allocated to a remote station and unavailable for allocation. A partial function get_trunk performs the allocation if there is a trunk available. We add to TYPES:

value
  get_trunk : Pstn_or_trunk-set $\overset{\sim}{\to}$ Trunk × Pstn_or_trunk-set,
  can_get_trunk : Pstn_or_trunk-set → **Bool**,
  can_get_trunk(pots) ≡ (∃ tr : Trunk • trunk_alloc(tr) ∉ pots)
axiom
  [get_trunk_ax]
    ∀ pots, pots$'$: Pstn_or_trunk-set, tr : Trunk •
      can_get_trunk(pots) ∧ (tr, pots$'$) = get_trunk(pots) ⇒
      pots$'$ = {trunk_alloc(tr)} ∪ pots ∧ trunk_alloc(tr) ∉ pots

Having defined the network resources to be **Trunk** and **Pstn_connection**, we can introduce a refinement of the sort **Connection** introduced in Section 4.4.1 to model the state of a connected line-card. We redefine in TYPES:

type
    Connection ==
      no_conn(no : No) |
      trunk_conn(trunk : Trunk) |
      pstn_conn(pconn : Pstn_connection)

A remote line-card can be connected to another in the same remote, or to a trunk and so to central. A PSTN line-card can be connected to a **Pstn_connection**.

The type **Trunk_alloc** does not mention the number which is allocated a trunk or the number associated with a **Pstn_connection**. That information is held indirectly in the number associated with a line-card whose state includes the connection. To allow us to determine the line-card allocated to a **Trunk** or to a **Pstn_connection**, we define an overloaded partial function **find_no** which given **Line_map** returns **No**. We add to TYPES:

value
    find_no : Line_map × Trunk $\overset{\sim}{\to}$ No,
    find_no : Line_map × Pstn_connection $\overset{\sim}{\to}$ No
axiom
    [find_no_trunk_ax]
      ∀ no : No, m : Line_map, tr : Trunk •
        m(no) = connected(trunk_conn(tr)) ∨
        m(no) = connecting(trunk_conn(tr)) ⇒
          no = find_no(m, tr),
    [find_no_pc_ax] ...

4.5.3 Adding Trunks

The scheme **CONNECT_1** adds an observer **trunks** that returns the subtype **Trunk_alloc**:

scheme CONNECT_1 =
    with T **in class**
      type State_base
      value
        lines : State_base → Line_map,
        trunks : State_base → Trunk_alloc
        ...
    end

We can now provide a definition for **has_connect_resources** as a test of the availability of resources. We can now say explicitly that two trunks are required for calls involving two different remote stations, etc. We add to CONNECT_1:

value
    has_connect_resources : No × No × State_base → **Bool**
    has_connect_resources(no, no', s) ≡
      if is_remote(no) **then**
        if is_remote(no') **then**
          remote_of(no) = remote_of(no') ∨
          (∃ tr, tr' : Trunk •
            tr ≠ tr' ∧
            {trunk_alloc(tr), trunk_alloc(tr')} ∩ **dom** trunks(s) = {})
        else ∃ tr : Trunk, pc : Pstn_connection •
          {trunk_alloc(tr), pstn_alloc(pc)} ∩ **dom** trunks(s) = {}
        end
      else
        is_remote(no') ⇒
        (∃ tr : Trunk, pc : Pstn_connection •
          {trunk_alloc(tr), pstn_alloc(pc)} ∩ **dom** trunks(s) = {})
      end

The definition of **no_of** (to calculate the telephone number connected to by a connection) in CONNECT_1 will use the information in the trunk allocation map: the number needs to be calculated at the central station. But its precondition, from CONNECT_0, is that there is a connection in the line map, which will later be distributed between the remote stations and the central station. We need to be sure that a trunk or PSTN connection stored in the line map implies the presence of a corresponding entry in the trunk allocation map. We define a function **connect_consistent** expressing this property, and use it to define a subtype of **State_base**:

type
    State = {| s : State_base • connect_consistent(s) |}
value
    connect_consistent : : State_base → **Bool**
    connect_consistent(s) ≡
      (∀ no : No •
        case lines(s)(no) **of**
          connected(trunk_conn(tr)) →
            trunk_alloc(tr) ∈ **dom** trunks(s),
          connected(pstn_conn(pconn)) →
            pstn_alloc(pconn) ∈ **dom** trunks(s),
          _ → **true**
        end),

no_of : Connection × State $\overset{\sim}{\to}$ No
no_of(cn , s) ≡ ...
pre ($\exists$ no : No • lines(s)(no) = connected(cn))

We now have enough machinery to define the main functions **connect** and **disconnect** in CONNECT_1.

We then verify that the properties of CONNECT_0 are preserved by proving that CONNECT_1 implements CONNECT_0.

4.5.4 Introducing Remote Stations

CONNECT_1 still takes a monolithic view of the telephone system by representing the set of line-cards as a single map. The system, however, is physically distributed with a remote managing a set of line-cards.

We therefore define a nested map from **Rid** to a mapping from **No** to **Line_state**. We introduce REM_Dist_map to be subtype of this map which is total. We also define a total mapping PSTN_map with domain of numbers not belonging to a remote. We add to TYPES:

type
  REM_Dist_map =
    {| m : Rid $\overrightarrow{m}$ No $\overrightarrow{m}$ Line_state • is_remote_complete(m) |},
  PSTN_map =
    {| m : No $\overrightarrow{m}$ Line_state •
      dom m = {no | no : No • ~is_remote(no)} |}
value
  is_remote_complete : (Rid $\overrightarrow{m}$ No $\overrightarrow{m}$ Line_state) $\to$ **Bool**
  is_remote_complete(m) ≡
    dom m = { rid | rid : Rid } $\wedge$
    ($\forall$ rid : Rid •
      dom m(rid) = { no | no : No • remote_of(no) = rid })

The types we have identified, provide us with a signature for a state observer **remote_lines** that represents all remotes and their associated line-cards. We also declare an observer **central_lines** to denote the line-cards in the PSTN.

value
  remote_lines : State $\to$ REM_Dist_map,
  central_lines : State $\to$ PSTN_map

These two signatures are defined in CONNECT_2, which is an extension of CONNECT_1. In addition, the function **remote_of** allows us to calculate an Rid from a number so that we can combine the distributed map into a flat map of type Line_map. We add to CONNECT_2 an axiom stating that the union of the line-cards in the PSTN and the combination of all the maps of the remotes is equivalent to the original complete line map of the telephone network:

axiom
[lines_def]
    ∀ s : State •
        lines(s) =
            central_lines(s) ∪
            [no ↦ remote_lines(s)(remote_of(no))(no) |
                no : No • is_remote(no)]

4.6 Decomposing the Network

The previous specifications have included connection resources, their allocation, partitioning of numbers and the distribution of Line_map. Each step introduced observers that enriched the properties of the network model. In the next step, we decompose the specification into component modules. These modules will provide a detailed description of the components and the telephone network architecture to be considered. It will also describe the interaction between the network components.

The observers **trunks**, **central_lines** and **remote_lines** which we introduced in the previous sections represent the components of the network. The decomposition involves providing modules for the remotes and the PSTN both managing a set of line-cards, as well as modules for the set of trunks maintained by the central. Considering PSTN in our development provides us with an assumption of its properties that will ensure that our system behaves correctly in the context of its environment. By following the RAISE method, we define schemes REMOTE_0, PSTN_0, and TRUNKS_0 for each observer respectively.

We include a scheme TRANSMISSION_0, that represents our assumptions of the transmission medium that uses TDM/TDMA. It is through this medium that we define the trunk assignment protocol. The protocol transmits messages over the medium with the property that there might be reordering or delay of these messages.

The previous models assumed that calls can be connected instantaneously. (i.e. a line-card immediately goes from being free to connected). In real systems, however, calls are set up in a step-by-step fashion from one exchange to the next until the final exchange is reached. This is accomplished by initially acquiring the necessary connection resources and then sending signalling messages to another exchange. In our system, we define the signalling between the remote stations and the central, and provide a simplified signalling for the PSTN.

4.6.1 Messages and Transmission

The components of the system communicate by sending and receiving messages on a transmission medium, which may cause reordering. Reordering occurs for messages between different remote stations due to their different distances from the central.

The use of TDM/TDMA schemes allow us to consider the system as having a set of unique trunk channels, and management channels. Trunk channels are used for sending signalling messages such as trunk disconnection or a connection request to connect to a certain number. Management channels are for sending messages that request and allocate trunks. Management channels are shared and it is a design requirement that the size of messages using them is minimised. So, for example, a remote wanting to get a trunk to make a connection to a number elsewhere first sends an initial management trunk request message, without including the required number. When it receives another management message allocating a trunk it uses this trunk for further messages to make the connection.

It is assumed that lower layers multiplex or combine these trunk and management channels onto a single channel where the receiver can demultiplex or split them later. At a higher layer, they are just unique channels having their own message types. For the system, we will have a pair of these sets of channels one for TDM and the other for TDMA. The messages transmitted on these channels are defined as variant types. **Signal_out** and **Signal_in** refer to messages sent from the central to remote (TDM) and in the other direction (TDMA) respectively. We add to **TYPES**:

type
    Signal_in = Mgt_in | Trunk_in,
    Signal_out = Mgt_out | Trunk_out,
    Mgt_in   == trunk_req(trunk_req_rid : Rid),
    Mgt_out   ==
        no_alloc(no_alloc_rid : Rid) |
        alloc(alloc_rid : Rid, alloc_trunk : Trunk) |
        connect(connect_no : Remote_no, connect_trunk : Trunk),
    Trunk_in ==
        connect_ack(connect_ack_trunk : Trunk) |
        cancel(canceltrunk : Trunk) |
        connect_req(connect_req_trunk : Trunk, connect_req_no : No) |
        in_data(in_data_trunk : Trunk, in_data_data : Data),
    Trunk_out==
        connect_ack(connect_ack_trunk : Trunk) |
        disconnect(disconnect_trunk : Trunk) |
        out_data(out_data_trunk : Trunk, out_data_data : Data),
    Opt_signal_in == nil_sig | mk_signal_in(signal : Signal_in),
    Opt_signal_out == nil_sig | mk_signal_out(signal : Signal_out)

Opt_signal_in and Opt_signal_out are added to allow the functions that receive messages to return nil_sig if there is no message.

Messages being sent on a particular trunk are modelled applicatively with the use of destructors of result type Trunk in the variant. Considering connect_ack(tr) of the variant Trunk_in, this means that connect_ack message is sent by a remote station on trunk tr. For management channels, consider alloc(alloc_rid:Rid, alloc_trunk: Trunk) of the variant Mgt_out. This means central allocates trunk tr to remote rid in response to its request for allocation. Since, at a higher layer, the remote rid only considers and responds to messages intended for it, we can consider this type of message as being received from a dedicated channel identified by rid. This technique allows us to specify the protocol applicatively by passing the tr or rid as part of the message to be sent.

We make proofs tractable by providing a function that can receive one message of any type in a direction. We must therefore assume that messages may be reordered in the transmission medium. The messages must have some property in terms of the order they can be received. We identify this property by considering what combination of messages may overtake each other in the medium. Messages may be reordered between different remotes owing to their particular distances from the central. Trunk messages may be reordered between different trunks because different trunks may have different sources or destinations. We assume that messages associated between central and each remote are not reordered.

To capture this property, the transmission medium in one direction is modelled as a map of message lists. The list captures messages not overtaking. The domain of the map denotes the trunks and the management channels. Receiving a message is then an implicit choice of which list in the map a message is removed from. Transmitting a message is simply appending the message to the list of the corresponding map element for the message.

These functions for transmitting and receiving messages in each direction are defined in TRANSMISSION_IN_0 and TRANSMISSION_OUT_0.

scheme TRANSMISSION_IN_0 =
with T **in class**
  type
    Messages :: mgt_msgs : Mgt_messages trunk_msgs : Trunk_messages,
    Mgt_messages =
      $\{| $ m : Rid $\overrightarrow{m}$ Mgt_in* • ($\forall$ rid : Rid • rid $\in$ **dom** m)$|\}$,
    Trunk_messages =
      $\{| $ m : Trunk $\overrightarrow{m}$ Trunk_in* • ($\forall$ tr : Trunk • tr $\in$ **dom** m)$|\}$
  value
    transmit_mgt : Mgt_in × Messages → Messages,
    transmit_trunk : Trunk_in × Messages → Messages,
    receive : Messages $\rightarrow$ Opt_signal_in × Messages
  ... **end**

TRANSMISSION_OUT_0 is similar.

For the purpose of modularity, we instantiate these schemes within one module TRANSMISSION_0 that provides functions that simply call the above functions. In succeeding sections, we describe how component modules use the message types and the transmission module just described.

4.6.2 Assumptions about the Public Network

The scheme PSTN_0 is a model of our assumptions about the system's environment involving the PSTN. It defines appropriate message types, like those between central and the remotes but simpler as no trunks are involved, and functions connect, disconnect, and handle (for dealing with messages from the PSTN).

4.6.3 Remote Stations

The scheme REMOTE_0 represents a model of a set of remote stations which communicate via a transmission medium shared with the central station. The scheme REMOTE_0 is parameterised with the TRANSMISSION_0 module to model a shared transmission between components.

The type of interest of REMOTE_0 is concretely defined as the nested map partitioned by remote station identifiers defined in Section 4.5.4:

scheme REMOTE_0(TR : TRANSMISSION_0) =
  with T **in class**
    type
      State = REM_Dist_map
    value
      connect : No × No × State × TR.State → State × TR.State
      connect(no, no', s, transs) ≡ ...,
      disconnect :
        No × State × TR.State → State × TR.State
      disconnect(no, s, transs) ≡ ...,
      handle_transmissions_out :
        Rid × State × TR.State → State × TR.State
      handle_transmissions_out(rid, s, transs) ≡ ...,
      ...
  end

The function connect performs connection requests for a phone associated with a remote. For a target number in the same remote, a connection to its line-card is set up if the phone is available. If the target number is not in the remote then a trunk request is transmitted to the central. On receiving this request, if resources are available, central allocates a trunk to the remote and allocates the other resources necessary to set up the connection with the other phone. If the resources are not available, central replies with a no_alloc message.

A function handle_transmission_out receives messages from the central station through the transmission medium and interprets the message by either sending new messages or modifying its line-map or both.

The function disconnect performs a disconnection initiated by a phone line in the remote. If the connection was within the remote, it modifies the line map accordingly, otherwise the line is freed and a trunk cancel message is transmitted to the central.

4.6.4 Trunks

Trunks are resources that are allocated by the system. This is defined as a separate module providing a set of functions to manage these trunks. We define State here to be a record composed of a set of pending trunks and the map of connected trunks connections of type Trunk_alloc representing our switch. Connected trunks are trunks already associated with another connection resource.

The set of pending trunks are trunks that have already been allocated but are not yet involved in a connection, or have been disconnected but have yet to be cancelled. Maintaining a set of pending trunks prevents trunks which are either waiting for a connection or trunks in the process of being disconnected from becoming allocated again. The invariant property is that the set of pending trunks and the domain of the trunk connections map are disjoint.

To reserve a trunk, get places an available trunk in the pending set if there is a trunk available that has not been used. Used trunks are either in pending or in connections.

For connecting together two resources (one of which must be a trunk), the function assign updates the connections map if the trunks were previously pending.

To remove the association of two connected resources, the function deassign removes both from the connections map. If a resource is a trunk, then it is placed in the pending set to be freed by a function make_free. make_free removes a trunk from the pending set to make it available for allocation.

```
scheme TRUNKS_0 =
  with T in class
    type
      Trunk_rec ::
        pending : Trunk-set ↔ change_pending
        connections : Trunk_alloc ↔ change_connections,
      State = {| s : Trunk_rec • is_disjoint(s) |}
    value
```

get : State $\stackrel{\sim}{\rightarrow}$ Trunk × State,
assign : Pstn_or_trunk × Pstn_or_trunk × State $\stackrel{\sim}{\rightarrow}$ State,
deassign : Pstn_or_trunk × State $\stackrel{\sim}{\rightarrow}$ State,
make_free : Trunk × State $\stackrel{\sim}{\rightarrow}$ State,
can_assign : Pstn_or_trunk × Pstn_or_trunk × State $\rightarrow$ **Bool**
can_assign(pot, pot$'$, s) $\equiv$
   pot $\neq$ pot$'$ $\wedge$ trunks_of_pots(pot, pot$'$) $\subseteq$ pending(s),
can_get : State $\rightarrow$ **Bool**,
is_disjoint : Trunk_rec $\rightarrow$ **Bool**
is_disjoint(s) $\equiv$ pending(s) $\cap$ connected(s) = {},
connected : Trunk_rec $\rightarrow$ Trunk-**set**
connected(r) $\equiv$
   { tr | tr : Trunk • trunk_alloc(tr) $\in$ **dom** connections(r) },
trunks_of_pots : Pstn_or_trunk × Pstn_or_trunk $\rightarrow$ Trunk-**set**
  ...
end

4.6.5 Connections

We have defined schemes corresponding to the main components of the system: REMOTE_0, PSTN_0, TRUNKS_0, and TRANSMISSION_0. These are instantiated as objects in CONNECT_3, and their types of interest provide a concrete definition for State as a record. To model remote stations sharing a communication medium with the central, the object instance of REMOTE_0 is parameterised with the object instance of TRANSMISSION_0. The generators connect, disconnect are defined in terms of the corresponding functions in REMOTE_0 and PSTN_0. In addition, a function handle_transmissions_in implements the protocol receiving messages sent by remotes.

scheme CONNECT_3 =
  class
    object
      TR : TRANSMISSION_0, R : REMOTE_0(TR),
      P : PSTN_0, TU : TRUNKS_0
    type
      State ::
        transmissions : TR.State $\leftrightarrow$ change_transmissions
        trunks : TU.State $\leftrightarrow$ change_trunks
        pstn : P.State $\leftrightarrow$ change_pstn
        remotes : R.State $\leftrightarrow$ change_remotes
      ...
  end

As we move towards a distributed system we need to be particularly careful about consistency. In Section 4.5.3, introducing CONNECT_1, which we want to implement with CONNECT_3, we defined a consistency condition connect_consistent that trunk and PSTN connections stored in the line map (now split between remotes and the PSTN) must imply the presence of corresponding entries in the trunk allocation map. We need to show that connect_consistent is maintained by our generators. We check that

- the line map at a remote is only changed to connected to a trunk on receipt of a connect message or a connect_ack message from the central station
- the central station only sends a connect or a connect_ack message after including the trunk in the trunk allocation map
- a trunk is only removed from the trunk allocation map after receiving a cancel message from a remote
- a remote only sends a cancel message for a connected trunk after removing the connection from its line map

and we check similar properties for the PSTN.

We illustrate the protocol by considering the message exchange involved in a (successful) remote-to-remote connection. Consider a remote station rid receiving a request from its phone no to connect to some other phone no' located at some other remote station rid'. The sequence of messages for a successful connection is illustrated in the message sequence chart in Figure 4.3. This figure also indicates how the two remotes change the states of the relevant line cards, and how the central station changes the pending and connections information about trunks.

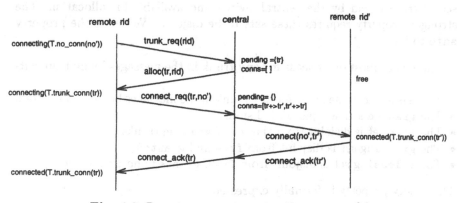

Fig. 4.3. Remote-to-remote connection - successful.

The protocol is therefore concerned with the allocation and deallocation of the trunk resources in the system. The central services a request for a trunk from a remote by responding with a trunk allocation message if a trunk is available. A remote can at any time send a cancel message to free a trunk assigned to it. A trunk can only become free by a cancel message from a remote. To relinquish a trunk assigned to a remote, the central must send a disconnect message for the trunk and make the trunk pending and so unavailable for allocation. The remote station receiving the disconnect message sends a cancel message for the trunk. This ensures that the central only allocates trunks that are no longer used by any remote.

We want to prove that this protocol maintains the property that at most one remote has access to a trunk at any time (i.e. trunks allocated to the remotes must be a set of disjoint sets), and the property that no trunks are lost (i.e. a trunk assigned in the central means that there is a remote using it for a connection). In the previous models of the network, CONNECT_1 and CONNECT_2, trunk assignment is performed instantaneously. It can easily be shown that the operations connect and disconnect in these models maintain these properties.

These properties cannot, however, be guaranteed to be preserved in a decomposed system using a protocol that transmits messages over a delaying medium: messages for allocating or freeing the trunk may be in transit in the medium. We prove that we satisfy such a property by asserting a stronger property that implies it. The first, "no confusion" property, we call safe. We take into account the messages in transit by considering messages in the medium as containing two sets of trunks. The granting set is composed of trunks with allocation messages not yet received by remotes. The releasing set consists of trunks with cancel messages from remotes not yet received by the central. Then there is the granted set composed of the set of trunks registered at each remote station. Finally there is the free set which is the set of trunks held by the central switch and available for allocation. The stronger property requires these sets to be disjoint. We define the property safe to be:

- There is at most one release for any trunk in the messages being transmitted.
- There is at most one grant for any trunk in the messages being transmitted.
- The granted sets are pairwise disjoint.
- The free set is disjoint from the set of granted trunks.
- The granting set is disjoint from free and granted.
- The releasing set is disjoint from free, granted and granting.

This safety property is formally expressed as:

value
    safe : State → **Bool**
    safe(s) ≡
      release_unique(transmissions(s)) ∧
      grant_unique(transmissions(s)) ∧
      ($\forall$ tr : Trunk •
        ($\forall$ rid_1, rid_2 : Rid •

$tr \in$ granted(rid_1, remotes(s)) $\land$ $tr \in$ granted(rid_2, remotes(s)) $\Rightarrow$
$rid_1 = rid_2$) $\land$
($tr \in$ free(trunks(s)) $\Rightarrow$
 ($\forall$ rid : Rid • $tr \notin$ granted(rid, remotes(s)))) $\land$
($tr \in$ granting(transmissions(s)) $\Rightarrow$
 $tr \notin$ free(trunks(s)) $\land$ ($\forall$ rid : Rid • $tr \notin$ granted(rid, remotes(s)))) $\land$
($tr \in$ releasing(transmissions(s)) $\Rightarrow$
 $tr \notin$ free(trunks(s)) $\land$
 ($\forall$ rid : Rid • $tr \notin$ granted(rid, remotes(s))) $\land$
 $tr \notin$ granting(transmissions(s)))))

The definitions of **safe, granted, free, granting, grants, releasing,
release_unique** and **grant_unique** are defined in an extension of CONNECT_3
called CONNECT_3_EXT.

The safety property is a system property. We need to prove theorems that
the state changing functions in CONNECT_3, **connect, disconnect**, etc. preserve **safe**:

in CONNECT_3_EXT ⊢
  $\forall$ no : No, s : State • safe(s) $\Rightarrow$ safe(disconnect(no, s)),
in CONNECT_3_EXT ⊢
  $\forall$ no, no' : No, s : State • safe(s) $\Rightarrow$ safe(connect(no, no', s)),
in CONNECT_3_EXT ⊢
  $\forall$ s : State • safe(s) $\Rightarrow$ safe(handle_transmissions_in(s))

To ensure that what we are proving is a property of the system, we need
to ensure that CONNECT_3_EXT is a conservative extension of CONNECT_3. this
follows from the use of explicit definitions in the extension.

There is a similar required property that no trunks are "lost", i.e. become
unavailable for use. This is expressed by a property that the union of **free,
granted, granted**, and **releasing** trunks is constant and is proved similarly.

4.6.6 Verification

With the introduction of a medium and defining the details that involve connection establishment, we say that CONNECT_3 *partially* implements CONNECT_2.
One module partially implements another module if given certain assumptions, the former is shown to have similar properties to the latter. We can
prove that for connections within a remote or within the PSTN we have
implementation. The other cases in CONNECT_3 which involve the medium require us to specify some assumptions for these to hold as implementation. It
follows that CONNECT_3 is a partial implementation of CONNECT_0.

To prove partial implementation for a connection between remotes we
formulate theorems for each message transmission that describe the effect on
the states of other components. In these theorems we make certain assumptions to arrive at a property similar to the abstract specification. Here is the

first such axiom that describes what a remote does on receiving a **connect** request for another remote – the line card is set to **connecting** and a trunk request message is sent:

axiom
  in CONNECT_3 ⊢
  ∀ s, s′ : State, rs, rs′ : R.State, no, no′ : No, ts, ts′ : TR.State,
    ps : P.State, rid, rid′ : Rid, tu : TU.State •
    s = mk_State(ts, tu, ps, rs) ∧ no ≠ no′ ∧ is_remote(no) ∧
    rid = remote_of(no) ∧ is_remote(no′) ∧
    rid′ = remote_of(no′) ∧ rid ≠ rid′ ∧
    rs(rid)(no) = connected(no_conn(no)) ∧
    s = mk_State(ts, tu, ps, rs) ∧ s′ = connect(no, no′, s) ⇒
      remotes(s′) =
        remotes(s) † [rid ↦ rs(rid) †
                        [no ↦ connecting(no_conn(no′))]]] ∧
      transmissions(s′) =
        TR.transmit_mgt_in(trunk_req(rid), transmissions(s)) ∧
      trunks(s′) = trunks(s) ∧ pstn(s′) = pstn(s)

Each such axiom corresponds to a single transmission of a remote or central corresponding to a user action, like **connect**, or receipt of a message on the transmission medium. If we merge the axioms by equating the result state s′ of one and the initial state s of another, i.e. we assume that there is at most one message in the system at any one time, we get the properties of CONNECT_2.

The other types of connections (between a remote and the PSTN) can be proved similarly.

4.7 Integration

We introduce a refinement, PHONE_2 which instantiates CONNECT_3 instead of CONNECT_1. Since CONNECT_3 is a partial implementation of CONNECT_0 and PHONE_2 is otherwise identical to PHONE_1 it then follows that PHONE_2 is a partial implementation, under the same conditions, of PHONE_1.

4.8 Implementation

Not all of this specification is intended to be implemented in software. The purpose is to check the correctness of the proposed protocols for communication between the central and remote stations (and the originally proposed protocols were in fact found to be defective), to design the software for the central and remote stations, and to design the hardware for doing the radio transmission. So the parts of the specification to be implemented are the functions in CONNECT_3 (which model the actions of the central station), TRUNKS_0 (which models the component of the central station dealing with trunk management), REMOTE_0, (which models the collection of remote stations), and (mainly in hardware) TRANSMISSION_0. PSTN_0 models our *assumptions* about the public network, and PHONES_2 shows how these connection components combine with assumptions about telephones to provide a system that implements the requirements of a POTS shown to be met by PHONES_0.

4.9 Related Work

There is substantial literature available that deals with specifying telephone systems using formal techniques. For example, a rely and guarantee method for Timed CSP was used to specify the behaviour of a POTS [78]. An instance of the Temporal Logic of Actions was used to describe modular specification of telephone services [79]. A stepwise refinement approach in developing telephony systems using LOTOS was described by [140]. [152] provides a case study of a telephone exchange. In this report we do not consider temporal properties. We are concerned with specifying a distributed network involving unknown (and arbitrary) delays in transmission. The data structures required, and their distribution between central and remote switches, means that a language supporting a range of data structures was appropriate for the initial stages of development. The description of the processes involved is deferred until after the decomposition into modules specifying the distributed components has been done: RAISE provides us with a modular language. Its suggested method, doing data development applicatively and later transforming to a concurrent architecture, proved appropriate to the problem. Proofs that the decomposition of the data structures (with appropriate functions to modify them) implement the basic requirements of POTS, and that resources are correctly allocated and released, can be done without the extra complications arising from concurrency.

4.10 Conclusions

This chapter shows how a step wise approach leads to a formal development of a telecommunications software. In particular, we use an *invent and verify* approach supported by the RAISE method. We began in Section 4.2 from an abstract specification of the POTS as a monolithic system. In Sections 4.4 to 4.5, we gradually refined this specification to reveal and address certain operational and architectural aspects of the system. These include: behaviour of the service, allocation of shared network resources, and the system's distributed architecture. The abstract specifications describe operations that atomically modify the global state of the system. It can be proved that these operations satisfy a critical system property that no trunk is ever lost or assigned to two remotes at the same time. In Section 4.6 we decomposed the abstract specification and defined its operations according to a resource assignment protocol with messages transmitted over a delaying communication medium. To prove that the operations maintain the property that no trunks are lost, we assert a stronger property that involves the medium and further assumes that messages sent on this medium never get lost. This assumption allows us to prove the correctness of the protocol with respect to this property. The other property that no trunks are confused between remotes can be proven similarly. We found, however, that with the introduction of intermediate operations and a delaying medium, the system will only partially implement the abstract specification. We therefore specified under what conditions we will have an implementation.

The work also demonstrates how an applicative style of specification in RSL can be used to formally develop a large communications system. It also demonstrate the expressive power of RSL in describing systems on different levels of abstraction, down to describing an implementation. This implementation can then be directly translated into a concurrent specification. An applicative style of specification makes formal reasoning tractable. In addition, the different techniques provided for by the method give us a high degree of assurance of the system's correctness. The use of a step-wise approach in the RAISE method, coupled with its compositional properties, facilities for modularisation, and parameterisation provides a general framework for developing systems that involve underlying layers of communication protocols.

4.10.1 Future Work

In the development of the system, we assumed a perfect transmission medium to be able to prove the correctness of the assignment protocol. We could refine our model for the transmission medium to involve modules that tolerate certain faults.

In addition, we have not considered here the problem of feature interaction common in most telephony systems. Feature interaction happens when new service features interfere with the behaviour of the original service. However, the technique developed in Section 4.4 could be extended to formalise this problem.

Background Information

This chapter is based on work [37] done by Roderick Durmiendo of the Advanced Science and Technology Institute (ASTI) under the Department of Science and Technology of the Republic of the Philippines, together with Chris George.

5. Developing a National Financial Information System

5.1 Introduction

This chapter is concerned with the specification of a very large system: a national financial information system for Vietnam. Other themes exemplified in this chapter are the use of prototyping to test parts of the specification, and the transformation from a synchronous to an asynchronous system.

Financial information is one of the most important kinds of information for society. It supports the government in macro-economic management by providing essential information for the purposes of planning and decision-making. In recent years, Vietnam has been shifting from a centrally-planned to a market-oriented economy. The development of a market-oriented economy requires a great volume of information exchange, provided in a timely, accurate, and reliable manner. Aware of its importance and based on promised funds from the World Bank, the Vietnamese Government decided to build an integrated financial information system for its Ministry of Finance.

The financial information system is an information system receiving, storing and processing important economic and financial information: on the state budget revenue and expenditure criteria, on the management of various settlement account systems through the treasury system, on the management of the taxpayers, on the management of financial operations of businesses, on the management of domestic and foreign debt, etc. The financial information system is formed from various components, but the central one is the management and operation of the state budget. Concerning this, there are the taxation system and the treasury system. The Ministry of Finance also provides financial information to other agencies like Government Office, Ministry of Planning and Investment, and State Bank, through some periodic reports.

5.1.1 Ministry of Finance

The Ministry of Finance is the Government agency performing nation-wide state management in the financial, accounting and state budget fields. The Ministry of Finance is responsible for implementing a wide range of financial planning, coordination and monitoring activities.

The treasury, taxation and budget systems are parts of the MoF. The treasury system manages state budget expenditure and the taxation system manages revenue collection. The State Budget department serves to synthesise information from the treasury and taxation systems. See the MoF data flow diagram in Figure 5.1.

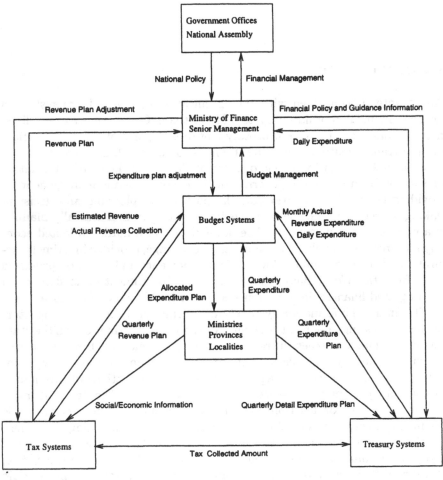

Fig. 5.1. MoF data flow diagram.

Budget planning is an annual event. As part of this a national revenue plan for tax collection is established, and allocated among the provinces and districts.

Taxpayers are allocated to either province or district tax offices. They report their income, profits, turnover etc. to that office, receive demands for taxes and pay the treasury department in the same province or district. Treasury departments report to tax departments on amounts collected. Tax departments make daily and annual reports up the tax system hierarchy. They also forecast and report on expected revenues.

Based on the approved expenditure plan which the state budget produces, budget holders make their detailed expenditure plans and get them approved (and perhaps modified). Proposed actual expenditures are then checked against the detailed expenditure plans and, if approved, made by the treasury department at the appropriate level. Treasury departments make daily and annual reports up the treasury system hierarchy.

A national summary report on budget performance is made at the end of the year.

This chapter concentrates mostly on the taxation system. The details of the treasury and budget systems can be found in the UNU/IIST reports [34, 35].

5.2 Tax Information System

The tax system is an important branch of the Ministry of Finance. Essentially its role is to manage the flow of money from taxpayers to the state budget. A *taxpayer* is an enterprise, either public or private, which is responsible for paying tax.

The state budget and the tax system have close relationships. The collected tax amount is the revenue of the state budget. The tax system is in charge of managing all taxpayers and performing tax collection activities for the whole country.

The tax system is mainly focused on two objectives:

- Identifying the tax incidence for each taxpayer, i.e. tax categories required and tax amount in each category.
- Administering the tax collection activities so that tax leakages can be avoided. Restricting tax leakages is performed both on the side of taxpayers and on the side of tax collectors.

5.2.1 Taxpayers

Taxpayers are first of all associated with a *specialisation*, a kind of business, such a farming, manufacturing, transport, and trading. Each specialisation has one or more *categories* of tax, such as profit tax, turnover tax, and sales tax. We define in a global object T:

type
  Specialisation,
  Category

We also add **Amount** to T, to be used for amounts of money, especially tax. **Amount** is defined as an abbreviation for **Nat**.

Associated with tax categories are corresponding tax rates and the method of calculating tax amounts, as well as exemption and collecting approaches. Each category will also have its tax *period* (typically a calendar month). The object T defines the abstract type **Date** and **Period**. Dates are totally ordered, but are otherwise abstract. Periods are modelled simply as natural numbers; the start and end dates corresponding to a period for a tax category can be calculated by knowing a start date and the length of tax periods for that category.

Tax Regime. This information of how to calculate taxes according to category and specialisation, which is independent of other details about taxpayers, is termed the tax *regime*. It may be changed from time to time by the Government. There are two functions in particular that are in the regime. First, from an amount of taxable profit, turnover, sales etc. the regime is used to calculate, according to the date and the specialisation and category, how much tax is to be paid for the period, the **tax_amount**. Second, when taxes remain unpaid beyond their due date, a penalty is added. This penalty is calculated on a daily basis according to a **penalty_rate** of interest that also depends on the date:

scheme REGIME =
  with T **in class**
    type Regime, Rate = {| r : **Real** • r $\geq$ 0.0 |}
    value
      tax_amount :
        Date × Specialisation × Category × Amount × Regime →
          Amount,
      penalty_rate : Date × Regime → Rate
  end

We do not define these functions further: we are simply stating that this information must be in the regime.

Taxpayer Roll. The association of a taxpayer with a specialisation and some categories of tax is not constant, because the rules may change. First, taxpayers are required to *register* information about their business. This is basic and relatively stable information like name and address, plus some description of the kind of business. We define it abstractly:

object RT :
  class
    type Register
  end

The details of all the registrations taxpayers make over time is called their their *roll*:

scheme ROLL =
  with T **in class**
    type
      Reg_list = (Date × RT.Register)*,
      Roll = {| rl : Reg_list • **len** rl > 0 ∧ date_ordered(rl) |}
  end

There are also various functions defined, such as **get_reg** to extract the registration information for a particular date.

The current register value is used to calculate the specialisations and categories they are currently involved in. This depends on the regime, so we add to REGIME:

value
  is_included :
    Specialisation × Category × RT.Register × Regime → **Bool**

Taxpayer Bases. Taxpayers then have to declare actual profits, turnover, sales, etc. in each tax period. This information is termed the *tax calculation base*. This consists of the tax categories of the taxpayer and the *tax calculation valuation* for each specialisation of the taxpayer. The tax calculation valuation is a common name; the actual amount used depends on the category. For instance, for sales tax the tax calculation valuation is the turnover, and for profit tax it is the profit.

A base is then a collection of amounts indexed by specialisation and category, which we can represent as a map. We add to T (since we use the type in several modules):

type
  Base = Specialisation × Category $\overrightarrow{m}$ Amount

Now we can use a value of type **Base**, together with the current date and regime, to calculate a set of amounts of tax that are due. These *tax amounts* are indexed just by category, since taxes for one taxpayer in the same category but different specialisations are accounted together. We define BASE:

scheme BASE(RG : REGIME) =
  hide SD, SM **in**
  with T **in class**
    value
      demand_amounts :
        Date × Base × RG.Regime → (Category $\overrightarrow{m}$ Amount)
      demand_amounts(d, b, rg) ≡
        [c ↦ demand_amount(d, c, b, rg) |
          c : Category • ∃ s : Specialisation • (s, c) ∈ b],

```
demand_amount :
  Date × Category × Base × RG.Regime → Amount
demand_amount(d, c, b, rg) ≡
  let
    sa =
      [s ↦ RG.tax_amount(d, s, c, b(s, c), rg) |
        s : Specialisation • (s, c) ∈ b]
  in
    SM.sum(0, sa)
  end
object
  SM : SUM(SD),
  SD :
    class
      type Domain = Specialisation, Range = Int
      value
        sum : Int × Int → Int
        sum(x, y) ≡ x + y
    end
end
```

The scheme SUM used here is a generic module that will apply a function sum (provided as part of the parameter scheme) to accumulate all the range values. Its parameter scheme is SUM_DATA:

```
scheme SUM_DATA =
  class
    type Domain, Range
    value sum : Range × Range → Range
  end
```

and SUM is:

```
scheme SUM(SD : SUM_DATA) =
  class
    type Map = SD.Domain ⇸ SD.Range
    value
      sum : SD.Range × Map → SD.Range
      sum(null, m) ≡
        if m = [ ] then null
        else
          let d : SD.Domain • d ∈ dom m in
            SD.sum(m(d), sum(null, m \ {d}))
          end
        end
  end
```

SUM is used not only, as here, to add amounts, but also to summarise reports.

The scheme BASES defines a type Bases as a list of taxpayer bases, used as a historical record of the taxpayer's declarations.

After tax demands are calculated, *tax bills* are issued and payments received. Amounts, payments and any exemptions are recorded in the *tax book*. A *tax summary book* is also produced from the tax book to summarise information for each specialisation.

Figure 5.2 is a dataflow diagram for taxpayer management.

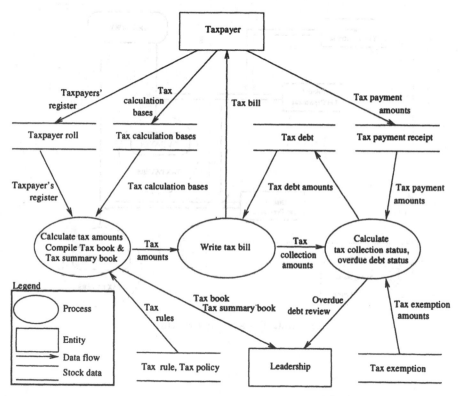

Fig. 5.2. Dataflow diagram for taxpayer management.

5.2.2 Tax System Structure

The tax system is organised into a hierarchy. The General Tax Department is at the highest level and is located in the capital; a Provincial Tax Department is at the middle level and is located in each province and a District Tax Department is at the lowest level and is located in each district.

At the moment, the activities of managing taxpayers are carried out at the level of provincial tax departments (which administer the great majority of public enterprises) and at the level of district tax departments (which administer small public enterprises and all private enterprises). In the general tax department this function is not carried out; it is instead responsible for guiding and monitoring the implementation of the tax collection plan. A provincial tax department manages both its tax payers and also its district tax offices. See Figure 5.3.

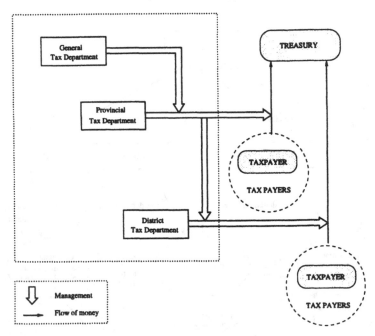

Fig. 5.3. Tax system structure.

5.2.3 Tax Accounting

There are rules of tax accounting that the specification needs to follow:

1. When a taxpayer pays an amount, debts from previous periods are settled first.
2. When the tax system generates a demand, it deducts any overpayment from previous periods.
3. Tax debts attract interest at a rate determined by the tax regime.
4. Tax transactions in different categories are independent.

This raises the question of the relation of rule 4 and the rules 1 and 2. In fact independence takes precedence; payments, debts, and overpayments are accounted for each category in which a taxpayer is involved. This is typical of the issues often hidden in requirements and clarified by specification.

Accounts. The scheme ACCOUNT defines the functions to do accounting: generating demands, recording payments and exemptions. This includes calculating debts (including interest if necessary) and overpayments. Accounts are modelled as date-ordered sequences of transactions:

scheme ACCOUNT(RG : REGIME) =
  with T **in class**
    type
      Account =
        {| trl : Tran* • date_ordered(trl) ∧ over_pos(trl) |},
      Tran ==
        demand(Date, Period, Amount) |
        pay(Date, Period, Amount) |
        exemption(Date, Period, Amount) |
        over_settle(Date, Amount) |
        pre_demand(Date, Amount),
     ...
  end

The first three kinds of transactions record demands made, payments received, and exemptions allowed.

If a taxpayer pays too much, an **over_settle** transaction is added to show an over-payment. When the demand is calculated in the next period, a **pre_demand** may be added to record the cancellation of all or part of the previous over-payment. For example, suppose the over-payment amount is 10. If the demand amount is at most the over-payment, say 8, a pre-demand transaction with amount 8 is added (and the bill sent will show an over-payment of 2). But if the demand is more than the over-payment, say 12, a demand of 2 and pre-demand of 10 are added (and the bill sent will demand 2). So the current over-payment is always the sum of the **over_settle** transactions minus the sum of the **pre_demand** transactions. The algorithm is such that over-payments are never negative: hence the second clause in the definition of the subtype **Account**, where **over_pos** expresses this condition.

Bills show debts from previous periods, any over-payment, and the new demand:

type
  Bill ::
    debt : Debts over_amount : Amount new_demand : Amount,
    Debts = Period $\overrightarrow{m}$ Amount

The function **demand** to calculate a bill is:

value
  demand :
    Date × Date × Period × Amount × Account × RG.Regime
    $\overset{\sim}{\to}$ Account × Bill
  demand(d_1, d_2, p, a, ac, rg) $\equiv$
    let o = over_amount(ac), ds = mk_debts(d_1, ac, rg) **in**
      (**if** o = 0 **then**
        add(demand(d_2, p, a), ac)
      elsif a $\leq$ o **then**
        add(pre_demand(d_1, a), ac)
      else
        add(demand(d_2, p, a − o), add(pre_demand(d_1, o), ac))
      end,
        mk_Bill(**if** a $\leq$ o **then** (ds, o − a, 0) **else** (ds, 0, a − o) **end**))
    end
  pre can_demand(d_1, d_2, ac)

where d_1 is the start of the current period, d_2 its due-date (the date by which taxes must be paid to avoid additional interest payments). The precondition can_demand checks that the dates are appropriately ordered and no earlier than the date of the latest transaction in the account.

There are also functions for crediting payments and recording exemptions.

The scheme ACCOUNTS defines a map from categories to accounts, used to model all the accounts of a taxpayer, and allowing each category to be accounted separately:

scheme ACCOUNTS(RG : REGIME) =
  hide AC **in with** T **in class**
    object AC : ACCOUNT(RG)
    type Accounts = Category $\twoheadrightarrow$ AC.Account
    ...
  end

5.2.4 Tax Payer Management

We can now bring together all the information needed about a particular taxpayer: the roll, the bases and the accounts. This is done in the scheme TAXPAYER_MANAGEMENT. Here are the main types and the function declare to generate a collection of Bills for a taxpayer from a declaration:

scheme TAXPAYER_MANAGEMENT(RG : REGIME) =
  hide RL, B, BS, AC **in with** T **in class**
    object
      RL : ROLL,

```
    B : BASE,
    BS : BASES,
    AC : ACCOUNTS(RG)
  type
    Taxpayer ::
      roll : RL.Roll ↔ re_roll
      bases : BS.BASES ↔ re_bases
      account : AC.Accounts re_account,
    Bills = Category ⇸ AC.Bill
  value
    declare :
      Date × Date × Period × Base × Taxpayer × RG.Regime
      ⥲ Taxpayer × Bills
    declare(d₁, d₂, p, b, t, rg) ≡
      let
        ca = B.demand_amounts(d₁, b, rg),
        bs = BS.declare(d₁, p, b, bases(t)),
        (ac, bills) = demand(d₁, d₂, p, ca, account(t), rg)
      in
        (re_bases(bs, re_account(ac, t)), bills)
      end
      pre can_declare(d₁, d₂, b, t),

    demand :
      Date × Date × Period × (Category ⇸ Amount) ×
        AC.Accounts × RG.Regime
      ⥲ AC.Accounts × Bills
    demand(d₁, d₂, p, ca, ac, rg) ≡
      if ca = [ ] then (ac, [ ])
      else
        let
          c : Category • c ∈ dom ca,
          (ac₁, bills) = demand(d₁, d₂, p, ca \ {c}, ac, rg),
          (ac₂, bill) = AC.demand(d₁, d₂, p, c, ca(c), ac₁, rg)
        in
          (ac₂, bills ∪ [c ↦ bill])
        end
      end
      pre
        d₁ ≤ d₂ ∧
        (∀ c : Category •
            c ∈ dom ca ⇒ AC.can_demand(d₁, d₂, c, ac)),
    ...
  end
```

The first function **declare** takes a base declaration from the taxpayer (the fourth parameter). From this a collection of amounts indexed by category is calculated using the **demand_amounts** function from **BASE** that we saw in Section 5.2.1. The bases component of the taxpayer is updated with the new base declaration. The updated accounts for the taxpayer, and the collection of bills (bills indexed by category), are calculated using the function **demand**. This uses the **demand** function in **ACCOUNTS**, which in turn uses for each account the function **demand** we saw in Section 5.2.3.

5.2.5 Reports

Each office in the taxation hierarchy has to report regularly to its superior office. The superior office makes summary reports from those coming from below.

Reports are described abstractly. A report has a format **Report_form** and a number of **Lines**, determined by the format. Each line in a report has an amount. Two reports may be summarised to generate a third, provided they have the same format, which will also be shared by the result. The amount in each line of the result is the sum of the amounts of the corresponding lines in the input reports:

object RP :
  with T **in class**
    type
      Report, Report_form, Line
    value
      form : Report $\rightarrow$ Report_form,
      is_in : Line $\times$ Report_form $\rightarrow$ **Bool**,
      amount : Line $\times$ Report $\overset{\sim}{\rightarrow}$ Amount,
      summary : Report $\times$ Report $\overset{\sim}{\rightarrow}$ Report
    axiom
      [form_summary]
      $\forall$ rp$_1$, rp$_2$: Report •
        form(summary(rp$_1$, rp$_2$)) $\equiv$ form(rp$_1$) **pre** form(rp$_1$) = form(rp$_2$),
      [amount_summary]
      $\forall$ l : Line, rp$_1$, rp$_2$: Report •
        amount(l,summary(rp$_1$, rp$_2$)) $\equiv$ amount(l, rp$_1$) + amount(l, rp$_2$)
        pre form(rp$_1$) = form(rp$_2$) $\wedge$ is_in(l, form(rp$_1$))
      ...
  end

5.2.6 Groups

The scheme **TAXPAYER** defines a function **mk_report** to report on a taxpayer.

The scheme GROUP_MANAGEMENT defines a group of taxpayers and its management functions. It does this by instantiating a scheme DATABASE with keys which are taxpayer identifiers Tids (defined in T) and data which are Taxpayer records:

scheme GROUP_MANAGEMENT(RG : REGIME) =
 hide D **in with** T **in class**
  object
   TP : TAXPAYER(RG),
   D : **class type** Key = Tid, **Data** = TP.Taxpayer **end**,
   DB : DATABASE(D)
 end

The scheme DATABASE is a standard, abstract specification of a DATABASE ([116], Section 7.13):

scheme DATABASE(D : DATA) =
 class
  type Database
  value
   /* generators */
   empty : Database,
   insert : D.Key × D.Data × Database → Database,
   remove : D.Key × Database → Database,
   /* observers */
   defined : D.Key × Database → **Bool**,
   lookup : D.Key × Database $\overset{\sim}{\rightarrow}$ D.Data
  axiom
   ...
 end

The scheme GROUP extends GROUP_MANAGEMENT with a report function for making a report about the whole group.

The structure of the specification modules forming the group is illustrated in Figure 5.4.

5.2.7 Tax Offices

We now construct the structure of tax offices, at the district (DTD – District Tax Office), province (PTD) and general (GTD) levels. The first two of these have their own groups of tax payers, and each of these have associated modules defining a planning function. The general level has a regime that is shared with the rest through parameterisation. The structure is illustrated in Figure 5.5.

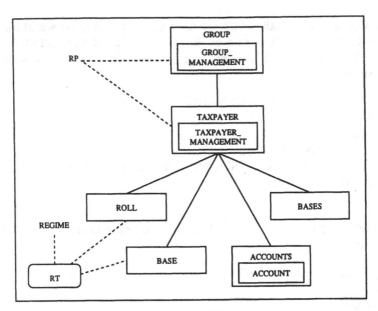

Fig. 5.4. The group specification structure.

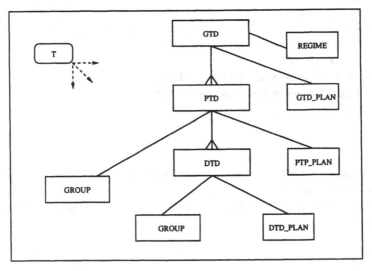

Fig. 5.5. The overall specification structure.

5.3 Prototype

We decided to make a prototype of (part of) the specification with three aims:

1. to check that the specification for calculating tax bills and accepting payments were correct
2. to investigate optimised algorithms for calculating tax bills
3. as an exercise in producing executable code from a specification.

5.3.1 Testing

The specification for calculating tax bills and accepting payments is fairly complicated. In particular, debts for previous periods (including interest) have to be calculated so that they can be presented in the bill, and so that payments can be allocated (on an "oldest debt first" basis). There are also unlikely but possible occurrences to be checked like over-payments. We were uncertain that the specification was correct, that it met the requirements. To gain confidence in the specification, it was decided to validate it by testing. This meant it first had to be executable, so it had to be translated to a programming language. We used the translator to C++ in the original RAISE tools [58].

In order to make the specification translatable it first had to be developed: abstract types had to be made concrete and implicit definitions and axioms replaced by explicit definitions of constants and functions.

The approach adopted was as simple as possible for things not directly affecting the calculation components we were interested in. For example, dates were represented as natural numbers. Once the specification was complete translation was straightforward.

Obtaining an executable prototype also involved writing by hand in C++ a "main" function. This is quite simple, essentially a number of `cin` and `cout` statements allowing the user to input test data and obtain results.

5.3.2 Test Results

Test data and expected results were produced and compared with the actual results. There were a few errors that were essentially "typos" in the specification, test data, or expected results and hence easily fixed. More significant problems were:

- One error in the test data caused the prototype to crash (making the start of the first period 0 when the `start_date` was defined as 1). This could have been detected if the concrete data used in defining the concrete `Regime` had been proved to implement the abstract version (or, in this case if it had just been put through the confidence condition checker and the conditions carefully inspected or justified). In practice it illustrates the need for validation functions to check input.
- A similar error (but with less drastic results) was caused by the test transactions being presented other than in date order. The tests produced erroneous output. Checking that transactions are input in date order was

included in the specification: another example of the need for input validation.

- There was one conceptual error discovered. When a demand is generated it includes demands for debts from previous periods. Debts incur interest. While amounts for the current period start to attract interest as debts after the due-date for the current period, debts from previous periods attract interest from the start of the current period. This difference in treatment for debts from previous periods was not specified, and some tests gave erroneous results. The correction was not very complicated, but this is the kind of error that it is important to find early in development.

- The interest on debts is specified as being calculated on a daily basis. In the original specification interest was calculated using real arithmetic and then converted to a natural number. Converting each day's amount in this way produced substantial rounding errors. Testing exposed this problem. It was corrected by delaying the conversion for each period until the total debt had been calculated.

5.3.3 Optimisation

Execution of tests demonstrated the exponentially increasing time complexity of the function on accounts used to calculate debts. These are calculated by each time recomputing the total debts from the start date. In specification terms the algorithm is clear and correct but it is unacceptably inefficient at run time. Two optimising strategies were defined, implemented and tested:

1. The first involved inserting an extra "balance" field in accounts: a standard kind of technique for avoiding duplicated calculation. This had the expected results in terms of run time but was insufficient: it merged the debts from all previous periods while the requirements were for these to be displayed separately in demands. This is an example of requirements not being clear even within a small team.

2. The second optimisation involved reducing the "one day at a time" mechanism to one that checked first for the previous significant date in the account, typically several days back, and computing in one step over this period.

3. A third possible optimisation, identified but not implemented, is a correction to the first, adding a debt map instead of a simple balance to each transaction.

The prototype was a useful vehicle for investigating such optimisations. The results can be used in the development of the main system.

5.4 Specifying a Distributed System

The specification described so far is purely applicative; it implies that, for example, a provincial tax office can obtain a report from one of its district offices merely by calling a function. This is not in general likely to be the case; they might at present not even be electronically connected. We need to define a distributed, more loosely coupled system. The first steps towards this were done by transforming the specifications to a concurrent form according to the RAISE method [117]. This is a systematic (though not automated) procedure: see Sections 2.3.1 and 2.3.2 of Chapter 2.

The result is that each office in the taxation system is represented by a process, a server offering the various functions to generate a tax demand, accept a payment, generate a report, etc., through communication on channels.

Similar specifications, though less detailed, were made of the treasury and budget systems. These have a similar structure to the taxation system, with offices at the national, provincial and district level (plus an extra commune level for the treasury system).

We therefore have a model of the "vertical" connections between the offices at different levels within each of the taxation, treasury, and budget systems. But this is inadequate in two ways:

1. There are also "horizontal" connections that cross the system boundaries. For example, tax is actually paid to a district or province treasury office. The treasury office reports the payment to the taxation office of that district or province so that the taxpayer's accounts can be updated.
2. The specification in terms of a process for each office is synchronous. For example, the specification says that when a provincial tax department asks for a periodic report from its constituent district offices, it waits for the responses, and can do nothing else until they have all arrived. The actual system is not like this: it is asynchronous.

The first problem is a challenge to the method we adopted for developing the specification. We tried to develop each system separately, which helps to keep the problem simple by reducing the amount of information to be considered at any one time. Is this a feasible approach, when they need to communicate with each other? Will we have to redo much of the work done already? This would be unfortunate, because as specifications are developed we put effort into not only writing them but also in reviewing them, checking them against requirements, sometimes prototyping and testing them, perhaps even proving important properties of them. Thus we invest in them and increase their quality. As soon as we change them we are likely to lose this quality level. The challenge therefore is to find a way of changing the specifications in such a way that we can guarantee that their quality is not affected.

5.4.1 Messages

To introduce asynchrony for the financial information system we use the standard technique of buffering. The buffers we use hold queues of messages for delivery (like the spool file in an email system). We associate a buffer with each office in each system: a buffer for the general taxation office, one for each provincial and district taxation office, and similarly for each treasury and budget office. Each office has an address, composed of a system (like tax or budget) and, for example, a pair of a province identifier and a district identifier for a district office. We define in an object M:

type
  Pid, Did, Cid,
  Address' ==
    general_address |
    province_address(pid : Pid) |
    district_address(dpid : Pid, did : Did) |
    commune_address(cpid : Pid, cdid : Did, cod : Cid),
  Address = {| a : Address' • is_address(a) |}

is_address is a predicate to check that the address actually exists. M represents a file of information about Vietnam.

We adopt the protocol that every message has its sender address embedded in it, together with a number. In a scheme FIS_TYPES we define:

type
  Num = **Nat**,
  Message_text,
  Message :: num : Num sender : Address text : Message_text,
  System == tax | treasury | budget | loans | aid,
  Address' :: system : System locality : M.Address,
  Address = {| a : Address' • is_address(a) |}

is_address is a predicate to check that the address exists within its system. For example, if the address is of a commune the system must be treasury.

When an office creates a message, such as a request for a report, or an instruction, or information about a tax payment, it assigns the message a number that is new for that office. The protocol is that all such *initial* messages are replied to, even if only an acknowledgement is needed, and the *response* message is given the same number as the initial message (and is obviously addressed to the sender). Numbers of initial messages are then unique within an office, allowing the response to be unambiguously associated with the initial message.

The specification of the message system asserts that all messages are delivered, but it is easy in a final implementation to cater for failure in the transmission system by introducing time-outs on responses.

5.4.2 Asynchronous Communication

In the concurrent synchronous specification, an office compiling a report from its constituent lower level offices collects their reports by calling their report-generating functions in parallel. In the asynchronous system this is achieved as follows:

1. The report compiling function sends initial messages to the lower level offices. These will appear in the lower level offices' message buffers.
2. Each office has a *secretary* process that takes messages from the office's message buffer. Requests for reports, which are initial messages, are handled by the secretary calling the appropriate function and using the result to create a response message, sent back to the originating office.
3. The upper level office also has a secretary. When a secretary receives a response message it places it in the office's *in-tray*.
4. The report compiling function is waiting for response messages to appear in its office's in-tray with the right message numbers. As these appear it extracts them, and when all have arrived it can compile its report exactly as it did in the synchronous system.

5.4.3 Secretaries

It should be apparent that the asynchronous system needs some extra components compared with the synchronous one:

- a secretary process that receives initial messages and sends responses, and receives responses and places them in the in-tray
- an in-tray which allows messages to be stored and retrieved by number
- a process to generate new numbers for initial messages to be sent.

Here is the **secretary** process from the **SECRETARY** module:

value
```
/* needs protection by delay in loop after null message */
secretary : Unit → in any out any Unit
secretary() ≡
 while true do
  let m = MSG.get(A.address) in
  if ∼ T.is_null(m) then
   let mt = C.decode(T.text(m)) in
   if A.can_handle(mt, T.sender(m)) then
    let res = C.code(A.handle(mt, T.sender(m))) in
    MSG.put
     (T.sender(m), T.mk_Message(T.num(m), A.address, res))
    end
   else IN.put(m)
   end end end end end
```

Here:

- A.Address is the secretary's office's address.

- MSG is the message system, and MSG.get(a) gets the next message for address a. This may be null (meaning there are no messages). Human secretaries probably make tea at this point; electronic ones have to wait for some period of time to avoid them just looping and consuming all the machine cycles. Inserting some time delay will be done in the final code, as indicated by a comment in the RSL.
- Messages may be encoded for security reasons, so must first be decoded using the C.decode function.
- A.can_handle is a function that checks if this is an initial message that the secretary can deal with, like making a report, or recording a tax payment, perhaps. If the secretary can handle this message, it creates a response with the A.handle function, encodes it, and sends the response to the sender of the initial message, using the put function of the message system MSG. Otherwise, the secretary places the message in the office in-tray (IN.put) for someone or something else to deal with it.

5.4.4 Stub Modules

The other change we need to make is to flatten the previous nesting of modules. For example, in the provincial tax office scheme PTD there is an array of objects instantiating the district tax office scheme DTD. These nested DTD objects are removed from the PTD, since they are now global. We replace the objects in PTD with *stub* objects. For each function previously offered directly by PTD, like mk_report, say, the stub has a function with the same name. This function gets a new message number and sends a "report request" message with that number to the address of the DTD object the stub is replacing. It then waits for a message with the same number to appear in its office's in-tray, whereupon it decodes it and returns the content. We have to ensure that the secretary in the DTD office can_handle a report request, and the handle function used there is precisely mk_report. Then the stub function will behave exactly as the original synchronous function, but with some time delay.

All the other functions in the office, such as tax accounting and report summarising, are unaffected. So we have achieved a transformation of the original system with minimal disturbance to its specification.

5.4.5 Encoding and Decoding Messages

Each system has its own version of CODE for encoding and decoding messages. For the taxation system, for example:

scheme TAX_CODE(T : FIS_TYPES) =
  class
    type
      Message_text ==
        summarise_req(form : RP.Report_form) |
        summarise_res(report : RP.Report) |
      —
    value
      code : Message_text $\rightarrow$ T.Message_text,
      decode : T.Message_text $\rightarrow$ Message_text
    axiom [decode_code] $\forall$ mt : Message_text • decode(code(mt)) = mt
  end

Only one kind of message – initial request and response for a report – is defined here. Clearly more would be needed.

Each system has its own module like TAX_CODE, which means that each system has its own collection of message types, and also that the coding systems in different systems can be different. There would have to be agreement about "horizontal" messages between systems, of course, but there is no reason why in general messages within the treasury should be readable by people within the taxation system, for example.

The SECRETARY module above has a CODE module as a parameter. We can instantiate CODE with TAX_CODE to make a taxation system secretary, with TREASURY_CODE to make a treasury system secretary, etc.

5.4.6 Module Structure

The resulting module structure of a provincial tax office DIST_PTD is shown in Figure 5.6.

The module for tax accounting the province's taxpayers, CC_GROUP (most of whose sub-modules are omitted), is on the left. The stub modules for the province's districts (STUB_DTD), the SECRETARY, IN_TRAY, MESSAGE system etc. are on the right.

5.4.7 Gradual Automation

Terms like "secretary" and "in-tray" intentionally reflect the common names of people and physical artifacts in non- or partly-automated offices. We don't necessarily see this system as one to be completely implemented by computers acting automatically. Indeed, to try to automate these processes across every office in a country in one big step of automation would almost certainly be disastrous even if it were feasible. Rather, we specify how, provided each office behaves according to certain rules, the whole system will behave. It doesn't matter to a provincial tax office whether its district offices are automated or not, just that they should behave as specified. Similarly, if all or part of

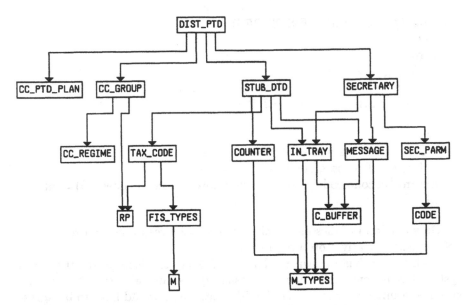

Fig. 5.6. Asynchronous provincial tax office: module structure.

the processes in one office are automated, it should be transparent to the others it deals with. This is a major aim of the work: to provide a model of the whole system that allows component parts to be automated step-by-step. Similarly, it doesn't matter whether messages are transmitted electronically, by fax, by phone, on paper, or even by someone stepping from a district tax office to the district treasury office in the next room, as long as the protocols are followed.

5.5 Conclusion

5.5.1 Summary

We show how a large and complex system can be successfully described using both abstraction (leaving out much of the detail) and modular structure (so that we concentrate on one part at a time). The modular structure also largely reflects the existing structure, which helps in both constructing and comprehending it. This applies both to the physical structure of general, province and district offices, but also to the conceptual structure of the taxation system, where rolls, bases, and accounts of taxpayers are separated, and all are separated from the regime (the current tax laws and regulations).

Second, we suggest how a rapid prototype can be constructed and used for testing at an early stage in design, to find errors and eventually give more confidence in correctness.

Third, we show how a collection of separate, concurrent but synchronous systems can be combined into a single asynchronous system by a standard transformation that minimises changes to what exists, follows a standard procedure, and hence allows us to predict the properties of the resulting asynchronous specification from the properties of the synchronous one.

5.5.2 Discussion

The specifications presented here are very abstract. They are intended as a means of analysis and description, more than as an immediate basis for implementation (although the work on optimisation is of direct relevance for implementing tax accounting). Before any system or subsystem were implemented based on these specifications there would need to be decisions on issues like security, and detailed information about the size and transaction rate of the offices involved. Implementation policy would also depend on the hardware available and the communications available within and between different systems. One advantage of this high level description is that it is quite independent of such details, and allows for a number of different implementation options, including in particular different options in different offices.

Reuse. We also suggest, though it would take further work to check this, that the description presented here would apply elsewhere, in other countries. Some of the accounting procedures would undoubtedly change, and the organisation structure might be different, but most of the components of this specification, we believe, could be easily adapted and reused in a system with similar purpose.

Background Information

This chapter describes the Ministry of Finance Information Technology (MoFIT) project undertaken in 1996–7 by UNU/IIST and the Vietnamese Ministry of Finance (MoF). The project was carried out by five software engineers from the MoF and the Vietnamese Institute of Information Technology (IoIT): Trần Mai Liên, Lê Linh Chi, Phùng Phương Nam, Đỗ Tiến Dũng, and Nguyễn Lê Thu, together with Chris George. Hoàng Xuân Huấn, an economist from Hanoi University, also worked on the project later.

The aims of the project were:

- in the long term, to specify a national financial information system as input to a major project in Vietnam to produce such a system
- in the short term, to specify the taxation system
- to train software engineers from the MoF and IoIT in the techniques of domain analysis, requirements capture, and specification of software systems.

The project specified the main components of the system [34, 35]:

- the taxation system, responsible for assessing, demanding and collecting various taxes
- the treasury system, responsible for all the monetary transactions in the system
- the budget system, responsible for drawing up national budgets, allocated between various ministries and their component offices, and monitoring performance against budgets
- the external loans system, responsible for administering loans from outside Vietnam
- the external aid system, responsible for administering external aid.

The resulting five specifications were then merged into a single system. In the process the previously synchronous communications within the components were transformed into asynchronous communications, extended to include communications between the components.

6. Multi-Lingual Document Processing

6.1 Introduction

There are several thousand languages in use in the world today, and increasing need for computer software systems which support these languages. A similar need applies also to historical languages which are no longer spoken in daily use: there is not only interest in studying such languages in their own right but also a desire to preserve the contents of decaying ancient documents written in these languages by transcribing them onto computers.

For some of these languages, notably those belonging to the oriental and Arabic families, there are inherent characteristics which make them more difficult to support than, for example, the European languages which can generally be implemented if necessary as simple extensions to some sort of "standard" (i.e. Latin-based) text or document processing system, this extension often requiring little more than the addition of a few extra characters to the font and the assignment of these characters to keys on the keyboard. One problem arises with languages which use character sets which are not simple extensions or modifications of the Latin character set, which means that existing fonts generally cannot be used and whole new fonts have to be designed to support such languages. Problems also exist with languages which have character sets which are much larger than those of the European languages, sometimes incorporating thousands of distinct characters as in, for example, the ideographic scripts used for Japanese, Chinese and Korean. For such languages there are clearly not sufficient keys on the computer keyboard to allow a simple mapping from a single key to a single character as is done on an English keyboard, and instead more complicated input methods are required, often involving the use of multiple keystrokes or some sort of graphical interface to generate a single character. Finally, different problems are encountered with languages which are not traditionally written in the same direction as the European languages, for example languages like Arabic, which is written horizontally from right to left, and Mongolian and Japanese, which are both written vertically downwards and in which the lines of text progress from left to right and from right to left respectively.

Despite these difficulties, there is a large and increasing number of software systems which support non-European languages. Where such support has been achieved by extending some existing Latin-based document processing system, the extension has tended to be concentrated on the provision of the extra character sets (fonts) and the modification or extension of the keyboard input mechanism, and the question of directionality of the text has mainly been ignored. Indeed many such systems strictly impose the horizontal, left-to-right directionality on all languages whatever their natural directionality, sometimes rotating the individual characters of scripts which are naturally written vertically so that they are at least correctly aligned with respect to each other.

To a large extent this is of course to be expected, as without the ability to display the characters of a language or to input them into the computer in some way the question of the reading and writing direction is largely academic. However, scripts written in an unnatural direction can be extremely difficult to read and they are often difficult to write in an unnatural direction too.

Software systems which were primarily designed to support non-Latin languages often do allow their users to write and read documents in the appropriate natural direction and sometimes allow the user to choose the reading and writing direction of a document. However, such systems generally support a very much smaller range of languages and scripts than the Latin-based systems, often having been designed to specifically support a single language or a small group of related languages.

While many of these systems are perfectly adequate for producing documents in a wide range of single languages and even documents which include more than one language or script intermixed, none of them can be said to be truly multi-lingual: those that do offer support for more than one direction either do not allow texts with different directionality to be intermixed arbitrarily in a single document or do not support all four different writing directions. Thus, for example, while many of the systems supporting different directionalities would have little difficulty generating the document shown in Figure 6.1, in which a Japanese text, written vertically in columns and beginning at the top right-hand corner, is followed by its English translation, there are few, if any, which could generate the document shown in Figure 6.2 in which blocks of Mongolian script, which are written vertically in columns beginning at the top left-hand corner, are embedded within German text.

However, multi-lingual documents, and hence also computer systems which support their creation, are becoming increasingly important in a wide range of applications, especially as international communication, collaboration and even tourism increase. Thus, for example, international trade and business agreements in many cases have to be written in the native languages of all parties concerned; institutions such as libraries, universities, hospitals and tourist information services often need to store or make available information in more than one language; and people need to learn to read, write and speak other languages, which requires multi-lingual teaching material, dictionaries, and so on. Moreover, there are some countries (for example In-

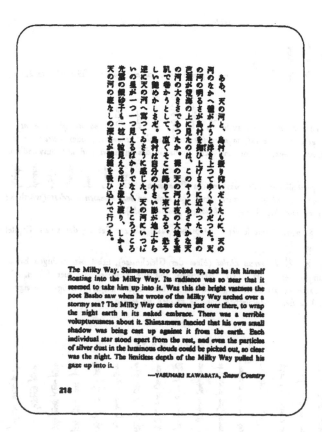

Fig. 6.1. Japanese text with English translation.

dia and many in Africa) in which a sometimes very wide range of different languages are in daily use. Similarly, there are countries in which different written forms of what is essentially the same language co-exist and indeed are often intermixed (for example Mongolia, where the different forms are even written in different directions, the Cyrillic script being written horizontally from left to right and the traditional Mongolian script vertically from left to right).

This chapter describes the design of a multi-lingual document processing system, the "MultiScript" system, in which particular emphasis is placed not only on supporting all four different writing directions used in the overwhelming majority of the world's languages but also on allowing all these four directions to be arbitrarily intermixed in the same document.

The first stage of the design process, the domain analysis, comprised a comprehensive study and analysis of a wide range of multi-lingual documents.

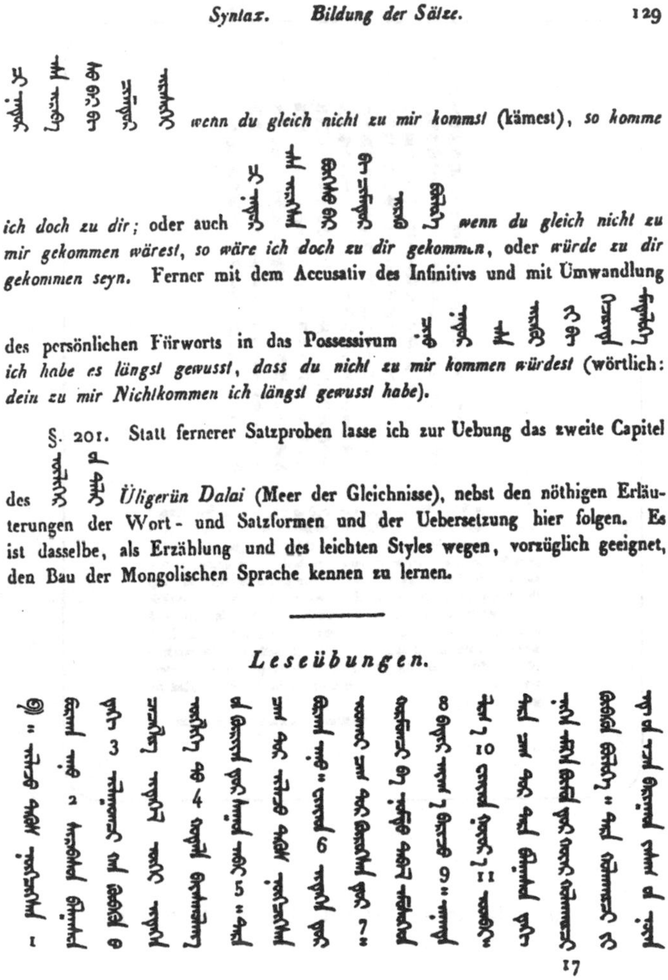

Syntax.   Bildung der Sätze.   129

᠁ *wenn du gleich nicht zu mir kommst* (kämest), *so komme*

ich doch zu dir; oder auch ᠁ *wenn du gleich nicht zu mir gekommen wärest, so wäre ich doch zu dir gekommen,* oder würde zu dir gekommen seyn. Ferner mit dem Accusativ des Infinitivs und mit Umwandlung

des persönlichen Fürworts in das Possessivum ᠁ *ich habe es längst gewusst, dass du nicht zu mir kommen würdest* (wörtlich: *dein zu mir Nichtkommen ich längst gewusst habe*).

§. 201. Statt fernerer Satzproben lasse ich zur Uebung das zweite Capitel

des ᠁ *Üligerün Dalai* (Meer der Gleichnisse), nebst den nöthigen Erläuterungen der Wort- und Satzformen und der Uebersetzung hier folgen. Es ist dasselbe, als Erzählung und des leichten Styles wegen, vorzüglich geeignet, den Bau der Mongolischen Sprache kennen zu lernen.

Leseübungen.

17

Fig. 6.2. German text with embedded Mongolian script.

This is described in Section 6.2. Then, based on this analysis, an abstract model of a generic multi-directional, multi-lingual document was developed and formally specified using the RAISE specification language RSL [116]. As well as standard text, this model also includes the notion of hyperlinks between different parts of a document and indeed between different parts of different documents. This is described in Section 6.3. In Section 6.4 we then go on to describe the specification of a range of atomic operations for editing multi-lingual documents.

Together with a series of informal requirements, the full specification was in fact used as the basis for an implementation of the MultiScript system.

6.2 Multi-Lingual Documents: Domain Analysis

In order to make sure that the MultiScript system would support the construction of multi-lingual documents in all their various forms, we began by carrying out a comprehensive study and analysis of existing multi-lingual documents in order to identify their essential properties and features. Figures 6.3 through 6.7 show some examples of multi-lingual documents which typify these properties and features.

Figure 6.3 shows Latin and Cyrillic scripts, both of which are written horizontally from left to right, intermixed with Arabic script, which is written from right to left.

МОНГОЛЬСКО-ТЮРКСКИЙ СЛОВАРЬ   113

·bariʿür ·ч. بارى‌وں — tutqa نوتقا	batu بانو — ч. beẓil بغيل скупой 661,
ручка 211‖ b. ügeị aruq باربوون اوكاى	börk (?) بورک — 905, berk بيرک крепкий
ч. kobin كوبين корзина без	909‖ b. bolba بولبه — ч. b. boldï стал кре-
ручки 209‖ b. ü. ẏuduẏa خودوضه	пок 598 895‖ b. b. bilïktü بيليـکـنو —ч.
ч. destesis küse دسنمسيز كون кувшин	b. b. ïlïmde стал крепок в науке 857‖
без ручки 106.	b. b. küči كوچى — ч. b. b. küči
barẓurdar ere اير	его сила стала крепкой 1083‖ b. b. te-
ч. barẓurdar er برغوردار ابر счаст-ли-	mür jidadu نيمور جيدادى — ч. berke
вый мужчина 470.	boldï temür süngüge بيرک بولدى نيمور
basa abuba tanqulaẏi (?) نسه ابوبه	стал крепок для железного
ч. yana aldï tabuẏni بنه —ننقولاغى	копья 581‖ b. b. üjle اويله —ч. berk
опять взял службу 697‖ اللرى نابوغنى	boldï iš بيرک بولدى ايش —ч. работа стала
b. baịba بايبه —ч. y. turdï نوردى	прочной 909‖ b. b. yama يامه —ч. b. b.
опять был 541‖ b. moduni burẏasut	neme نيمه вещь стала крепкой 1036‖
ч. dari yïẏačning مودونى بورغاسوت	b. ẏajar فاجار —ч. b. yer بير крепкая

Fig. 6.3. Mixing horizontally-oriented scripts.

Figure 6.4 depicts traditional Mongolian script in which Tibetan script, together with transliterations of the Tibetan into Cyrillic script, are embedded. The traditional Mongolian script is mostly written in its normal orientation, namely vertically with lines progressing from left to right, though it appears horizontally, in fact rotated through 90° anti-clockwise, in the first line of the table in the centre of the example. Both the Tibetan and Cyrillic scripts are written in their standard orientation throughout, i.e. horizontally from left to right.

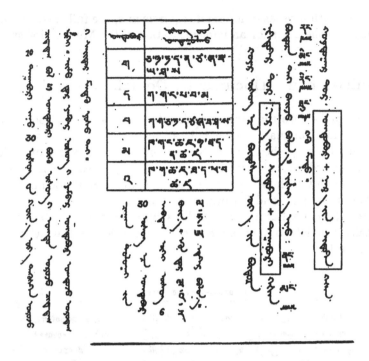

Fig. 6.4. Embedding horizontal text in vertical script (1).

The example shown in Figure 6.5 is taken from a Japanese dictionary in which Japanese text is intermixed with traditional Mongolian, Latin and Tibetan scripts. The Japanese text is written in its traditional orientation, that is vertically with the lines of text proceeding from right to left, and the other scripts follow the same directionality. Since each block of Mongolian script is always confined to a single line it in fact reads entirely naturally, though the characters of the normally horizontally oriented Latin and Tibetan scripts are rotated through 90° clockwise to fit in with the altered orientation.

Figure 6.6 shows a page from a Mongolian-English dictionary [87]. Both the traditional and the Cyrillic forms of Mongolian are featured, as well as a transliteration of the traditional script into Latin characters. All scripts are written in their standard orientation.

Figure 6.7 shows an extract from the index of the same dictionary [87]. Here, all the text is horizontally oriented, but the traditional Mongolian script is rotated through 90° clockwise so that the first letter of each piece of traditional Mongolian script is adjacent to the first letter of the corresponding piece of Latin script. The directionality of the traditional Mongolian script therefore does not follow that of its transliteration into Latin script. Rather, the directionality is chosen so that the pieces of Mongolian script are aligned

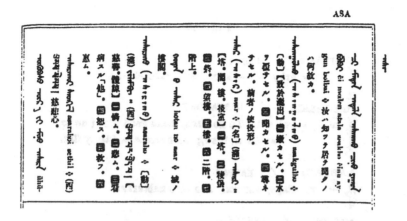

Fig. 6.5. Embedding horizontal text in vertical script (2).

in such a way that they read naturally in alphabetical order when the page
is rotated so that the Mongolian script has its correct vertical orientation.

Each of the different scripts featured in the above examples is naturally
written in one of four different orientations: horizontally from left to right
with lines of text proceeding downwards (Latin, Cyrillic, and Tibetan); horizontally from right to left, also with lines of text proceeding downwards (Arabic); vertically downwards in columns, the columns proceeding from left to
right (traditional Mongolian); and vertically downwards but with the columns
proceeding from right to left (Japanese). In fact the vast majority of the
world's scripts follow the same four orientations[1]. We can therefore cate-
gorise the scripts into four groups according to the direction in which they
are naturally read and written. We call these groups the "HL", "HR", "VL"
and "VR" groups respectively. Thus, for example, in addition to Latin and
Cyrillic scripts, the HL group includes Thai, Greek and Bengali. Similarly,
Hebrew belongs to the HR group, Manchu and Todo to the VL group, and
Chinese and Korean to the VR group.

The examples also show that there are basically only two ways in which
pieces of text in different scripts can be intermixed in a single document:
either pieces of text in one script are embedded within pieces of text in another so that the entire text is effectively read sequentially as in the examples
in Figures 6.3 and 6.5; or the pieces of text in the different scripts are clearly
separated from each other and are read independently as in the examples in
Figures 6.6 and 6.7. We first deal with each of these cases separately, then go
on to consider the more general situation in which both cases appear in the
same document as in the example in Figure 6.4.

---

[1] We are only aware of one script which has a different orientation: the ancient
Orkhon script which is read horizontally from right to left but from bottom to
top; see [29], section 49.

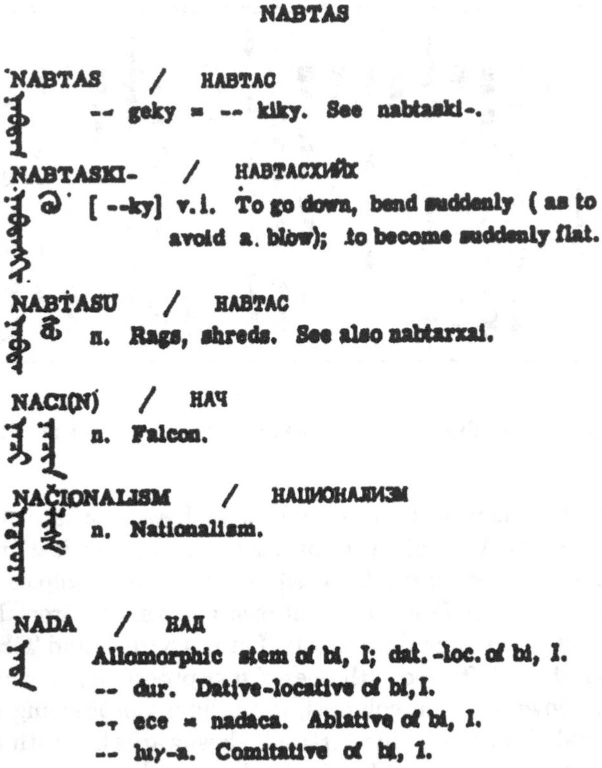

NABTAS

NABTAS   /   НАВТАС

-- geky = -- kiky. See nabtaski-.

NABTASKI-   /   НАВТАСХИЙХ

℈ [--ky] v.i. To go down, bend suddenly (as to
avoid a. blow); to become suddenly flat.

NABTASU   /   НАВТАС

n. Rags, shreds. See also nabtarxai.

NACI(N)   /   НАЧ

n. Falcon.

NACIONALISM   /   НАЦИОНАЛИЗМ

n. Nationalism.

NADA   /   НАД

Allomorphic stem of bi, I; dat.-loc. of bi, I.
-- dur. Dative-locative of bi, I.
-т ece = nadaca. Ablative of bi, I.
-- luy-a. Comitative of bi, I.

Fig. 6.6. Mixing horizontal and vertical scripts (1).

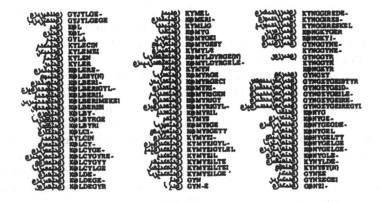

Fig. 6.7. Mixing horizontal and vertical scripts (2).

6.2.1 Embedded Text

When one script is embedded in another which has the same natural orientation this orientation is used by both as in the intermixing of Latin and Cyrillic scripts in Figure 6.3. However, if the two scripts have different natural orientations then there are two different basic ways in which the insertion can be made: either the embedded script adopts the orientation of the script in which it is embedded or it retains its own natural orientation. In the former case the embedded script is often written with its characters rotated when one of the natural orientations is horizontal and the other vertical as can be seen in the example in Figure 6.5.

The first of these possibilities is illustrated by the example in Figure 6.5. The normally horizontally oriented Latin and Tibetan scripts which are embedded in the vertical Japanese script are written in the same orientation as the Japanese script, the individual Latin and Tibetan characters being rotated through 90° clockwise. Other examples of this can be found in the top and bottom examples in Figure 6.8. The first of these consists of English text in which Mongolian script is embedded, the Mongolian being written with the same orientation as the English text (horizontal, left to right and top to bottom) and with its individual characters rotated through 90° anti-clockwise. The second example is similar except that it shows Chinese text, written in its traditional orientation (vertical, top to bottom and right to left), in which English text is embedded. The English text is written with the same orientation as the Chinese, and again its individual characters are rotated, in this case through 90° clockwise. In all cases, the rotation of the characters is performed in such a way that the characters are correctly aligned relative to each other when they are combined to form words. This additionally ensures that the characters of cursive scripts connect together correctly (as in the Mongolian text in the last line of the first example in Figure 6.8).

To model text with this kind of structure, we consider it as a sequence of pieces of *formatted text*, each of which has the same orientation (i.e. is written and read in the same direction) and consists of some *formatting information* and a sequence of *characters*. The formatting information effectively specifies the properties of each of the characters in that particular piece of text, for example their typeface, their size, their rotation, their colour, etc. In this way, the first (English/Mongolian) example in Figure 6.8 is represented as a sequence of pieces of formatted text, alternately consisting of English characters alone and rotated Mongolian characters alone. More concretely: the first piece of formatted text contains the English text 'For example ... begining'; the second a single rotated Mongolian character; the third the English text '(code ... middle'; the fourth another single rotated Mongolian character; and so on. Similarly, the third (Chinese/English) example in the same figure is represented as a sequence of pieces of formatted text, alternately Chinese and rotated English.

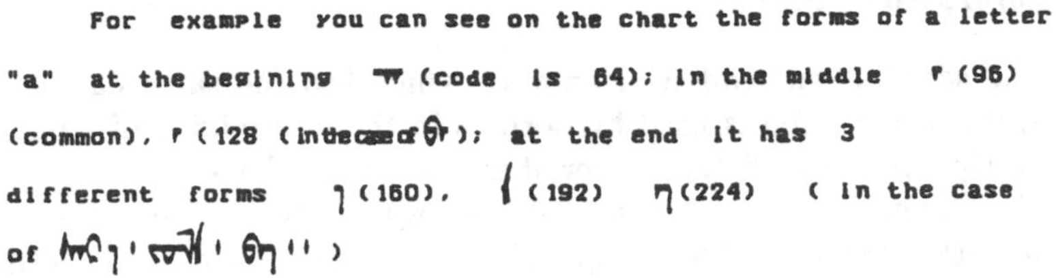

For example you can see on the chart the forms of a letter "a" at the begining (code is 64); in the middle (96) (common), (128 (in the case of)); at the end it has 3 different forms (160), (192) (224) (in the case of)

(a)

The words الإسلام and العرب mean Islam and the Arabs.
The words الإسلام و العرب mean Islam and the Arabs.

(b)

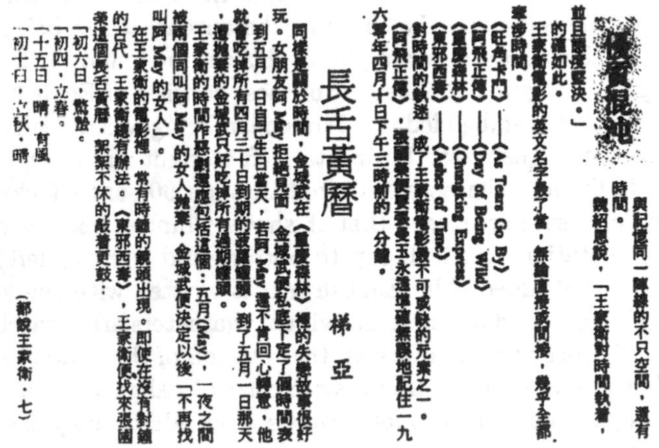

與記憶同一陣線的不只空間，還有
時間。
魏紹恩說，「王家衛對時間執着，
並且態度堅決。」
的確如此。
王家衛電影的英文名字最了當，無論直接或間接，幾乎全部
牽涉時間。
《旺角卡門》——《As Tears Go By》
《阿飛正傳》——《Day of Being Wild》
《重慶森林》——《Chungking Express》
《東邪西毒》——《Ashes of Time》
對時間的執迷，成了王家衛電影最不可或缺的元素之一。
《阿飛正傳》，張國榮便要張曼玉永遠準確無誤地記住一九
六零年四月十日下午三時前的一分鐘。

長舌黃曆　梯亞

同樣是關於時間，金城武在《重慶森林》裡的失戀故事很好
玩。女朋友阿May拒絕見面，金城武便私底下定了個時間表
，到五月一日自己生日當天，若阿May還不肯回心轉意，他
就會吃掉所有四月三十日到期的菠蘿罐頭。到了五月一日那天
，遭拋棄的金城武只好吃掉所有過期罐頭。
王家衛的時間作懸劇還應包括這個：五月(May)，一夜之間
被兩個同叫阿May的女人拋棄，金城武便決定以後「不再找
叫阿May的女人」。
在王家衛的電影裡，常有時鐘的鏡頭出現。即使在沒有對鐘
的古代，王家衛總有辦法。《東邪西毒》，王家衛便找來張國
榮這個長舌黃曆，絮絮不休的敲着更鼓：
「初六日，驚蟄。
「初四，立春。
「十五日，晴，有風
「初十日，立秋，晴
（郁說王家衛．七）

(c)

Fig. 6.8. Three examples of multi-lingual documents.

The second possibility, where the embedded script retains its natural orientation, is illustrated by the example in Figure 6.3 as well as by the middle example of Figure 6.8, in which English text is interrupted by insertions in Arabic, the English text being read horizontally from left to right and the Arabic horizontally from right to left.

To model text with this kind of structure, we consider each block of embedded text as being enclosed in a *frame*, with the reading and writing direction of the text within a frame being defined by the *orientation* of the frame. The orientation of a frame is in turn determined by its *entry point* and its *line stream.*

The entry point defines the position (for instance on a printed page of text or in a window on a computer screen) at which reading or writing within the frame begins, and is situated at the top left-hand corner of the frame for the

HL and VL groups of scripts and at the top right-hand corner of the frame for the HR and VR groups. This definition could very easily be extended to include the bottom corners of the frame, thereby additionally supporting exceptional scripts such as the Orkhon script which are read from bottom to top.

The line stream defines the direction in which the text within the frame is read or written, and is either horizontal (for the HL and HR groups of scripts) or vertical (for the VL and VR groups). Consecutive lines of text are aligned perpendicular to the line stream and proceed away from the entry point, so that for horizontal line stream they proceed downwards if the entry point is at the top and upwards if it is at the bottom while for vertical line stream they proceed to the right if the entry point is at the left and to the left if it is at the right.

The second example in Figure 6.8 is thus represented as a single piece of English text with three frames embedded in it, one containing each separate piece of Arabic text. Each of these three frames has right entry point and horizontal line stream and is read in its entirety when the appropriate point in the English text is reached. A frame embedded in a piece of text in this way is thus effectively considered as a single complex "character" within that text. The example in Figure 6.3 has a similar but slightly more complicated structure.

6.2.2 Separated Text

Text may appear in a document as separated blocks in two different ways. First, one block of text may logically follow some other text in the sense that it is intended to be read immediately after that other text. This is illustrated most clearly in the example in Figure 6.1 where a Japanese text, written vertically in columns and beginning at the top right-hand corner, is followed by its English translation, though the examples in Figures 6.6 and 6.7 essentially follow the same structure except that in these cases it is repeated many times.

In fact this type of example is just a special case of embedded text with different orientation as in the English/Arabic example discussed immediately above at the end of Section 6.2.1, the embedding simply coming at the end of the text. It is therefore modelled in exactly the same way: the English text is enclosed in a frame, whose entry point is left and whose line stream is horizontal, and that frame appears after the last character of the Japanese text (possibly with a line break character inserted between them).

The other way in which text may appear as separated blocks in a document is when the contents of one block have only a loose connection, or even no connection at all, with the contents of the other. In this case, the two blocks, if loosely related, must appear "close" to each other but not necessarily at a given (fixed) position as would be the case for embedded text.

This is illustrated in Figure 6.2, which in fact shows a page from a German book about Mongolian grammar [127]. In this example, the text below the horizontal line, which consists of the German word 'Leseübungen' (which means 'reading exercises') together with a block of Mongolian script, is related to the text in §.201 above the horizontal line, but it could in principle appear anywhere within that section. In fact it is somewhat like a figure or a table in the sense that its position may effectively float, at least within some bounds, so the table in the centre of the example in Figure 6.4 is in fact another example of loosely related text.

In order to model text with this kind of structure, we introduce the notion of a *free frame*. This has exactly the same properties as a frame used to describe embedded text apart from the fact that its position is not fixed absolutely in relation to the text with which it is associated when that text is printed or displayed.

The text below the horizontal line in Figure 6.2 is therefore considered as a free frame, with left entry point and horizontal line stream, which contains the characters making up the German word 'Leseübungen' followed by another frame, with left entry point and vertical line stream, containing the block of Mongolian text. Similarly, the table in Figure 6.4 is represented as a single free frame, also with left entry point and horizontal line stream, which contains one line of Mongolian script, written with the characters rotated through 90° anti-clockwise, together with 5 lines of Tibetan script in its normal orientation.

6.2.3 The General Case

Of course in general a document may contain both embedded and separated pieces of text, as is in fact the case in the examples shown in Figures 6.2 and 6.4. Thus, in Figure 6.2 the part above the horizontal line consists of German text with embedded Mongolian script, both scripts retaining their natural orientation, and the part below the horizontal line consists of a separated piece of text loosely connected to the text in §.201 above the line. In general, therefore, we consider that a piece of text consists of two parts: a *string* and some *free frames*.

The string effectively represents the *ordered* part of the text, that is the part that is read sequentially from beginning to end, and consists of a sequence of *tokens*, each of which may be either a character or a frame. This sequence is split into pieces of formatted text as described in Section 6.2.1 in order to accommodate changes in typeface, character rotation, colour, etc. within the text. Frames within the sequence contain embedded text whose reading and writing direction is different from that of the containing text.

Conversely, the free frames represent the *unordered* part of the text, that is things which have only a loose connection, or even no connection at all, with the ordered part of the text or with each other. A free frame might contain text, as in the example shown in Figure 6.2 and discussed in Section 6.2.2,

but more generally it might also, for example, contain a figure, a picture or
a table. A good example of a document which only contains free frames is a
newspaper. This essentially consists of a set of unrelated or loosely related
individual articles, possibly with photographs or other pictorial items, so it
can be represented simply as a collection of free frames, one for each individual
article or pictorial item.

When a piece of text is printed or displayed, the position of each object
in the string part is completely determined by the orientation of the text
and by the position and size of the preceding object in the string, if any,
and frames embedded in the string act just like characters, albeit probably
ones of abnormal size. The free frames, on the other hand, can effectively be
positioned at will.

The whole of the example shown in Figure 6.2 is thus represented as
an ordered string part plus one free frame. The string part represents the
text above the horizontal line, that is the German text with the embedded
Mongolian, and the free frame represents the part below the horizontal line
as explained in Section 6.2.2. The changes in typeface between normal and
italic characters in the German text are effected by dividing the string into a
sequence of pieces of formatted text, and each individual piece of Mongolian
text is represented as an embedded frame within this string. The text within
the free frame consists only of a string part, this in turn consisting of a
single piece of formatted text comprising the characters of the German word
'Leseübungen' followed by a frame containing the block of Mongolian text.
The Mongolian text also consists only of a string part constructed from a
single piece of formatted text, this formatted text being made up from the
individual Mongolian characters in sequence.

6.2.4 Documents and Libraries

As we have seen above in the German/Mongolian example of Figure 6.2, a
frame may contain other frames or *subframes*. In fact these may occur in the
string part or in the free frames part, and could in principle be arbitrarily
nested with subframes also containing subframes. We can therefore make
use of this nesting and simply consider a whole document as a frame, the
orientation of that frame determining the sense in which the document should
be read and the contents (string and free frames) of the frame representing
the text within the document.

In this way, the German/Mongolian document [127] as a whole, of which
Figure 6.2 shows one page, is represented as a frame with left entry point
and horizontal line stream (corresponding to the natural orientation of the
German text, i.e. of the main text of the document), the contents of that
frame being a string containing the main German text with the embedded
Mongolian (as in the upper part of Figure 6.2) and a collection of free frames
representing the various exercises associated with the different subsections of
the main text (as in the lower part of Figure 6.2).

Documents are collected together in *libraries*, each library consisting of a set of documents, and the ultimate scope of our model is a collection of libraries. Each library might, for example, represent a collection of documents owned by a particular individual, with the collection of libraries as a whole representing all documents owned by all individuals.

6.3 The Formal Model of Multi-Lingual Documents

In this section we introduce the basic RSL types we use to model a generic multi-directional, multi-lingual document as described in Section 6.2, as well as the various well-formedness conditions these types must satisfy in order to ensure the consistency of the model. We also introduce some useful auxiliary concepts and functions. Then we go on to define operations on the system in Section 6.4.

6.3.1 The Basic Definitions

We define a type Doc as an RSL record type containing three components, one for each of the three basic constituents of a document: its *root*, its *frame map*, and its *hyperlinks*.

The frame map of a document effectively records the properties and contents of each frame (both embedded subframes and free frames) in the document. This is modelled as a map type in RSL, from an abstract type (or sort) FrameId of *frame identifiers* to the type Frame which represents the actual frame, to make it possible to distinguish different frames which happen to have the same orientation and contents.

The root of a document represents the frame identifier of the topmost (or main) frame of that document, that is of the frame which corresponds to the document as a whole.

Finally, the hyperlinks field records referential links from some part of a document to some other part of the same document or to some part of some other document, possibly in some other library. This is modelled as a map type from frame identifiers in the current document to other frame identifiers, the *library identifier* (represented by the abstract type LibId) and the *document identifier* (represented by the abstract type DocId) components of the *product* type in the range of the map indicating the library and the document within that library to which these latter frames belong.

type
  Doc ::
    root : FrameId
    frame_map : FrameId $\rightarrow$ Frame
    hyper_links : FrameId $\rightarrow$ (LibId × DocId × FrameId),
  FrameId, DocId, LibId

The fields of the type Doc must satisfy various consistency conditions in order for the type to represent only valid (or well-formed) documents, namely:

1. the root of the document must occur in the domain of the frame map in order for the contents of the document to be defined;
2. the frame map must be non-circular to ensure that the contents of the document are finite. This is equivalent to the condition that no frame of the document should be contained in (a subframe of) itself;
3. any frame identifier which is defined as the source of some hyperlink in the document must belong to the document;
4. the frame map of the document must record all frames belonging to the document, including the root frame, and no others;
5. each frame in the document must have a unique identifier. This is to ensure that it is possible to distinguish two frames in the document which have the same contents, for example when editing the document.

These conditions are formalised in the function is_wf_document. The auxiliary function is_non_circular embodies the second condition, while condition 5 is captured by stating that the list of all frame identifiers in the contents of the document (the result of the function all_frames) contains no duplicates (the function is_non_repeating).

value
  is_wf_document : Doc $\rightarrow$ **Bool**
  is_wf_document(d) $\equiv$
    let mk_Doc(r, fm, hm) = d **in**
      r $\in$ **dom** fm $\wedge$
      is_non_circular(fm) $\wedge$
      dom hm $\subseteq$ **dom** fm $\wedge$
      let id_list = all_frames(r, fm) **in**
        is_non_repeating(id_list) $\wedge$ (**elems** id_list = **dom** fm $\setminus$ {r})
    end end

One might also naively suppose that an additional consistency condition on libraries and hyperlinks is necessary to ensure that the library, document and frame identifiers appearing as the destination of any hyperlink must all exist, that is that it must always be possible to follow any hyperlink to its destination. However, in a multi-user environment where different libraries are assumed to be owned by different users, this would effectively imply that a document appearing as the destination of some hyperlink can only be edited in such a way as to maintain the validity of that hyperlink. This is clearly unreasonable, particularly if the documents at the source and the destination of the hyperlink have different owners. The best we can do, therefore, is to allow a hyperlink to reference a non-existent destination but to provide a function for removing such obsolete hyperlinks from a document automatically.

The next step is to use the function is_wf_document as the defining predicate of a subtype of the type Doc. This subtype, Document, then represents

well-formed documents, i.e. those values of type Doc which satisfy all the
appropriate consistency conditions.

type
Document = {| d : Doc • is_wf_document(d) |}

The document identifier distinguishes individual documents in a library,
and a library is then simply represented using a map type from document
identifiers to documents. Similarly, the library identifier distinguishes individual libraries within the whole collection of libraries, represented by the
type Libraries.

type
Library = DocId $\overrightarrow{m}$ Document,
Libraries = LibId $\overrightarrow{m}$ Library

The type Frame, which represents frames, is also modelled as a record
type. This consists of three parts: the orientation of the frame, represented
by the type Orientation; its string, represented as a list of pieces of formatted text, each piece represented by the type FormattedText; and its free
frames, represented as a list of frame identifiers. The string and the free
frames together constitute the contents of the frame.

type
Frame ::
  orient : Orientation
  string : FormattedText*
  freeFrames : FrameId*

The orientation is defined as a record type comprising an entry point and
a line stream. Both entry point and line stream are defined using variant
types which simply enumerate all possible values of those types.

type
Orientation :: entry : Entry_Point stream : Line_Stream,
Entry_Point == left | right,
Line_Stream == horizontal | vertical

Formatted text is also defined as a record type consisting of some formatting information and a list of tokens. A token is either a character or a
frame identifier, as represented by the union type. Formatting information
and characters are defined only abstractly as sorts.

type
FormattedText :: format : FormatInfo chars : Token*,
Token = Character | FrameId,
FormatInfo,
Character

6.3.2 Positioning within a Document

We now extend the model by introducing the notion of an *index* to define the abstract "position" of characters and frame identifiers within a document. This is particularly useful in the specification of editing operations on documents (see Section 6.4). For example, we can give a single index to define the point at which new text is to be added to a document (this index representing something like the current position of the cursor in typical computer systems) or two indexes to define the bounds of a block of text which is to be deleted from a document.

We represent a position as an index using a product type which consists of a frame identifier and two positive integers (the type **Index** below). The type Nat_1 represents the positive integers as a subtype of the natural numbers.

type
$$Nat_1 = \{| \; n : \textbf{Nat} \cdot n \neq 0 \; |\},$$
$$Index = FrameId \times Nat_1 \times Nat_1$$

The frame identifier in an index identifies the particular frame within which the indexed position is located, and the two positive integers fix the position within the contents of that frame. If the first integer is less than or equal to the number of pieces of formatted text contained in the frame then it determines a particular piece of formatted text, namely the one at that numerical position in the list, and the second integer in turn defines a similar position in the list of tokens within that piece of formatted text. If the first integer is one greater than the number of pieces of formatted text contained in the frame then it refers to the list of free frames of the frame, and the second integer then determines a particular free frame in that list of free frames.

An index is said to be *valid* if it refers to the position of some character or frame identifier within the document, that is if the frame identifier in the index refers to some frame in the document and if the two positive integers define some valid location within the contents of that frame according to the interpretation given above. The two functions is_valid_index define this property.

value
> is_valid_index : Document $\times$ Index $\rightarrow$ **Bool**
> is_valid_index(d, (f, n_1, n_2)) $\equiv$
>   **let** m = frame_map(d) **in**
>   f $\in$ **dom** m $\land$ is_valid_index(m(f), n_1, n_2) **end**,

> is_valid_index : Frame $\times$ Nat_1 $\times$ Nat_1 $\rightarrow$ **Bool**
> is_valid_index(f, n_1, n_2) $\equiv$
>   **let** mk_Frame(or, st, ff) = f, l = **len** st **in**
> $n_1 \leq l \land n_2 \leq$ **len** chars(st(n_1)) $\lor n_1 = l + 1 \land n_2 \leq$ **len** ff **end**

Additional functions on indexes, including functions which determine the token situated at some given valid index position and the next valid index position, are defined in [43].

6.4 Operations for Editing Multi-Lingual Documents

In the full specification we have defined a set of atomic operations for editing a document which is sufficiently complete to allow any desired editing operation to be realised as a combination of them. We have also generalised the top-level model of a simple collection of libraries to include the notion of an editing environment into which a user of the MultiScript system can load documents from the libraries for editing or browsing and within which documents can be created and edited.

In general we have specified these editing operations by first specifying an atomic editing operation which acts on a single frame of a document, then raising this operation to the level of the document itself and then to the level of the editing environment. Since the full specification of all editing operations is quite long, we illustrate the process by concentrating on a single operation here, namely adding a new token to a frame. Specifications of other operations can be found at this book's web site (see page 395) and in [42].

One way of adding a new token to a frame is to insert the token immediately before the "current" one. This is illustrated in the first two elements of Figure 6.9 for the cases where the current token lies respectively at the end or at the beginning of some piece of formatted text.

However, with this functionality alone it is impossible to insert a token at the position shown in the third element of the figure, or indeed into a piece of formatted text which is currently empty. We therefore define two functions for inserting a token into a frame: the function **insert_tkn**, which inserts a new token immediately before the existing token at some given index, and the function **add_token**, which adds a new token to the end of some given piece of formatted text in the frame.

The function **insert_tkn** uses the auxiliary function **insert** to insert the new token at position m in the nth piece of formatted text, then installs the resulting piece of formatted text back into the string using the function **chg_ft**. Its precondition ensures that the nth piece of formatted text and the mth token within it both exist.

value
    insert_tkn : Token × Frame × Nat$_1$ × Nat$_1$ $\overset{\sim}{\to}$ Frame
    insert_tkn(t, f, n, m) ≡
      let ft = string(f)(n),
          new_ft = insert(t, ft, m)
      in chg_ft(new_ft, f, n) **end**
      pre n ≤ **len** string(f) ∧ m ≤ **len** chars(string(f)(n))

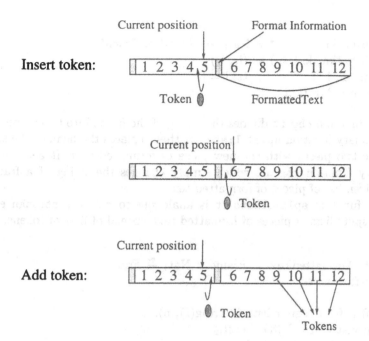

Fig. 6.9. Inserting and adding a token.

The auxiliary function **insert** used above is written in terms of another auxiliary function of the same name which uses the function **split_lists_tkn** to divide the list of tokens in the nth piece of formatted text at the mth position, then inserts the new token at this position, and finally recombines the divided list.

The first list of tokens returned by the function **split_lists_tkn** comprises the first $m - 1$ tokens in the nth piece of formatted text in the string, where m is the input parameter of the function (which represents the position of the token in the piece of formatted text), while the second list comprises the remainder of the tokens. This second list therefore always contains at least one token although the first may be empty.

value
　insert : Token × FormattedText × Nat$_1$ $\overset{\sim}{\to}$ FormattedText
　insert(tn, ft, m) ≡
　　mk_FormattedText(format(ft), insert(tn, chars(ft), m))
　　pre m ≤ **len** chars(ft),

　insert : Token × Token* × Nat$_1$ $\overset{\sim}{\to}$ Token*
　insert(t, tknl, m) ≡
　　let (tl$_1$, tl$_2$) = split_lists_tkn(tknl, m) **in** tl$_1$ ⌢ ⟨t⟩ ⌢ tl$_2$ **end**
　　pre m ≤ **len** tknl,

split_lists_tkn : Token* × Nat$_1$ $\overset{\sim}{\to}$ Token* × Token*
split_lists_tkn(tknl, m) as (l$_1$, l$_2$)
  post len l$_1$ = m − 1 ∧ tknl = l$_1$ ⌢ l$_2$
  pre m ≤ **len** tknl

The function **chg_ft** divides the string of the frame into two pieces using the auxiliary function **split_lists_ft**, then replaces the head of the second of those two pieces with the new piece of formatted text. It also uses the auxiliary function **chg_st**, which simply changes the string of a frame to some given list of pieces of formatted text.

The function **split_lists_ft** is analogous to **split_lists_tkn** except that it splits lists of pieces of formatted text instead of lists of tokens.

value
  chg_ft : FormattedText × Frame × Nat$_1$ $\overset{\sim}{\to}$ Frame
  chg_ft(ft, f, n) ≡
    let
      (ftl$_1$, ftl$_2$) = split_lists_ft(string(f), n),
      new_st = ftl$_1$ ⌢ ⟨ft⟩ ⌢ **tl** ftl$_2$
    in chg_st(new_st, f) **end**
    pre n ≤ **len** string(f),

  split_lists_ft :
    FormattedText* × Nat$_1$ $\overset{\sim}{\to}$ FormattedText* × FormattedText*
  split_lists_ft(ftl, n) **as** (l$_1$, l$_2$)
    post len l$_1$ = n − 1 ∧ ftl = l$_1$ ⌢ l$_2$
    pre n ≤ **len** ftl,

  chg_st : FormattedText* × Frame → Frame
  chg_st(ftl, f) ≡
    let mk_Frame(o, st, ff) = f **in** mk_Frame(o, ftl, ff) **end**

The function **add_tkn** adds a new token to the end of the *n*th piece of formatted text in a frame. The new piece of formatted text is constructed using the auxiliary function **add**, which simply appends a token to the end of a piece of formatted text, then the frame is updated using the function **chg_ft** defined above.

value
  add_tkn : Token × Frame × Nat$_1$ $\overset{\sim}{\to}$ Frame
  add_tkn(t, f, n) ≡
    let ft = string(f)(n), new_ft = add(ft, t) **in**
      chg_ft(new_ft, f, n) **end**
    pre n ≤ **len** string(f),

add : FormattedText × Token → FormattedText
add(ft, t) ≡ mk_FormattedText(format(ft), chars(ft) ⌢ ⟨t⟩)

When we raise the operation **insert_tkn** to the level of a document, we have to write separate operations for characters and frames because the two operations have different effects on the frame map of the document: when we add a subframe we additionally have to add it to the frame map of the document, together with any frames it contains[2].

Here, we only describe the function **insert_char** which inserts a character at the given index, that is at the mth position in the nth piece of formatted text. The frame identifier in the parameters of the function indicates the frame in the document to which the operation is to be applied, and the actual frame is extracted from this using the function **frame_at_fid**, which simply looks up the identifier in the frame map of the document. This frame is then edited appropriately using the frame-level version of the operation defined above, and the edited frame is inserted back into the document using the function **new_frame**. The precondition **at_token** of the function **insert_char** checks that the given frame identifier fid is one of the frames of the document d (the function **frames**), that the integer n of the index corresponds to some actual piece of formatted text within that frame, and that this piece of formatted text, which is extracted using the function **current_ft**, contains at least m tokens. The first two conditions are combined in the auxiliary function **at_string**.

value
   insert_char : Character × Index × Document $\xrightarrow{\sim}$ Document
   insert_char(c, (fid, n, m), d) ≡
     let new_f = insert_tkn(c, frame_at_fid(fid, d), n, m) **in**
      new_frame(fid, new_f, d) **end**
    pre at_token((fid, n, m), d),

   at_token : Index × Document → **Bool**
   at_token((fid, n, m), d) ≡
    at_string(fid, n, d) ∧ m ≤ **len** chars(current_ft(fid, n, d)),

   at_string : FrameId × Nat$_1$ × Document → **Bool**
   at_string(fid, n, d) ≡
    fid ∈ frames(d) ∧ n ≤ **len** string(frame_at_fid(fid, d)),

---

[2] In fact we only consider the addition of empty frames (and empty pieces of formatted text) at the document level. This allows us to more easily maintain the well-formedness constraints on a document and involves no loss of generality because we can of course add a non-empty frame or a non-empty piece of formatted text by first of all adding an empty one and then adding the required contents item by item. Non-empty frames can also be added to documents using the *paste* operations defined in [42].

current_ft : FrameId × Nat$_1$ × Document $\overset{\sim}{\rightarrow}$ FormattedText
current_ft(fid, n, d) ≡
    let f = frame_at_fid(fid, d) **in** string(f)(n) **end**
    pre at_string(fid, n, d)

In addition to the atomic operations discussed above, we have defined a series of operations for creating new documents by copying frames or blocks of text of existing ones, for inserting (pasting) the contents of one document into another, and for cutting a block of text from a document. A *clipboard* is used both to hold copied text and as a source of items to be pasted. We give an abstract definition of the clipboard here and refer to [42] for the details of the copy, cut and paste functions.

We represent the clipboard using the abstract type `Clipboard`, and give the signatures of three functions: the function `doc`, which returns a document from the clipboard; the function `is_empty`, which checks whether the clipboard is empty; and the function `copy`, which copies a new document to the clipboard.

These three functions are related by two axioms. The first of these states that the clipboard is not empty after the `copy` operation has been performed, while the second states that the document returned by the `doc` operation is the last one which was copied using the `copy` operation.

The final axiom states that the function `doc` is well-defined for non-empty clipboards, that is when the clipboard is not empty we can always retrieve a document from it.

type Clipboard

value
    doc : Clipboard $\overset{\sim}{\rightarrow}$ Document,
    is_empty : Clipboard → **Bool**,
    copy : Document × Clipboard → Clipboard

axiom
    ∀ d : Document, c : Clipboard • ~ is_empty(copy(d, c)),
    ∀ d : Document, c : Clipboard • doc(copy(d, c)) = d,
    ∀ c : Clipboard • doc(c) **post true pre** ~ is_empty(c)

These functions are sufficiently abstract to permit a range of implementations of the clipboard: it could simply be a buffer holding a single document; a list of documents, with the `doc` function returning the head of the list and the `copy` function adding a new document to the front of the list; an endless (i.e. circular) list with similar functionality; etc. Of course, when the clipboard has a composite structure, as in the last two examples, functions for manipulating that structure would be needed in addition to the ones defined

here. We do not specify such functions, preferring to leave the decision on
the precise form of the clipboard to the implementation level.

6.4.1 An Editing Environment for Collections of Documents

So far we have concentrated on editing operations on a single document in
isolation. We now move on to define an editing environment within which a
user of the MultiScript system can interact with a collection of documents.

Following the informal discussion of the MultiScript system given in Section 6.2.4, documents are grouped together into a set of libraries. Each library
in the set of libraries has a unique identifier, and similarly for each document
in any given library, though documents in different libraries may have the
same identifiers. In Section 6.3.1 this is represented formally as:

type
    Library = DocId $\nrightarrow$ Document,
    Libraries = LibId $\nrightarrow$ Library

We assume that a user of the MultiScript system does not edit documents
in the libraries directly, but rather loads (copies) them into some *user environment*, then edits the copy in this environment, and finally installs (saves)
the edited version of the document back into the library. We further assume
that a user can at any given time be working on or with several different
documents, all of which will be loaded into the user environment.

We model these *working documents* using the type WorkingDocs. This is
somewhat similar to the type Libraries except that it associates a document identifier in a library with a *document environment* instead of with a
document.

type
    WorkingDocs = LibId $\nrightarrow$ (DocId $\nrightarrow$ DocEnv)

The document environment records working parameters for a particular
document in the user environment, including the working position within the
document (that is the position at which editing operations will be applied),
some history of the editing operations carried out on the document (to facilitate the provision of *undo* operations which reverse the effects of a previous
sequence of editing operations), and some "local" defaults, which might include perhaps some other marked location in the document (for example
representing the beginning or the end of a block), some default orientation,
some default formatting information, etc.

The working position consists basically of the working frame, the working
string within that frame, and the working token within that string, which is
precisely the current index as defined in Section 6.3.2.

The editing history of a document represents one or more saved states of
the document which undo operations can return to, including the initial state

of the document at the time at which it was loaded into the user environment. We can use the order of the elements in a sequence to model relative time, for example by assuming that each element in the sequence is newer than the next. We therefore define the type **History** as a non-empty list of documents (non-empty because the initial state of the document at the time at which it was loaded into the user environment must always be in the list[3]). The position in the history list then represents the version of the document which is currently being edited, and the ability to return to a previous version of a document is then provided by simply allowing the user to change the position in this history list.

The document environment **DocEnv** is then defined as a subtype of the record type **DocEnv0** whose fields are as described above, with an additional field representing some unspecified local defaults (the type **DocDefaults**). The defining predicate of this subtype (the function **is_valid_docenv**) simply ensures that the given working version number is valid, that is that it represents some position in the history. Note, however, that there is no corresponding check that the working frame, string and token are sensible and actually represent valid entities within the document. This is checked, at least as much as necessary, in the preconditions of the editing operations: an operation can only be carried out if the working parameters are reasonable enough to define the position at which it should be performed. For example, a new free frame can only be added to a document if the working frame is reasonable, although the working string and the working token may in this case be unreasonable.

type
   History = {| dl : Document* • dl ≠ ⟨⟩ |},
   DocEnv0 ::
     working_frameId : FrameId ↔ chg_frame
     working_string : Nat_1 ↔ chg_string
     working_token : Nat_1 ↔ chg_token
     defaults : DocDefaults ↔ chg_def
     history : History ↔ chg_history
     working_version : Nat_1 ↔ chg_version,
   DocEnv = {| denv : DocEnv0 • is_valid_docenv(denv) |},
   DocDefaults

value
   is_valid_docenv : DocEnv0 → **Bool**
   is_valid_docenv(denv) ≡ working_version(denv) ≤ **len** history(denv)

The user environment records the current status of all the documents which are currently loaded into the editor, that is the user's working docu-

---

[3] In fact with the assumption that later in the list equates to earlier in time it must always be the last element of the list.

ments, and also records which of them is the current working document, that
is the document to which editing operations will be applied. The working
documents are modelled using the map type **WorkingDocs** introduced above
and the current working document is identified by its document identifier
together with the identifier of the library to which the document belongs[4].
However, a user cannot necessarily edit all the libraries in the system, and
we assume that a given document can be edited if and only if it belongs to a
library which can be edited. The user environment thus needs to additionally
record which libraries can be edited, which is done simply by recording their
identifiers. In addition, we assume the user environment contains a clipboard
and the definitions of some (unspecified) user defaults, which we represent
by the abstract type **UserDefaults**.

It is again natural to use a record type to model the user environment.
However, it is perfectly reasonable for documents which cannot be edited
to be among the working documents, perhaps so that a piece of text can
be copied or simply in order to be read, and we must ensure that these
documents cannot be edited. This is done by requiring that such a document
should have a history which consists only of a single document, which will
of course be the document in its original state. This condition is captured in
the function **is_valid_userenv** which is then used as the defining predicate
of the subtype **UserEnv** of the record type $UserEnv_0$. Note that, just as for
the working positions within the document environment, we do not impose
any constraints on the working library or the working document in order to
ensure that they actually represent some document in the current working
documents. Instead, we again check this in the preconditions of the editing
operations: an editing operation can only be applied if the current working
document is well-defined.

type
  $UserEnv_0$ ::
    working_libId : LibId $\leftrightarrow$ chg_lib
    working_docId : DocId $\leftrightarrow$ chg_doc
    working_docs : WorkingDocs $\leftrightarrow$ chg_wd
    defaults : UserDefaults $\leftrightarrow$ chg_def
    clipboard : Clipboard $\leftrightarrow$ chg_clip
    my_libs : LibId-**set** $\leftrightarrow$ chg_own,
  UserEnv = {| uenv : $UserEnv_0$ • is_valid_userenv(uenv) |},
  UserDefaults

value
  is_valid_userenv : $UserEnv_0$ $\rightarrow$ **Bool**
  is_valid_userenv(uenv) $\equiv$
    let mk_$UserEnv_0$(_, _, wd, _, _, libs) = uenv **in**

---

[4] The library identifier is necessary because there is no reason why the same document identifier could not be used in several different libraries.

$\forall$ lid : LibId, denv : DocEnv •
  lid $\in$ **dom** wd $\land$ lid $\notin$ libs $\land$ denv $\in$ **rng** wd(lid) $\Rightarrow$
    len history(denv) = 1
end

6.4.2 Editing Documents in the User Environment

The next step is to raise the editing operations on a document to the level of the user environment.

Essentially, invoking an editing operation within the user environment applies that operation to (the working version of) the current working document as defined by the working library and working document components of the user environment. However, as explained above, there is no constraint on these components to ensure that they do in fact represent one of the working documents: instead, we check this in the preconditions of the operations.

In fact the majority of the editing operations affect only the document environment of the working document, in particular its history, and otherwise do not change the user environment (the exceptions to this are the copy operations which only affect the clipboard in the user environment). We therefore write each of these operations in terms of a specific function which performs the particular editing operation on the document environment and the general function chg_docenv which simply changes the document environment of the current working document in the user environment. This general function has a precondition which ensures that the working document is well-defined.

value
  chg_docenv : DocEnv $\times$ UserEnv $\xrightarrow{\sim}$ UserEnv
  chg_docenv(denv, uenv) $\equiv$
    let
      mk_UserEnv$_0$(lid, did, wd, def, cb, libs) = uenv,
      lib = wd(lid),
      new_lib = lib $\dagger$ [did $\mapsto$ denv],
      new_wd = wd $\dagger$ [lid $\mapsto$ new_lib]
    in
      mk_UserEnv$_0$(lid, did, new_wd, def, cb, libs)
    end
    pre has_working_document(uenv)

Many of the functions which apply the specific editing operations to the document environment have the same general structure: first, the input parameters required by the analogous operations at the document level are extracted from the document environment; this analogous operation is then applied to the working version of the document as defined by the history and the working version number in the document environment, thus producing the new (edited) version of the document; and finally the history in the document environment is updated appropriately to record the edited version of the document.

When the working version number in the document environment is 1, meaning that the latest (i.e. newest) version of the document is the current working version, the edited document is simply added to the front of the history list and the working version number is unchanged. This means that the newly added edited version becomes the current working version because it is now the first document in the history.

If the current working version number is greater than 1, indicating that one or more undo operations have been performed, the current working version of the document is first copied onto the front of the history, then the edited version is added in front of that. This is done so as to preserve the information about actions carried out by the user: in this situation, the user created the version of the document currently at the head of the history, then returned to an earlier version, then edited the earlier version, and copying the current working version to the front of the history corresponds to recording the decision to return to an earlier version. In this case, the working version number is reset to 1.

In practice we probably do not want to update the history every time the document is changed – if we did this it would mean, for example, that editing a document by typing some text on a keyboard would update the history every time a new character is typed. We thus introduce a Boolean parameter into each editing operation which is used to indicate whether the history should be updated or not – if the parameter is true then the history is updated as described above, but if it is false the latest version of the document in the history is *replaced* by the new edited version of that document. However, we insist that the first editing operation which is applied to a document after it is loaded into the user environment must add a new document to the history – this is so that we can always return to the document in its original unedited state by a series of undo operations. In addition, we only allow the newest version of a document to be edited directly without adding a new document to the history – if we want to go back and edit an earlier version we must first make it the current version (by copying it to the front of the history) and then edit it, otherwise we would destroy the integrity of the history. These restrictions are encapsulated in the function can_edit_docenv.

value

  can_edit_docenv : DocEnv × **Bool** → **Bool**
  can_edit_docenv(denv, b) ≡
    ∼ b ⇒ **len** history(denv) ≥ 2 ∧ working_version(denv) = 1

This function now forms the precondition of the function edit_document which updates the history of a document environment with a given document according to the above description: if we are working on the latest version of the document (i.e. if the working version number is 1) then the given document is added to the front of the current history if the Boolean parameter is true but is added to the front of the tail of the current history (i.e. replaces the current version) if the Boolean parameter is false; if we are not working on the latest version of the document, then the current version is copied to the front of the history, then the given document is added in front of that. The case where we are not working on the latest version of the document and where the Boolean parameter is false is ruled out by the precondition.

value
 edit_document : Document $\times$ DocEnv $\times$ **Bool** $\overset{\sim}{\to}$ DocEnv
 edit_document(d, denv, b) $\equiv$
  let
   mk_DocEnv$_0$(fid, n, m, def, h, v) = denv,
   new_h =
    if v = 1 **then**
     if b **then** $\langle d \rangle$ $^\frown$ h **else** $\langle d \rangle$ $^\frown$ tl h **end**
    else $\langle d, h(v) \rangle$ $^\frown$ h **end**
  in mk_DocEnv$_0$(fid, n, m, def, new_h, 1) **end**
  pre can_edit_docenv(denv, b)

The editing operations at the level of the document environment essentially apply the basic atomic operations to the current working version of the document, determining their input parameters from the working parameters of the document environment where possible, then update the history accordingly using the function **edit_document** defined immediately above. Each operation defined in this way thus requires a precondition which ensures that the precondition of the corresponding basic operation as well as that of the function **edit_document** are both satisfied. All functions also have the additional Boolean parameter which indicates whether the history should be updated by addition or by replacement. Thus, for example, the definition of the function **insert_char** is as follows:

value
 insert_char : Character $\times$ DocEnv $\times$ **Bool** $\overset{\sim}{\to}$ DocEnv
 insert_char(c, denv, b) $\equiv$
  let
   i = working_index(denv),
   d = working_document(denv),
   new_d = insert_char(c, i, d)
  in
   edit_document(new_d, denv, b)
  end
  pre can_edit_token(denv, b)

At the level of the user environment, the appropriate operation is applied to the document environment, then the document environment is updated in the user environment using the function **chg_docenv** defined above:

value
    insert_char : Character × UserEnv × **Bool** $\xrightarrow{\sim}$ UserEnv
    insert_char(c, uenv, b) ≡
      let
        denv = working_docenv(uenv),
        new_denv = insert_char(c, denv, b)
      in
        chg_docenv(new_denv, uenv)
      end
      pre can_edit_token(uenv, b)

6.4.3 The MultiScript System

Finally, we move on to define the MultiScript system as a whole, linking the notion of the user environment with the notion of a collection of documents structured as a set of libraries. An example of this structure is illustrated in Figure 6.10.

In this example, the collection of documents consists of five libraries, which are labelled with library identifiers L1 through L5. Libraries L3 and L4 cannot be edited by the user, and library L5 is currently empty. A document from any library can be loaded into a document environment in an equivalent library in the user environment for editing or browsing. Documents d1, d2 and d3 from library L2 have been loaded in this way into document environments e1, e2 and e3 respectively. In addition, a further three documents from library L1 and a single document (which cannot be edited) from library L3 have also been loaded. After editing, a document can be written back to the libraries using various *save* operations.

In order to model this system, we introduce the record type MS$_0$, which simply consists of a user environment and a collection of libraries, then represent the MultiScript system as the subtype MS of this. The defining predicate of this subtype is the function is_valid_ms, which ensures that the libraries which the user can edit (that is those recorded in the field my_libs in the user environment) actually belong to the system.

type
    MS$_0$ ::
      libraries : Libraries
      user_env : UserEnv ↔ chg_uenv,
    MS = {| ms : MS$_0$ • is_valid_ms(ms) |}

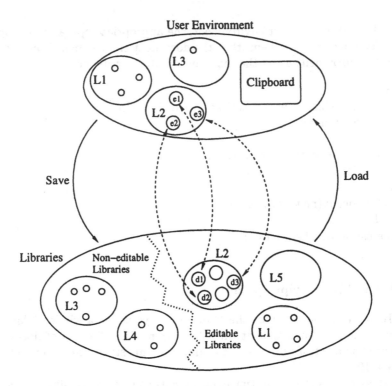

Fig. 6.10. The MultiScript system.

value
  is_valid_ms : $MS_0 \to$ **Bool**
  is_valid_ms(ms) $\equiv$ my_libs(user_env(ms)) $\subseteq$ **dom** libraries(ms)

At this top level, the editing operations extract the user environment from the MultiScript system, apply the corresponding operation which edits the document within the user environment, and finally reinstall the modified user environment into the MultiScript system using the reconstructor function chg_uenv defined in the record type MS_0. Each function has a precondition which ensures that the user environment within the MultiScript system satisfies the appropriate precondition for the particular operation.

The function insert_char at this level is defined as follows:

value
  insert_char : Character $\times$ MS $\times$ **Bool** $\overset{\sim}{\to}$ MS
  insert_char(c, ms, b) $\equiv$
    let uenv = user_env(ms),
        new_uenv = insert_char(c, uenv, b)
    in chg_uenv(new_uenv, ms) **end**
    pre can_edit_token(ms, b)

6.5 Conclusions

In this chapter we have described the specification of a model of a general multi-lingual document in which text in any of four different orientations can be arbitrarily mixed. We have shown how an analysis of existing multi-lingual documents helped us to identify the essential properties of multi-lingual documents and led us to an appropriate level of abstraction for our model, and we have also shown how "standard" editing functions can be specified in the model. These include simple operations for copying, cutting and pasting text in a document, and we have given a very abstract definition of a clipboard which can be used to store and provide text in such processes.

Background Information

This work, which represents a summary of the majority of the specification phase of the MultiScript project [40, 41, 43, 42, 99], was undertaken by Myatav Erdenechimeg and Yumbayar Namsrai from the National University of Mongolia, Ulaanbaatar, Mongolia, in collaboration with Richard Moore.

The specification presented here has in fact been extended to incorporate aspects of displaying and printing documents [103, 44], and this extended specification has been used as the basis for an implementation by Myatav Erdenechimeg of a prototype MultiScript system which supports the essential features of multi-lingual documents described in this chapter, namely text written in all four different orientations and intermixing of such text in a single document. The system also allows text created by other document processing systems to be incorporated into documents, though if the coding system used by this text is not compatible with the ISO 10646/Unicode standard encoding [69, 26] used in the MultiScript system it needs to be preprocessed before it can be incorporated into a MultiScript document.

The project has also contributed to the development of the ISO/Unicode international standard encoding for the traditional Mongolian script [104, 45, 102] and has developed a Unicode-compliant font for this script.

7. Formalising Production Processes

7.1 Introduction

Business process modelling can have many applications. It can be used to: understand the flow of work in an organisation; monitor and control progress of work; measure and optimise work performance; predict the effects of changes in management and operations; plan for implementation of changes; design interaction patterns between processes running in different organisations; and specify, develop and deploy software to further organisational/business goals, etc. Formal analysis is a particularly good reason to carry out such modelling, as it can disclose problems long before the process is actually deployed in an organisation. This early detection is especially important for processes that cross organisational boundaries where errors, as in all distributed systems, are inherently hard to detect and expensive to correct.

One approach to model a business process is to describe its concrete execution in an enterprise, using enterprise resources to produce tangible results like products or services. Typically, such descriptive modelling would be carried out to explore the analogy between business and computing and would concentrate on the mechanics of a process. A prescriptive model, in contrast, aims to express the intended purpose of each process. The challenge for business process modelling is, we believe, finding suitable abstractions that can be applied at both levels. By formally relating such descriptive and prescriptive models, we could verify if a process is correct (satisfies its intended purpose) and further develop an engineering approach to design such processes in a rigorous way. This chapter is set to contribute to this general goal.

We consider a particular, although broadly defined, business domain: customer-driven production. Production refers to the process of creating goods – tangible products like cars, phones or shovels. Products are produced by assembly from sub-products, carried out within independent business entities called production cells. Each cell contains the resources to store, manufacture and deliver products to its customers. On a certain level, a cell represents formally what is a manufacturing enterprise with its resources like a warehouse, shop-floor and product stocks. The behaviour of a cell is driven by the orders received from the customers and how such orders are implemented. The customers include other production cells. The implementation of a customer order is described by a production process. The aim of this chapter is to define formally what it means for such a process to be feasible (possible to carry out given the resources delegated for its execution) and correct (satisfying a customer order, if feasible). We adopt the following business model, explained for sequential, concurrent and distributed production:

1. Sequential production (one process, one cell). Each process responds to a customer order which specifies the product to deliver, the number of items and possibly the latest time of delivery. The process operates within a production cell which offers the resources for its execution, in terms of product stocks, storage space, and capacity to carry out manufacturing and transportation. It describes in detail what operations should be performed on the cell and in which sequence. The process is feasible if the cell has enough resources for its execution. A feasible process is correct if its execution satisfies the order: the stocks for the products reach the required volumes within the deadline.

2. Concurrent production (many processes, one cell). A cell may contain several processes, each created in response to a particular customer order and all executed concurrently. In order to resolve conflicts for the shared resources (such as product stocks, manufacturing workstations or a transportation system), processes are assigned priorities to represent their importance. Feasibility means the cell has enough resources for all such processes, executed concurrently. Correctness means all processes satisfy their corresponding customer orders, when executed concurrently under a priority-based scheduler.

3. Distributed production (many processes, many cells). Several processes running in different cells may satisfy an order in a cooperative way. Trying to utilise the resources that one cell lacks and another has available, they form customer-supplier relations dynamically, by receiving customer orders and implementing with their own processes, perhaps sending more orders at the same time. As a result, each cell may be running several processes, each contributing part of the original order. This mechanism leads to the distribution of production activities. Feasibility means each cell has enough resources for its processes executed concurrently. Correctness means a process satisfies its customer order provided all supplier processes satisfy their own. Moreover, when several such processes run in the same cell, they must satisfy their orders concurrently.

The rest of this chapter is as follows. Section 7.2 is about product modelling. Section 7.3 presents a descriptive production model, including the concepts like production cells, operations and processes, and defines what it means for a process to be feasible. Section 7.4 presents a corresponding prescriptive model. Section 7.5 defines what it means for a feasible process to be correct, by relating such descriptive and prescriptive models. It starts with sequential production, then introduces concurrency, distribution, and real-time constraints. Section 7.6 describes related work and provides some conclusions.

7.2 Modelling Products

The aim of this section is to provide a definition for products, to be used by both descriptive and prescriptive models.

Products are either atomic, in which case their internal structure is invisible or uninteresting, or are composed of sub-products. Sub-products are products in their own right – they can be further decomposed into sub-sub-products as well as reused by different products. Formally, we introduce the type Product to represent products, Quantity to represent numbers of products, and Products to represent sets of products with quantities:

type
    Product,
    Quantity = **Nat**,
    Products = Product $\overrightarrow{m}$ Quantity

We introduce two functions on the type Product: given a product p, size returns a natural number size(p) to represent the storage requirement of p (encoded in some way as **Nat**); given a product p, bill returns a product map bill(p) which represents the immediate sub-products q of p and how many items of q a single item of p requires.

type
    Size = **Nat**
value
    size: Product → Size,
    bill: Product → Products

Alternatively, we could make size depend on the product as well as the quantity, to represent the fact that products are stored in containers, such that products of different types are not mixed in the same container. Then, given a product p and a quantity n, size(p, n) would return the size of a container which holds n items of p. We do not pursue this idea further.

We constrain those functions in three ways: the value of size is always greater than zero, bill never returns a map with a zero value and it does not allow for a product which is a sub-product of itself. Here is the axiom:

axiom
    ∀ p: Product • size(p) > 0 ∧ ~issub(p, p) ∧ 0 ∉ **rng** bill(p)

Function issub takes two products as arguments and returns **true** or **false**, depending if one is a sub-product (immediate or not) of another.

value
    issub: Product × Product → **Bool**
    issub(q, p) ≡
        q ∈ **dom** bill(p) ∨
        (∃ r: Product • issub(q, r) ∧ issub(r, p))

We also define some auxiliary functions on product maps. Function **sum** adds the quantities in the product map. It is defined recursively:

value
  sum: Products $\rightarrow$ Quantity
  sum(ps) $\equiv$
    if ps $=$ [ ] **then** 0 **else**
      let p: Product • p $\in$ **dom** ps **in** ps(p) + sum(ps \ {p}) **end**
    end

Function **add** takes a product map **ps**, a product **p** and a quantity **n**, and increases the quantity **p** in **ps** by **n**. It is extended into the function **add** which adds in a similar way two product maps. As both functions are called **add**, the context decides which definition is meant.

value
  add: Products $\times$ Product $\times$ Quantity $\rightarrow$ Products
  add(ps, p, n) $\equiv$
    if p $\notin$ **dom** ps **then** ps $\cup$ [p $\mapsto$ n]
    else ps † [p $\mapsto$ ps(p) + n] **end**,
  add: Products $\times$ Products $\rightarrow$ Products
  add(ps$_1$, ps$_2$) $\equiv$
    [p $\mapsto$ ps$_1$(p) | p: Product • p $\in$ **dom** ps$_1$ \ **dom** ps$_2$] $\cup$
    [p $\mapsto$ ps$_2$(p) | p: Product • p $\in$ **dom** ps$_2$ \ **dom** ps$_1$] $\cup$
    [p $\mapsto$ ps$_1$(p) + ps$_2$(p) | p: Product • p $\in$ **dom** ps$_1$ $\cap$ **dom** ps$_2$]

Example 7.2.1. Following [144], consider an example product, a snow shovel. The figure below shows the product on the left and the sub-product graph on the right, which includes the values of the functions **size** (numbers in boxes) and **bill** (arrows and labels). In particular, a shovel has the storage requirement of 151 and it contains one connector, one top handle, one shaft, four rivets, one scoop assembly and four a-type nails (different from b-type nails). It is easy to check that the sub-product graph satisfies the axioms.

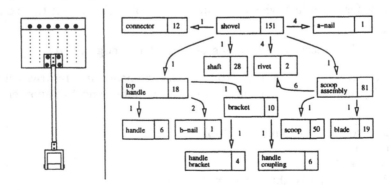

7.3 Descriptive Production Modelling

This section presents a descriptive production model, using the concepts like production cells, production operations and processes. We also define what it means for a process to be feasible given the resources allocated for its execution. Each concept is described and illustrated in the following sections.

7.3.1 Production Cell

Production is carried out within a production cell, modelled as an abstract type Cell. Each cell provides four kinds of resources to enable production: storage, stocks, assembly and transportation. They are described as follows:

1. Storage defines the maximum number of products the cell is able to store internally, weighted by their storage requirements (function size). It is represented by the function storage from Cell to Size.
2. Stocks denote the quantity of each product present in the cell. They are represented by the function stocks from Cell to Products.
3. Assembly describes how the cell can manufacture products from their sub-products (function bill), using the workstations available in the cell (abstract type Workstation). Given a cell and a workstation, function assemble returns a map in Products. The map describes the set of products that can be assembled on this workstation and how many items can be produced during a shift (assuming an uninterrupted assembly process).
4. Transportation describes how the cell can move the products between the workstations. Given a cell and a pair of workstations, the function transport returns the maximum number of products (weighted by their storage requirements) the cell can transport between them within a shift.

The definitions are as follows:

type
  Cell,
  Workstation
value
  storage: Cell → Size,
  stocks: Cell → Products,
  assembly: Cell × Workstation → Products,
  transport: Cell → ((Workstation × Workstation) → Size)

Such functions are constrained in three ways: (1) the occupancy of the cell (product volumes multiplied by storage requirements) must not exceed its storage capacity; (2) each manufacturable product has a non-empty set of sub-products and the quantity manufacturable per-shift is at least one; and (3) no product can be transported from a workstation to itself.

axiom
  ∀ c: Cell •
    storage(c) ≥
    sum([p ↦ size(p) * stocks(c)(p) | p:Product • p ∈ **dom** stocks(c)]) ∧
    (∀ w: Workstation •
      transport(c)(w, w) = 0 ∧
      (∀ p: Product •
        p ∈ **dom** assembly(c, w)
        ⇒ bill(p) ≠ [] ∧ assembly(c, w)(p) > 0
)
)
)

We define a new total function **stocks** from **Cell** and **Product** to **Quantity**, based on the function with the same name from **Cell** to **Products**. The function returns the stock of a product, if there is some stock, and otherwise zero.

value
  stocks: Cell × Product → Quantity
  stocks(c, p) ≡
    if p ∈ **dom** stocks(c)
    then stocks(c)(p) **else** 0 **end**

Example 7.3.1. Consider a cell to produce snow shovels, $cell_0$. Table 7.1 describes the values of the functions **storage, stocks, assembly** and **transport**. In particular, the cell has the storage capacity of 200000. Product stocks include zero shovels, 500 scoop assemblies, 5000 rivets, 1000 connectors, 500 top handles, and so on. The added occupancy is 145000, so the cell is three quarters full. The cell contains three workstations: ws_1 can assemble 150 shovels per-shift; ws_2 can assemble 100 shovels or 150 top handles per-shift; and ws_3 can assemble 200 brackets or 150 scoop assemblies per-shift. The workstations are connected by the transportation system which allows the movement of: 5000 storage units from ws_2 to ws_1; 15000 storage units from ws_3 to ws_1; and 2500 storage units from ws_3 to ws_2, all per-shift. There is no capacity to transport products between any other workstations. We can see that the axioms for a well-formed production cell are all satisfied for $cell_0$.

7.3.2 Operations on Stocks

We assume that **storage, assembly** and **transport** are static attributes, they constrain production but themselves do not change. This is not the case for **stocks**. We consider two stock-changing operations: **receive** and **deliver**. **receive** increments the stock for a given product by a given quantity, both specified as its arguments. It leaves all other stocks and attributes of the

Table 7.1. Production cell cell$_0$.

cell$_0$

storage	stocks		assembly		transport			

storage	stocks		assembly			transport	ws$_1$	ws$_2$	ws$_3$
200000	shovel	0	ws$_1$			ws$_1$	0	0	0
	scoopass	500	shovel	150		ws$_2$	5000	0	0
	rivet	5000				ws$_3$	15000	2500	0
	connector	1000	ws$_2$						
	tophandle	500	shovel	100					
	shaft	1000	tophandle	150					
	anail	2000							
	blade	500	ws$_3$						
	scoop	500	bracket	200					
	bnail	1000	scoopass	150					
	bracket	250							
	handle	500							
	hcoupling	250							
	hbracket	250							
	occupancy	145000							

cell unchanged. The precondition **enough_receive** requires that the cell has enough storage space to accommodate the additional products.

value

receive: Product × Quantity × Cell $\overset{\sim}{\to}$ Cell

receive(p, n, c) **as** c$'$

 post stocks(c$'$, p) = stocks(c, p) + n ∧ ...

 pre enough_receive(p, n, c),

enough_receive: Product × Quantity × Cell → **Bool**

enough_receive(p, n, c) ≡

 storage(c) ≥ n * size(p) +

 sum([p ↦ size(p) * stocks(c)(p) | p: Product • p ∈ **dom** stocks(c)])

The function **deliver** is defined similarly. It decrements the stock for a given product, provided the stock is sufficient (**enough_deliver**).

value

deliver: Product × Quantity × Cell $\overset{\sim}{\to}$ Cell

deliver(p, n, c) **as** c$'$

 post stocks(c$'$, p) = stocks(c, p) − n ∧ ...

 pre enough_deliver(p, n, c),

enough_deliver: Product × Quantity × Cell → **Bool**

enough_deliver(p, n, c) ≡ stocks(c, p) ≥ n

Such functions give rise to the corresponding functions on product maps, both defined recursively in terms of the basic functions. Here is **receive** and its precondition **enough_receive**.

value

　receive: Products × Cell $\xrightarrow{\sim}$ Cell

　receive(ps, c) ≡

　　if ps = [ ] **then** c **else**

　　　let p: Product • p ∈ **dom** ps

　　　in receive(ps \ {p}, receive(p, ps(p), c)) **end**

　　end pre enough_receive(ps, c),

　enough_receive: Products × Cell → **Bool**

　enough_receive(ps, c) ≡

　　sum([p ↦ size(p) * stocks(c)(p) | p: Product • p ∈ **dom** stocks(c)]) +

　　sum([p ↦ size(p) * ps(p) | p: Product • p ∈ **dom** ps])

　　≤ storage(c)

Here is the function **deliver**. Its precondition **enough_deliver** requires that the cell has enough stock for all products in the product map.

value

　deliver: Products × Cell $\xrightarrow{\sim}$ Cell

　deliver(ps, c) ≡

　　if ps = [ ] **then** c **else**

　　　let p: Product • p ∈ **dom** ps

　　　in deliver(ps \ {p}, deliver(p, ps(p), c)) **end**

　　end pre enough_deliver(ps, c),

　enough_deliver: Products × Cell → **Bool**

　enough_deliver(ps, c) ≡

　　(∀ p: Product • p ∈ **dom** ps ⇒ stocks(c, p) ≥ ps(p))

Example 7.3.2. Consider the operation to receive 2000 a-nails and 2000 rivets by $cell_0$. The additional products occupy 6000 storage units, therefore can be still accommodated by the cell. The resulting cell ($cell_1$) is described in Table 7.2, obtained by changing the stocks for those two products.

7.3.3 Production Operations

Production is carried out by the allocation of work to workstations. Throughout the shift, each workstation is programmed to assemble a number of items of a given product from its sub-products. Such sub-products come either from the warehouse, therefore decreasing product stocks, or from other workstations, therefore decreasing the volumes they produced. For each workstation, the program decides which part of the volume is forwarded to which specific workstations (perhaps using a conveyor system) for further processing. Such quantities should add up to the volume which does not exceed the total volume produced by the workstation. The remaining part is returned to the warehouse at the end of the shift, therefore increasing the stock.

Table 7.2. Production cell $cell_1$.

$$cell_1 = receive(\begin{bmatrix} rivet \mapsto 2000 \\ anail \mapsto 2000 \end{bmatrix}, cell_0)$$

storage
200000

stocks	
shovel	0
scoopass	500
rivet	7000
connector	1000
tophandle	500
shaft	1000
anail	4000
blade	500
scoop	500
bnail	1000
bracket	250
handle	500
hcoupling	250
hbracket	250
occupancy	151000

assembly

ws_1	
shovel	150

ws_2	
shovel	100
tophandle	150

ws_3	
bracket	200
scoopass	150

transport

	ws_1	ws_2	ws_3
ws_1	0	0	0
ws_2	5000	0	0
ws_3	15000	2500	0

Formally, we describe the allocation of work to workstations using the record type Work. It contains three fields:

- product and volume are respectively the product and the volume the workstation is programmed to assemble during the current shift and
- forward decides how to partition this volume between other workstations.

A well-formed work is such that the total volume produced and the volumes forwarded are all non-zero, and the sum of the quantities forwarded does not exceed the volume produced.

type
  Work'::
    volume: Quantity
    product: Product
    forward: Workstation $\overrightarrow{m}$ Quantity,
  Work = {| w: Work' • iswf(w) |}
value
  iswf: Work' → **Bool**
  iswf(w) ≡
    volume(w) > 0 ∧
    0 ∉ **rng** forward(w) ∧
    sum(forward(w)) ≤ volume(w)

An operation decides how to allocate work to all workstations. Defined as a map from Workstation to Work, it is subject to three constraints. First, if a workstation w in the domain of the operation op is programmed to forward part of its volume to workstation w′, then w′ is also in the domain of op. So the operation must be closed with respect to the workstations used. Second, the products received by the workstation (from other workstations) are all immediate sub-products of the product it currently manufactures. Third, for each sub-product, the total number of items received by the workstation from other workstations does not exceed the number needed to carry out production in the current shift.

type
  Operation′ = Workstation $\overrightarrow{m}$ Work,
  Operation = {| op: Operation′ • iswf(op) |}
value
  iswf: Operation′ → **Bool**
  iswf(op) ≡
    (∀ ws: Workstation •
      ws ∈ **dom** op ⇒
      dom forward(op(ws)) ⊆ **dom** op ∧
      dom from_work(op,ws) ⊆ **dom** bill(product(op(ws))) ∧
      (∀ p: Product •
        p ∈ **dom** from_work(op, ws) ⇒
        from_work(op, ws)(p) ≤ volume(op(ws)) * bill(product(op(ws)))(p)
)
)

The latter two properties are defined in terms of the function **from_work**. It returns the quantities received by the workstation **ws** from other workstations, as specified by the operation **op**. Such quantities are recorded in a map from **Product** to **Nat**. The function inspects **op** by examining the **forward** field of each workstation **ws′** which is different from **ws**, adds the quantity the workstation **ws′** is to transfer to **ws** (if any), removes **ws′** from op and continues recursively until op contains only **ws**.

value
  from_work: Operation′ × Workstation $\overset{\sim}{\to}$ Products
  from_work(op, ws) ≡
    if op = [ws ↦ op(ws)] **then** [] **else**
      let ws′: Workstation • ws′ ∈ **dom** op ∧ ws′ ≠ ws **in**
        let w′ = op(ws′), ps = from_work(op \ {ws′}, ws) **in**
          if ws ∉ **dom** forward(w′) **then** ps
          else add(ps, product(w′), forward(w′)(ws)) **end**
        end
      end
    end pre ws ∈ **dom** op

Example 7.3.3. Consider the operation op$_1$ in Table 7.3. It assigns the workstations ws$_1$, ws$_2$ and ws$_3$ the tasks to assemble 150 shovels, 150 top handles and 150 scoop assemblies respectively. The entire volume of shovels is sent to the inventory. Half of the volume of top handles and scoop assemblies is forwarded to ws$_1$ to produce shovels and half is sent to the inventory.

Table 7.3. Operation op$_1$.

op$_1$						
workstation	ws$_1$		ws$_2$		ws$_3$	
product	shovel		tophandle		scoopass	
volume	150		150		150	
forward	where	vol	where	vol	where	vol
	stocks	150	ws$_1$	75	ws$_1$	75
			stocks	75	stocks	75

Example 7.3.4. Consider the operation op$_2$ in Table 7.4. It assigns the workstation ws$_1$ to produce 150 shovels, ws$_2$ to produce 150 top handles and ws$_3$ to produce 200 brackets. 150 brackets are forwarded to ws$_2$ and 50 are sent to the inventory. The entire volume of top handles is forwarded to ws$_1$ to produce shovels. The entire volume of shovels is sent to the inventory.

Table 7.4. Operation op$_2$.

op$_2$						
workstation	ws$_1$		ws$_2$		ws$_3$	
product	shovel		tophandle		bracket	
volume	150		150		200	
forward	where	vol	where	vol	where	vol
	stocks	150	ws$_1$	150	ws$_2$	150
					stocks	50

7.3.4 Production Operations: Feasibility

Given an operation op and a cell c, in order to describe the effect of executing op on c, we have to first decide if c has enough resources to carry out op. The checking is done by the function **enough** from Operation and Cell to **Bool**. There are three conditions: (1) each workstation is able to carry out the work assigned to it, independently from other workstations; (2) the cell has enough stocks to satisfy the requirement for sub-products from all work assignments (minus the sub-products received from other workstations); and (3) the cell has enough space to accommodate manufactured products. Here is the definition of this function:

value
    enough: Operation × Cell → **Bool**
    enough(op, c) ≡
        enough_receive(to_stock(op), c) ∧
        enough_deliver(from_stock(op), c) ∧
        (∀ ws: Workstation • ws ∈ **dom** op ⇒ enough(op, ws, c))

We applied three auxiliary functions: **to_stock**, **from_stock** and **enough**. The function **enough** considers individual workstations in an operation. It checks if a workstation is able to carry out the work assigned to it: it can assemble the product; the volume can be obtained within a shift; and the cell has enough capacity to transport the required quantities from this workstation to others (weighted by the storage requirements of the transported products). The function is defined as follows:

value
    enough: Operation × Workstation × Cell $\overset{\sim}{\to}$ **Bool**
    enough(op, ws, c) ≡
        product(op(ws)) ∈ **dom** assembly(c, ws) ∧
        volume(op(ws)) ≤ assembly(c, ws)(product(op(ws))) ∧
        (∀ ws′: Workstation •
            ws′ ∈ **dom** forward(op(ws)) ⇒
            transport(c)(ws, ws′) ≥
            size(product(op(ws))) ∗ forward(op(ws))(ws′)
) **pre** ws ∈ **dom** op

Function **from_stock** decides how many sub-products the operation needs from the stock to carry out all work assignments. It is defined recursively on the set of workstations, using the auxiliary function **from_stock′** which adds such product requirements for all workstations.

value
    from_stock: Operation → Products
    from_stock(op) ≡ from_stock′(op, **dom** op),

    from_stock′: Operation × Workstation-**set** $\overset{\sim}{\to}$ Products
    from_stock′(op, wss) ≡
        if wss = {} **then** [ ] **else**
            let ws: Workstation • ws ∈ wss
            in add(from_stock(op, ws), from_stock′(op, wss \ {ws})) **end**
        end
        pre wss ⊆ **dom** op

The auxiliary function **from_stock** calculates the products needed from the stock by individual workstations. For each sub-product, it calculates how many items are needed to carry out the work assignment, minus the number to be received from other workstations (function **from_work**).

value
   from_stock: Operation × Workstation $\overset{\sim}{\to}$ Products
   from_stock(op, ws) ≡
     let p = product(op(ws)),
        v = volume(op(ws)),
        ps = from_work(op, ws)
     in [
         q ↦ **if** q ∉ **dom** ps **then** v ∗ bill(p)(q)
             else v ∗ bill(p)(q) − ps(q) **end** |
        q: Product • q ∈ **dom** bill(p)
      ]
   end
   pre ws ∈ **dom** op

The function **to_stock** accumulates the results produced by each individual workstation: the product and the volume assigned to be produced by the workstation, minus the amounts sent to other workstations for further processing. The function is defined below.

value
   to_stock: Operation′ → Products
   to_stock(op) ≡
     if op = [ ] **then** [ ] **else**
       let ws: Workstation • ws ∈ **dom** op
       in let w = op(ws),
           p = product(w),
           v = volume(w) − sum(forward(w))
       in add(to_stock(op \ {ws}), p, v) **end**
     end
   end

Example 7.3.5. The operation op_1 (Table 7.3) is feasible for its execution on the cell $cell_1$ (Table 7.2). Each assigned product is in the **assembly** map of the corresponding workstation and the volumes do not exceed what the workstations can assemble within a shift. In fact, they are all at their maximum: ws_1 with 150 shovels, ws_2 with 150 top handles and ws_3 with 150 scoop assemblies. 150 top handles is equivalent to 2700 storage units, which amount can be transported from ws_2 to ws_1 (5000 maximum). 150 scoop assemblies is equivalent to 12150 storage units, which amount can be transported from ws_3 to ws_1 (15000 maximum). There are also enough sub-products on stock, as illustrated in Table 7.5.

Table 7.5. Existing versus required stocks for the operation op$_1$.

product	stocks	needed
shovel	0	0
scoopass	500	150-150
rivet	7000	600+900
connector	1000	150
tophandle	500	150-150
shaft	1000	150
anail	4000	600
blade	500	150
scoop	500	150
bnail	1000	300
bracket	250	150
handle	500	150
hcoupling	250	0
hbracket	250	0

7.3.5 Production Operations: Execution

Consider a cell c and an operation op which is feasible for execution on this cell. The function exec describes the effect of executing op on c, which results in a modified production cell exec(op, c). This new cell has its product stocks increased according to the function to_stock(op) – the products manufactured but not consumed by the operation op. Also, the new cell has its product stocks decreased according to the function from_stock(op) – the products consumed by the operation op, all coming from the inventory (not from workstations). In order to modify the cell, exec applies the functions receive and deliver, as in Section 7.3.2. When op is infeasible for its execution on c, the result of exec is unspecified. Here is the definition:

value
    exec: Operation × Cell $\xrightarrow{\sim}$ Cell
    exec(op, c) ≡
        deliver(from_stock(op), receive(to_stock(op), c))
        pre enough(op, c)

Example 7.3.6. Consider the execution of the operation op$_1$ on the cell cell$_1$, as shown in Table 7.6. The result, cell$_2$, was obtained by increasing the stock for shovel and decreasing the stocks for all sub-products of shovel, top handle and scoop assembly. However, the stocks for top handle and scoop assembly themselves remain unchanged, as the entire volume needed to produce 150 shovels is obtained by production. Occupancies of the cell before and after production also remain the same, as the storage requirement of each product is the sum of the storage requirements of its sub-products (see Example 7.2.1).

Table 7.6. Production cell `cell`$_2$.

cell$_2$ = exec(op$_1$, cell$_1$)

storage	stocks		assembly			transport			
200000	shovel	150	ws$_1$				ws$_1$	ws$_2$	ws$_3$
	scoopass	500	shovel	150		ws$_1$	0	0	0
	rivet	5500				ws$_2$	5000	0	0
	connector	850	ws$_2$			ws$_3$	15000	2500	0
	tophandle	500	shovel	100					
	shaft	850	tophandle	150					
	anail	3400							
	blade	350	ws$_3$						
	scoop	350	bracket	200					
	bnail	700	scoopass	150					
	bracket	100							
	handle	350							
	hcoupling	250							
	hbracket	250							
	occupancy	151000							

7.3.6 Production Operations: Concurrency

In order for two operations op$_1$ and op$_2$ to be executed concurrently, they must not give conflicting work assignments for the shared workstations. In particular, any workstation ws in the domains of both op$_1$ and op$_2$, is set to produce the same product. This is captured by the function `compatible`:

value

    compatible : Operation × Operation → **Bool**
    compatible(op$_1$, op$_2$) ≡
      (∀ ws: Workstation •
        ws ∈ **dom** op$_1$ ∩ **dom** op$_2$ ⇒
        product(op$_1$(ws)) = product(op$_2$(ws))
)

Given two compatible operations op$_1$ and op$_2$, their composition is done by the function `compose`. It takes all work assignments from the non-shared workstations without change and combines the work assignments for the shared workstations. The latter is done by the auxiliary function `compose`.

value

    compose: Operation × Operation $\overset{\sim}{\to}$ Operation
    compose(op$_1$, op$_2$) ≡
      let
        ws$_1$ = **dom** op$_1$,
        ws$_2$ = **dom** op$_2$
      in

$[$ ws $\mapsto$ op$_1$(ws) | ws: Workstation • ws $\in$ ws$_1$ \ ws$_2$ $]$ $\cup$
$[$ ws $\mapsto$ op$_2$(ws) | ws: Workstation • ws $\in$ ws$_2$ \ ws$_1$ $]$ $\cup$
$[$ ws $\mapsto$ compose(op$_1$(ws), op$_2$(ws)) |
    ws: Workstation • ws $\in$ ws$_1$ $\cap$ ws$_2$
$]$
end
pre compatible(op$_1$, op$_2$)

Composition of work assignments leaves the product unchanged and adds the volumes produced and forwarded to the corresponding workstations. The function assumes that both work assignments refer to the same product. The function is defined as follows:

value
  compose: Work $\times$ Work $\overset{\sim}{\to}$ Work
  compose(w$_1$, w$_2$) **as** w **post**
    product(w) = product(w$_1$) $\wedge$
    volume(w) = volume(w$_1$) + volume(w$_2$) $\wedge$
    let f$_1$ = forward(w$_1$),
        f$_2$ = forward(w$_2$)
    in
      forward(w) =
        $[$ ws $\mapsto$ f$_1$(ws) | ws: Workstation • ws $\in$ **dom** f$_1$ \ **dom** f$_2$ $]$ $\cup$
        $[$ ws $\mapsto$ f$_2$(ws) | ws: Workstation • ws $\in$ **dom** f$_2$ \ **dom** f$_1$ $]$ $\cup$
        $[$ ws $\mapsto$ f$_1$(ws) + f$_2$(ws) | ws:Workstation • ws $\in$ **dom** f$_1$ $\cap$ **dom** f$_2$ $]$
    end
    pre product(w$_1$) = product(w$_2$)

Given a cell c and two compatible operations op$_1$ and op$_2$, their feasibility on c means feasibility of the operation compose(op$_1$,op$_2$).

value
  enough: Operation $\times$ Operation $\times$ Cell $\overset{\sim}{\to}$ **Bool**
  enough(op$_1$, op$_2$, c) $\equiv$
    enough(compose(op$_1$, op$_2$), c)
    pre compatible(op$_1$, op$_2$)

If feasible, concurrent execution of op$_1$ and op$_2$ is realised as the usual sequential execution of compose(op$_1$,op$_2$).

value
  exec: Operation $\times$ Operation $\times$ Cell $\overset{\sim}{\to}$ Cell
  exec(op$_1$, op$_2$, c) $\equiv$ exec(compose(op$_1$, op$_2$), c)
    pre compatible(op$_1$, op$_2$) $\wedge$ enough(op$_1$, op$_2$, c)

Example 7.3.7. Consider the operations op_{1a} and op_{1b} in Table 7.7. The operation op_{1a} programs the workstation ws_1 to produce 75 shovels, all sent to the inventory, and the workstation ws_2 to produce 150 top handles, half of which is forwarded to ws_1 and half sent to the inventory. The operation op_{1b} programs ws_1 to produce 75 shovels, all sent to the inventory, and ws_3 to produce 150 scoop assemblies, half forwarded to ws_1 and half to the inventory. The operations are compatible. They manufacture together 150 shovels, producing the required quantities of top handles and scoop assemblies. Their concurrent composition compose(op_{1a}, op_{1b}) is the operation op_1 (Table 7.3).

Table 7.7. Two concurrent operations.

op_{1a}					op_{1b}				
workstation	ws_1		ws_2		workstation	ws_1		ws_3	
product	shovel		tophandle		product	shovel		scoopass	
volume	75		150		volume	75		150	
forward	where	vol	where	vol	forward	where	vol	where	vol
	stocks	75	ws_1	75		stocks	75	ws_1	75
			stocks	75				stocks	75

7.3.7 Production Processes

A production process is a sequence of production operations, executed on a single production cell. It is defined as the type **Process**:

type
  Process = Operation*

Functions **enough** and **exec** check if a given cell has enough resources for a process (the process is feasible) and to execute a process, respectively. The functions are defined by recursion on processes, using the corresponding functions **enough** and **exec** to check feasibility and to execute individual operations. Feasibility, in particular, has to take into account the state changes caused by the execution of individual operations.

value
  enough: Process × Cell → **Bool**
  enough(p, c) ≡
    p = ⟨⟩ ∨
    enough(**hd** p, c) ∧ enough(**tl** p, exec(**hd** p, c)),
  exec: Process × Cell $\xrightarrow{\sim}$ Cell
  exec(p, c) ≡
    if p = ⟨⟩ **then** c **else** exec(**tl** p, exec(**hd** p, c))
    end pre enough(p, c)

Example 7.3.8. Consider the process p composed of the six operations op_1 to op_6, as described in Table 7.8. The purpose of p is to produce 1000 items of the shovel using the resources of $cell_1$. In order to obtain that number, p has to manufacture enough scoop assemblies (500 items) and top handles (500 items). In order to obtain 500 top handles, p has to first manufacture enough brackets (250 items). The process is feasible for execution on $cell_1$: all the workstations are assigned the workloads which they can manufacture within a shift, there is enough transportation capacity to forward all products between the workstations and there are enough sub-products in stock to ensure that successive operations are feasible, taking into account how the stocks change during the execution of p. Those changing stocks are described in Table 7.9, recorded after each successive operation. We can see that the final state includes 1000 shovels but zero quantities of all other products. Throughout the execution, the occupancy remains constant at 151000 storage units.

Table 7.8. Production process p.

		ws_1		ws_2		ws_3	
p	op_1	shovel		tophandle		scoopass	
		150		150		150	
		stocks	150	ws_1	75	ws_1	75
				stocks	75	stocks	75
	op_2	shovel		tophandle		bracket	
		150		150		200	
		stocks	150	ws_1	150	ws_2	150
						stocks	50
	op_3	shovel		shovel		scoopass	
		150		100		150	
		stocks	150	stocks	100	ws_1	150
	op_4	shovel		tophandle		scoopass	
		150		150		150	
		stocks	150	ws_1	75	ws_1	75
				stocks	75	stocks	75
	op_5	shovel		tophandle		bracket	
		150		50		50	
		stocks	150	ws_1	50	ws_2	50
	op_6	shovel		shovel		scoopass	
		50		100		50	
		stocks	50	stocks	100	ws_1	50

Table 7.9. Execution of the process p and its effect on stocks.

product	init	op$_1$	op$_2$	op$_3$	op$_4$	op$_5$	op$_6$
shovel	0	150	300	550	700	850	1000
scoopass	500	500	350	250	250	100	0
rivet	7000	5500	4900	3000	1500	900	0
connector	1000	850	700	450	300	150	0
tophandle	500	500	500	250	250	150	0
shaft	1000	850	700	450	300	150	0
anail	4000	3400	2800	1800	1200	600	0
blade	500	350	350	200	50	50	0
scoop	500	350	350	200	50	50	0
bnail	1000	700	400	400	100	0	0
bracket	250	100	150	150	0	0	0
handle	500	350	200	200	50	0	0
hcoupling	250	250	50	50	50	0	0
hbracket	250	250	50	50	50	0	0

7.3.8 Production Processes: Concurrency

Given the processes p_1 and p_2, their concurrent execution means to execute concurrently their first operations **hd** p_1 and **hd** p_2 (if possible, otherwise one of them), and then continue concurrently with **tl** p_1 and **tl** p_2. We express this concurrent execution as sequential execution with operation composition. The simulation of two concurrent processes by a corresponding sequential process is described by the function **compose**.

value

compose: Process × Process × Cell $\overset{\sim}{\to}$ Process
compose(p_1, p_2, c) ≡ ...
   pre enough(p_1, p_2, c)

The function takes two processes p_1 and p_2 and a cell c, such that p_1 and p_2 are to be executed concurrently on c, and returns a new process compose(p_1, p_2, c). In order to define this process, we have to first decide what it means for two concurrent processes to be feasible on a given cell.

It is not enough to require that enough(p_1, c) and enough(p_2, c) hold together, as in the presence of the shared resources the feasibility of one of them can contradict the feasibility of another. Instead, at any moment during the execution, the cell c must have enough resources to allow at least one of p_1 or p_2 to make progress, therefore both processes to complete eventually. Establishing this property requires a decision which of p_1 or p_2 should proceed first if the cell has insufficient resources for both of them. We decide in favour of the first process, therefore implicitly adopting a static priority-based scheduling. The function **enough** decides if the cell has enough resources for concurrent execution of two processes:

value
  enough: Process × Process × Cell → **Bool**
  enough(p_1, p_2, c) ≡
    $p_1 = \langle\rangle \wedge p_2 = \langle\rangle$ ∨
    $p_1 = \langle\rangle \wedge$ enough(p_2, c) ∨
    $p_2 = \langle\rangle \wedge$ enough(p_1, c) ∨
    $p_1 \neq \langle\rangle \wedge p_2 \neq \langle\rangle \wedge$
    let $h_1 =$ **hd** p_1, $h_2 =$ **hd** p_2, $t_1 =$ **tl** p_1, $t_2 =$ **tl** p_2
    in if compatible(h_1, h_2) $\wedge$ enough(h_1, h_2, c)
      then enough(t_1, t_2, exec(h_1, h_2, c))
      else enough(h_1, c) $\wedge$ enough(t_1, p_2, exec(h_1, c)) ∨
          enough(h_2, c) $\wedge$ enough(p_1, t_2, exec(h_2, c))
    end
  end

The function **compose** reduces two concurrent processes p_1 and p_2 to an "equivalent" sequential process, for a given production cell c. The processes must be feasible for concurrent execution on c. The function implements static priority scheduling, where p_1 has higher priority than p_2.

value
  compose: Process × Process × Cell $\overset{\sim}{\rightarrow}$ Process
  compose(p_1, p_2, c) ≡
    if $p_1 = \langle\rangle \wedge p_2 = \langle\rangle$ **then** $\langle\rangle$ **else**
      if $p_1 = \langle\rangle \vee p_2 = \langle\rangle$
      then if $p_1 = \langle\rangle$ **then** p_2 **else** p_1 **end**
      else let $h_1 =$ **hd** p_1, $h_2 =$ **hd** p_2,
            $t_1 =$ **tl** p_1, $t_2 =$ **tl** p_2
        in if compatible(h_1, h_2) $\wedge$ enough(h_1, h_2, c)
          then $\langle$compose(h_1, h_2)$\rangle$ $\frown$ compose(t_1, t_2, exec(h_1, h_2, c))
          else if enough(h_1, c)
              then $\langle h_1\rangle$ $\frown$ compose(t_1, p_2, exec(h_1, c))
              else $\langle h_2\rangle$ $\frown$ compose(p_1, t_2, exec(h_2, c)) **end**
          end
        end
    end
  end
  pre enough(p_1, p_2, c)

Then to execute p_1 and p_2 concurrently on c means to execute the process compose(p_1, p_2, c) sequentially.

value
  exec: Process × Process × Cell $\overset{\sim}{\rightarrow}$ Cell
  exec(p_1, p_2, c) ≡
    exec(compose(p_1, p_2, c), c) **pre** enough(p_1, p_2, c)

Example 7.3.9. Consider the processes p_1 and p_2 in Table 7.10. Each process is responsible for manufacturing 500 shovels using the resources of the production cell $cell_1$. However, p_1 must not use the stock of top handles but manufacture them (500 items) from existing sub-products; also the missing number of brackets (250 items). Top handles are left to be used by p_2. On the other hand, p_2 must not use the stock of scoop assemblies, reserved for p_1, but manufacture them from sub-products. Concurrent composition of p_1 and p_2 gives the process p described in Table 7.8.

Table 7.10. Concurrent processes p_1 and p_2.

p_1

ws_1		ws_2		ws_3	
shovel		tophandle			
75		150			
stocks	75	ws1	75		
		stocks	75		
shovel		tophandle		bracket	
75		150		200	
stocks	75	ws1	75	ws2	150
		stocks	75	stocks	50
		shovel			
		100			
		stocks	100		
shovel		tophandle			
75		150			
stocks	75	ws1	75		
		stocks	75		
shovel		tophandle		bracket	
75		50		50	
stocks	75	ws1	50	ws2	50
		shovel			
		100			
		stocks	100		

p_2

ws_1		ws_3	
shovel		scoopass	
75		150	
stocks	75	ws1	75
		stocks	75
shovel			
75			
stocks	75		
shovel		scoopass	
150		150	
stocks	150	ws1	150
shovel		scoopass	
75		150	
stocks	75	ws1	75
		stocks	75
shovel			
75			
stocks	75		
shovel		scoopass	
50		50	
stocks	50	ws1	50

7.3.9 Production with Several Production Cells

With only one cell involved in production, its resources determine what kind of products can be produced, how many, and when the customers could receive them. Concurrent processes allow responses to several customer orders simultaneously, but, like sequential processes, they are constrained by the resources existing in the cell. A departure from this single-cell scenario is allowing several cells to share their resources as part of a distributed production environment. This leads to collaboration between production cells, where different cells play the roles of customers who issue customer orders and suppliers who implement them; it is also possible for a single cell to play both roles. The aim of this section is to formalise a small fragment of this distributed environment.

Consider a function **enough** to carry out the simplest possible check of the availability of resources in this distributed environment. It takes four arguments: a process p, a product map ps and two cells c_1 and c_2. It checks if c_2 can deliver ps and c_1 can receive ps and subsequently has enough resources to execute p. The function is defined as follows:

value
    enough: Process × Cell × Products × Cell → **Bool**
    enough(p, c_1, ps, c_2) ≡
        enough_deliver(ps, c_2) ∧
        enough_receive(ps, c_1) ∧ enough(p, receive(ps, c_1))

If **enough** is satisfied for the process p, products ps and the cells c_1 and c_2, then **exec** carries out the execution. This will affect both cells: c_2 delivers the products ps and c_1 first receives them and then executes p.

value
    exec: Process × Cell × Products × Cell $\overset{\sim}{\rightarrow}$ Cell × Cell
    exec(p, c_1, ps, c_2) ≡
        (exec(p, receive(ps, c_1)), deliver(ps, c_2))
        pre enough(p, c_1, ps, c_2)

The functions formalise an interaction between a single customer and a single supplier. A step further is to consider a set of suppliers. Consider a map cp from production cells representing suppliers d, to Products representing how many products of different kinds the customer c is expected to receive from each d. Assuming c is not among the suppliers, the function **enough** decides if each supplier is able to deliver the corresponding products and c has enough space to receive the products from all suppliers and subsequently has enough resources to execute the process p.

value
    enough: Process × Cell × (Cell $\overset{}{\underset{m}{\rightarrow}}$ Products) $\overset{\sim}{\rightarrow}$ **Bool**
    enough(p, c, cp) ≡
        enough_receive(add(cp), c) ∧
        enough(p, receive(add(cp), c)) ∧
        (∀ d: Cell • d ∈ **dom** cp ⇒ enough_deliver(cp(d), d))
        pre c ∉ **dom** cp

Assuming this function is satisfied, **exec** carries out the execution. This affects the consumer cell which first receives the products from all suppliers and then executes the process p. It also affects all supplier cells by delivering the products to the consumer. The function returns a pair of a cell, representing the modified consumer, and a set of cells, representing the modified suppliers. There is an implicit assumption here that two different production cells cannot become one by performing state-changing operations. Such identical cells would then disappear from the resulting set. We could implement this assumption by introducing a function from Cell to identifiers, such that different cells are assigned different identifiers and identifiers remain constant when performing state-changing operations. We do not pursue this development further. The function exec is defined below.

value
    exec: Process × Cell × (Cell $\overrightarrow{m}$ Products) $\overset{\sim}{\to}$ Cell × Cell-**set**
    exec(p, c, cp) ≡
    (
        exec(p, receive(add(cp), c)),
        { deliver(cp(d), d) | d: Cell • d ∈ **dom** cp }
)
    pre c ∉ **dom** cp ∧ enough(p, c, cp)

7.4 Prescriptive Production Modelling

Section 7.3 introduced a concrete model for describing production, including production resources, operations on them, what it means for such operations to be feasible for execution and what is the execution effect in this case. The concepts were developed gradually, from the tasks assigned to individual workstations, the operations performing such tasks on several workstations, to production processes. Here we look at such operations from the point of view of their purpose, not their execution.

The purpose of each production cell is to continuously satisfy the needs of its customers, expressed in terms of products, quantities and deadlines. This "mission statement" translates down to the goals of individual processes, each designed to respond to a particular customer order. We define such orders using the variant type Order, as below. The type is defined using five different functions (variants) with arguments: produce takes a product map; deliver and receive each takes a product map and a customer order; and takes two customer orders; and deadline takes a natural number (representing time) and an order. The type is defined as follows:

type
    Time = **Nat**,
    Order ==
        produce(Products) |
        deliver(Products, Order) | receive(Products, Order) |
        and(Order, Order) | deadline(Time, Order)

The meaning of different orders is as follows:

1. produce(ps), where ps is a product map, describes the simplest customer order: the set of products the customer needs and how many items of each such product. It does not say how to achieve this order, it only describes the aim for a possible implementation. Any other customer order is built from produce, as all are built from pre-existing orders (recursively).
2. deliver(ps, o), where ps is a product map and o is an order, means to satisfy o after delivering the products ps. Any implementations of o must not rely on the products ps to still exist in the cell. For instance, deliver(ps$_1$,produce(ps$_2$)) means to deliver the products ps$_1$ and then produce ps$_2$ on the resulting cell.
3. receive(ps, o), where ps is a product map and o is an order, is symmetric to deliver. It means to satisfy the order o after receiving the products ps. For instance, receive(ps$_1$,produce(ps$_2$)) means to receive the products ps$_1$ and then produce ps$_2$ on the resulting cell.
4. and(o$_1$, o$_2$), where o$_1$ and o$_2$ are customer orders, means to satisfy the orders o$_1$ and o$_2$ simultaneously, where neither depends on the results produced by the other. For instance, and(produce(ps$_1$), produce(ps$_2$)) means to produce the products ps$_1$ and ps$_2$ simultaneously.
5. deadline(n, o), where n is a natural number and o is an order, means to satisfy o within the number of shifts described by n.

Example 7.4.1. Consider a customer order to produce 1000 shovels (described by the product map ps$_1$), to be ready within 6 shifts from the moment a production cell receives 2000 rivets and 2000 a-nails (described by the product map ps$_2$). The order is described using the table below.

deadline(6, receive(ps$_2$, produce(ps$_1$)))				
ps$_1$		ps$_2$		
products	shovel	products	rivet	anail
volume	1000	volume	2000	2000

7.5 Relating Descriptive and Prescriptive Models

Customer orders defined in Section 7.4 provide a prescriptive model for production, which complements the descriptive model in Section 7.3. Here we show how to formally relate those two models.

Consider a production process p, a customer order o and a cell c. Function satisfies defines what it means for a process to satisfy the order when executed on the cell. The precondition requires that the process is feasible for this cell (function enough). The type of function satisfies is as follows:

value
  satisfies: Process × Order × Cell $\overset{\sim}{\to}$ **Bool**

Assuming the process is feasible, we define this function for different kinds of customer orders, according to the type Order. The simplest case is produce(ps): after executing the process on the cell (function exec), the resulting levels of stocks must satisfy the quantities in the product map ps. Here is the axiom expressing this:

axiom
  $\forall$ p: Process, ps: Products, c: Cell •
    enough(p, c) $\Rightarrow$
    satisfies(p, produce(ps), c) =
    ($\forall$ r: Product •
      r $\in$ **dom** ps $\Rightarrow$ stocks(exec(p, c), r) $\geq$ ps(r)
)

Example 7.5.1. Consider the process p in Table 7.8, the cell $cell_1$ defined in Table 7.2 and the customer order to produce 1000 shovels, produce(ps_1) as in Example 7.4.1. The process is feasible for execution on $cell_1$, see Example 7.3.8, and it satisfies the order when executed on this cell. This could be verified by checking the levels of stocks in Table 7.9.

The following sections proceed by considering the remaining orders:

1. sequential production implementing deliver,
2. concurrent production implementing and,
3. distributed production implementing receive, and
4. production under time constraints implementing deadline.

7.5.1 Sequential Production

Consider a production process p, a production cell c, and a customer order deliver(ps, o) where ps is a product map and o is another customer order. Suppose p is feasible for execution on c. When is it possible to say that p satisfies deliver(ps, o) when executed on c?

In the simplest case, we could deliver the products ps from the cell c, if they exist, and then recursively check the satisfaction of the order o by p using the resulting cell deliver(ps, c). However, this is too strong a definition, as it requires that the products exist in c even before p is executed.

Instead, we allow the products ps to be first manufactured using the resources in c, according to the initial part (prefix) p_1 of p. Formally, we require p_1 to be feasible for execution on c and this execution to satisfy the order produce(ps). The remaining part p_2 is then used to satisfy the order o, based on the cell obtained by executing p_1 on c (cell c_1) and then delivering the products ps (cell c_2). This way we ensure that p_2 will not consume, and therefore rely on, the products ps. Formally, we require that the process p_2 is feasible for execution on the cell c_2 and that this execution satisfies the customer order o. Here is the axiom expressing this:

axiom
$\forall$ p: Process, c: Cell, ps: Products, o: Order •
   enough(p, c) $\Rightarrow$
     satisfies(p, deliver(ps, o), c) =
     ($\exists$ p_1, p_2: Process •
       p = p_1 $\widehat{}$ p_2 $\wedge$
       enough(p_1, c) $\wedge$ satisfies(p_1, produce(ps), c) $\wedge$
       let c_1 = exec(p_1, c), c_2 = deliver(ps, c_1)
       in enough(p_2, c_2) $\wedge$ satisfies(p_2, o, c_2) **end**
)

Example 7.5.2. Consider the processes p_1 and p_2 in Table 7.10, the cell $cell_1$ in Table 7.2, and the customer order deliver(ps, produce(ps)) where ps is [shovel $\mapsto$ 500]. The order asks to deliver 500 shovels and then produce again the same amount. The process $p_1\widehat{}p_2$ satisfies this order when executed on $cell_1$. This can be verified by investigating how the levels of stocks in $cell_1$ change when executing $p_1\widehat{}p_2$, with 500 shovels delivered after the execution of p_1 and before the execution of p_2. Table 7.11 demonstrates this, with mid marking the point after p_1 and before p_2. We can see that the execution of p_1 results in 500 shovels in stock and, after delivering this amount, enough of sub-products to produce the next 500 by p_2.

Table 7.11. Sequential execution of p_1 and p_2 and its effect on stocks.

product	init	p_1						mid	p_2					
shovel	0	75	150	250	325	400	500	0	75	150	300	375	450	500
scoopass	500	425	350	250	175	100	0	0	75	0	0	75	0	0
rivet	7000	6700	6400	6000	5700	5400	5000	5000	3800	3500	2000	800	500	0
connector	1000	925	850	750	675	600	500	500	425	350	200	125	50	0
tophandle	500	575	650	550	625	600	500	500	425	350	200	125	50	0
shaft	1000	925	850	750	675	600	500	500	425	350	200	125	50	0
anail	4000	3700	3400	3000	2700	2400	2000	2000	1700	1400	800	500	200	0
blade	500	500	500	500	500	500	500	500	350	350	200	50	50	0
scoop	500	500	500	500	500	500	500	500	350	350	200	50	50	0
bnail	1000	700	400	400	100	0	0	0	0	0	0	0	0	0
bracket	250	100	150	150	0	0	0	0	0	0	0	0	0	0
handle	500	350	200	200	50	0	0	0	0	0	0	0	0	0
hcoupling	250	250	50	50	50	0	0	0	0	0	0	0	0	0
hbracket	250	250	50	50	50	0	0	0	0	0	0	0	0	0

7.5.2 Concurrent Production

Consider a cell c, a process p and a customer order and(o_1, o_2), requesting to deliver the orders o_1 and o_2 concurrently. Suppose p is feasible for execution on c. What does it mean for p to satisfy and(o_1, o_2) when executed on c?

It means that p is a concurrent composition of two sub-processes p_1 and p_2, compose(p_1, p_2, c) (Section 7.3.8), such that:

1. p_1 satisfies o_1 in the presence of p_2 executing concurrently: p_1 is feasible for execution on the cell c_2 obtained from c by removing the products that p_2 needs for its execution, and it satisfies o_1 on c_2.
2. p_2 satisfies o_2 in the presence of p_1 executing concurrently: p_2 is feasible for execution on the cell c_1 obtained from c by removing the products that p_1 needs for its execution, and it satisfies o_2 on c_1.

This way we ensure that the processes do not interfere with each other's goals. Here is the axiom which formalises these conditions:

axiom
$\forall$ p: Process, c: Cell, o_1, o_2: Order •
  enough(p, c) $\Rightarrow$
    satisfies(p, and(o_1, o_2), c) =
    ($\exists$ p_1, p_2: Process •
      enough(p_1, p_2, c) $\land$ p = compose(p_1, p_2, c) $\land$
      let c_2 = deliver(from_stock(p_2), c)
      in enough(p_1, c_2) $\land$ satisfies(p_1, o_1, c_2) **end** $\land$
      let c_1 = deliver(from_stock(p_1), c)
      in enough(p_2, c_1) $\land$ satisfies(p_2, o_2, c_1) **end**
)

The function from_stock(p) calculates the products that p needs from stock. It is defined by accumulating the products needed by every operation op of p, using a similar function from_stock(op) (Section 7.3.4).

value
  from_stock: Process $\rightarrow$ Products
  from_stock(p) $\equiv$
    if p = $\langle\rangle$ **then** [ ]
    else add(from_stock(**hd** p), from_stock(**tl** p)) **end**

Example 7.5.3. Consider the process p in Table 7.8, the cell cell$_1$ in Table 7.2, and the customer order to produce 500 shovels concurrently with producing another 500 shovels: and(produce(ps), produce(ps)) where ps is [shovel $\mapsto$ 500]. The process is feasible for execution on cell$_1$, as shown in Example 7.3.8, and it satisfies the order above. To justify this claim, consider the decomposition of p into two concurrent processes p_1 and p_2, as in

Table 7.10. Consider the process p_2. Table 7.11 demonstrates the levels of stocks when p_1 is executed first and then p_2 is executed. It shows that p_2 is both feasible for execution on $cell_1$ after removing the products needed by p_1 (mid column), and it satisfies the order produce(ps). Consider the process p_1. This case is illustrated in Table 7.12. Again, we can certify that p_1 is both feasible for execution on $cell_1$ after removing the products needed by p_2, and it satisfies the order produce(ps).

Table 7.12. Execution of p_1 after removing the products needed by p_2.

product	init	ps$_2$ = from_stock(p$_2$)	deliver (ps$_2$,init)	p$_1$					
shovel	0	0	0	75	150	250	325	400	500
scoopass	500	0	500	425	350	250	175	100	0
rivet	7000	5000	2000	1700	1400	1000	700	400	0
connector	1000	500	500	425	350	250	175	100	0
tophandle	500	500	0	75	150	50	125	100	0
shaft	1000	500	500	425	350	250	175	100	0
anail	4000	2000	2000	1700	1400	1000	700	400	0
blade	500	500	0	0	0	0	0	0	0
scoop	500	500	0	0	0	0	0	0	0
bnail	1000	0	1000	700	400	400	100	0	0
bracket	250	0	250	100	150	150	0	0	0
handle	500	0	500	350	200	200	50	0	0
hcoupling	250	0	250	250	50	50	50	0	0
hbracket	250	0	250	250	50	50	50	0	0

7.5.3 Distributed Production

Consider a production process p, a production cell c, and a customer order receive(ps, o) where ps is a product map and o is another customer order. Suppose p is feasible for execution on c. Then p satisfies the order receive(ps, o) when executed on c iff it satisfies o on c, after c has received the products ps. This new cell can be described as receive(ps, c). The assumption is that c has enough space to accommodate these additional products. Here is the axiom expressing this definition:

axiom
$\forall$ p: Process, c: Cell, ps: Products, o: Order •
    enough(p, c) $\Rightarrow$
        satisfies(p, receive(ps, o), c) =
        (enough_receive(ps, c) $\wedge$ satisfies(p, o, receive(ps, c)))

The order receive(ps, o) effectively delegates part of production to outside the process. It is the responsibility of p to fulfill the order o, but delivery of the products ps must be ensured from outside, typically by an external production cell.

Example 7.5.4. Consider the process p in Table 7.8, the cell $cell_0$ in Table 7.1, and the customer order receive(ps_2, produce(ps_1)) where ps_1 is [shovel $\mapsto$ 1000] and ps_2 is [rivet $\mapsto$ 2000, a-nail $\mapsto$ 2000]. The order requires the production of 1000 shovels provided the cell first receives 2000 rivets and 2000 a-nails. As the resulting cell is $cell_1$ (Table 7.2) and p satisfies the order produce(ps_1) on $cell_1$ (Example 7.5.1), p indeed satisfies the order receive(ps_2, produce(ps_1)) on $cell_0$.

7.5.4 Real-Time Production

Consider the process p, the cell c and the customer order deadline(n, o) where n is a natural number and o is another customer order. p satisfies deadline(n, o) iff it satisfies the order o and completes its execution within the time n. As time is measured in shifts, n represents how many shifts can elapse from the moment c receives all external products to the moment p completes its execution.

Formally, we use the length of p to calculate how long it takes for p to complete, and bound this length by n. This takes into account all the operations in p, each executed within one shift, but ignores the waiting time for any external products. Here is the definition:

axiom
  $\forall$ p: Process, c: Cell, n: **Nat**, o: Order •
    enough(p, c) $\Rightarrow$
      satisfies(p, deadline(n, o), c) =
      (satisfies(p, o, c) $\land$ **len** p $\le$ n)

Example 7.5.5. Consider the process p in Table 7.8, the cell $cell_0$ in Table 7.1, and the order deadline(6, receive(ps_2, produce(ps_1))) in Example 7.4.1. The order requires the production of 1000 shovels within 6 shifts, after receiving 2000 rivets and 2000 a-nails. As p contains 6 operations and it satisfies receive(ps_2, produce(ps_1)) on $cell_0$ (Example 7.5.4), it also satisfies the order deadline(6, receive(ps_2, produce(ps_1))) on $cell_0$.

7.6 Conclusions

Being able to assert correctness of a computer program by mathematical reasoning, rather than testing is the cornerstone and so-far unfulfilled promise of formally-based software development. A number of programming theories now exist, with their own definitions and the means to verify program correctness. Such theories express correctness in different terms: program variables, relations between inputs and outputs, sequences of state-changes, possible interactions of the program with its environment, etc. Program feasibility is either a non-issue (data is easy to replicate), abstracted away (assuming enough resources exist) or addressed by static or dynamic scheduling.

This chapter is an attempt at defining correctness for business processes, using the concepts from the business domain to express what this correctness really means. In order to make such definitions concrete we focused on a particular business domain: manufacturing of discrete-parts products. For this domain, we defined models to describe what is a business process, what are the resources the process needs for its execution, when there are enough resources for the process and what the execution really means. We expressed such definitions formally, using what we considered a "minimal" number of modelling concepts. In addition to this descriptive model, we also defined a corresponding prescriptive model to capture the purpose of each process. Correctness was then defined as a relation between such descriptive and prescriptive models. It was defined incrementally, first for sequential processes, then considering concurrency, distribution and real-time constraints.

There is a vast literature concerning business process modelling, considering the topic from different perspectives: management, operations and production research, industrial engineering, software development, information systems development, artificial intelligence, etc. For instance, [30] promotes a process-oriented view of an enterprise in order to best utilise the promise of enterprise systems to further organisational/business goals. [64] describes a concrete graphical notation to carry out process analysis by simulation. The approach is informal. Well-known examples of industrial-strength frameworks are ARIS [125] and CIMOSA [81]. [139] contains an overview of such frameworks from the point of view of enterprise modelling and integration. [60] describes the need to base enterprise/process description languages on formal semantics. [73] contains an evaluation of the existing languages and tools, considering formality as one of the issues. [47] contains an operations management perspective on modelling of business process flows. The models are formal and problem-specific, allowing in particular quantitative analyses of process performance. Among formally-based approaches, [46] describes a modelling language allowing various kinds of qualitative and quantitative analyses by translation into different semantic models. Petri Nets is one of the most popular formal approaches, in particular for modelling manufacturing processes [32], but also for modelling workflow systems [138, 145]. Both papers consider verification of workflows but express properties like absence of control-flow errors, soundness or termination in technical rather than business terms. For us, such properties would be used to establish that a process is well-formed, which is necessary but insufficient to establish its correctness.

Future work in this area has several possible directions. First, to further develop the model: add more structure to process definitions [150]; support different ways to schedule concurrent processes; make the semantics of the prescriptive model more explicit, instead of relying on the descriptive model; derive algebraic laws to prove equivalences between orders; etc. Second, to automate the construction of a process to satisfy a given customer order [71]. Third, to describe the model with XML [27] and use this representation to develop an implementation. Finally, to build some real-life case studies.

Background Information

This chapter is based on work [107] done by Adegboyega Ojo of the Computer Science Department, University of Lagos, Nigeria, and Tomasz Janowski.

8. Model-Based Travel Planning

8.1 Introduction

Travel planning can be a challenge these days. There is an abundance of travel-related information in the magazines, newspapers, guides, brochures, on the internet. The information covers all imaginable aspects of travel including flights, hotels, cars, restaurants, maps, events and others. Travel is offered in the form of individual products or complete packages, its contents predefined or customised to individual needs, definite or based on waiting lists, sold for a regular price or as special deals (under different restrictions when, where and for whom the deal applies). With so many options available and so many constraints involved, there is a great deal of uncertainty how to carry out the process of travel planning.

Internet contributes significantly to making this information available for individual travellers, including on-line availability-checking, reservations and sale. However, internet-based travel agents tend to focus more on the presentation of information and less on its actual contents. Moreover, they implement little in the way of a method for the process of systematic travel planning – formulating the requirements and then moving gradually toward the solution. Here are some observations when visiting such agents: (1) a visitor has to know in detail what service he looks for before he can learn this for himself; (2) when presented with an offer a visitor can only accept or reject it, but cannot explore the alternatives; (3) an error message communicates to the visitor the presence of an error but not the reasons for it or how to avoid it; (4) there is no recollection of previous interactions with a visitor – the system always returns to its pre-defined state; (5) when a little amount of automation is possible in support of visitors' decisions it is not implemented.

This chapter is about methods and tools in support of travel planning. We show how to approach travel planning as essentially an engineering problem. We define precisely what constitutes travel requirements, what is a travel plan, and in what sense the plan correctly implements the requirements. The approach is model-based, with models representing all stages of travel planning, from abstract requirements to concrete itineraries. Such models are designed, analysed and redesigned to represent decisions made by the travel engineer (the person who designs the travel plan). The models are minimal – expressed with the minimum number of modelling concepts – but also open-ended – new concepts can be added when needed. They are also formally-based – their syntax is well-defined and their semantics is expressed in precise mathematical terms, using numbers, sets, maps, functions, abstract and concrete types. The formal machinery used for semantic definitions is basic set theory and logic. Formality makes it possible to prove correctness of a travel plan with respect to travel requirements, and also to justify the soundness of the design rules that allow travel plans to be made more concrete. Such rules are applied during a development process, leading gradually from the abstract travel requirements to concrete solutions. We present such rules and discuss their soundness.

In presenting such models we have four goals in mind. First, we want to formalise some of the travel-related concepts in a way which is independent of the current technology, providing the basis for an engineering approach. The latter means that the models must capture different levels of abstraction as well as relate those levels by the concept of correctness. Second, we want to apply such models to define a formally-based method for systematic travel planning, including definitions of the design rules and justification of why they are sound. Third, we want to explore the opportunities and limitations for automation in support of travel-related decision-making. The models will be used to formulate precise problems and seek possibly automated solutions. Fourth, we would like to seek an implementation of a prototype travel assistant, based on the models, in support of the method.

The rest of this chapter is as follows. Section 8.2 introduces the basic concepts. Section 8.3 describes the models for travel planning, with definitions and examples. As the models capture different levels of abstraction, Section 8.4 defines what it means for a concrete travel plan to correctly implement an abstract plan. Section 8.5 presents a method for systematic travel planning, based on the models in Section 8.3 and the notion of correctness in Section 8.4. Section 8.6 describes the ideas for a travel assistant, a software system to support travel development. Finally, Section 8.7 contains some conclusions.

8.2 Basic Concepts

Two basic concepts to build models for travel planning are Time, representing time instances, and Place, representing locations one may like to visit while travelling. We are not going to decide a priori if time is to be measured in days, hours, minutes or seconds, nor consider particular properties of locations. Instead, we define both concepts as abstract types.

type
  Time, Place

By defining Time as an abstract type we leave open the question of granularity and representation of time. Both can be decided later, if needed. But we do need to relate time instances, deciding if one instance (t) happens no later than another (t′), written t≤t′. This relation is defined as an operation that takes two time instances and returns **true** or **false**. The operation has the properties of a linear order, meaning it is reflexive, antisymmetric, transitive and total. The definition includes the signature of the function and the axioms to define its properties.

value
  ≤ : Time × Time → **Bool**
axiom
  ∀ t: Time • t ≤ t,
  ∀ t, t′: Time • t ≤ t′ ∧ t′ ≤ t ⇒ t = t′,
  ∀ t, t′, t″: Time • t ≤ t′ ∧ t′ ≤ t″ ⇒ t ≤ t″,
  ∀ t, t′: Time • t ≤ t′ ∨ t′ ≤ t

Given two time instances t and t′ such that t≤t′, we can use them to represent a period of time from t to t′. Then t′-t represents how many time units have elapsed from t to t′. We define this duration as a natural number. It has two properties: for any t, duration from t to itself is zero, and given t, t′ and t″ such that t≤t′≤t″, duration from t to t″ is the sum of the durations from t to t′ and from t′ to t″.

type
  Duration = **Nat**
value
  − : Time × Time $\overset{\sim}{\to}$ Duration
axiom
  ∀ t: Time • t − t = 0,
  ∀ t, t′, t″: Time •
    t ≤ t′ ∧ t′ ≤ t″ ⇒
    t″ − t = (t″ − t′) + (t′ − t)

One more operator is +, applied to a time instance t and a duration d: t+d produces a new time instance t′ such that t≤t′ and the duration from t to t′ is d.

value
  + : Time × Duration → Time
axiom
  ∀ t: Time, d: Duration •
    t ≤ (t + d) ∧ (t + d) − t = d

It would seem that introducing distances between places is necessary for travel planning. In order to keep the models simple and avoid introducing different modes of transport, we will express this distance in terms of the minimum travel time. The function **traveltime** takes two places and returns a duration – the minimum time to travel directly from one place to another. We constrain this function with three axioms: the minimum time to travel from any place to itself is zero; the time does not depend on the direction of travel; and the minimum time to travel between two places is less than or equal to the time of travelling via a third place.

value
   traveltime: Place × Place → Duration
axiom
   ∀ p, p′, p″: Place •
      traveltime(p, p) = 0 ∧
      traveltime(p, p′) = traveltime(p′, p) ∧
      traveltime(p, p″) ≤ traveltime(p, p′) + traveltime(p′, p″)

8.3 Modelling for Travel Planning

The type of interest is Journey. Its purpose is to record decisions made at all stages of travel planning, from initial requirements to concrete itineraries. The idea is that starting from the former, we arrive at the latter in a gradual way. The type Journey describes the outcomes from all stages in this process.

type
   Journey

The model is built upon six basic concepts: home, visit, order, successor, duration and timing. All are explained in the following sections.

8.3.1 Home

By home we mean the start place of a journey. Typically, this is the place where the traveller is located when not travelling, his place of residence. We define this location by the function home from Journey to Place.

value
   home: Journey → Place

The function is total, meaning that for any journey there is a unique home location. Moreover, this location will not change during development. As well as being the start point of the journey, it may also be the place where the journey ends, but this is not enforced by the model which allows for both return and one-way journeys.

Example 8.3.1. Suppose the traveller's home location is Macau. This is where his journey is going to start and perhaps also end. Below we can see a skeletal travel plan which only contains the traveller's home. It contains one row and two columns. The first column describes the contents of its corresponding row; here the row contains the **home** place of the traveller.

home	Macau

8.3.2 Places

Suppose the traveller wishes to visit a number of places during his journey. Initially, the order of visits or particular timing are not decided. We assume for simplicity that each place is visited exactly once. The exception is the home location which may be visited either once (one-way journey) or twice (return journey). The function **visit** returns the set of places to be visited during a journey. It is declared as follows:

value

visit: Journey → Place-**set**

If the home location is present in the set then it implies a return journey, otherwise a one-way journey. The function is total, meaning any journey defines the set of places to visit. With no further axioms to constrain this function, the set of places may be empty. Strange as it may seem, this value may be considered as the start point of the systematic planning process, which adds more places as the process is carried out. So unlike the home location, the set of places to visit is not constant during development.

Example 8.3.2. Suppose the traveller from Macau wishes to visit five cities: Hong Kong, Singapore, Toronto, Havana and Mexico City. Then he would like to return back to Macau. This expanded travel plan is displayed below. It now contains two rows, the first is the home location, the second is the set of places the traveller wishes to visit. The ordering is immaterial, for instance Singapore occurring before Hong Kong does not mean we want to visit them in this order. However, as the home location is present in the visit set, the traveller wishes to return to Macau.

home	Macau					
visit	Macau	Singapore	Hong Kong	Toronto	Mexico	Havana

8.3.3 Ordering

Except for home being visited at the beginning of the journey and perhaps at the end, the ordering of other visits is left undecided. However, the traveller may wish to be more specific about this ordering. The model allows the traveller to decide that one place must be visited after another one. The function **later** represents such constraints. It takes a journey and returns a set containing pairs of places, as below.

value
   later: Journey $\rightarrow$ (Place $\times$ Place)-set

If p_1 and p_2 are places and j is a journey then $(p_1,p_2) \in later(j)$ means that according to j, p_2 can only be visited after p_1. It does not enforce that p_2 must be visited immediately after p_1, just some time afterwards. As the plan is developed, the traveller may decide to add more pairs to this relation, becoming increasingly more specific about the ordering of visits.

We have four axioms to constrain the value of this function:

1. Any place included in the relation later(j), in the first or the second position in a pair, is either a home location home(j) or belongs to the set visit(j).

   axiom
   $\forall$ j: Journey, p_1, p_2: Place $\bullet$
   $(p_1, p_2) \in later(j) \Rightarrow \{p_1, p_2\} \subseteq visit(j) \cup \{home(j)\}$

2. For any journey j, home(j) is the first place to visit during j, formally $(home(j),p) \in later(j)$ for any place $p \in visit(j)$. Second, for any return journey j, home(j) is the last place to visit during j, formally $(p,home(j)) \in later(j)$ for any $p \in visit(j)$.

   axiom
   $\forall$ j: Journey, p: Place $\bullet$
   $(p \in visit(j) \Rightarrow (home(j), p) \in later(j)) \land$
   $(p \in visit(j) \land home(j) \in visit(j) \Rightarrow (p, home(j)) \in later(j))$

3. The relation later(j) is transitive: if p_1 must be visited before p_2 and p_2 must be visited before p_3, then also p_1 must be visited before p_3, therefore $(p_1,p_3) \in later(j)$.

   axiom
   $\forall$ j: Journey, p_1, p_2, p_3: Place $\bullet$
   $(p_1, p_2) \in later(j) \land (p_2, p_3) \in later(j) \Rightarrow (p_1, p_3) \in later(j)$

4. Every place is visited at most once, except home(j) which may be visited once (for a one-way journey) or twice (for a return journey). We formalise this by saying that later(j) is not reflexive, except $(home(j),home(j)) \in later(j)$ when j is a return journey.

   axiom
   $\forall$ j: Journey, p: Place $\bullet$
   $p \in visit(j) \Rightarrow (p, p) \notin later(j) \lor p = home(j)$

Example 8.3.3. Consider again the traveller from Macau. To make the example more concrete, suppose our traveller is a researcher and university teacher, and the trip is related to his professional activities. He has specific goals to visit different cities: Hong Kong to obtain visas for Canada and Cuba; Toronto to attend a conference; Singapore to discuss a presentation at the conference with his co-author; Mexico to present a course at the local university; and Havana to interview external participants for the course in Mexico as well as prospective students for his institute. It follows that he must visit: Hong Kong before Toronto and Havana (to obtains visas); Singapore before Toronto (to discuss conference presentation); and Havana before Mexico (to interview students). Moreover, Macau being the start and the end location, is visited before as well as after any other city. In the table below, the row later contains a list of places for each place in the upper visit row, all that must be visited after this place. For instance, the column below Singapore contains Macau and Toronto, both to be visited after Singapore.

home	Macau					
visit	Macau	Singapore	Hong Kong	Toronto	Mexico	Havana
later	Macau	Macau	Macau	Macau	Macau	Macau
	Singapore	Toronto	Toronto			Mexico
	Hong Kong		Havana			
	Toronto		Mexico			
	Mexico					
	Havana					

8.3.4 Sequencing

The ordering does not decide in what particular sequence the traveller should visit places. It may require that before he visits p_1 and p_2, he must first visit p, but does not say which of p_1 or p_2 must immediately follow p.

The function next decides which two places should be visited consecutively. It takes a journey and returns a map from places to places.

value
    next: Journey → (Place ↦ Place)

For each place in the domain of the map, it returns a unique place to be visited immediately afterwards. In particular, the map may be empty, meaning none of the places has its immediate successor determined. If non-empty, however, the contents must be consistent with the later relation, in the sense that for all places p in the domain of next(j), the pair (p,next(j)(p)) belongs to later(j). Moreover, for two different places p_1 and p_2 in the domain of next(j), their immediate successors must also be different. The axioms below express these constraints.

axiom

> ∀ j: Journey, p: Place •
>   p ∈ **dom** next(j) ⇒ (p, next(j)(p)) ∈ later(j),
> ∀ j: Journey, p_1, p_2: Place •
> $p_1 \neq p_2$ ∧ {p_1, p_2} ⊆ **dom** next(j) ⇒ next(j)(p_1) ≠ next(j)(p_2)

Example 8.3.4. Given that the traveller from Macau must visit Singapore before Macau and Toronto, and Hong Kong before Macau, Toronto, Havana and Mexico, his first visit after Macau must be either Hong Kong or Singapore. Based on proximity, we decide for Hong Kong. From Hong Kong we again have two options: Singapore or Havana. For the same reason we choose Singapore. However, the axioms require that we first include Singapore in the later set for Hong Kong, before it is selected as the immediate successor. These decisions are included in the travel plan below.

home	Macau					
visit	Macau	Singapore	Hong Kong	Toronto	Mexico	Havana
later	Macau Singapore Hong Kong Toronto Mexico Havana	Macau Toronto	Macau Toronto Havana Mexico Singapore	Macau	Macau	Macau Mexico
next	Hong Kong		Singapore			

8.3.5 Durations

So far, we have described the elements of the model which are completely time-independent, expressed solely in terms of places and relations between them. The first time-related concept is duration: the minimum time the traveller wishes to stay in a place. Initially, we may not have this value defined for all or even any of the places. The information will be added gradually during the planning process. Formally, given a journey, the function `duration` returns a map from places to durations.

value

> duration: Journey → (Place ⇸ Duration)

The map may be empty, when no place has its duration decided. If non-empty, its domain includes only the places the traveller wants to visit, except the home location. As the traveller stays at the home location before the journey begins and perhaps after it has finished, allocating how long he should stay there is unnecessary or even confusing (would the duration refer to the stay before or after the journey?). Second, the duration must be non-zero. Allocating a zero duration to a place is like not allocating any duration at all, from the point of view of travel planning. In this case we choose not to include the place in the map. The following axiom formalises these constraints.

axiom
  ∀ j: Journey •
    0 ∉ **rng** duration(j) ∧
    dom duration(j) ⊆ visit(j) \ {home(j)}

The auxiliary function **duration** takes a journey j and a place p and returns the duration assigned to p by j if one exists and otherwise zero.

value
  duration: Journey × Place → Duration
  duration(j, p) ≡
    if p ∈ **dom** duration(j) **then** duration(j)(p) **else** 0 **end**

Example 8.3.5. Back to the example. Considering the purpose of his journey, the traveller needs to allocate certain minimum times for his stays in different places: one day in Singapore for discussion, one day in Hong Kong to collect a visa, three days in Toronto to attend the conference, 12 days in Mexico to present a course, one day in Havana to interview students. The resulting travel plan in described below.

home	Macau					
visit	Macau	Singapore	Hong Kong	Toronto	Mexico	Havana
later	Macau Singapore Hong Kong Toronto Mexico Havana	Macau Toronto	Macau Toronto Havana Mexico Singapore	Macau	Macau	Macau Mexico
next	Hong Kong		Singapore			
duration		1	1	3	12	1

8.3.6 Arrivals

A step further from deciding on the durations of stay in different places is to allocate the actual timing: what is the latest time the traveller should arrive in each place. We assume at this point that the duration is already decided, so timing involves setting only the arrival time, the intended end time being calculated accordingly. Formally, the function **arrive** returns a map from places to time instances.

value
  arrive: Journey → (Place $\overrightarrow{m}$ Time)

We have three axioms to constrain this function. The first decides what places can be included in the domain of the **arrive** map – it includes all the places the traveller wants to visit which have their period of stay determined. Formally, the domain of **arrive(j)** must be contained in the domain of duration(j). However, we treat the home location in a special way. Although we decided not to allocate any duration to this place, when dealing with a return journey we may wish to assign an arrival time to the home location to represent the latest we wish to arrive home. The following axiom represents this constraint.

axiom
    ∀ j: Journey •
        dom arrive(j) ⊆ **dom** duration(j) ∪ {home(j)} ∧
        (home(j) ∈ **dom** arrive(j) ⇒ home(j) ∈ visit(j))

The second axiom deals with the impossibility of overlaps between visits in two consecutive places. Given a place p and its successor next(j)(p), both having their arrival times allocated, departure from p (obtained by adding the time of arrival and the duration of stay) and arrival in next(j)(p) must allow at least the minimum time for the journey (traveltime(p,next(j)(p))).

axiom
    ∀ j: Journey, p: Place •
        p ∈ **dom** next(j) ∧
        {p, next(j)(p)} ⊆ **dom** arrive(j) ⇒
        arrive(j)(next(j)(p)) − arrive(j)(p) ≥
            traveltime(p, next(j)(p)) + duration(j, p)

From the transitivity of later this constraint should extend to any sequence of places. Consider a function traveltime which for any pair (p_1, p_2) of places such that p_1 is visited before p_2 returns the minimum time needed to travel from p_1 to p_2 via the places decided by the travel plan. The function also accepts pairs of equal places, for which it has to return zero.

value
    traveltime: Journey → (Place × Place 〰 Duration)
axiom
    ∀ j: Journey •
        dom traveltime(j) =
          later(j) ∪ { (p, p) | p: Place • p ∈ visit(j)} ∧
        (∀ p: Place • p ∈ visit(j) ⇒ traveltime(j)(p, p) = 0)

The function is defined by two properties:

1. The delay must not be less than the minimum time to travel directly from p_1 to p_2 (irrespective of any travel plan).

    axiom
        ∀ j: Journey, p_1, p_2: Place •
          (p_1, p_2) ∈ later(j) ⇒
          traveltime(j)(p_1, p_2) ≥ traveltime(p_1, p_2)

2. If there is a place p which is visited after p_1 and before p_2, then the minimum travel time to get from p_1 to p_2 is greater than or equal to the sum of the travel times to get from p_1 to p and from p to p_2, plus the duration of stay in p (if that is decided).

axiom

$\forall$ j: Journey, p, p_1, p_2: Place •
$(p_1, p) \in$ later(j) $\wedge$ (p, p_2) $\in$ later(j) $\Rightarrow$
traveltime(j)(p_1, p_2) $\geq$
traveltime(j)(p_1, p) + traveltime(j)(p, p_2) + duration(j, p)

With this function defined, the following axiom expresses that there is enough time between arrival times to places which may or may not be visited consecutively, allowing for the minimum travel times and durations of visits. Formally, given two places p_1 and p_2 such that p_2 must be visited after p_1 and both have their arrival times decided, the time elapsing between arrivals to p_1 and p_2 is greater than or equal to the minimum time to travel from p_1 to p_2 plus the duration of stay in p_1.

axiom

$\forall$ j: Journey, p_1, p_2: Place •
$p_1 \neq p_2$ $\wedge$
$\{p_1, p_2\} \subseteq$ **dom** arrive(j) $\wedge$ (p_1, p_2) $\in$ later(j) $\Rightarrow$
arrive(j)(p_2) $-$ arrive(j)(p_1) $\geq$ traveltime(j)(p_1, p_2) + duration(j, p_1)

Example 8.3.6. Suppose the traveller from Macau has two timing constraints on this journey. The first constraint is to arrive in Toronto in time for the conference, which starts on 6/12/2000. Given the minimum duration of stay in Toronto (three days), he wants to leave Toronto on 9/12/2000 at the earliest, while arriving on 6/12/2000 at the latest. The second constraint is to arrive back in Macau no later than 23/12/2000. Is it a feasible plan?

Suppose all journeys between places can be achieved within one day. We have to apply special care to allow enough timing between the stays in Toronto and Macau. From the ordering decided by the travel plan there are two possibilities: either we travel directly from Toronto to Macau or we first visit Havana, Mexico and then return to Macau. The first option will take us only four days, three days of conference in Toronto plus one day for travel back to Macau, arriving the earliest on 11/12/2000, well before the 23/12/2000 deadline. The second option: three days in Toronto; one day of journey to Havana and another for interviews; one day to Mexico; 12 days of the course; one day for returning to Macau. This gives 19 days altogether. The second option shows that setting those two dates only 16 days apart is insufficient, at least to maintain both options. Instead, we decide at this stage that the return time to Macau is 31/12/2000.

home	Macau					
visit	Macau	Singapore	Hong Kong	Toronto	Mexico	Havana
later	Macau Singapore Hong Kong Toronto Mexico Havana	Macau Toronto	Macau Toronto Havana Mexico Singapore	Macau	Macau	Macau Mexico
next	Hong Kong		Singapore			
duration		1	1	3	12	1
time	31/12/2000			6/12/2000		

8.4 Correctness: Relating Travel Plans

The model in Section 8.3 allows the expression of travel decisions at various levels of abstraction. A basis for an engineering approach to travel planning is that such plans be related in a formal way. We need to define formally what it means for a concrete plan to implement an abstract plan. The purpose of this section is to provide such a definition.

Consider two travel plans, j_1 and j_2. When is it possible to say that j_2 implements j_1? We formalise this property using the function correct, defined using the list of properties below.

value
    correct: Journey × Journey → **Bool**
    correct(j_1, j_2) ≡ ...

1. The homes for j_1 and j_2 are the same.

    home(j_1) = home(j_2)

2. All places visited according to j_1 are also visited according to j_2, but j_2 may introduce more places to visit. In particular, if j_1 is a one-way journey then j_2 can be a one-way or a return journey, but if j_1 is a return journey then j_2 must also be a return journey.

    visit(j_1) ⊆ visit(j_2)

3. The ordering decided by j_1 is maintained by j_2: if j_1 decides that p_1 is to be visited before p_2 then j_2 makes the same decision. However, j_2 may introduce more order constraints than j_1.

    later(j_1) ⊆ later(j_2)

4. Decisions made by j_1 to visit two places consecutively are maintained by j_2. However, j_2 may assign the immediate successors of more places. So j_2 is more deterministic than j_1.

∀ p: Place •
    p ∈ **dom** next(j_1) ⇒
    p ∈ **dom** next(j_2) ∧ next(j_1)(p) = next(j_2)(p)

5. If j_1 assigns a duration to p then j_2 does as well. The value decided by j_2 must be greater than or equal to the value decided by j_1. So we can extend the duration, therefore delaying the departure, but we cannot reduce it. This is consistent with our interpretation of the **duration** value as the minimum period of stay. At the same time, j_2 may allocate duration to more places than j_1 does.

∀ p: Place •
    p ∈ **dom** duration(j_1) ⇒
    p ∈ **dom** duration(j_2) ∧ duration(j_1)(p) ≤ duration(j_2)(p)

6. If j_1 assigns the time of arrival to a place p then j_2 does as well. The arrival at p according to j_2 can be earlier than or equal to the arrival to p according to j_1. So not only can we extend the duration of stay, we can also advance the time of arrival. This is consistent with our interpretation of the **arrive** value as the latest time of arrival in a place. At the same time, j_2 may allocate a time of arrival to more places than j_1.

∀ p: Place •
    p ∈ **dom** arrive(j_1) ⇒
    p ∈ **dom** arrive(j_2) ∧ arrive(j_2)(p) ≤ arrive(j_1)(p)

There are clearly three ways we can define one travel plan to be more concrete than another one: by extending the journey with more places to visit; by adding more constraints on the ways those places are actually visited, the ordering of visits, duration and timing; and by extending the time of stay in different places, deciding to arrive earlier and/or depart later.

The definition above implies certain general properties of the correctness ordering. First, any travel plan is correct with respect to itself. Second, if j_2 is correct with respect to j_1 and j_3 is correct with respect to j_2, then j_3 is also correct with respect to j_1. In other words, correctness is transitive.

8.5 Development: Building Travel Plans

Development of a travel plan proceeds incrementally. It starts from the minimal plan which has the home location assigned but no places to visit. It then proceeds by gradually adding places to visit, constraints about the ordering of visits, minimum durations of stay in different places and the latest arrival times. As part of the development we can also advance arrival times and postpone departures. Each step means making the travel plan more concrete and complete. We assume such design decisions are made by well-defined operations which preserve correctness of a new travel plan with respect to an old plan. The purpose of this section is to define such operations. We conjecture but do not prove that each preserves correctness.

8.5.1 Empty Plan

Typically, the start point of the travel development is the empty plan which has the home location assigned but no places to visit. This plan is described by the function empty below. The function takes a place (to become a home location) as its argument and returns an empty journey. Formally:

value
    empty: Place $\rightarrow$ Journey
axiom
    $\forall$ p: Place • home(empty(p)) = p $\land$ visit(empty(p)) = {}

Example 8.5.1. The initial plan with Macau as home and an empty set of visits, as described in Example 8.3.1.

8.5.2 Adding Places

One of the basic operations done during development is to add new places to visit. We describe this operation using the function addplace, which takes a journey j and a place p as its arguments and returns a new journey j'. This new journey contains all places that j wants to visit plus p, under the precondition that p is not already present among the visited places.

However, by simply adding p to the set visit(j), the resulting journey may not be well-formed. We have to add the pair (home(j),p) to the later(j) relation, to make sure home(j) is visited before p. If j is a return journey, we also have to add (p,home(j)). Otherwise, if p=home(j), meaning we want to develop a one-way journey into a return journey, we also have to add all (q,home(j)) where q∈visit(j) to make sure that home(j) represents the final destination. The function is defined below.

value
    addplace: Journey $\times$ Place $\xrightarrow{\sim}$ Journey
    addplace(j, p) **as** j' **post**
        visit(j') = visit(j) $\cup$ {p} $\land$
        later(j') = later(j) $\cup$ {(home(j), p)} $\cup$
            if home(j) $\in$ visit(j) **then** {(p, home(j))}
            else if p $\neq$ home(j) **then** {}
                else { (q, home(j)) | q: Place • q $\in$ visit(j)} **end**
            end $\land$

home(j') = home(j) ∧ next(j') = next(j) ∧
duration(j') = duration(j) ∧ arrive(j') = arrive(j)
pre p ∉ visit(j)

We conjecture that given a travel plan j and a place p satisfying the precondition, the function `addplace` produces the plan `addplace(j,p)` which is correct with respect to j. We formulate this property as follows:

∀ j: Journey, p: Place •
  p ∉ visit(j) ⇒ correct(j, addplace(j, p))

We conjecture similar properties for the remaining operations in this section, without describing or formalising them explicitly.

Example 8.5.2. Suppose we want to add five cities to visit: Singapore, Hong Kong, Toronto, Mexico and Havana. We do this one-by-one, making sure that Macau is the start point of the journey. As the next step, we add Macau itself to the plan, developing a one-way journey into a return journey. We make sure that Macau is visited before as well as after any other place.

home	Macau					
visit	Macau	Singapore	Hong Kong	Toronto	Mexico	Havana
later	Macau Singapore Hong Kong Toronto Mexico Havana	Macau	Macau	Macau	Macau	Macau

8.5.3 Adding Order Constraints

When a new place is added into the travel plan, its relative ordering with respect to other places is not constrained. The exception to this is the home location, as the new place is automatically constrained to be visited after and perhaps before it. So, adding more order constraints is crucial to travel development as it leads to making the journey more concrete, getting closer to determining in what sequence the places should be visited.

The function `addlater` introduces a dependency between two places p_1 and p_2 in the travel plan, that p_1 must be visited before p_2. As the function has to ensure that the resulting relation is still transitive, it adds to the relation `later(j)` the set of pairs (p_0, p_3) such that p_0 is equal to p_1 or is visited before p_1 and p_3 is equal to p_2 or is visited after p_2. Other attributes remain unchanged. Here is the definition:

value
  addlater: Journey × Place × Place $\overset{\sim}{\to}$ Journey
  addlater(j, p_1, p_2) **as** j' **post**

$$later(j') = later(j) \cup$$
$$\{ (p_0, p_3) \mid p_0, p_3: Place \cdot$$
$$(p_0 = p_1 \vee (p_0, p_1) \in later(j)) \wedge (p_3 = p_2 \vee (p_2, p_3) \in later(j))$$
$$\} \wedge$$
$$home(j') = home(j) \wedge$$
$$visit(j') = visit(j) \wedge next(j') = next(j) \wedge$$
$$duration(j') = duration(j) \wedge arrive(j') = arrive(j)$$
pre $\{p_1, p_2\} \subseteq visit(j) \wedge$
$$(p_1, p_2) \notin later(j) \wedge$$
$$no\_cycle(j, p_1, p_2) \wedge enough\_time(j, p_1, p_2)$$

The function has a number of preconditions to make sure the resulting journey is well formed and correct with respect to the initial journey:

1. Both places are to be visited during journey, $\{p_1, p_2\} \subseteq$ `visit(j)`, but they are not in the `later` relation, $(p_1, p_2) \notin$ `later(j)`.

2. For any place p_0 equal to p_1 or visited before p_1 and p_3 equal to p_2 or visited after p_2, it is not the case that p_3 is visited before p_0: $(p_3, p_0) \notin$ `later(j)`. This is to avoid introducing circularity into `later`.

value
>   no_cycle: Journey × Place × Place → **Bool**
>   no_cycle(j, p_1, p_2) ≡
>   (∀ p_0, p_3: Place •
>   (p_0 = p_1 ∨ (p_0, p_1) ∈ later(j)) ∧
>   (p_3 = p_2 ∨ (p_2, p_3) ∈ later(j))
>   ⇒ (p_3, p_0) ∉ later(j)
>   )

3. For any place p_0 to be visited before p_1 and p_3 to be visited after p_2, if both have arrival times, there must be enough time for all intermediate visits and travel. This includes the durations of stay in p_0, p_1 (if decided) and p_2 (if decided) and the travel times between p_0 and p_1, p_1 and p_2, and p_2 and p_3. The function **enough_time** is defined as follows:

value
>   enough_time: Journey × Place × Place → **Bool**
>   enough_time(j, p_1, p_2) ≡
>   (∀ p_0, p_3: Place •
>   (p_0 = p_1 ∨ (p_0, p_1) ∈ later(j)) ∧
>   (p_3 = p_2 ∨ (p_2, p_3) ∈ later(j)) ∧
>   {p_0, p_3} ⊆ **dom** arrive(j)
>   ⇒ arrive(j)(p_3) − arrive(j)(p_0) ≥
>   duration(j, p_0) + duration(j, p_1) + duration(j, p_2) +
>   traveltime(j)(p_0, p_1) + traveltime(j)(p_1, p_2) +
>   traveltime(j)(p_2, p_3)
>   )

Example 8.5.3. We add the constraint that the traveller must visit Toronto after Singapore (to discuss presentation at the conference with his co-author) and Mexico after Havana (to interview students for the course). Moreover, he must obtain visas in Hong Kong in order to enter Canada and Cuba. So we add two more constraints: visit Toronto and Havana after Hong Kong. He must also visit Mexico after Hong Kong, as Mexico is visited after Havana. The result is as described in Example 8.3.3.

8.5.4 Choosing Successors

The ordering may not determine which particular place should be visited immediately after a given one. One aspect of making the plan more concrete is to make such decisions, to choose which place the traveller should visit next. The function **choosenext** takes two places p_1 and p_2 and selects p_2 to be visited immediately after p_1. The precondition requires that: p_2 is to be visited after p_1; no immediate successor of p_1 exists; and p_2 is not an immediate successor of any visited place.

value
    choosenext: Journey $\times$ Place $\times$ Place $\overset{\sim}{\to}$ Journey
    choosenext(j, p_1, p_2) **as** j' **post**
        next(j') = next(j) $\cup$ [$p_1 \mapsto p_2$] $\wedge$
        home(j') = home(j) $\wedge$
        visit(j') = visit(j) $\wedge$ later(j') = later(j) $\wedge$
        duration(j') = duration(j) $\wedge$ arrive(j') = arrive(j)
        pre (p_1,p_2) $\in$ later(j) $\wedge$
            $p_1 \notin$ **dom** next(j) $\wedge$ $p_2 \notin$ **rng** next(j)

Example 8.5.4. Consider the traveller from Macau. According to the previous travel plan, from Macau he can only proceed directly to Singapore or Hong Kong. At this point we make a decision that this place is going to be Hong Kong, taken for its proximity (say). Then clearly he must next proceed to Singapore. The result is as described in Example 8.3.4.

8.5.5 Adding Durations

Another decision is how long the traveller is going to stay in different places. This duration of stay is added by the function **addduration**. The function takes a journey j, a place p and a duration d as its arguments, and returns a new journey j'. In this new journey p is assigned d in the **duration** map. The rest of the map and other attributes of j remain unchanged. The function takes a number of preconditions: p is present in the **visit** set but not equal to **home**; the duration of p is undefined; and d is greater than zero but small enough to maintain the existing timing constraints.

value
  addduration: Journey × Place × Duration $\xrightarrow{\sim}$ Journey
  addduration(j,p,d) **as** j' **post**
    duration(j') = duration(j) ∪ [p ↦ d] ∧
    home(j') = home(j) ∧ visit(j') = visit(j) ∧
    later(j') = later(j) ∧ next(j') = next(j) ∧
    arrive(j') = arrive(j)
  pre p ∈ visit(j) ∧ p ≠ home(j) ∧
    p ∉ **dom** duration(j) ∧ d > 0 ∧ enough_time(j, p, d)

Consider two places p_1 and p_2 such that p_1 is either equal to p or visited before p, p_2 is either equal to p or visited after p, and the arrivals for p_1 and p_2 are decided in the plan. Then the precondition must guarantee enough time between the departure from p_1 and the arrival to p_2 to accommodate: the duration of stay at p_1, the travel time from p_1 to p, the stay at p for the time d, and the travel time from p to p_2. The assumption is expressed by the auxiliary function **enough_time**:

value
  enough_time: Journey × Place × Duration → **Bool**
  enough_time(j, p, d) ≡
    (∀ p_1, p_2: Place •
      (p_1 = p ∨ (p_1, p) ∈ later(j)) ∧
      (p_2 = p ∨ (p, p_2) ∈ later(j)) ∧
      {p_1, p_2} ⊆ **dom** arrive(j) ⇒
      arrive(j)(p_2) − arrive(j)(p_1) ≥
      duration(j, p_1) + traveltime(j)(p_1, p) + d + traveltime(j)(p, p_2)
)

Example 8.5.5. With the places to be visited defined and their ordering partly decided, we are in a position to assign durations. In particular, we decide that the traveller will stay a minimum of three days in Toronto (to attend the conference), one day in Hong Kong (to collect visas to Canada and Cuba), one day in Singapore (to discuss with his co-author), one day in Havana (to interview students) and 12 days in Mexico (to teach a course). As no timing has yet been introduced into the plan, we only need to check that all five places are defined and do not yet have durations. The result is as described in Example 8.3.5.

8.5.6 Adding Arrivals

Once the plan includes the places to visit, their relative ordering and durations of stay, it is time to decide when the traveller should arrive at those places. The operation to add the time of arrival is carried out by the function `addarrival`. It takes a travel plan j, a place p and the time t as its arguments, and modifies j to include t as the time of arrival at p.

value
    addarrival: Journey × Place × Time $\xrightarrow{\sim}$ Journey
    addarrival(j, p, t) **as** j' **post**
    arrive(j') = arrive(j) ∪ [p ↦ t] ∧
    home(j') = home(j) ∧
    visit(j') = visit(j) ∧ later(j') = later(j) ∧
    next(j') = next(j) ∧ duration(j') = duration(j)
    pre p ∉ **dom** arrive(j) ∧
        (p ∈ **dom** duration(j) ∨ p ∈ visit(j) ∧ p = home(j)) ∧
        enough_before(j, p, t) ∧ enough_after(j, p, t)

The function has a number of preconditions:

1. The time of arrival at p is not already decided in j.
2. The duration of stay in p is already decided or p is the home location (we want to determine the arrival time at the final destination).
3. For any place p' which is visited before p and has its arrival time fixed, there is enough time between arrivals at p' and p (t) to accommodate the stay in p' and the travel time from p' to p. This assumption is captured by the function enough_before:

value
    enough_before: Journey × Place × Time → **Bool**
    enough_before(j, p, t) ≡
        (∀ p': Place •
            p' ∈ **dom** arrive(j) ∧ (p', p) ∈ later(j) ⇒
            t − arrive(j)(p') ≥ duration(j, p') + traveltime(j)(p', p)
)

4. For any place p'' which is visited after p and has its arrival time fixed, there is enough time between arrivals at p (t) and p'' to accommodate the stay in p and the travel time from p to p''. This assumption is captured by the function enough_after:

value
    enough_after: Journey × Place × Time → **Bool**
    enough_after(j, p, t) ≡
        (∀ p'': Place •
            p'' ∈ **dom** arrive(j) ∧ (p, p'') ∈ later(j) ⇒
            arrive(j)(p'') − t ≥
            duration(j, p) + traveltime(j)(p, p'')
)

Example 8.5.6. There is only one date which is fixed for the journey – the start time of the conference in Toronto, 6/12/2000. We add this date of arrival to the plan. We then proceed to add another date, the arrival date at the final destination. Suppose the traveller wishes to be back in Macau on 23/12/2000. Is it possible to add this date, satisfying all preconditions? Following the same analysis as in Example 8.3.6, we show this is not the case. With 16 days between those two dates, there is not enough time for both alternatives allowed by the journey: from Toronto back to Macau or from Toronto to Havana, Mexico and then Macau. While the former requires only four days, the latter requires 19 days, assuming one day of travel between any two places. As a result, we decide to postpone the arrival until 31/12/2000. Example 8.3.6 describes the plan.

8.5.7 Extending Durations

As part of the development we make it possible to increase the period of stay in different places. This way the initial duration represents the minimum time of stay. We represent this operation as the function extendduration. This function modifies a given travel plan by increasing the duration of stay in a place p. The place must have its duration already assigned. The added duration must not violate the timing constraints already in the plan: for any places p_1 and p_2, if p_1 happens before p and p_2 after p and both have their arrival times decided, then the added duration of stay in p must fit within the allowed time limits. The function is defined below.

value
    extendduration: Journey × Place × Duration $\overset{\sim}{\to}$ Journey
    extendduration(j, p, d) **as** j′ **post**
        duration(j′) = duration(j) † [p $\mapsto$ duration(j)(p) + d] ∧
        home(j′) = home(j) ∧
        visit(j′) = visit(j) ∧ later(j′) = later(j) ∧
        next(j′) = next(j) ∧ arrive(j′) = arrive(j)
        pre p ∈ **dom** duration(j) ∧
            (∀ p_1, p_2: Place •
                (p_1 = p ∨ (p_1, p) ∈ later(j)) ∧
                (p_2 = p ∨ (p, p_2) ∈ later(j)) ∧
                {p_1, p_2} ⊆ **dom** arrive(j)
                ⇒ arrive(j)(p_2) − arrive(j)(p_1) ≥
                    duration(j, p_1) + traveltime(j)(p_1, p) +
                    duration(j, p) + d + traveltime(j)(p, p_2)
)

Example 8.5.7. Consider the traveller from Macau. With 24 days from the arrival at Toronto to returning to Macau and 19 allocated, we can afford to spend more time in one of the places. We choose Havana, increasing the duration from one to three days.

home	Macau					
visit	Macau	Singapore	Hong Kong	Toronto	Mexico	Havana
later	Macau Singapore Hong Kong Toronto Mexico Havana	Macau Toronto	Macau Toronto Havana Mexico Singapore	Macau	Macau	Macau Mexico
next	Hong Kong		Singapore			
duration		1	1	3	12	3
time	31/12/2000			6/12/2000		

8.5.8 Advancing Arrivals

Development can also advance the arrival times at different places. The original arrival time serves as the latest time the traveller wishes to arrive in a place, and can be advanced later. We represent this operation as the function advancearrival which modifies a travel plan by changing the time of arrival at a place. This new time must be earlier than the time already in the travel plan. The function is defined below.

value

    advancearrival: Journey $\times$ Place $\times$ Time $\overset{\sim}{\rightarrow}$ Journey

    advancearrival(j, p, t) **as** j' **post**

      arrive(j') = arrive(j) † [p ↦ t] $\wedge$

      home(j') = home(j) $\wedge$

      visit(j') = visit(j) $\wedge$ later(j') = later(j) $\wedge$

      next(j') = next(j) $\wedge$ duration(j') = duration(j)

      pre p $\in$ **dom** arrive(j) $\wedge$

        t $\leq$ arrive(j)(p) $\wedge$

        enough_before(j, p, t) $\wedge$

        enough_after(j, p, t)

As before, the function must not violate any existing timing constraints, in particular for any places p' to be visited before p and p'' to be visited after p that have their arrival times assigned. To express such preconditions we use the functions enough_before and enough_after, as defined before.

Example 8.5.8. Consider the traveller from Macau. With 24 days from the arrival at Toronto to returning to Macau and 21 allocated (in the worst case), we can afford to advance the return time to Macau by three days, from 31/12/2000 to 28/12/2000. The result is described below.

home	Macau					
visit	Macau	Singapore	Hong Kong	Toronto	Mexico	Havana
later	Macau Singapore Hong Kong Toronto Mexico Havana	Macau Toronto	Macau Toronto Havana Mexico Singapore	Macau	Macau	Macau Mexico
next	Hong Kong		Singapore			
duration		1	1	3	12	3
time	28/12/2000			6/12/2000		

8.6 Model-Based Travel Assistant

We present in this section the ideas for implementation of a model-based travel assistant. The assistant is a software system that helps to carry out development of travel plans according to the methodology described here. We envision the assistant should carry out the following functions:

1. Creating and modifying travel plans. According to this function, the travel assistant acts much like a syntax-directed editor. It helps to conveniently write down and change the components of the travel plan.
2. Checking if a given travel plan is well-formed according to the rules defined in Section 8.3, for instance whether every place in later is among the places the traveller wants to visit, whether every successor maintains an order constraint, etc. This function could be activated in two ways: on-request, to check if the plan is well-formed, or automatically, to prohibit any changes in the editor that would violate well-formedness.
3. Checking if modifications to the travel plan maintain correctness; if the modified plan is correct with respect to the initial plan (Section 8.4). This is an extension of the function for checking well-formedness. It could also be performed automatically or on-request.
4. Keeping track of the travel development, from initial to final stage. Allowing one to move back and forth along the development history, to undo and redo design decisions.

We plan to implement this software using the emacs editor and its programming language, emacs LISP. This would involve defining a special mode for travel planning. The mode would define the format of the buffer containing a travel description, with proper highlights and colours applied to the fields in this buffer. This mode would also define the operations the user can perform, to make the changes to the buffer (according to one of the operations in Section 8.5), to check those changes, undo and redo them, etc.

The software should serve as a research prototype. In particular, we would like to investigate what features should be added to the model according to practical needs. Should features be added directly, or is it possible to express them with existing concepts? Should we extend or restrict the rules of development? Is correctness defined adequately or is it too rigid? We hope to be able to answer those and other questions using the travel assistant.

8.7 Conclusions

The main technical content of this chapter is to present a model-based approach to travel planning. The approach consists of three parts: a model for travel planning, correctness between travel plans and systematic development from abstract toward concrete plans. In particular, our models represent all levels of travel plans, from abstract requirements to concrete itineraries. They are based on six concepts: (1) places to be visited; (2) the place where journey starts and perhaps ends; (3) order constraints, deciding when one place should be visited before another; (4) a relation deciding which particular place should be visited after a given one; (5) minimum duration of stay in different places; and (6) the latest arrival time. We defined what it means for one travel plan (concrete) to be correct with respect to another (abstract). We also defined a development approach which starts from the initial empty travel plan and proceeds by introducing more places, order constraints, successors, durations and arrival times. During development, we may also increase the durations and advance arrivals. We defined each operation as a function with pre- and post-conditions. The functions are designed to make sure the resulting travel plan is correct with respect to the initial journey, provided its arguments satisfy the precondition. This fact is conjectured but not proven. We illustrated this approach with a simple example and presented an initial idea of an automated travel assistant.

With the massive growth of the internet and related technology, and the necessity to use them in the tourism sector, the need for travel planning applications is a major concern for the travellers and people involved with the travel and tourism business. The International Federation of Information Technology and Tourism (IFITT) is working on the promotion of the international discussion about tourism-related IT. The federation has identified key issues for tourism and IT, with application- and business-oriented points of view [149]. The Open Travel Alliance (OTA) [82] is working on the strategies for the travel industry to take advantage of the internet. OTA released in particular the specification of messages for communicating customer profiles based on XML [65]. The specifications include mandatory requirements and recommendations for the format of messages, covering issues like security and privacy, travel business content, and administrative exchanges. The European Project called Tourism Toward the Information Society is working to increase the productivity of tourism professionals and to improve the satisfaction of tourists through the use of advanced technologies (http://tourist.madinfo.pt/). IBM's Travel and Transport solution presents the idea of tools to support travel applications (www.ibm.com/solutions).

[135] applies Constraint Satisfaction to retrieve relevant information from huge amounts of travel-related data on the internet. How to base travel planning on tourism information systems is discussed in [90]. The Foundation for Intelligent Physical Agents (FIPA) promotes the applications of agent technology in various domains. In particular, [16] shows the experience in developing personal travel applications. [132] demonstrates how to develop a travel application (The London Travel Demonstrator) in a collaborative virtual environment. [28] presents a formal model of airline operations, related to future demand forecasting and frequent flyer programs. [93] discusses how to use software agents in travel reservation systems. Most of the airlines are gearing up to provide customised services to their clients. Airlines like United, Lufthansa and Scandinavian present their own sites to give customised services to the clients. There are also integrated travel service providers like Traveldesk, Travelocity or Trip, but none of them supports the process of travel planning in the sense described in this chapter.

We would like to continue this work by implementing the travel assistant, based on the models presented here. We plan to base this software on the emacs editor and program the operations in emacs LISP. This should help to validate the model with some real-life examples, to see if the models should be extended with some new features, e.g. the time difference between different places. We also envision other possible directions: formally proving that all operations described in the development section are sound; introducing travel resources to decide feasibility of the design decisions; and generating queries to check availability of the resources in support of design decisions. The travel assistant could generate such queries as XML documents [65], to be exchanged between client applications and travel resource providers.

Background Information

This chapter is based on work [130] done by Nitesh Shrestha, originally from Kathmandu University, Nepal, currently a PhD student at Fraunhofer-IPSI, Darmstadt, Germany, and Tomasz Janowski.

9. Proving Safety of Authentication Protocols

9.1 Introduction

Authentication protocols are vital to the internet. When we decide to buy something from an on-line supplier, they ask for our credit card details, and we encrypt these and send them back, how do we know they are going to the right place, that they are safe from other people reading them? Authentication protocols are the mechanisms used for checking, authenticating, that the agent we think we are connected to is actually the agent we think it is, and the only agent able to decrypt what we send.

There are various approaches to proving the safety of authentication protocols, including special belief logics like BAN [17], model checking [122, 92], and theorem proving. Most theorem proving and model checking has been based on trace histories [113, 18], in particular using CSP and its trace model [38].

In this chapter we demonstrate that a simpler approach based on sets of events can suffice to prove safety properties of authentication protocols. Sets have the advantage over sequences that they carry less information. They therefore reduce the risk of unwarranted assumptions being included. They are also likely to produce simpler proofs precisely because there is less information and hence perhaps fewer cases to consider. Paulson [113] remarks that "Making the model more detailed makes reasoning harder and, eventually, infeasible." Set induction also tends to be simpler than list induction, though this advantage may disappear with good proof tool support.

We present proofs of the Needham-Schroeder (N-S) protocol and of the Secure Sockets Layer (SSL) protocol widely used on the internet. The approach and some of the theory developed is general and could be used for other protocols. The specifications were proved with the RAISE justification editor [58].

The remainder of this chapter is organised as follows. Section 9.2 informally introduces the N-S protocol. Section 9.3 presents the formal specification of the protocol, including sub-sections 9.3.1 listing our assumptions, 9.3.2 defining the rules of the protocol, 9.3.3 specifying what we mean for the protocol to be safe, 9.3.4 outlining the proof of safety, and 9.3.5 discussing validity. Section 9.4 sketches the SSL protocol and its proof. Section 9.5 states the principles followed here that we believe appropriate for proving such protocols.

Section 9.6 makes comparisons with other work and draws some conclusions. The full details are in the UNU/IIST report [57].

9.2 The Needham-Schroeder Protocol

The N-S protocol is an example of an authentication protocol. The aim of such a protocol is to allow agents (users) to establish encrypted and hence private connections between each other over a communication medium which may allow eavesdropping, interception, alteration, etc. of messages. So when agent A says to agent B "Can we communicate?", and gets a reply, agent A needs to authenticate that the reply does indeed come from B. The N-S protocol is a symmetric protocol that also allows agent B to authenticate that it is A that it is in communication with.

The protocol is based on *keys* which are used to "lock" (encrypt) and "unlock" (decrypt) messages. Each key comes as a pair, a *public* key and a *private* one. These are such that only the private key can decrypt messages encrypted with the public key. As well as having an identifier, each agent is assigned a pair of keys, and the public one only is available to other agents. The idea is that if I want to send a message to agent A, I encrypt it with A's public key. This should ensure that only A can read it. If I put in this message something "secret", that only I know, and it comes back to me, I can feel confident that it is A that I am talking to, because no other agent could have read my message and discovered the secret. Secrets are commonly called "nonces", and are random numbers sufficiently large for the chance of them being guessed by another agent or being used twice to be vanishingly small.

In practice keys are not constant. If you go on using a public key for long enough then there is a chance someone will be able to discover the corresponding private key. We do not deal here with the part of the full protocol devoted to the assignment of public keys. We assume that public keys are already distributed. Neither do we consider the problem of old keys: we assume keys are sufficiently new for only the owner of a public key to be able to decrypt messages encrypted with that key. In other words, we consider only a session of limited duration in time.

The protocol, in the corrected form of Lowe [92], is illustrated in Figure 9.1.

Agent A creates a nonce Na and sends it and A's identity to agent B, in a message encrypted with B's public key, Kb. The notation "{M}K" is conventional for information M encrypted with key K. B responds with a message containing Na, a new nonce Nb, and (in the corrected version) B's identity, encrypted with A's public key, Ka. A responds with Nb encrypted with Kb. Only B should be able to read the first message, and only A the second. When A receives the second it can check that its nonce Na is correctly returned, so if only B could read it, the second message must come from B.

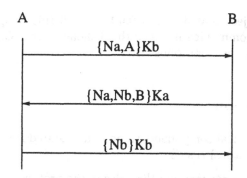

Fig. 9.1. The (corrected) Needham-Schroeder protocol.

Similarly B concludes from the third message that it must be in contact with A.

This informal analysis does not explain why B needs to include its identity in the second message. Lowe [92] showed that without it, if A sent the first message to an agent C, it was possible for C to successfully impersonate A in communicating with another honest agent (see Figure 9.2). A starts communicating with C, sending a nonce Na. C reads this and sends it on to B (so C is impersonating A). B replies, supposedly to A. C cannot decrypt B's message, but it can forward it to A. A thinks this message comes from C, because it contains the nonce Na it sent to C, and so thinks that Nb is C's nonce, and sends it back. Now C can read a message containing the nonce Nb that B thinks is known only to A. C completes the protocol with B, and has successfully impersonated A.

If, as Lowe suggested, the identity of the sender is included in the second message, then A can discover it has a message containing B's identity and a nonce it sent to C, and the attack fails.

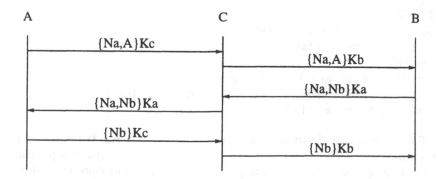

Fig. 9.2. Lowe's attack.

One might object that it is A's fault that all this happened: it should not have started communicating with the dishonest agent C. But it is B, the innocent party, who is compromised.

9.3 Formalisation

There are three critical components to be clearly stated if we wish to show a communication protocol is safe:

1. What honest agents may do: the rules of the protocol.
2. What dishonest agents can do.
3. What the required safety property is.

The proof that the safety property always holds is then inductive: if honest agents obey the rules, and dishonest agents do their worst, then from any safe state only other safe states can be achieved.

We need to model a state. We would like this model to be as simple as possible, to make the proofs tractable and to make our assumptions as clear as possible. An obviously necessary component of the state is the messages that have been sent. Typically, histories or traces (i.e. lists) of triples involving message, sender, and (intended) receiver are used. We find this too rich a state, and would ideally like to have only the set of messages sent.

This turns out not to be sufficient for the N-S protocol. We need to record whether a message is "genuine", i.e. sent according to the rules, or not. See Section 9.3.1.

So our state is a set of pairs containing message plus genuine or fake *status*:

type
  Nonce,
  Agent,
  Pub_key,
  State = (Message × Status)-**set**,
  Status == genuine | fake,
  Message ==
    $m_1(n_1 : \text{Nonce}, a_1 : \text{Agent}, k_1 : \text{Pub\_key})$ |
    $m_2(n2a : \text{Nonce}, n2b : \text{Nonce}, a_2 : \text{Agent}, k_2 : \text{Pub\_key})$ |
    $m_3(n_3 : \text{Nonce}, k_3 : \text{Pub\_key})$

Nonce, Agent, and Pub_key are abstract types or *sorts*. We make no assumptions about them. Status is just like an enumerated type in a programming language: its specification implies that genuine and fake are different and are the only members of the type.

This definition of Message as an RSL *variant type* implies that messages are equal only if they are both the same variant (e.g. both of variant m_1)

and have equal components. It also implies that the three different kinds of message are distinguishable: an m_1 cannot be confused with an m_2, etc. This "type correctness" of protocol messages is easy to ensure, as Paulson [113] points out, with the addition of a few extra bits of information. Failing to ensure it can be the cause of attacks, so the validity of such assumptions in an implementation needs to be carefully checked, and is again an argument for minimality in the specification: the fewer such assumptions that are built into the model the better.

The modelling of a message written in conventional notation as "{N,A}K" as a message m_1(N,A,K), which contains the encryption key K, looks rather odd. How can a message contain its own encryption key? But in fact it is precisely the condition needed to ensure that only the holder of the corresponding private key can decrypt the message. That is, uniqueness of reader is another way of saying that the reader is implicitly encoded in the message.

Next we assert that agents may be honest or not and that agents have unique public keys:

value
   honest : Agent $\rightarrow$ **Bool**,
   pub_key : Agent $\rightarrow$ Pub_key,
   owner : Pub_key $\rightarrow$ Agent
axiom [pub_key_inj]
   $\forall$ a : Agent • owner(pub_key(a)) $\equiv$ a

We also add useful functions to return the encryption key of a message, and to return the set of nonce(s) in a message.

9.3.1 Assumptions

We stated earlier how important it is to be clear (i.e. formal) about the assumptions that are made. We now state our assumptions and show how we specify them.

Nonces cannot be guessed. Nonces are very large random numbers, so the chance of anyone guessing one is regarded as negligible enough to be zero. And, clearly, if anyone could guess your secrets no protocol could be secure. We capture this notion in two steps. First, we specify that nonces have unique creators:

value
   created : Agent $\times$ Nonce $\rightarrow$ **Bool**
axiom
  [created_inj]
   $\forall$ a,b : Agent, n : Nonce •
     created(a, n) $\wedge$ created(b, n) $\Rightarrow$ a = b

As we see later, we then specify that an agent (even a dishonest one) can only send a nonce if the agent either created it or knows it by reading it in a message.

Encryption is safe. We assume every agent has a public key (stated earlier). We now add the predicate that states whether a nonce is known to an agent: it must be in a message that the agent **received**. We assume that an agent has received any message that was sent and encrypted with that agent's public key. (Since knowledge of nonces is what threatens the protocol, assuming that all messages are received, none get lost, is the safest assumption.) But only messages encrypted with the agent's public key are received: private keys are secure and unique. We noted above that this assumption is in practice regarded as true only for a limited amount of time.

value
received : Agent × Message × State → **Bool**
received(a, m, s) ≡ m ∈ s ∧ key(m) = pub_key(a),

known : Agent × Nonce × State → **Bool**
known(a, n, s) ≡
    (∃ m : Message • received(a, m, s) ∧ n ∈ nonces(m))

We have overloaded ∈: m ∈ s means the message is in the state with either **genuine** or **fake** status.

Nonces are fresh. It is a requirement of the protocol that the nonces Na and Nb are *fresh*, i.e. not used before. This is achieved in practice by using very large random numbers for nonces, and assuming that the same number will not be chosen twice. We specify it by saying that a **fresh** nonce is used, and a nonce is fresh if it has not appeared in any messages:

value
fresh : Nonce × State → **Bool**
fresh(n, s) ≡ (∀ m : Message • m ∈ s ⇒ n ∉ nonces(m))

Safety is about honest agents not being compromised. Our main function **safe** expresses the safety of the protocol:

value
safe : State → **Bool**
safe(s) ≡
    (∀ a, b : Agent, n : Nonce •
        honest(a) ∧ honest(b) ∧ shared(a, b, n, s) ⇒
            (∀ x : Agent • known(x, n, s) ⇒ x = a ∨ x = b))

which says that if two honest agents share a nonce, they are the only agents who know it. But we have to be careful about **shared**. It doesn't just mean known, else this could be broken by a dishonest agent C creating a nonce and sending it to A and B. We must understand "shared(A, B, Na, S)" as "A wants to share Na with B and has received confirmation." **shared** is defined by:

value
  shared : Agent × Agent × Nonce × State → **Bool**
  shared(a, b, na, s) ≡
    sent_genuine(m_1(na, a, pub_key(b)), s) ∧
    (∃ nb : Nonce • received(a, m_2(na, nb, b, pub_key(a)), s)) ∨
    (∃ nb : Nonce •
      received(a, m_1(nb, b, pub_key(a)), s) ∧
      sent_genuine(m_2(nb, na, a, pub_key(b)), s)) ∧
    received(a, m_3(na, pub_key(a)), s),

  sent_genuine : Message × State → **Bool**
  sent_genuine(m, s) ≡ (m, genuine) ∈ s

So a nonce Na is **shared** between agents A and B if either

- there is a genuine m_1 message from A to B containing Na and readable by B, and an appropriate m_2 message apparently from B received by A, or
- there is an m_1 message apparently from B to A, a genuine m_2 message from A to B containing Na, and the appropriate m_3 message back to A.

We see below that a message is **genuine** only if it follows the rules of the protocol (fresh and created by the agent also identified in the message). So safety is only concerned with the secrecy of nonces involved in the protocol.

It is tempting to think that the genuine/fake flag could be replaced by using, instead of **sent_genuine(m_1(na, a, pub_key(b)), s)**, the conjunction

  created(a, na) ∧ m_1(na, a, pub_key(b)) ∈ s

but this conjunction also holds in the situation that a sends na to dishonest c, and c impersonates a in sending the message to b. We do not want to make **shared(a, b, na, s)** true in this situation, since a is trying, albeit foolishly, to share na with c, not b.

An alternative to flagging the messages as genuine or fake would be to store as part of the state the set of nonces shared by honest agents. This is a slightly less abstract model as it requires an invariant that a nonce recorded as shared by an agent implies the presence of appropriate messages in the state. The approach would then be very close to that of Bolignano [14], which includes local states for the agents.

Dishonest agents can behave honestly. This is not an assumption, but is added here for clarity. We shall see that only messages created according to the rules may be associated with the genuine status. But if a dishonest agent chooses sometimes to follow the rules, then the corresponding message can be marked as genuine.

9.3.2 Rules of the Protocol

We are now ready to specify the key ideas in the method. We specify:

- that a well_formed state is either empty or the result of adding a message to an existing well_formed state
- that messages can only be added according to certain rules, defined in a function can_add

can_add specifies what honest and dishonest agents can do:

- genuine messages must conform to various rules; these are the rules of the protocol
- fake messages can only be sent by dishonest agents, and they are only limited by what they know or can create

value
    can_add : Agent × Message × Status × State → **Bool**
    can_add(a, m, st, s) ≡
      if st = fake **then**
        ∼ honest(a) ∧
        (∀ n : Nonce •
          n ∈ nonces(m) ⇒ created(a, n) ∨ known(a, n, s))
      else case m **of**
        m_1(na, a′, k) →
          a = a′ ∧ fresh(na, s) ∧ created(a, na),
        m_2(nb, na, a′, k) →
          a = a′ ∧
          received(a, m_1(nb, owner(k), pub_key(a)), s) ∧
          fresh(na, s) ∧ created(a, na),
        m_3(nb, k) →
          (∃ na : Nonce •
            sent_genuine(m_1(na, a, k), s) ∧
            received(a, m_2(na, nb, owner(k), pub_key(a)), s))
      end
    end

We see that honest agents may not send fake messages, but dishonest ones may send genuine ones. We also see that the only time the genuineness of a message is involved is when a genuine m_3 message is being sent: for the

m_3 message to be considered genuine the agent sending it must have sent a genuine m_1 message. There is no problem with this assumption because it is the same agent involved in the two messages.

well_formed is defined inductively in terms of can_add:

value
  well_formed : State → **Bool**
  well_formed(s) ≡
    s = {} ∨
    (∃ m : Message, st : Status, a : Agent •
     (m, st) ∈ s ∧
     well_formed(s \ {(m, st)}) ∧
     can_add(a, m, st, s \ {(m, st)}))

In other words, a state is well-formed if there is some possible history by which it was built from empty by a sequence of additions satisfying can_add. In general, a well-formed state may have many such possible histories.

We are now ready to specify what it means for our protocol to be safe. But first we raise a general concern about such a specification: we must be sure it is consistent, or else we could prove anything about it. We ensure consistency by using constructive definitions and checking individually that they are well defined. The only axioms are pub_key_inj and created_inj which cause no problems. The only recursive definition is well_formed, and the cardinality of the set forming the state provides a measure to show that the recursion is well-founded.

We might also check that it is possible for a non-empty state to be created. Technically this is a liveness property, but such a basic one should be considered! It is easy to check, for example, that two honest agents can complete the three steps of the protocol provided they can invent nonces. Paulson [113] calls such properties *possibility properties*.

9.3.3 Safety of the Protocol

A protocol is safe if a well_formed state is safe:

$$\forall s : State • well\_formed(s) \Rightarrow safe(s) \tag{1}$$

This property may be stated as part of an abstract specification which the protocol specification is shown to implement, or stated as a RAISE theorem about the protocol. The two formulations are equivalent: they give exactly the same proof obligation.

9.3.4 Proof of Safety

The following lemma genuine$_1$, together with a similar one genuine$_2$ for m_2 messages, allows the proof obligation (1) to be proved trivially:

[genuine$_1$]
 ∀ a, b : Agent, na : Nonce, s : State •
   honest(a) ∧ honest(b) ∧ well_formed(s) ∧
   (m$_1$(na, a, pub_key(b)), genuine) ∈ s ⇒
   (∀ x : Agent • known(x, na, s) ⇒ x = a ∨ x = b)

   genuine$_{1/2}$ require lemmas **secret**$_{1/2}$ that state that nonces sent by honest agents to other honest ones cannot become known to dishonest ones. Here is **secret**$_2$:

[secret$_2$]
∀ a, b : Agent, na, nb: Nonce, s : State •
 honest(a) ∧ honest(b) ∧ well_formed(s) ∧
 (m$_2$(na, nb, a, pub_key(b)), genuine) ∈ s ⇒
 (∀ x : Agent • known(x, nb, s) ⇒ honest(x))

   These four lemmas are proved by complete set induction. A number of other lemmas were also stated and proved. Many of these are trivial, but a few need the following can_add_lemma:

[can_add_lemma]
 ∀ m : Message, st : Status, s : State •
   well_formed(s) ∧ (m, st) ∈ s ⇒
   (∃ a : Agent, s' : State •
     s' ⊂ s ∧ can_add(a, m, st, s'))

can_add_lemma is not dependent on the actual definition of can_add, but only on the way that well_formed is defined in terms of can_add. It therefore holds for any protocol defined in this manner. It is useful in proving properties that are invariant under the addition of more messages. can_add_lemma is proved easily by complete set induction.

9.3.5 Validation

There is still perhaps a danger that our specification somehow assumes what we want to prove, and so really says nothing, is worthless. We can gain some more confidence in the specification by looking at attacks and seeing how the specification deals with them. In the case of the N-S protocol we are fortunate in having Lowe's attack [92] to consider.
   We can express his attack in terms of the state

{(m$_1$(Na, A, pub_key(C)), genuine),
 (m$_1$(Na, A, pub_key(B)), fake),
 (m$_2$(Na, Nb, B, pub_key(A)), genuine),
 (m$_3$(Nb, pub_key(C)), genuine),
 (m$_3$(Nb, pub_key(B)), fake)}

A sends Na to (dishonest) C. C impersonates A in sending Na to B. B responds according to the protocol with a new nonce Nb sent to A. A completes the protocol with C, who again impersonates A in completing with B. B has shared Nb with A, but C also knows it: the state is not safe.

We can try to prove a contradiction: that the state is well-formed, under the assumptions that A and B are honest, C is dishonest, Na and Nb are created by A and B respectively and are different. This proof fails: when we try to prove that A can send the first m_3 message we arrive at the goal "C = B", which must be false. This goal arises because A reads the m_2 message as coming from B but is trying to establish a connection with C.

Lowe's correction to the original protocol was to include the third argument of the m_2 message. If we change the specification, removing this third component (and the corresponding check in can_add), then the proof that the state is well-formed can be completed, and hence the specification cannot be correct.

We can also try to discover this problem in the proof. We did the proof of the lemma $secret_2$ for the changed specification. We failed to complete the proof in one case involving the following assumptions:

honest(A)
created(A, Na)
$(m_1(N, C, pub\_key(X)), genuine) \in S$
$(m_1(N, C, pub\_key(A)), ST) \in S$
$(m_2(N, Na, pub\_key(C)), genuine) \in S$
$(m_3(Na, pub\_key(X)), genuine) \in S$

The goal to be proved is honest(X). We can see that there are two possibilities. Either A and X are the same, and the proof is immediate, or we recognise Lowe's attack where X is dishonest (and the status ST is fake).

It is dangerous to draw conclusions from failure to prove something: we might merely have failed to find a sufficient proof approach. But the fact that we can verify the incorrectness of the protocol without Lowe's improvement does suggest that our specification is not merely assuming what it seeks to prove.

9.4 The SSL Protocol

This section is based on version 3.0 of the Secure Sockets Layer protocol described in [54].

There are many optional variants on the SSL protocol, and here we analyse only one particular (but standard) sequence of messages aimed at allowing a client to authenticate a server. This is the most common internet situation, when you want to check that the information you are about to send an internet server, such as your credit card details, can only be decrypted by the server that you intend it to be read by. So we will only consider a one-way authentication, though the protocol can be used for mutual authentication, and we will not be concerned with the details of agreeing the cryptographic algorithms or the establishing of session IDs (that allow resumption of sessions without re-authentication).

The message sequence is illustrated in Figure 9.3.

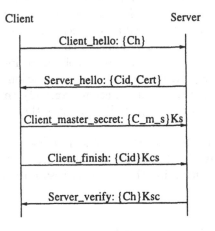

Fig. 9.3. The SSL protocol.

The client generates and sends a random challenge Ch in the clear (not encrypted). The server replies with a random connection identifier Cid and its certificate Cert, also sent in the clear. The client generates a nonce C_m_s called the "master secret" which it sends encrypted with the server's public key Ks. The client and server should now both be in possession of Ch, Cid and the master secret C_m_s. From these they can construct a symmetric pair of keys Kcs and Ksc which they use to encrypt and decrypt following messages. The idea is that if an intruder cannot discover the master secret it cannot create or discover the keys to decrypt following messages (or to encrypt false ones). The final Server_finish message is not shown above, as it is the Server_verify that we are concerned with.

The structure of the specification is very similar to N-S. The state is a set of messages: it turns out that we don't need the genuine/fake status component. Instead of just honest and dishonest agents we have clients (honest agents who play the role of client), servers (honest agents who play the role of server), and dishonest ones (who may do their worst). There is a can_add function that specifies that clients and servers follow the relevant rules and dishonest agents may exploit anything they know.

It is less clear how to set up the types for the SSL protocol. The initial challenge is described as a 28-byte random number [54] and the connection identifier as something "different from (and independent of) the challenge".

We decided to make these the same type, i.e. they can only be distinguished by value, not by structure. We also decided to make the master secret belong to the same type, although it is probably acceptable to make it different since it is described as having 48 bytes. (We heartily concur with Paulson [112] that specifiers of protocols should give abstract descriptions so it is clear what is assumed, and also what security properties are being claimed.)

The specification of safe says that if the rules of the protocol have been followed only the intended server can add the Server_verify message. It follows, if this message is received, that only the intended server could have sent it.

safe : State → **Bool**
safe(s) ≡
  (∀ ch, cid, ms : Random, a, b, c : Agent, k : Key •
    kind(a) = client ∧ c_hello(ch) ∈ s ∧
    created(a, ch) ∧ kind(b) = server ∧
    s_hello(cid, cert(b)) ∈ s ∧
    c_m_s(ms, pub_key(cert(b))) ∈ s ∧
    created(a, ms) ∧ ~ plain(ms, s) ∧
    can_add(c, s_ver(ch, k), s) ∧
    k = rd(make_keys(ms, ch, cid)) ⇒ c = b)

~ plain(ms, s) specifies that ms does not appear unencrypted in any message in s. rd extracts one of the symmetric keys, the one the client uses to read (and the server to write).

As with N-S, the protocol is safe if well-formedness implies safe (1). This is proved by complete set induction, but again needs some lemmas. The first lemma states that if a client follows the rules it will only send a master secret to a server, and is proved by case analysis:

[c_m_s_lemma$_1$]
  ∀ a, b : Agent, ms : Random, s : State •
  well_formed(s) ∧ kind(a) = client ∧
  created(a, ms) ∧ ~ plain(ms, s) ∧
  c_m_s(ms, pub_key(cert(b))) ∈ s ⇒ kind(b) = server

The second states that a master secret created by a client will only ever be readable by one server. This needs induction:

[c_m_s_lemma$_2$]
  ∀ a, b : Agent, ms : Random,
    cert : Certificate, s : State •
  well_formed(s) ∧ kind(a) = client ∧
  created(a, ms) ∧ ~ plain(ms, s) ∧
  kind(b) = server ∧
  c_m_s(ms, pub_key(cert(b))) ∈ s ∧
  c_m_s(ms, pub_key(cert)) ∈ s ⇒ cert = cert(b)

The similarities to the N-S proofs, and to the kinds of lemma required, are quite striking.

9.5 Principles

We have adopted a number of principles in making these specifications:

- There should be the minimum of state information. Such information can be used in the specification of the problem but may also bias the specification by making the actions of agents dependent on information to which they should have no access. A simple state also helps with the proof.
- The assumptions used must be stated clearly as well as precisely so that reviewers can check what is being assumed.
- The actions of dishonest agents (conventionally termed *intruders*) should be specified as weakly as possible. The fewer assumptions there are about intruders the smaller the risk of precluding an intruder tactic that might in practice be possible. We avoid identifying just one agent as the intruder and therefore allow the possibility of several (possibly collaborating) intruders. There is generally in the literature an assumption that one intruder can do what several can do, and an argument why one is sufficient is presented in [33]. It seems a reasonable assumption, but we have to be very careful about assumptions. Dolev et. al. [33] is often quoted as settling the issue that one is enough, but they make assumptions about message generation that are not true for either of our protocols.
- Safety of encryption-based protocols should be independent of the way in which messages are transmitted. The only safe assumption is that any agent can access a message, regardless of whether it is addressed to that agent. So including information about the addressees of messages may again lead to assumptions that are not fully justified; omitting them avoids any need for discussion about intruders "redirecting", "copying", and "forwarding" messages. Avoiding explicit modelling of communication also avoids discussion of issues like broadcast or point-to-point communication.
- The inclusion of information about the sender of a message, unless included in the message itself, should be avoided. In practice agents can only act on the contents of messages, and having information about the sender may lead to unwarranted assumptions.

The above principles lead to the idea that the only information in the "state" of the protocol should be the messages already sent.

We were unable to keep entirely to this principle. We found the need for the N-S protocol to include a status flag indicating whether the message was "genuine" or "fake". The only information we include in the message, apart from its contents, is the key it was encrypted with. We need this to define which agents might read it.

It seems perhaps natural to use a list (trace) of events for the state but we have shown that a set is sufficient. Sets have an immediate advantage over lists in terms of minimal assumptions: there is no distinction between single and multiple transmissions. Hence the possibility of the latter is automatically included. This method would not be possible if a protocol depended on agents receiving more than one identical message, when bags would be needed. However, dishonest agents can always copy messages (since copying does not require decryption) and so such a protocol seems unlikely to be of use.

A possible objection to sets rather than lists is that distinguishing messages by their order of arrival is not possible. But Paulson [113] points out that such a feature is a weakness; a dishonest agent can intercept and change the order of messages.

9.6 Related Work

Many authors have pointed out that belief logics like BAN are simple and give short abstract proofs but have proved unreliable in practice: Burrows et al. [17] using BAN did not notice the attack that Lowe [92] noticed and then confirmed by model checking. Model checking is good for finding effective attacks but necessarily requires limits in the state space which may not be justified. Bolignano [14, 15] suggests a combined approach using model checking plus proofs that the abstractions to tractable finite state spaces are justified, but he has hand proofs and only one initiator, one responder and one intruder. Lowe [92] offers similar arguments but also with hand proofs.

This work is closest to Paulson's inductive approach [112, 113] in which he uses traces of events which include the receiver and purported sender of messages. His work is considerably more extensive and he discusses other protocols such as Otway-Rees.

Paulson uses the Isabelle/HOL prover and has considerably automated his proofs. For N-S he proves the presence of the other agent and our secret$_1$ and secret$_2$ lemmas. These two lemmas are, as Butler [18] points out, the critical properties. But it seems useful to be assured that messages are not being read by third parties, rather than merely to be assured that any such eavesdroppers must be honest. The RAISE justification editor has no facility for replay and only a limited amount of simplification. The proofs have to be done interactively, and redoing them after changes to the specification is very tedious. This does, however, give the user rather finer control and better understanding of the precise position in a proof than an automated tool sometimes does.

We have tried rewriting the specifications in the specification language of PVS [111] and redone the proofs. The case analyses that arise in the proofs often depend on finding quite subtle contradictions in the assumptions and it would seem to require some skill by the user to find tactics to discharge all the cases automatically. But serious work in this area clearly depends on finding and employing such tactics.

Wagner and Schneier [146] concentrate on the cryptographic details of the SSL protocol.

This work was inspired by Michael Butler's work on N-S [18] in which agents are modelled using Abrial's B method [1], specifically AMN, extended with traces. Trying to mimic this work in RSL soon convinced us that it could be considerably simplified. In particular Butler seems to go further than necessary in explicitly modelling agents, including the (sole) intruder. Lack of theorems about traces in the B-tool he used forced him to do most of the proofs by hand.

The use of `created` in this chapter deserves more discussion. The usual approach is to axiomatise what the intruder can learn from previous messages. In the case of N-S in which keys are public this can be simplified to an intruder only being able to know nonces contained in messages it can decrypt. But the possibility of an intruder inventing a new nonce should also be included. We have to then axiomatise the idea that the probability of an intruder creating a nonce created by another agent is so small as to be regarded as impossible. Butler [18] allows his intruder to create a nonce unless an honest agent has invented it already. So the intruder's ability to invent nonces paradoxically decreases with the amount of information in the system. The use of `created` is a slightly stronger assumption but a more natural one.

The advantages of using sets of (minimal) events rather than traces was discussed in Section 9.5. Dutertre and Schneider [38] argue that Paulson's inductive approach [113] of only specifying how a trace may be extended, which is very similar to the approach in this chapter, "gives no control over when rules may apply". We would argue the exact opposite: there is danger in modelling too precisely what an agent might do, because of the danger of assuming that intruders will apply rules when they might very well break them. Dutertre and Schneider also rely on the construction of rank functions which, as they point out, need to be discovered for a particular protocol.

Background Information

Toshiyuki Tanaka, of the Graduate School of Information Science and Electrical Engineering, Kyushu University, Fukuoka, Japan, worked with Chris George on a more concrete description of the N-S protocol [133]. This chapter is based on the more abstract descriptions and proofs of the N-S and the SSL protocols done later [57].

10. Formalisation of Realm-Based Spatial Data Types

10.1 Introduction

This chapter describes work done as part of a project on Geographical Information Systems (GIS). It shows how an approach previously presented and understood in terms of an algorithm can be specified abstractly and presented systematically.

Computer mapping and spatial database management are the bases for GIS technology, which allows users to effectively organise, update and query mapped data. Technically speaking, all maps are composed of three basic features: points, lines and areas. In the GIS world, map features are most commonly represented by x, y coordinates. Points are identified by a single coordinate pair, line segments are identified as pairs of (different) points, lines as sequences of segments, and areas as sequences of points defining their borders as sequences of segments (see Figure 10.1). So the fundamental notions are points and segments. Good database management of spatial data of these two kinds contribute to the high quality of GIS.

For this purpose, in 1993, Güting and Schneider in [61] introduced a concept of a *realm*. A realm is a planar graph over a finite resolution grid consisting of a finite set of grid points and non-intersecting line segments. This structure is defined by users dynamically for the underlying spatial data types. The purpose of using the realm structure to define spatial data types is to ensure [61]:

- The geometric consistency of related spatial objects. For instance, two adjacent regions should have a common border.
- The closure properties for the computations with its spatial data types. For instance, the intersection of a region with a line (the part of the line lying within the region) should also be a realm-based line, and the common points of line segments should always lie on the grid.
- The adequacy of finite representations available in computers, thus avoiding the problem of numerical and consequently topological errors.

We will see later how these aims are achieved by using a realm to define the spatial data type. In their paper, Güting and Schneider emphasised the role of the numerical robustness and the topological correctness of realms, and gave an algorithmic description of them. They proposed algorithms as a

259

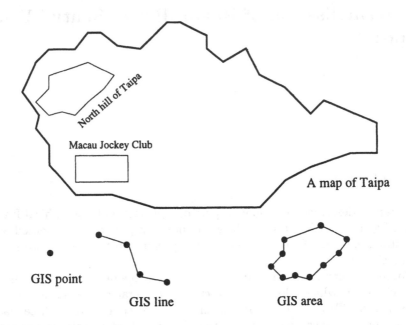

Fig. 10.1. GIS map and features.

semantics for some concepts in realms such as segment-envelope, and realm update. Such a semantics is operational and difficult to use. We need a more abstract semantics for realms which can be used to reason formally about their properties and the operations on them. Starting from an implementation of a realm by Güting and Schneider [61], we are looking for its meaning in mathematics. We try to work out "what we do" expressed at the abstract level rather than "how we do it" expressed at implementation level.

In this chapter we give a formal and abstract specification of realms in the RAISE specification language that can be used as an abstract semantics for them. With this formal specification, we can reason formally about the algorithmic description, to check numerical robustness and topological correctness, using RAISE tools. Concepts such as segment-envelope, and realm-insertion, are made intuitive and precise in this specification.

This work can also be the basis for work on map generalisation, for defining cartographic operators for map generalisation such as simplification, smoothing, classification, displacement, and collapse (see for example [106] for these concepts).

The primitives for building a realm are finite *grids*, grid points, and grid segments. In the next two sections we introduce these primitives and the relationships between them. We focus on the concept of a segment *envelope*, which is a base for defining extended realms. Starting from the aims mentioned earlier, we derive the requirement for a segment and a point in a realm. That requirement is formalised in Section 10.4 using segment envelopes. A realm of which the segments and points satisfy the requirement is called an *extended* realm. Therefore extended realms serve as a basis for defining spatial data types which can be managed and manipulated efficiently and easily. The data types which are often used in GIS (see, for example [9, 10]) are cycle, face, unit and block. These data types are specified in Section 10.5.

10.2 Basic Types: Grid, Grid Point, and Grid Segment

Given a non-zero natural number n, a *grid* is the set of points in a two-dimensional space with integer coordinates ranging from 0 to $n-1$. Let N be the set of integers from 0 to $n-1$ inclusive. A point in a two-dimensional space with the coordinates in N, a point on the grid, is called an *N-point* and is expressed as a record consisting of coordinates x and y in N. A segment in two-dimensional space with (different) *N*-points as its end points is called an *N-segment* and can be represented as a set of two *N*-points. Given two different *N*-points p and q, to define the segment with p and q as its end points, we use the function mk_seg(p,q).

type
   N = $\{|$ i : **Nat** • i < n $|\}$,
   N_point :: x : N   y : N,
   N_seg = $\{|$ s : N_point-**set** • **card** (s) = 2 $|\}$,
   ZeroOne = $\{|$ x : **Real** • $0.0 \leq x \wedge x \leq 1.0$ $|\}$
value
   n : **Nat** • n > 0,

   mk_seg : N_point × N_point $\overset{\sim}{\to}$ N_seg
   mk_seg(p, q) $\equiv$ {p, q} **pre** p ≠ q

We will commonly in discussion assume a conventional graphical presentation of a grid in which x coordinates increase horizontally left-to-right, and y coordinates increase vertically upwards. This allows us to use convenient terms like "vertical" rather than "having end points with equal x coordinates".

When defining a segment as a set of two *N*-points, we do not have any order between these two points, and hence do not enforce any direction for a segment. However, we can give the left-right order between end points of a segment as follows. If there is a vertical segment separating them, then the *left end point* is the one lying on the left of the segment, and the *right end point* is the other. When there is no such a vertical segment separating them, i.e. they form a vertical, the lower point is called left, and the other is called right. Let l and r be the functions returning left end point and right end point of a given segment respectively:

value
  l, r : N_seg → N_point
axiom
  [left_right_p]
    ∀ s : N_seg • (x(l(s)) < x(r(s)) ∨
      (x(l(s)) = x(r(s)) ∧ y(l(s)) < y(r(s)))) ∧
    s = {l(s), r(s)}

A point (x, y) where at least one of x and y is not an integer is called a *real-point*. Sometimes, for a segment, we have to determine the real-point that divides the segment by a given ratio α ($0 \leq \alpha \leq 1$), and for a real-point we have to determine its nearest N-point (grid point). For this purpose, we introduce the functions ψ, to generate the real-point, and **round**, to generate the nearest grid point.

In general, a real-point will have several closest grid points. For example, when a real-point is at the center of a grid square, there are four grid points equidistant from the real-point which are closer to it than any other grid points. By convention, in theses cases we always choose the one which is highest and rightmost among those candidates to be the nearest grid point.

value
  ψ : **Real** × N_seg → **Real** × **Real**
  $\psi(\alpha, s) \equiv$
    (α∗**real** x(l(s))+(1.0−α)∗**real** x(r(s))),
    α∗**real** y(l(s))+(1.0−α)∗**real** y(r(s))),

  round : **Real** × **Real** → N_point
axiom
  [round_p]
    ∀ x_1, y_1 : **Real** • round(x_1, y_1) **as** p
    post real x(p)−0.5 ≤ x_1 ∧ x_1 < **real** x(p)+0.5 ∧
      real y(p)−0.5 ≤ y_1 ∧ y_1 < **real** y(p)+0.5

The natural topological relationships between an N-point p and an N-segment s are: the point p may (or may not) be in or on the segment s.

- The predicate ps_on(p,s) holds exactly when p is on s.

    ps_on : N_point × N_seg → **Bool**
    ps_on(p,s) ≡ ∃α : ZeroOne • (**real** x(p), **real** y(p)) = $\psi(\alpha,s)$

When an N-point p is on the segment s, we say that p is a grid point of s.
- The predicate ps_in(p,s) holds exactly when ps_on(p,s) holds and p is not an end point of s.

    ps_in : N_point × N_seg → **Bool**
    ps_in(p,s) ≡ ps_on(p,s) ∧ p ∉ s

The possible relationships between two N-segments s and t are that s and t may meet, overlap, intersect, be collinear, be aligned, or be parallel. We introduce the following predicates to express these relationships.

- The predicate ss_meet(s,t) holds iff N-segments s and t have exactly one common point which is an end point of both of them.

    ss_meet : N_seg $\times$ N_seg $\rightarrow$ **Bool**
    ss_meet(s,t) $\equiv$ **card**(s $\cap$ t)=1

- The predicate ss_overlap(s,t) holds for N-segments s and t iff they have at least two common N-points.

    ss_overlap : N_seg $\times$ N_seg $\rightarrow$ **Bool**
    ss_overlap(s, t) $\equiv$
        card ({ p | p : N_point • ps_on(p, s) $\wedge$ ps_on(p, t) }) ≥ 2

- The predicate ss_collinear(s,t) holds iff s and t overlap with the same line segment.

    ss_collinear : N_seg $\times$ N_seg $\rightarrow$ **Bool**
    ss_collinear(s, t) $\equiv$
        ($\exists$ u : N_seg • ss_overlap(s, u) $\wedge$ ss_overlap(t, u))

- The predicate ss_aligned(s,t) holds if s and t are collinear but do not overlap.

    ss_aligned : N_seg $\times$ N_seg $\rightarrow$ **Bool**
    ss_aligned(s, t) $\equiv$ ss_collinear(s, t) $\wedge$ $\sim$ss_overlap(s, t)

- The predicate ss_intersect(s,t) holds iff s and t have exactly one common point which is not a common end point. When ss_intersect(s,t) holds, the function intersection(s,t) returns the nearest N-point of the real intersection point of s and t.

    ss_intersect : N_seg $\times$ N_seg $\rightarrow$ **Bool**
    ss_intersect(s,t) $\equiv$
        ($\exists!$ α, β : ZeroOne • $\psi(\alpha,s)=\psi(\beta,t)$) $\wedge$ $\sim$ss_meet(s,t),

    intersection : N_seg $\times$ N_seg $\overset{\sim}{\rightarrow}$ N_point
    intersection(s, t) $\equiv$
        let α : ZeroOne, β : ZeroOne • $\psi(\alpha, s) = \psi(\beta, t)$
        in round($\psi(\alpha, s)$) **end**
        pre ss_intersect(s, t)

- The predicate ss_parallel(s,t) holds iff s and t are in parallel. Because the two end points of a segment must be different, the two segments s and t are in parallel iff $(y(r(s)) - y(l(s))) * (x(r(t)) - x(l(t))) = (y(r(t)) - y(l(t))) * (x(r(s)) - x(l(s)))$.

ss_parallel : N_seg × N_seg → **Bool**
ss_parallel(s, t) ≡
    let slope_st=(y(r(s))−y(l(s))) * (x(r(t))−x(l(t))),
        slope_ts=(y(r(t))−y(l(t))) * (x(r(s))−x(l(s)))
    in slope_st = slope_ts
    end

- The predicate ss_disjoint(s,t) holds iff if s and t do not have any common point.

ss_disjoint : N_seg × N_seg → **Bool**
ss_disjoint(s,t) ≡
∼ (∃ α,β : ZeroOne • $\psi(\alpha,s)=\psi(\beta,t)$)

10.3 Polygonal Lines and Segment Envelopes

As we have mentioned earlier, the spatial data at the lowest level of abstraction can always be viewed as a set of points and line segments which can intersect, while the spatial data will be represented in computers in the form of realms which do not allow intersecting line segments. Therefore, the spatial data needs to be first transformed into a realm. The main problem of numerical correctness with segments is that two segments will in general not intersect at a grid point, and therefore the intersection point must be moved to the nearest grid-point. So a segment may be transformed into a chain of segments going through grid points to preserve topological correctness. Consider the example in Figure 10.2.

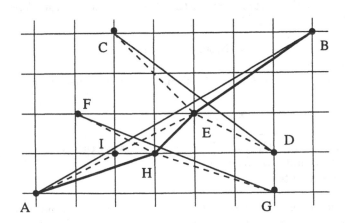

Fig. 10.2. An example of geometric correctness.

The intersection point of segments AB and CD is taken to be the nearest grid point E. This gives a redrawing as four non-intersecting segments AE, EB, CE and DE. Now we insert a new segment FG and the intersection point of segments FG and AE is the closest grid point H. Another redrawing replaces the original segment AB by the chain of segments $AHEB$. However, in this way a segment can drift through a series of intersections by an arbitrary distance from its original position. For example, the intersection H of AB with the segment FG is some way from the intersection point I that it would have been redrawn to originally. In addition, we can also see the following topological inconsistency: the point I was originally below the segment AB, but is now above the chain representing this segment.

In order to overcome these problems, the segments are considered to be virtually "thick" enough to always include a grid-point in the common part of intersecting segments. A virtually thick segment of a segment is called its *thick cover*. The thick cover of an N-segment s can be considered as a set of polygonal lines connecting the end points of s which topologically preserve possible redrawings of s caused by rounding the intersection with other segments to an N-point. The thicker a segment is the less precise it is. Hence only the smallest thick cover is interesting. This leads to the concept of an *envelope*.

We introduced the function round(x,y) in the previous section, which returns the nearest N-point to the real-point (x,y). round(x,y) is the N-point p for which the square $Sq(p)$ defined by

$$Sq(p) = [x(p) - 0.5, x(p) + 0.5) \times [y(p) - 0.5, y(p) + 0.5),$$

contains the real-point (x,y), where for real numbers a, b, $[a, b)$ denotes the set of all real numbers c such that $a \leq c < b$.

We also need a precise definition of some topological properties. To express possible redrawings, we introduce the notion of a *simple polygonal line* which is the result of redrawing a segment. A redrawing of a segment should have a natural linear ordering between its points just as a segment does. So, a simple polygonal line should have a linear ordering over its vertices. Intuitively, we define:

- A simple polygonal line $pl =< p_1, p_2, \ldots, p_m >$, $m \geq 2$ is a sequence of N-points such that the sequences of integers $< x(p_i) >$ and $< y(p_i) >$, $1 \leq i \leq m$, are monotonic. Each N-point p_i, $i \in \{1, \ldots, m - 1\}$ is called a *vertex* of pl and each N-segment formed from two vertices p_i and p_{i+1} ($1 \leq i < m$), is called an edge of pl. The type Simple_Pl consists of simple polygonal lines.

type
    Simple_Pl = {| pl : N_point* • is_simple(pl) |}
value
    is_simple : N_point* → **Bool**
    is_simple(pl) ≡ **len** pl ≥ 2 ∧

$$(\forall\ i : \mathbf{Nat} \bullet i > 0 \wedge i < \mathbf{len}\ pl \Rightarrow pl(i) \neq pl(i+1))\ \wedge$$
$$((\forall\ i : \mathbf{Nat} \bullet i > 0 \wedge i < \mathbf{len}\ pl \Rightarrow x(pl(i)) \leq_x (pl(i+1)))\ \vee$$
$$\quad (\forall\ i : \mathbf{Nat} \bullet i > 0 \wedge i < \mathbf{len}\ pl \Rightarrow x(pl(i)) \geq x(pl(i+1))))\ \wedge$$
$$((\forall\ i : \mathbf{Nat} \bullet i > 0 \wedge i < \mathbf{len}\ pl \Rightarrow y(pl(i)) \leq y(pl(i+1)))\ \vee$$
$$\quad (\forall\ i : \mathbf{Nat} \bullet i > 0 \wedge i < \mathbf{len}\ pl \Rightarrow y(pl(i)) \geq y(pl(i+1))))$$

- For two points p and q having the same horizontal coordinate, i.e. $x(p) = x(q)$, if the vertical coordinate of p is greater than the vertical coordinate of q, then p is said to be above q, and q is said to be below p.

value
    pp_above : N_point × N_point → **Bool**
    pp_above(p,q) ≡ $(y(q) > y(p) \wedge x(p) = x(q))$

- A point p is above (below) a segment s iff p is above (below) some point on s and not on s. A point p is above (below) a simple polygonal line pl iff p is above (below) some segment of pl and not below (above) any other segment of pl. These relationships are formalised by the Boolean functions **ps_above, ps_below, ppl_above** and **ppl_below** in RSL.

value
    ps_above : N_point × N_seg → **Bool**
    ps_above(p, s) ≡
        $(\exists(x,y) : \mathbf{Real} \times \mathbf{Real} \bullet \exists\ \alpha : ZeroOne \bullet (x,y)=\psi(\alpha,s)\ \wedge$
        real $x(p)=x \wedge$ **real** $y(p)>y)\ \wedge$ ~ps_on(p,s),

    ps_below : N_point × N_seg → **Bool**
    ps_below(p, s) ≡
        $(\exists(x,y) : \mathbf{Real} \times \mathbf{Real} \bullet \exists\ \alpha : ZeroOne \bullet (x,y)=\psi(\alpha,s)\ \wedge$
        real $x(p)=x \wedge$ **real** $y(p)<y)\ \wedge$ ~ ps_on(p,s),

    ppl_above : N_point × Simple_Pl → **Bool**
    ppl_above(p, pl) ≡
        $(\exists\ i : \mathbf{Nat} \bullet i > 0 \wedge i < \mathbf{len}\ pl \wedge$ ps_above(p,mk_seg(pl(i),pl(i+1)))) $\wedge$
        $(\forall\ i : \mathbf{Nat} \bullet i > 0 \wedge i < \mathbf{len}\ pl \Rightarrow$
          ~ ps_below(p, mk_seg(pl(i), pl(i+1)))),

    ppl_below : N_point × Simple_Pl → **Bool**
    ppl_below(p, pl) ≡
        $(\exists\ i : \mathbf{Nat} \bullet i > 0 \wedge i < \mathbf{len}\ pl \wedge$ ps_below(p,mk_seg(pl(i),pl(i+1)))) $\wedge$
        $(\forall\ i : \mathbf{Nat} \bullet i > 0 \wedge i < \mathbf{len}\ pl \Rightarrow$
          ~ ps_above(p, mk_seg(pl(i), pl(i+1))))

- Two grid points are on one side of a segment s iff they are both above or below s, or at least one of them is on s. A set of points is said to be on one side of a segment iff any two points of the set are on one side of the segment.

value

oneside : N_point × N_point × N_seg → **Bool**

oneside(p, q, s) ≡
    (ps_above(p,s) ∧ ps_above(q,s)) ∨
    (ps_below(p,s) ∧ ps_below(q,s)) ∨ ps_on(p,s) ∨ ps_on(q,s)

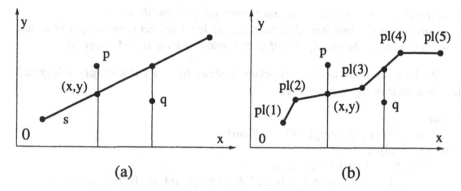

Fig. 10.3. The above - below relation.

Figure 10.3 illustrate these relations between a point and a segment, and between a point and a polygonal line. In Figure 10.3(a), p is above, while q is below, the segment s. In Figure 10.3(b), p is above, and q is below the polygonal line pl.

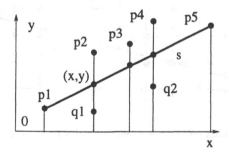

Fig. 10.4. The one-side relation.

In Figure 10.4 the points $p2$ and $p3$ are on one side of the segment s, and so are the points $q1$ and $q2$; the points $p3$ and $q1$ do not lie on one side of the segment s, while the set of points $\{p1, p2, p3, p4, p5\}$ is on one side of the segment s.

We have seen the need to redraw a segment to ensure that the intersection with another segment is a grid point. However, redrawing a segment should preserve topological properties. The requirement for redrawing is given as:

Definition 10.3.1. *A simple polygonal line pl is a redrawing of a grid segment s iff it satisfies:*

- *pl joins two end points of s and passes all grid points of s,*
- *pl preserves the topological structure, i.e. for any grid point g, if g is above s then g is not below pl, and if g is below s then g is not above pl.*

We introduce the Boolean function **redraw** to verify if a simple polygonal line is a redrawing of a segment.

value
  redraw : N_seg × Simple_Pl → **Bool**
  redraw(s,pl) ≡
    (∀ p : N_point • ps_on(p,s) ⇒
      (∃ i : **Nat** • i > 0 ∧ i < **len** pl ∧ ps_on(p, mk_seg(pl(i), pl(i+1)))))) ∧
    {l(s), r(s)} = {pl(1),pl(**len** pl)} ∧
    (∀ g : N_point • ps_above(g,s) ⇒ ~ppl_below(g,pl)) ∧
    (∀ g : N_point • ps_below(g,s) ⇒ ~ppl_above(g,pl))

Now, we are ready to give an intuitive and abstract definition of what we mean by a thick cover. An example of a thick cover of a segment is given in Figure 10.5.

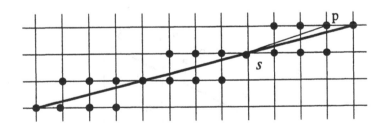

Fig. 10.5. A thick cover of segment s, and a redrawing of s to pass p.

Definition 10.3.2. *A thick cover of a segment s is a set B of grid points such that the following conditions are satisfied:*

1. (Covering s) The end points of s are in B,

2. *(Including all possible intersections with other segments) All the nearest grid points of real-points in s are also in B,*

3. *(Including all possible redrawing of segments when intersected with other segments) For any grid point p in B, there is a simple polygonal line pl which is a redrawing of s via p, and all the nearest points of pl are in B.*

At least one thick cover exists for any segment. One is the set of all grid points that lie either on the segment s or at the corner of grid cells that are crossed by s (where grid cells are the smallest squares with grid points at their corners).

The Boolean function thick is introduced to verify if a set of grid points is a thick cover of a segment:

value
    thick : N_seg × N_point-set → **Bool**
    thick(s, B) ≡
    (l(s) ∈ B ∧ r(s) ∈ B) ∧
    (∀ α : ZeroOne • round(ψ(α, s)) ∈ B) ∧
      (∀ p : N_point • p ∈ B ⇒
        (∃ pl : Simple_Pl • redraw(s,pl) ∧ p ∈ **elems** pl ∧
          (∀ i : **Nat**,α : ZeroOne • i > 0 ∧ i < **len** pl ⇒
          round(ψ(α,mk_seg(pl(i),pl(i+1)))) ∈ B)))

Our goal is now to give an abstract definition of a segment envelope. We require that an envelope of a segment is a minimal thick cover of the segment.

Definition 10.3.3. *An* envelope *of a segment s is a thick cover of s that does not include any other thick cover of s.*

The function env for returning the envelope of a segment is formalised as

value
    env : N_seg → N_point-set
axiom
[envelope_s]
    ∀ s : N_seg • thick(s,env(s)) ∧
      (∀ B : N_point-set • thick(s,B) ∧ B ⊆ env(s) ⇒ B = env(s))

Definition 10.3.3 ensures that the envelope of a segment is not too large, and we see below that envelopes exist uniquely. One can therefore identify a segment with its envelope whenever necessary. Definition 10.3.2 guarantees that not only the intersections of segments are inside their envelopes, but also that redrawing a segment results in a polygonal line that, together with its nearest grid points, is inside its envelope. This guarantees that the topological structure is not damaged.

Figure 10.5 shows a thick cover of a segment s (which is also the envelope of s). Let p be a grid point in $env(s)$ and above the segment s. Redrawing s

to pass p will replace the segment s by a polygonal line in the thick cover of s, each vertex of which is above or on s.

Note that our definition of envelopes coincides with the definition given in [61], but is more abstract, and can be used to reason about their properties. For example from this definition we can prove that the envelope of a segment s exists uniquely. The proof proceeds as follows. Take two thick covers B_1 and B_2 of a segment s and consider their intersection $B_1 \cap B_2$. In order to show $B_1 \cap B_2$ is also a thick cover of s, we have to verify three items of Definition 10.3.2 are satisfied for it. Items 1 and 2 are satisfied trivially. To verify item 3 take a grid point p in $B_1 \cap B_2$ and show the existence of a redrawing of s, say a polygonal line pl which goes though p and which has all the nearest points in $B_1 \cap B_2$. For B_1 and B_2, the existence of such polygonal lines, say pl_1 and pl_2 respectively, satisfying the item 3 has been guaranteed by the assumption. The idea of the proof is to construct pl by modifying pl_1 and pl_2, in fact by deleting some of their vertices. This construction is shown in the following sequence of auxiliary lemmas. We use RSL to formalise the lemmas but present their proofs informally.

Lemma 10.3.1.

$\forall \ B : N\_point\text{-}set, \ p : N\_point, \ s : N\_seg \ \bullet$
$\quad (thick(s,B) \land p \in B \land (ps\_above(p,s) \Rightarrow$
$\qquad \forall \ q : N\_point \bullet pp\_above(p,q) \land ps\_above(q,s) \Rightarrow q \in B)) \land$
$\quad (thick(s,B) \land p \in B \land (ps\_below(p,s) \Rightarrow$
$\qquad \forall \ q : N\_point \bullet pp\_below(p,q) \land ps\_below(q,s) \Rightarrow q \in B))$

Proof. Assume that p is above s. Since B is the thick cover of s, and p is in B, there is a simple polygonal line pl as in the item 3 of Definition 10.3.2. Therefore any grid point lying above s is not below pl. So, a grid point lying above s and below p must be a point of pl, and therefore is in B. The case that p is below s is proved similarly.

For simplicity, we introduce a partial function **appr** to express a relationship between two grid points, a segment, a simple polygonal line, and a set of grid points, that we often use in this section. Intuitively, for a segment s, for two grid points p, q lying on one side of s, for a simple polygonal line pl and for a set of grid points B, $\mathbf{appr}(p,q,s,pl,B)$ says that polygonal line pl is from p to q and satisfies:

- vertices of pl are on one side of s,
- pl preserves the topological structure, i.e. for all grid points g, if g is above s then g is not below pl, and if g is below s then g is not above pl, and
- all the nearest grid points of pl are in B.

value
$\quad$ appr : N_point $\times$ N_point $\times$ Simple_Pl $\times$ N_point-set $\overset{\sim}{\to}$ **Bool**

$appr(p,q,s,pl,B) \equiv pl(1) = p \wedge pl(\textbf{len } pl) = q \wedge$
$\quad (\forall\ q',\ q'' : \text{N\_point} \bullet q' \in \textbf{elems } pl \wedge q'' \in \textbf{elems } pl \Rightarrow$
$\quad\quad\quad\quad\quad\quad\quad\quad oneside(q',\ q'',\ s)) \wedge$
$\quad (\forall\ g : \text{N\_point} \bullet ps\_above(g,s) \Rightarrow \sim ppl\_below(g,pl)) \wedge$
$\quad (\forall\ g : \text{N\_point} \bullet ps\_below(g,s) \Rightarrow \sim ppl\_above(g,pl)) \wedge$
$\quad (\forall\ i : \textbf{Nat}, alpha : \text{ZeroOne} \bullet i>0 \wedge i<\textbf{len } pl \Rightarrow$
$\quad\quad round(\psi(\alpha, mk\_seg(pl(i), pl(i+1)))) \in B)$
$\textbf{pre } oneside(p,q,s)$

Lemma 10.3.2.

$\forall\ B : N\_point\text{-}set,\ p,q : N\_point,\ s : N\_seg \bullet$
$\quad (thick(s,B) \wedge oneside(p,q,s) \wedge$
$\quad\quad (\exists\ pl : Simple\_Pl \bullet appr(p,q,s,pl,B))) \Rightarrow$
$\quad (\exists\ pl' : Simple\_Pl \bullet appr(p,q,s,pl',B) \wedge$
$\quad ((ps\_above(p,s) \vee ps\_above(q,s)) \Rightarrow$
$\quad\quad (\forall\ i : \textbf{Nat} \bullet 1 < i \wedge i < \textbf{len } pl' \Rightarrow$
$\quad\quad \sim ps\_above(pl'(i),mk\_seg(pl'(i-1),pl'(i+1))))) \wedge$
$\quad ((ps\_below(p,s) \vee ps\_below(q,s)) \Rightarrow$
$\quad\quad (\forall\ i : \textbf{Nat} \bullet 1 < i \wedge i < \textbf{len } pl' \Rightarrow$
$\quad\quad \sim ps\_below(pl'(i),mk\_seg(pl'(i-1),pl'(i+1))))))$

In words, this lemma is formulated as follows. Let B be a thick cover of a segment s, and p and q be on one side of s. If there is a simple polygonal line pl such that $appr(p, q, s, pl, B)$ (which implies that p, q are in B), there is a polygonal line pl' for which $appr(p, q, s, pl', B)$ holds, and if one of p and q is above (below) s, then for no three consecutive vertices p_{i-1}, p_i, p_{i+1} of pl' does p_i lie above (below) the segment $\{p_{i-1}, p_{i+1}\}$.

Proof. We first assume that one of p and q lies above s. We assume that pl is a simple polygonal line from p to q that satisfies item 2 of Definition 10.3.1, and has all the nearest points in B. We construct a simple polygonal line pl' by modifying pl. Let at the beginning $pl' = pl$. If there exist three consecutive vertices p_{i-1}, p_i, p_{i+1} of pl' such that p_i is either above or on the segment $\{p_{i-1}, p_{i+1}\}$, we delete p_i from pl'. This process is repeated until there are no three consecutive vertices p_{i-1}, p_i, p_{i+1} of pl' satisfying that p_i is above the segment $\{p_{i-1}, p_{i+1}\}$. The replacing process guarantees that any real-point u in pl' is either below or on pl. Therefore, for any real-point u in pl', there are real-points u' on pl and u'' on s such that $round(u)$ is either the same as $round(u')$ or the same as $round(u'')$ or it holds $round(u)$ is above s and below $round(u')$. For the first two cases, $round(u)$ is in B by the definition of B and pl. For the last case, it follows from Lemma 10.3.1 that $round(u)$ is also in B. As a result, any grid point lying above s is not below pl'. Furthermore, all the vertices of pl' lie on one side of s, because they are in the set of vertices of pl, and pl' is also a simple polygonal line, because a subsequence of a monotonic sequence is also monotonic.

The case when the points p and q are below or on s is proved in the same way.

Lemma 10.3.3.

$\forall B_1, B_2 : N\_point\_set, s : N\_seg \bullet$
  $thick(s, B_1) \land thick(s, B_2) \Rightarrow$
    let $B = B_1 \cap B_2$ **in**
    $\forall p,q : N\_point \bullet$
      $p \in B \land q \in B \land oneside(p, q, s) \land$
      $(\exists pl_1, pl_2 : Simple\_Pl \bullet appr(p,q,s,pl_1,B_1) \land appr(p,q,s,pl_2,B_2)) \Rightarrow$
      $(\exists pl : Simple\_Pl \bullet appr(p,q,s,pl,B))$ **end**

This lemma is formulated in words as follows. Let B_1 and B_2 be two thick covers of a segment s, let $B = B_1 \cap B_2$ and $p, q \in B$ be two grid points lying on one side of s. If there exist two simple polygonal lines pl_1 and pl_2 from p to q satisfying the conditions of items 2 and 3 of Definition 10.3.1 such that all the nearest grid points of real-points in pl_1 are in B_1 and all the nearest grid points of real-points in pl_2 are in B_2, then there is a simple polygonal line pl from p to q satisfying items 2 and 3 of Definition 10.3.1 such that the nearest grid points of points in pl are in B.

Proof. First we assume that one of p and q is above s (hence, the other should be either on or above s). By Lemma 10.3.2 and Definition 10.3.1, we can assume that the two simple polygonal lines pl_1 and pl_2 (perhaps after redrawing) from p to q satisfy that any three consecutive vertices u, v, w of pl_1 or of pl_2 satisfy that v is below the segment $\{u, w\}$. From the properties of pl_1 and pl_2 mentioned in the definition of redrawing, all the vertices of pl_1 are not below pl_2 (and conversely). Therefore, by Lemma 10.3.2 any point in any segment of pl_1 is not below pl_2 (and conversely). With the same argument as in the proof of the previous lemma, and from Lemma 10.3.1, we have that all the nearest grid points of real-points in pl_2 are in B_1. Therefore, all the nearest grid points of points in pl_2 are in $B_1 \cap B_2$, and we can take pl to be pl_2. The case that one of p and q is below s is proved in the same way, and this completes the proof of Lemma 10.3.3.

Lemma 10.3.4. *(Closure property under intersection of the family of thick covers of a segment)*

$\forall B_1, B_2 : N\_point\_set, s : N\_seg \bullet$
  $thick(s,B_1) \land thick(s,B_2) \Rightarrow thick(s, B_1 \cap B_2)$

Proof. Let $B = B_1 \cap B_2$, where B_1 and B_2 are thick covers of a segment s. We verify that B satisfies Definition 10.3.2. Assume that p is a grid point in B and above s. Let p_1 and p_2 be the two end points of s. By Definitions 10.3.2 and 10.3.1, there are two polygonal lines pl_1 and pl_2 from p_1 to p_2 via p such that $\text{appr}(p_1, p_2, s, pl_1, B_1) \wedge \text{appr}(p_1, p_2, s, pl_2, B_2)$. We can decompose the polygonal line pl_1 into the polygonal lines $pl_{1,p1}$ from p_1 to p and $pl_{1,p2}$ from p to p_2, and decompose the polygonal pl_2 into the two polygonal lines $pl_{2,p1}$ from p_1 to p and $pl_{2,p2}$ from p to p_2.

By Lemma 10.3.3, there are simple polygonal lines pl_{p1} from p_1 to p and pl_{p2} from p to p_2 which satisfy $\text{appr}(p_1, p, s, pl_{p1}, B)$ and $\text{appr}(p, p_2, s, pl_{p2}, B)$. Let pl be the concatenation of pl_{p1} and pl_{p2}. Then, $\text{redraw}(s, pl)$ holds and all the nearest grid points of pl are in B.

When p is a grid point in B and below s, the proof is similar. Therefore, B is also a thick cover of s.

Theorem 10.3.1.

$\forall\ s : N\_seg \bullet env(s) =$
    $\{\ p \mid p : N\_point \bullet \forall\ B : N\_point\text{-}set \bullet thick(s,B) \Rightarrow p \in B\ \}$

This theorem means that for any segment s, there is a unique thick cover of s that does not include any other thick cover of s, which is the envelope of s. Therefore, the function **env** may be refined to

value
    env : N_seg $\rightarrow$ N_point-**set**
    env(s) $\equiv$
        $\{\ p \mid p : N\_point \bullet \forall\ B : N\_point\_set \bullet thick(s,B) \Rightarrow p \in B\ \}$

A complete specification of basic data types for map data is given as the scheme GRID, which is an extension of the scheme GRID$_1$ by adding the above types and values.

10.4 Realms

Having obtained a precise understanding and characterisation of envelopes, we can give an abstract and formal specification of realms.

To offer the advantages mentioned in the introduction of the chapter, a realm R is a set of grid points and grid segments defined over a finite grid such that:

- all (grid) end points of the segments of R are also in R,
- there is no point of R which is inside a segment of R, and
- two different segments of R do not intersect.

Although the definition of realms is simple, maintaining basic properties of a realm after modification is not simple. The main contribution of our specification is to find out the requirements for maintaining the properties of a realm. The fundamental operations for modification of realms are the insertion and deletion of points and segments. These operations must preserve the topological structure presented over the grid as well as be close to their intuitive meaning. As we have shown earlier, when we insert a new segment to a realm, this segment may intersect with another segment of the realm. If the intersection point is a grid point, this point is added to the realm, and segments are broken into smaller segments to maintain the definition of realms. If the intersection point is not a grid point, its nearest grid point must be included in the common part of their envelopes. Since we identify a segment with its envelope, we can take this point as the grid intersection point, and then break the "thick" segments into smaller segments. When we identify a segment with its envelope, the constraint "there is no point of R which is inside a segment of R" becomes *there is no point in the realm included in a proper envelope of any of its segments*, where the "proper envelope" proper_env(s) of a segment s is defined to contain all grid points in the envelope of s except for its end points. We call a realm that satisfies the additional rule "there is no point in the realm included in a proper envelope of any of its segments" an *extended realm*. A definition of realms in RSL is given as follows. Let SP be a union type of N-point and N-segment. The functions rpoint(sps) and rseg(sps) return the set of points and the set of segments, respectively, in the set sps of elements of type SP. Checking whether a set of elements of type SP is a realm is done by the predicate is_realm, and checking whether a realm is an extended realm is done by the predicate is_exrealm. The auxiliary function pl_sps, when applied to a polygonal line pl, returns the set of vertices and segments of pl. Realms and extended realms are formalised in RSL as:

object Grid : GRID
type
    SP = Grid.N_point | Grid.N_seg,
    Realm = {| R : SP-**set** • is_realm(R) |},
    ExRealm = {| R : SP-**set** • is_exrealm(R) |}
value
    rpoint : SP-**set** → Grid.N_point-**set**
    rpoint(sps) ≡ { p | p : Grid.N_point • p ∈ sps },

    rseg : SP-**set** → Grid.N_seg-**set**
    rseg(sps) ≡ { s | s : Grid.N_seg • s ∈ sps },

    proper_env : Grid.N_seg → Grid.N_point-**set**
    proper_env(s) ≡ Grid.env(s) \ s,

is_realm : SP-set → **Bool**
is_realm(sps) ≡
   (∀ s : Grid.N_seg • s ∈ rseg(sps) ⇒
     Grid.l(s) ∈ rpoint(sps) ∧ Grid.r(s) ∈ rpoint(sps)) ∧
   (∀ s : Grid.N_seg, p : Grid.N_point • p ∈ rpoint(sps) ∧ s ∈ rseg(sps) ⇒
     ~Grid.ps_in(p,s)) ∧
   (∀ s, t : Grid.N_seg • s ∈ rseg(sps) ∧ t ∈ rseg(sps) ∧ ~ (s = t) ⇒
     ~ Grid.ss_intersect(t, s)),

is_exrealm : SP-set → **Bool**
is_exrealm(sps) ≡ is_realm(sps) ∧
   (∀ p : Grid.N_point, s : Grid.N_seg •
     p ∈ rpoint(sps) ∧ s ∈ rseg(sps) ⇒ p ∉ proper_env(s)),

pl_sps : Grid.Simpl_Pl → SP-set
pl_sps(pl) ≡ **elems** (pl) ∪
   { Grid.mk_seg(pl(i),pl(i+1)) | i : **Nat** • i > 0 ∧ i < **len** pl }

The deletion of an element from an extended realm will result in an extended realm again. So, the requirement for the deletion operator is obvious. When inserting an element *sp* (a grid point or a grid segment) into an extended realm *R*, we expect to generate a new extended realm *R'* to include the inserted element and the elements of the old one. However, taking the set union of *R* and *sp* may not result in an extended realm. As said earlier, only redrawing segments can maintain the constraints for realms. Because redrawing leads to loosening of the precision, we should use it with care. So, intuitively, our requirement for the insertion of an element *sp* (a grid point or a grid segment) into an extended realm *R* is to achieve a new extended realm *R'* which is minimal (according to set inclusion) among those extended realms that include the points of *R* and of *sp* such that each segment of *R*∪*sp* should have a redrawing in *R'*. Therefore the operation **insert** is defined as follows.

value
  insert : ExRealm × SP → ExRealm
axiom
  [insert_sp_into_R]
    ∀ R : ExRealm, sp : SP •
    insert(R, sp) **as** R'
      post local
         value relation : ExRealm × ExRealm → **Bool**
         axiom
           ∀ RR,RR' : ExRealm • relation(RR, RR') ≡
           rpoint(RR) ∪ rpoint(sp) ⊆ rpoint(RR') ∧
           (∀ s : Grid.N_seg • s ∈ rseg(RR) ∪ rseg(sp) ⇒

$$(\exists \ pl : Grid.Simple\_Pl \bullet Grid.redraw(s,pl) \ \land$$
$$pl\_sps(pl) \subseteq RR'))$$

in

  relation(R,R') $\land$
  ($\forall$ R'' : ExRealm $\bullet$ relation(R,R'') $\land$
   (rpoint(R'') $\subseteq$ rpoint(R') $\lor$ rseg(R'') $\subseteq$ rseg(R')) $\Rightarrow$
    R'' = R')

end

In the definition of **insert**, the predicate **relation**(RR, RR') is a local predicate describing that, given sp (a grid point or a grid segment), the extended realm RR' is a modification of the extended realm RR to include points and redrawings of segments of RR and sp.

Now we can prove that algorithms proposed in [61] for inserting a point and a segment to a realm are implementations of the operation **insert** specified above, and the proof can be verified by using the Raise tools. The idea of the implementation of the operation **insert** by algorithms proposed in [61] is that, when inserting a point p into a realm, it marks all the segments in the realm whose proper envelopes contain p. Then, all these segments are redrawn to pass through p, and p is added to the realm. When inserting a segment s, it behaves as follows:

- The end points of the segment s are inserted in the realm as above
- The grid points in the realm that are in the proper envelope of s are marked
- For each segment in the realm that intersects s, the grid intersection point (Section 10.2) is associated with the segment
- The realm segments associated with points are redrawn to pass through the associated points, and the associated points are added to the realm
- s is redrawn to pass through the marked points and the points associated with realm segments.

Checking that these algorithms satisfy our specification for insertion, i.e. are a refinement of our specification, is just procedural. In our recent work [25], we have translated these specifications and implementations into **B** [1] and performed the verification with the **B-toolkit**.

10.5 Realm-Based Geometry

We give a formal definition of the basic topological structures on a realm and their relations. These structures are *Cycle*, *Face*, *R-unit* and *Block*, and are used to represent the spatial data types. As the structures are built from sets of segments in a realm, they inherit the properties of the realm.

10.5.1 Cycles

A *cycle* is simply a closed polygonal line in a realm, and is defined as follows. A sequence of N-segments $c = <s_1, \ldots, s_m>$, $m > 2$ is called a cycle if the following conditions are satisfied:

- the set of segments of c and their end points form a realm, and
- consecutive segments meet, and the last and the first segments meet, but no others do.

type Cycle = {| c : Grid.N_seg* • is_cycle(c) |}
value
  segset_sps : Grid.N_seg-**set** → SP-**set**
  segset_sps(ss) ≡
    ss ∪ { p | p : Grid.N_point • ∃ s : Grid.N_seg • p ∈ s ∧ s ∈ ss },

  is_cycle : Grid.N_seg* → **Bool**
  is_cycle(c) ≡
    len c > 2 ∧
    is_exrealm(segset_sps(**elems** c)) ∧
    (∀ i, j : **Nat** •
      {i,j} ⊆ {1..**len** c} ⇒
      Grid.ss_meet(c(i),c(j)) = (j = 1 + i**len** c))

Recall that Grid is an object of type GRID. Given a set of grid segments ss, segset_sps(ss) returns the set of the given segments ss and their end points, and the predicate is_cycle(ss) holds iff the sequence of segments ss forms a cycle.

The predicates on_cycle, outside_cycle, and inside_cycle express whether a point is on, outside, and inside a cycle, respectively. These predicates are defined as:

value
  on_cycle : Grid.N_point × Cycle → **Bool**
  on_cycle(p, c) ≡
    (∃ s : Grid.N_seg • s ∈ **elems** c ∧ Grid.ps_on(p, s)),

  inside_cycle : Grid.N_point × Cycle → **Bool**
  inside_cycle(p, c) ≡ Grid.y(p) < Grid.n − 1 ∧
    let q : Grid.N_point • Grid.x(q) = Grid.x(p) ∧
          Grid.y(q) = Grid.n − 1,sp = Grid.mk_seg(p, q),
      si = { s | s : Grid.N_seg • s ∈ **elems** c ∧ (Grid.ss_intersect(s,sp) ∧
        ∼Grid.ps_on(Grid.l(s),sp)) }
    in ∼on_cycle(p,c) ∧ **card**(si)\2 = 1 **end**,

  outside_cycle : Grid.N_point × Cycle → **Bool**
  outside_cycle(p,c) ≡ ∼on_cycle(p,c) ∧ ∼ inside_cycle(p,c)

The basic functions defined on cycles are as follows.

- p_in_cycle(c) returns the set of all N-points inside the cycle c.
- p_on_cycle(c) returns the set of all N-points on the cycle c.
- cycle_points(c) is the set of all N-points inside or on c. When p belongs to cycle_points(c), we say that p is a grid point of the cycle c.

value
  p_in_cycle : Cycle $\to$ Grid.N_point-**set**
  p_in_cycle(c) $\equiv$ { p | p : Grid.N_point • inside_cycle(p,c) },

  p_on_cycle : Cycle $\to$ Grid.N_point-**set**
  p_on_cycle(c) $\equiv$ { p | p : Grid.N_point • on_cycle(p,c) },

  cycle_points : Cycle $\to$ Grid.N_point-**set**
  cycle_points(c) $\equiv$ p_in_cycle(c) $\cup$ p_on_cycle(c)

We use the following predicates to describe two relationships between a segment s and a cycle c:

- the predicate sc_areainside(s, c) holds iff any grid point on s is also a grid point of c, which means that any grid points on s is either on or inside the cycle c,
- the predicate sc_edgeinside(s, c) holds iff sc_areainside(s, c) holds and s is not a segment of c.

value
  sc_areainside : Grid.N_seg $\times$ Cycle $\to$ **Bool**
  sc_areainside(s, c) $\equiv$
      ($\forall$ p : Grid.N_point • Grid.ps_on(p, s) $\Rightarrow$ p $\in$ cycle_points(c)),

  sc_edgeinside : Grid.N_seg $\times$ Cycle $\to$ **Bool**
  sc_edgeinside(s,c) $\equiv$
      sc_areainside(s,c) $\wedge$ s $\notin$ **elems** c

The relationships between two cycles c_1 and c_2 within a realm are captured by the following predicates.

- The predicate cc_areainside(c_1, c_2) holds iff c_1 is area-inside c_2 which means that any grid point of c_1 is also a grid point of c_2, i.e.
  cc_areainside(c_1, c_2) $\equiv$ (cycle_points(c_1) $\subseteq$ cycle_points($c2$));
- The predicate cc_edgeinside(c_1, c_2) holds iff c_1 is edge-inside c_2 which means that c_1 and c_2 have no common segment and c_1 is area-inside c_2;
- The predicate cc_vertexinside(c_1, c_2) holds iff c_1 is vertex-inside c_2 which means that c_1 is edge-inside c_2 and there is no N-point that lies on both c_1 and c_2;

- The predicate cc_areadisjoint(c_1, c_2) holds iff c_1 and c_2 are area-disjoint which means that c_1 and c_2 have no common point inside and there is no edge point of one cycle lying inside the other;
- The predicate cc_edgedisjoint(c_1, c_2) holds iff c_1 and c_2 are edge-disjoint which means c_1 and c_2 have no common edge and are area-disjoint;
- The predicate cc_adjacent(c_1, c_2) holds iff c_1 and c_2 are adjacent which means that cc_areadisjoint(c_1, c_2) and c_1 and c_2 have at least one edge in common;
- The predicate cc_vertexdisjoint(c_1, c_2) holds iff c_1 and c_2 are edge-disjoint and there is no N-point that lies on both of them;
- The predicate cc_meet(c_1, c_2) holds iff c_1 and c_2 are edge-disjoint and have a common vertex;
- the function realm_cycles returns all the cycles of a realm.

Formal definition of these relations is given as:

value

cc_areainside : Cycle × Cycle $\overset{\sim}{\to}$ **Bool**
cc_areainside(c_1, c_2) ≡
  cycle_points(c_1) ⊆ cycle_points(c_2)
  pre is_exrealm (segset_sps(**elems** c_1 ∪ **elems** c_2)),

cc_edgeinside : Cycle × Cycle $\overset{\sim}{\to}$ **Bool**
cc_edgeinside(c_1, c_2) ≡
  cc_areainside(c_1, c_2) ∧ **elems** c_1 ∩ **elems** c_2 = {}
  pre is_exrealm(segset_sps(**elems** c_1 ∪ **elems** c_2)),

cc_vertexinside : Cycle × Cycle $\overset{\sim}{\to}$ **Bool**
cc_vertexinside(c_1, c_2) ≡
  cc_edgeinside(c_1, c_2) ∧ p_on_cycle(c_1) ∩ p_on_cycle(c_2) = {}
  pre is_exrealm(segset_sps(**elems** c_1 ∪ **elems** c_2)),

cc_areadisjoint : Cycle × Cycle $\overset{\sim}{\to}$ **Bool**
cc_areadisjoint(c_1, c_2) ≡
  p_in_cycle(c_1) ∩ cycle_points(c_2) = {} ∧
  cycle_points(c_1) ∩ p_in_cycle(c_2) = {}
  pre is_exrealm(segset_sps(**elems** c_1 ∪ **elems** c_2)),

cc_edgedisjoint : Cycle × Cycle $\overset{\sim}{\to}$ **Bool**
cc_edgedisjoint(c_1, c_2) ≡
  cc_areadisjoint(c_1,c_2) ∧ **elems** c_1 ∩ **elems** c_2 = {}
  pre is_exrealm(segset_sps(**elems** c_1 ∪ **elems** c_2)),

cc_adjacent : Cycle × Cycle $\overset{\sim}{\to}$ **Bool**
cc_adjacent(c_1,c_2) ≡

cc_areadisjoint(c_1,c_2) $\wedge$ **elems** c_1 $\cap$ **elems** c_2 $\neq$ {}
pre is_exrealm(segset_sps(**elems** c_1 $\cup$ **elems** c_2)),

cc_vertexdisjoint : Cycle $\times$ Cycle $\xrightarrow{\sim}$ **Bool**
cc_vertexdisjoint(c_1,c_2) $\equiv$
    cc_edgedisjoint(c_1,c_2) $\wedge$ p_on_cycle(c_1) $\cap$ p_on_cycle(c_2) = {}
pre is_exrealm(segset_sps(**elems** c_1 $\cup$ **elems** c_2)),

cc_meet : Cycle $\times$ Cycle $\xrightarrow{\sim}$ **Bool**
cc_meet(c_1, c_2) $\equiv$ cc_edgedisjoint(c_1, c_2) $\wedge$
    p_on_cycle(c_1) $\cap$ p_on_cycle(c_2) $\neq$ {}
pre is_exrealm(segset_sps(**elems** c_1 $\cup$ **elems** c_2)),

realm_cycles : Realm $\rightarrow$ Cycle-**set**
realm_cycles(R) $\equiv$ { c | c : Cycle • **elems** c $\subseteq$ rseg(R) }

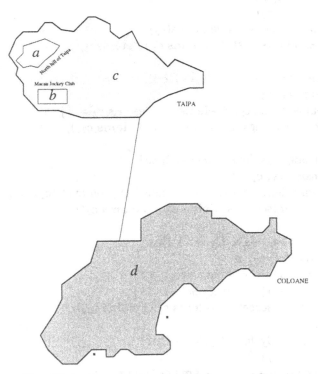

Fig. 10.6. An example of cycles, faces and R-units.

Figure 10.6 shows an example of cycles and their relationships taken from the map of the Macau territory. Taipa and Coloane are two islands linked by a causeway. In the figure, a, b, c and d are cycles, and cc_vertexinside(a, c), cc_vertexinside(b, c), cc_edgeinside(a, c), cc_vertexdisjoint(a, b), cc_vertexdisjoint(c, d), cc_edgeinside(b, c), cc_edgedisjoint(a, b), and cc_edgedisjoint(c, d) hold on them.

A complete specification of cycles is given as the scheme CYCLE.

10.5.2 Faces

A region in a realm formed from a main cycle and, possibly, some cycles within it is called a *face*. A face f of the realm is defined as a pair (c, H), where c is a cycle, and H is a (possibly empty) set of cycles (called *holes* of f) which satisfies the following conditions:

- there is an extended realm containing all the cycles in $H \cup \{c\}$, or equivalently, the set of all segments of the cycles and their end points form an extended realm,
- for each cycle h in H we have cc_edgeinside(h, c),
- for two different elements h and h' of H we have cc_edgedisjoint(h, h'),
- no other cycle can be formed from the set of segments of the cycles in the face f.

Figure 10.6 contains exactly four faces $(c, \{a, b\})$, $(d, \emptyset)$, $(a, \emptyset)$ and $(b, \emptyset)$.

A formal specification of faces includes, as usual, auxiliary functions to convert types and predicates for expressing relationships between faces and other geometrical objects:

- ccs_sps(c, H) returns the set of segments, plus their end points, of a cycle c and a set of cycles H.
- is_face(f) holds iff f is a face.
- face_points(f) returns the set of all grid points belonging to a face $f = (c, H)$; it is defined as the set of those N-points that belong to the cycle c and are not inside any cycle h in H.
- The predicate pf_areainside(p, f) holds iff p belongs to face_points(f).
- If s is a segment and $f = (c, H)$ then the predicate sf_areainside(s, f) holds iff s is area-inside f which means that sc_areainside(s, c) and for each cycle h in H we have $\neg$ sc_edgeinside(s, h).
- realm_faces(R) returns the set of all faces of a realm R.

type Face = {| f : Cycle × Cycle-**set** • is_face(f) |}
value
 ccs_sps : Cycle × Cycle-**set** → SP-**set**
 ccs_sps(c, H) ≡
  { sp | sp : SP • ∃ h : Cycle • h ∈ H ∪ {c} ∧
                sp ∈ segset_sps(**elems** h) },
 is_face : Cycle × Cycle-**set** → **Bool**
 is_face(c, H) ≡

is_exrealm(ccs_sps(c, H)) $\land$
(H $\neq$ {} $\Rightarrow$
  ($\forall$ h : Cycle • h $\in$ H $\Rightarrow$ cc_edgeinside(h, c)) $\land$
  ($\forall$ h, h' : Cycle • h $\in$ H $\land$ h' $\in$ H $\Rightarrow$
    cc_edgedisjoint(h,h')) $\land$
  ($\forall$ c' : Cycle • **elems** c' $\subseteq$ rseg(ccs_sps(c, H)) $\Rightarrow$
    c' $\in$ H $\cup$ {c})),

face_points : Face $\to$ Grid.N_point-**set**
face_points(f) $\equiv$
  let (f_0, F_0) = f **in**
    cycle_points(f_0) \
    { p | p : Grid.N_point• $\exists$ h : Cycle • inside_cycle(p,h) $\land$ h $\in F_0$ }
  end,

pf_areainside : Grid.N_point $\times$ Face $\xrightarrow{\sim}$ **Bool**
pf_areainside(p,f) $\equiv$
  p $\in$ face_points(f)
  pre is_exrealm(ccs_sps(f) $\cup$ {p}),

sf_areainside : Grid.N_seg $\times$ Face $\xrightarrow{\sim}$ **Bool**
sf_areainside(s, f) $\equiv$
  let (c, H) = f
  in sc_areainside(s, c) $\land$
    ($\forall$ h : Cycle • h $\in$ H $\Rightarrow$ $\sim$ sc_edgeinside(s, h))
  end
  pre is_exrealm(ccs_sps(f) $\cup$ segset_sps({s})),

realm_faces : Realm $\to$ Face-**set**
realm_faces(R) $\equiv$ { f | f : Face • ccs_sps(f) $\subseteq$ R }

We also introduce the following predicates to express the relationships between two faces $f = (f_0, F_0)$ and $f' = (f'_0, F'_0)$:

- ff_areainside(f, f') holds iff we have cc_areainside(f_0, f'_0) and for each cycle h' in F'_0 either we have cc_areadisjoint(h', f_0) or we can find a cycle h in F_0 satisfying cc_areainside(h', h).
- ff_areadisjoint(f, f') holds iff we have ff_areadisjoint(f_0, f'_0), or there exists a cycle h' in F'_0 satisfying cc_areainside(f_0, h'), or there exists a cycle h in F_0 such that cc_areainside(f'_0, h).
- ff_edgedisjoint(f, f') holds iff we have ff_edgedisjoint(f_0, f'_0), or there exists a cycle h' in F'_0 satisfying cc_edgeinside(f_0, h') or there exists a cycle h in F_0 such that cc_edgeinside(f'_0, h).

For example, in Figure 10.6, two faces $(c, \{a, b\})$ and $(d, \emptyset)$ are area disjoint. These predicates are specified as:

value
  ff_areainside : Face × Face $\overset{\sim}{\to}$ **Bool**
  ff_areainside(f, f') ≡
    let (f_0, F_0) = f, $(f0', F0')$ = f' **in**
    cc_areainside$(f_0, f0')$ ∧
    (∀ h' : Cycle • h' ∈ F0' ⇒
      cc_areadisjoint(h', f_0) ∨
      (∃ h : Cycle • h ∈ F_0 ∧ cc_areainside(h', h)))
    end
    pre is_exrealm(ccs_sps(f) ∪ ccs_sps(f')),

  ff_areadisjoint : Face × Face $\overset{\sim}{\to}$ **Bool**
  ff_areadisjoint(f, f') ≡
    let (f_0, F_0) = f, $(f0', F0')$ = f' **in**
    cc_areadisjoint$(f_0, f0')$ ∨
    (∃ h' : Cycle • h' ∈ F0' ∧ cc_areainside(f_0, h')) ∨
    (∃ h : Cycle • h ∈ F_0 ∧ cc_areainside(f0', h))
    end
    pre is_exrealm(ccs_sps(f) ∪ ccs_sps(f')),

  ff_edgedisjoint : Face × Face $\overset{\sim}{\to}$ **Bool**
  ff_edgedisjoint(f, f') ≡
    let (f_0, F_0) = f, $(f0', F0')$ = f' **in**
    cc_edgedisjoint$(f_0, f0')$ ∨
    (∃ h' : Cycle • h' ∈ F0' ∧ cc_edgeinside(f_0, h')) ∨
    (∃ h : Cycle • h ∈ F_0 ∧ cc_edgeinside(f0', h))
    end
    pre is_exrealm(ccs_sps(f) ∪ ccs_sps(f'))

Putting them together gives the scheme FACE as a specification of faces.

10.5.3 R-Units

A minimal face in a realm is called an *R-unit* of that realm. More precisely, a face f of a realm R is called an R-unit in R iff it does not contain any other face of R, i.e. there is no other face g of R such that ff_areainside(g, f). To indicate that f is an R-unit in the realm R, we use the predicate is_unit(f, R). In Figure 10.6, the faces $(a, \emptyset)$, $(b, \emptyset)$, $(c, \{a, b\})$ and $(d, \emptyset)$ are R-units, and they are the only R-units.

A specification of R-units is written as the scheme RUNIT below. it has been shown that one can decompose a set of edge-disjoint faces into set of R-units. We denote by units(F, R) the set of R-units resulting from the decomposition from a set of faces F in a realm R . Let realm_units(R) denote the set of all R-units of a realm R. Scheme RUNIT, a specification of R-units, can be now written as follows.

scheme RUNIT = **extend** FACE **with**
class
  value
    is_unit : Face × Realm → **Bool**,
    is_unit(f, R) ≡ f ∈ realm_faces(R) ∧
        (∀ g : Face • g ∈ realm_faces(R) ∧
            ff_areainside(g,f) ⇒ g = f),

    units : Face-**set** × Realm → Face-**set**
    units(F, R) ≡
      { f | f : Face • f ∈ F ∧ is_unit(f,R) },

    realm_units : Realm → Face-**set**
    realm_units(R) ≡ units(realm_faces(R), R)
end

An immediate theory from this specification is that `realm_units(R)` is
exactly the set of all R-units in a realm R.

10.5.4 Blocks

In this subsection we give a definition of *blocks*. We say that a set S of N-
segments is connected iff any two segments of S are joined by a sequence
of segments in which consecutive segments meet. A block is defined as a
connected set of N-segments in a realm. This type is defined in RSL as

type Block = {| bl : Grid.N_seg-**set** • is_block(bl) |}
value
  is_block : Grid.N_seg-**set** → **Bool**
  is_block(bl) ≡
    is_exrealm((bl)) ∧
      (∀ s, t : Grid.N_seg • {s, t} ⊆ bl ∧ s ≠ t ⇒
        (∃ sl : Grid.N_seg* •
          sl ≠ ⟨⟩ ∧ **elems** sl ⊆ bl ∧
          (∀ i : **Nat** •
             1 ≤ i ∧ i < **len** sl ⇒
               Grid.ss_meet(sl(i), sl(i + 1)) ∧ s = sl(1) ∧ t = sl(**len** sl)))),

  realm_blocks : Realm → Block-**set**
  realm_blocks(R) ≡
    { bl | bl : Block • bl ⊆ rseg(R) }

where, as usual, the predicate `is_block` is for checking whether a set of
segments is a block, and the function `realm_blocks(`R`)` returns the set of all
blocks of a realm R.

The possible relationships between two blocks are as follows. Two blocks are disjoint iff every segment of one block is disjoint from every segment of the other block. Two blocks meet iff they do not have a common segment and there exists exactly one N-point which is a meeting point of a segment in one block and a segment in the other. Formally,

value
    blockdisjóint : Block × Block → **Bool**
    blockdisjoint(bl_1, bl_2) ≡
      ($\forall$ s, s' : Grid.N_seg • s ∈ bl_1 ∧ s' ∈ bl_2 ⇒
        Grid.ss_disjoint(s, s'))
      pre is_exrealm(segset_sps(bl_1 ∪ bl_2)),

    blockmeet : Block × Block → **Bool**
    blockmeet(bl_1, bl_2) ≡
      bl_1 ∩ bl_2 = {} ∧
      ($\exists$ p : Grid.N_point, s_1, s_2 : Grid.N_seg •
        s_1 ∈ bl_1 ∧ s_2 ∈ bl_2 ∧ Grid.ss_meet(s_1, s_2) ∧
        ($\forall$ s, s': Grid.N_seg •s ∈ bl_1 ∧ s' ∈ bl_2 ∧
          Grid.ss_meet(s,s') ⇒ p ∈ s ∩ s'))
      pre is_exrealm(segset_sps(bl_1 ∪ bl_2))

In Figure 10.7, *block*1 (the coast of Taipa), *block*2 (the causeway), and *block*3 (the coast of Coloane) are blocks. The relationships between them are blockdisjoint(*block*1, *block*3), blockmeet(*block*1, *block*2), and blockmeet(*block*3, *block*2).

10.6 Conclusion

This chapter presents a specification of the realm-based geometrical structures in the RSL. Realm-based structures can be used to define quite general spatial data types, and their formal specification can be used for the verification of the algorithms implementing spatial objects.

The chapter has shown in particular that the clear definition of an envelope is sufficient for solving numerical correctness problems. The properties of an envelope of a segment guarantee that the operations on a realm are always carried out inside an envelope and avoid topological errors. The set of the points of the envelopes of segments forming the polygonal line obtained by redrawing a segment s is always included in the envelope of s. Hence, we can replace s by this polygonal line without introducing any topological errors. The fundamental operations on realms (insertion, deletion) always use redrawing in the envelopes. The criteria for verifying the implementation of insertion and deletion of a grid point or a segment into a realm are also given. The specification of data types Cycle, Face and Block are based only

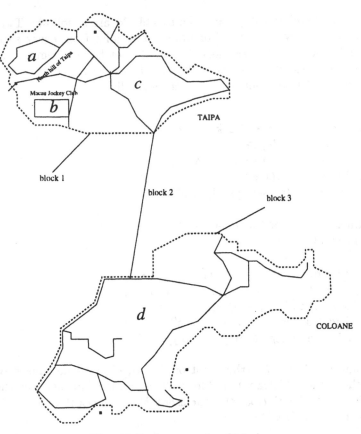

Fig. 10.7. An example of blocks.

on the concept of realm, and do not depend on a fixed given realm. Therefore these specifications give more freedom for implementing realm-based objects on maps.

Background Information

This work [134] was carried out in 1995–6 as part of a project on Geographical Information Systems (GIS) by a software engineer from the Vietnamese Institute of Information Technology, Quoc Tao Ngo, and Hung Dang Van.

11. Object-Oriented Design Patterns

11.1 Introduction

Software *design patterns* offer designers a way of reusing proven solutions to particular aspects of design rather than having to start each new design from scratch – the patterns are generic and abstract and embody "best practice" solutions to design problems which recur in a range of different contexts [4].

One specific and popular set of software design patterns, which are independent of any specific application domain, are the so-called "GoF"[1] patterns which are described in the catalogue of Gamma et al. [55]. The GoF catalogue is thus a description of the know-how of expert designers in problems appearing in various different domains.

The patterns in the GoF catalogue are described using a consistent format which is based on an extension of the general object-oriented design technique OMT (Object Modelling Technique [123]). A graphical notation is used to represent the main constituents of the pattern – classes, methods, and relationships between classes – and this is supplemented with natural language descriptions of the intent and motivation of the pattern and the roles and responsibilities of its constituents. In addition, examples of the use of the patterns, in the form of both designs and sample code, are included. This notation has in fact effectively been adopted as the standard way of presenting software design patterns.

This form of presentation gives a very good intuitive picture of the patterns, but it is not sufficiently precise to allow a designer to demonstrate conclusively that a particular problem matches a particular pattern or that a proposed solution is consistent with a particular pattern. Moreover, it also makes it difficult to be certain that the patterns themselves are meaningful and contain no inconsistencies. Indeed, in some cases the descriptions of the patterns are intentionally left loose and incomplete to ensure that they are applicable in as wide a range of applications as possible, which can make it difficult for designers to be sure that they have interpreted and understood the patterns correctly. A formal model of patterns can help to alleviate these problems.

---

[1] Gang of Four.

In this chapter we present a formal model of a generic object-oriented design based upon the extended OMT notation, and show how designs can be formally linked with patterns in this model. Finally, we show how the properties of individual patterns can be specified in the model, thus giving a basis for formally checking whether a given design and a given pattern are consistent with each other.

11.2 A Formal Model of Object-Oriented Design

Both a general object oriented design in OMT and a description of a design pattern in the extended OMT are based around various kinds of diagram, the most important of which are class diagrams and interaction diagrams. Class diagrams show the different classes that make up the design together with their instance variables and methods, and also show the relationships between different classes. Interaction diagrams represent sequences of method calls and thus partly define the functionality of particular methods. Examples in the extended OMT notation of a class diagram and an interaction diagram, which in fact represent respectively the structure and collaborations of the Command pattern (see [55]), are shown in Figures 11.1 and 11.2.

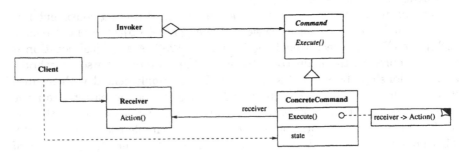

Fig. 11.1. Class diagram: Command pattern structure.

We begin by describing the main elements and properties informally in Section 11.2.1, then go on to develop a formal specification of these in Section 11.2.2.

11.2.1 The Extended OMT Notation

In the class diagram classes are depicted as rectangles containing the name of the class in bold face type at the top and below this the signatures (i.e. the names and the parameters) of the methods of the class followed by its instance variables. Every class in the design must have a unique name.

Classes and methods may be either *abstract* or *concrete*, an abstract class being one from which no instances (objects) can be created and an abstract

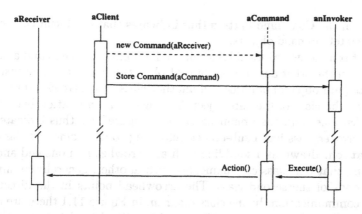

Fig. 11.2. Interaction diagram: collaborations of the Command pattern.

method one which cannot be executed (perhaps because the method is only completely defined in subclasses). An abstract class or method is indicated in the class diagram by writing its name in italic script instead of upright script.

Concrete methods, which can be executed, may additionally have *annotations* in the class diagram. These annotations indicate what actions the method should perform and they appear within rectangles with a "folded" corner which are attached to a method within the class description rectangle by a dashed line ending in a small circle.

Thus, for example, the class diagram in Figure 11.1 indicates that the class ConcreteCommand is a concrete class which contains a concrete method called Execute and a state variable called state, while the class Command is an abstract class in which the method called Execute is abstract. In addition, the annotation attached to the Execute method in the ConcreteCommand class indicates that the action of this method is to invoke the Action method on the variable called receiver.

The relationships in the class diagram indicate connections or communications between classes. They are represented as lines linking classes, four different kinds of lines being used to distinguish four different types of relations as follows:

inheritance: drawn as a solid line with a triangle in the middle and indicating that one class is a subclass of another. The base of the triangle lies towards the subclass. The inheritance relation between the Command class and the ConcreteCommand class in Figure 11.1 thus indicates that the ConcreteCommand class is a subclass of the Command class.

instantiation: drawn as a dashed line with an arrowhead on one end and indicating that one class creates objects belonging to another class. The arrowhead points to the class from which the objects are created. The instantiation relation between the Client class and the ConcreteCommand class in the Command pattern thus indicates that the Client class creates ConcreteCommand objects.

aggregation: drawn as a solid line with a diamond on one end and an arrowhead on the other and indicating that objects of one class are constituent parts (sub-objects) of objects of another class. The arrowhead points towards the class of the sub-object. The aggregation relation between the Invoker class and the Command class in Figure 11.1 thus indicates that the Invoker class has a sub-object belonging to the Command class.

association: drawn as a solid line with an arrowhead on one end and indicating that one class communicates with another, generally by invoking methods of the second class. The arrowhead points in the direction of the communication. In the class diagram in Figure 11.1 there are association relations between the Client and the Receiver classes and between the ConcreteCommand and the Receiver classes corresponding to the invocation of methods in the Receiver class by methods in the Client class and the ConcreteCommand class.

Association and aggregation relations also have an associated *arity* and may additionally have an associated name. The arity indicates the number of objects participating in the relation, and may be either one or many according to whether each object of one class communicates with or is composed of a single object or a collection of objects of the other class. Relations of arity many are indicated by adding a solid black circle to the front of the arrowhead, as shown in the aggregation relation between the MacroCommand and the Command classes in Figure 11.3. Names of relations, which generally correspond to state variables (although the state variables may not be explicitly shown), are written above the line representing the relation as in the name commands of the same aggregation relation.

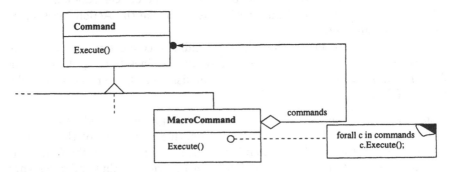

Fig. 11.3. The structure of the Macro Command.

The interaction diagram in Figure 11.2 gives details about the interactions between the Client, Invoker, Receiver and ConcreteCommand classes. It shows that the Client first creates a new instance of the ConcreteCommand class and instantiates the receiver instance variable in that instance, then it passes this concrete command to the Invoker by invoking its StoreCommand method with the concrete command as its parameter.

11.2.2 Formalising the Components of the Model

The basic building blocks of design which are used in the class diagram are classes, methods, state variables, and relations. These are distinguished by their names, which we specify as sort types. However, the names of relations are in fact the same as the names of the state variables with which they are associated, so we only introduce types representing class names, method names, and variable names:

type
    Class_Name, Method_Name, Variable_Name

We deal with each of the four elements separately.

Methods. The definition of a method in the extended OMT notation consists in general of two parts – its *signature*, which comprises its name, its input parameters and its result and which is written inside the rectangle representing the class to which the method belongs, and its (optional) *body*, which gives an indication of the actions that the method performs and which takes the form of a list of interactions appearing as an annotation in a separate rectangle which is linked to the signature.

In fact there are essentially only two different kinds of interactions that appear in the method body: invocations and instantiations.

An invocation represents an interaction in which objects of one class request objects of another (possibly the same) class to perform some action by executing some method. In the case where the two classes are different (see for example the description of the body of the Execute method in the ConcreteCommand class in the Command pattern illustrated in Figure 11.1), this corresponds to a communication between two classes and there will be either an association or an aggregation relation which links the two classes and which represents that communication. In addition, the name of the relation is the name of a variable which represents the receiver of the invocation (the variable receiver in the Execute method).

In the case where the two classes are the same, the invocation could be to a method in the same class or to a method in a superclass of that class. In general, however, there are no specific variables in the design which correspond to the receivers of these invocations, so we introduce two reserved variable names self and super, which respectively represent the receivers of invocations to the same class and to a superclass of the current class (cf. the variables of the same name in Smalltalk). The fact that these are different values is enforced by an axiom.

value
   self, super : Variable_Name

axiom
   self $\neq$ super

An invocation then consists of a variable name, which may be a variable defined in the design or **self** or **super**, together with the name of the method being invoked and the actual parameters passed to that method.

The actual parameters are basically just a list of variables, though they may not include the reserved variable **super**. We therefore introduce the subtype **Wf_Variable_Name** of **Variable_Name** whose defining predicate **wf_vble_name** excludes the value **super**, then use this subtype to define the type **Actual_Parameters** which represents the parameters of an invocation:

type
   Wf_Variable_Name = {| v : Variable_Name • wf_vble_name(v) |},
   Actual_Parameters = Wf_Variable_Name*

value
   wf_vble_name : Variable_Name $\rightarrow$ **Bool**
   wf_vble_name(v) $\equiv$ v $\neq$ super

Next, we define the record type **Actual_Signature** to represent the name of the method being invoked together with its actual parameters, and an invocation as a whole is then represented by the record type **Invocation** which consists of the name of the variable representing the receiver of the request plus the appropriate signature:

type
   Actual_Signature ::
      meth_name : Method_Name a_params : Actual_Parameters,
   Invocation ::
      call_vble : Variable_Name call_sig : Actual_Signature

An instantiation represents an interaction in which one class requests another class to create a new object. In most object-oriented programming languages there are essentially two ways in which this can be done: either the class might create a "default" instance of itself and then set the state variables of this instance appropriately using other methods; or the class may have other local creation methods which have parameters which are used to create customised instances directly. We cover both of these situations in our model by representing an instantiation as the type **Instantiation** which consists of the name of the class to be instantiated together with a possibly empty list of actual parameters to be used by the instantiation method.

type
  Instantiation ::
    class_name : Class_Name a_params : Actual_Parameters

A design may also indicate the results returned by methods and assignments to variables within the bodies of the methods, including assignments to both state variables and local (dummy) variables.

In an actual implementation, the result of a method is likely to be a tuple or a list of variables, but we model this abstractly and use just a set of variables since this is sufficient to capture all the necessary properties. However, it is clear that the result cannot include the variable **super**, so we use the type **Wf_Variable_Name** to define the type **Result**.

type
  Variables = Wf_Variable_Name-**set**,
  Result = Variables

Assignments come in two different forms: one in which the result of some *request* (i.e. instantiation, invocation, etc.) is assigned to one or more variables, generally so that it can be used as parameters or receivers of subsequent actions; and one where the parameters of the method are assigned to variables, generally state variables. We model the first of these as a mapping from sets of variables to requests, where requests are modelled using the union type **Request**, and the second as a mapping from sets of variables to sets of variables.

In both cases the domain value of the mapping should not include the variables **self** or **super** since it doesn't make sense to assign values to those variables, and in the second case the range value of the mapping should also not include the variable **super** but it may include the variable **self**. We therefore introduce another subtype (**Wf_Vble_Name**) of **Variable_Name** whose defining predicate **not_self_super** excludes these two values. Then both kinds of assignment are modelled by the map type **Variable_Change**, which maps sets of variables to either requests or sets of variables (the union type **Request_or_Var**) and which is also defined as a subtype, its defining predicate **is_wf_vchange** requiring that we do not make an assignment to the empty set of variables. Additional constraints on this "variable change map" are defined below as part of the well-formedness condition on a method as a whole.

type
  Wf_Vble_Name = {| v : Variable_Name • not_self_super(v) |},
  Request = Invocation | Instantiation | _ ,
  Request_or_Var = Request | Variables,
  Variable_Change =
    {| m : Wf_Vble_Name-**set** $\overrightarrow{m}$ Request_or_Var • is_wf_vchange(m) |}

value
 not_self_super : Variable_Name $\rightarrow$ **Bool**
 not_self_super(v) $\equiv$ v $\neq$ self $\wedge$ v $\neq$ super,

 is_wf_vchange : (Wf_Vble_Name-**set** $\overrightarrow{m}$ Request_or_Var) $\rightarrow$ **Bool**
 is_wf_vchange(m) $\equiv$ {} $\notin$ **dom** m

As explained in Section 11.2.1, methods may be abstract or concrete. In general, only the signature is defined for an abstract method, which means that the method cannot be executed, whereas a concrete method is defined completely and can be executed. Abstract methods are commonly defined in superclasses, concrete definitions of the same method being given in the subclasses. However, in some cases it is useful to define some methods abstractly in a superclass even if they should not be executable or do not make sense in all subclasses. (See for example the Composite pattern in [55] in which the child management operations Add, Remove, and GetChild do not make sense at all in the Leaf classes although they are in principle available because they are inherited from the Component class.) In this case, the method should be concrete in all concrete subclasses but it is not executable. We therefore subdivide the classification of a concrete method into *error* methods and *implemented* methods in order to be able to distinguish these two cases.

Like an abstract method, an error method cannot be executed. Thus, both perform no actions and therefore have no body, so we represent their bodies simply by the constants **defined** and **error** respectively. An implemented method, on the other hand, must actually perform some action and so does have a body, though this could be empty since the actions of the method might not be specified in the design. In this case, the body consists of the requests and assignments contained in the annotation to the method, and we therefore model it using the **Variable_Change** mapping defined above together with a list of requests which represents the actions performed by the method in the order in which they are performed. The bodies of the three kinds of methods are then modelled using the variant type **Method_Body** as follows:

type
 Method_Body ==
   defined |
   error |
   implemented(variable_change: Variable_Change, request_list: Request*)

Finally, we come to the input parameters appearing in a method's signature, which we refer to as its formal parameters in order to distinguish them from the actual parameters used in invocations of the method. There are in fact two ways in which these formal parameters can be defined in the extended OMT notation: in the first case only the name of the parameter is given, while in the second the parameter name is accompanied by a class name which indicates the class of the object the parameter represents. Formal parameters may not include the values **self** or **super** since they represent generic "placeholders" for actual variables, and all variable names used in the formal parameters must be different so that the variables can be distinguished in the body of the method.

We use the variant type **Parameter** to represent the two different kinds of formal parameters, the variable names in both variants being represented by the type **Wf_Vble_Name** which automatically excludes the unwanted values **self** and **super**. Then the formal parameters of a method are described by the subtype **Wf_Formal_Parameters**, which is a list of parameters in which no two parameters have the same variable name.

The defining predicate **is_wf_formal_parameters** of the subtype, which represents the above consistency condition, is written in terms of the auxiliary function **type_parameter** which simply extracts the variable name from a parameter.

type
  Parameter ==
    var(Wf_Vble_Name) |
    paramTyped(paramName : Wf_Vble_Name, className : Class_Name),
  Wf_Formal_Parameters =
    {| p : Parameter* • is_wf_formal_parameters(p) |}

value
  is_wf_formal_parameters : Parameter* $\rightarrow$ **Bool**
  is_wf_formal_parameters(p) $\equiv$
    ($\forall$ i, j : **Nat** •
      {i, j} $\subseteq$ inds p $\wedge$
      type_parameter(p(i)) = type_parameter(p(j)) $\Rightarrow$
      i = j),

  type_parameter : Parameter $\rightarrow$ Variable_Name
  type_parameter(p) $\equiv$
    case p **of** var(v) $\rightarrow$ v, paramTyped(v, c) $\rightarrow$ v **end**

Putting all these various components together, we define a method as a whole using a record type which comprises the method's body, its result, and its formal parameters.

type
  Method ::
    f_params : Wf_Formal_Parameters
    meth_res : Result
    body : Method_Body

There are a number of consistency conditions which this record type must satisfy in order for it to be a valid representation of a method. These are:

receiver_in_call_vble: any request which appears in the range of the variable change mapping of an implemented method must appear in the list of requests comprising the body of that method;

correct_list_ins: the result of every instantiation in the body of an implemented method must be assigned to a variable in the variable change mapping and therefore must appear in the range of that mapping. This condition is in fact not strictly necessary but corresponds to a sort of "no waste" condition – the instantiation must return a new object and if this is not assigned to a variable it is just lost and there was therefore no point in creating it;

is_correct_fparams: the variable change mapping cannot make assignments to formal parameters of an implemented method;

is_error_method: an error method cannot return a result (i.e. its result must be an empty set of variables);

correct_inst_assig: if an instantiation appears in the variable change map, the set of variables to which it is assigned must contain exactly one variable (because the result of an instantiation is always a single variable; i.e. only one object is created);

correct_vble_assig: when the variable change map assigns one set of variables to another, the two sets must contain the same number of variables;

correct_collel_assig: if an invocation of the method collectionelement[2] appears in the variable change map, the set of variables to which it is assigned must contain exactly one variable (because its result is a single variable).

These seven functions are combined together in the function is_wf_method, and this is used as the defining predicate for the subtype Wf_Method of the type Method. This completes our definition of a method.

value
  is_wf_method : Method $\rightarrow$ **Bool**
  is_wf_method(m) $\equiv$
    receiver_in_call_vble(m) $\wedge$
    correct_list_ins(m) $\wedge$
    is_correct_fparams(m) $\wedge$
    is_error_method(m) $\wedge$

---

[2] This is one of a group of three reserved method names – collectionadd, collectionremove and collectionelement – which are introduced in order to model various operations on collections of objects which are not specified explicitly but which are implicit in the names of the methods used in a particular design or pattern, for instance the methods Attach and Detach in the Observer pattern in [55]. The method collectionelement returns one element from a collection.

correct_inst_assig(m) ∧
correct_vble_assig(m) ∧ correct_collel_assig(m)

type
  Wf_Method = {| m : Method • is_wf_method(m) |}

The last step in this section is to define the collection of all methods in a class. This is done using the map type **Map_Methods**, which associates the name of each method with its definition. Using a finite map here automatically ensures that no two methods in the same class have the same name. At this level there is only one constraint, namely that the reserved method names **collectionadd**, **collectionremove** and **collectionelement** cannot be used as the names of methods in the design. This is expressed using the function **is_wf_class_method** and this is in turn used as the defining predicate of the subtype **Class_Method** which then represents the well-formed collection of all methods in a class.

type
  Map_Methods = Method_Name $\overrightarrow{m}$ Wf_Method,
  Class_Method = {| m : Map_Methods • is_wf_class_method(m) |}

value
  is_wf_class_method : Map_Methods → **Bool**
  is_wf_class_method(m) ≡
    collectionadd ∉ **dom** m ∧
    collectionremove ∉ **dom** m ∧ collectionelement ∉ **dom** m

State Variables. The state variables of a class can simply be described as a set of variables, except that the set cannot include the two reserved variables **self** and **super**. We therefore use the subtype **Wf_Vble_Name** of **Variable_Name** introduced above to define the type **State** which represents the state variables of a class:

type
  State = Wf_Vble_Name-**set**

Classes. Its state variables and methods are the main elements of a class, and these are modelled by the types **Class_Method** and **State** introduced above. However, as explained in Section 11.2.1, a class may be either abstract or concrete. We model this *class type* using the variant type **Class_Type**, and a class is then modelled as the record type **Design_Class** which is composed of the appropriate three components:

type
  Class_Type == abstract | concrete,

Design_Class ::
  class_state : State
  class_methods : Class_Method
  class_type : Class_Type

Again, the basic record type requires some constraints, though in this case only one, namely that state variables cannot be used as formal parameters of methods since this would lead to ambiguity when referring to the name in the body of the method. We define the function **is_wf_class** to capture this property and use this as the defining predicate for the subtype **Wf_Class** of well-formed classes. The function **method_in_class** used in the definition of **is_wf_class** simply checks that a given method belongs to a given class.

value
  is_wf_class : Design_Class → **Bool**
  is_wf_class(c) ≡
  (
    ∀ m : Wf_Method •
      method_in_class(m, c) ⇒
      class_state(c) ∩ set_f_params(f_params(m)) = {}
  ),

  method_in_class : Wf_Method × Design_Class → **Bool**
  method_in_class(m, c) ≡ m ∈ **rng** class_methods(c)

type
  Wf_Class = {| c : Design_Class • is_wf_class(c) |}

The collection of all classes in a design is then modelled analogously to the collection of all methods in a class – the map type **Classes** associates the name of each class with its definition. Again, using a finite map here automatically ensures that no two classes in the design have the same name.

type
  Classes = Class_Name $\overrightarrow{m}$ Wf_Class

Relations. A relation is basically a link between classes which has one of four distinct types (inheritance, association, aggregation, or instantiation) and which may also (in the case of association and aggregation relations only) have an arity. All relations except inheritance relations are binary and link a single *source* class to a single *sink* class. Inheritance relations are in general one-to-many, linking a superclass with an arbitrary number of subclasses. However, it is possible to view a single one-to-many inheritance relation which links one superclass to (say) n subclasses as n binary inheritance relations, each linking the superclass to one of the subclasses. This allows us to consider all relations as binary relations and thus simplify our model.

In the case of instantiation and (binary) inheritance relations, there can be at most one such relation between any pair of classes. The relation type together with the source and sink classes is thus sufficient to identify the relation uniquely. However, it is possible to have more than one association or aggregation relation between the same two classes, with different relations being distinguished by their names, which are essentially variable names except that the names self and super may not be used. Association and aggregation relations also have associated source and sink cardinalities, which may be one or many.

We use the type Ref to record the name and cardinalities of association and aggregation relations, the name being modelled using the type Wf_Vble_Name in order to exclude the unwanted values and the cardinality by the variant type Card which simply comprises the two possible values. The variant type Relation_Type similarly models the type of a relation: for inheritance and instantiation relations it is just a constant of the appropriate name, while for aggregation and association relations it is a function of the appropriate name applied to a value of type Ref. A relation as a whole is then modelled by the record type Design_Relation, which comprises the type of the relation and the names of its source and sink classes as explained above.

type
  Card == one | many,
  Ref ::
    relation_name : Wf_Vble_Name
    sink_card : Card
    source_card : Card,
  Relation_Type ==
    inheritance | association(as_ref : Ref) |
      aggregation(ag_ref : Ref) | instantiation,
  Design_Relation ::
    relation_type : Relation_Type
    source_class : Class_Name
    sink_class : Class_Name

The well-formedness condition wf_relation on a relation states that instantiation relations are not explicitly shown between a class and itself in the extended OMT diagram (every class is generally assumed to be able to instantiate itself) and that there cannot be inheritance relations between a class and itself since this would lead to essentially infinite inheritance structures. This is used as the basis for defining the subtype Wf_Relation of well-formed relations. The auxiliary function is_assoc_or_aggr simply checks whether a relation is either an association or an aggregation relation.

value
　wf_relation : Design_Relation → **Bool**
　wf_relation(r) ≡
　　~ is_assoc_or_aggr(r) ⇒ source_class(r) ≠ sink_class(r),

　is_assoc_or_aggr : Design_Relation → **Bool**
　is_assoc_or_aggr(r) ≡
　　relation_type(r) ≠ inheritance ∧ relation_type(r) ≠ instantiation

type
　Wf_Relation = {| r : Design_Relation • wf_relation(r) |}

Because it is impossible to have two identical relations between the same two classes (we cannot have two instantiation relations or two inheritance relations between the same two classes, and if we have two association or aggregation relations between the same two classes then those two relations must have different names), it is sufficient to model the collection of all relations in a design using a set. However, this set of relations must satisfy certain constraints as follows:

no_circularity: it is not possible for a class to have a "meaningless" relationship with itself arising implicitly as a result of a loop of relations. For example, we cannot have a collection of relations in which classes c_1, ..., c_n are linked by inheritance relations in such a way that c_{i+1} is a subclass of c_i for all i and c_1 is a subclass of c_n;

is_compatible_relation: if two classes are related by an inheritance relation then there cannot be any other relation between the same two classes and in the same direction (though relations in the opposite direction are of course possible);

different_variable_name: association and aggregation relations must be uniquely identified by their names.

The function is_valid_relation combines the last two constraints together, and the function is_correct_relation then extends the properties from two relations to an arbitrary set of relations:

value
　is_valid_relation : Wf_Relation × Wf_Relation → **Bool**
　is_valid_relation(e_1, e_2) ≡
　　is_compatible_relation(e_1, e_2) ∧ different_variable_name(e_1, e_2),

　is_correct_relation : Wf_Relation-set → **Bool**
　is_correct_relation(rs) ≡
　　(∀ e_1, e_2 : Wf_Relation •
　　　e_1 ∈ rs ∧ e_2 ∈ rs ⇒ is_valid_relation(e_1, e_2))

Finally, we combine all constraints in the function wf_relations and use this as the defining predicate for the subtype Wf_Relations of well-formed sets of relations in the usual way:

value
    wf_relations : Wf_Relation-**set** → **Bool**
    wf_relations(rs) ≡ no_circularity(rs) ∧ is_correct_relation(rs)

type
    Wf_Relations = {| rs : Wf_Relation-**set** • wf_relations(rs) |}

11.2.3 A Formal Model of an Object-Oriented Design

A design as a whole then simply consists of a collection of classes and a collection of relations, the collection of classes being represented by the type Classes and the collection of relations by the type Wf_Relations defined in Section 11.2.2. A design is therefore modelled as a simple Cartesian product of these two types.

type
    Design_Structure = Classes × Wf_Relations

There are of course many constraints that must apply to this combination of classes and relations in order for it to correctly model an object-oriented design. These include, for example, that an abstract class must have subclasses, that state variables cannot be redefined in subclasses, that the sink of an instantiation relation cannot be an abstract class (because we cannot build instances of an abstract class), that a concrete class contains no abstract methods, etc. etc. All these constraints are combined into the function is_wf_design_structure and this forms the defining predicate of the subtype Wf_Design_Structure which then represents a general object-oriented design in the extended OMT notation:

type
    Wf_Design_Structure =
      {| ds : Design_Structure • is_wf_design_structure(ds) |}

11.3 Linking Designs to Patterns

A pattern represents an abstract "outline" or "skeleton" of a design. It shows a collection of classes, together with some of their properties and some relationships between the various classes.

In order for a part of a design to match a particular pattern, there must be classes in the design which have the same properties as each of those in the pattern and which are related in the same way. To be able to check whether a design matches a particular pattern we therefore need to link the model of a general object-oriented design described and specified above to the design patterns. In this section we restrict to defining how to link a design to a single instance of a single pattern. We extend this to matching a design against multiple instances of one or more patterns simultaneously in Section 11.5.

The relationship between a design and a pattern is defined using a *renaming map*, which associates the names of entities (classes, methods, state variables and parameters) in the design with the names of corresponding entities in the pattern. A typical example of this is shown in Figure 11.4. Note that because the pattern only represents an abstract skeleton of a design some entities in the design may have no corresponding entity in the pattern as is in fact the case in the example shown.

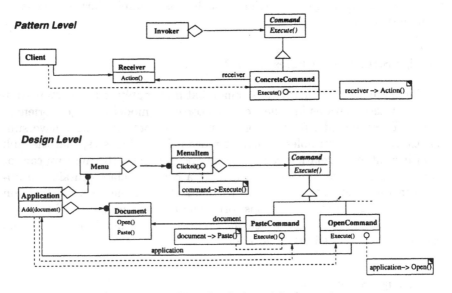

Fig. 11.4. Linking the design with the pattern.

The correspondence between state variables as well as that between parameters involves only a relationship between variables. We describe this using a *variable renaming*, which simply links names of variables in the design to those in the pattern. We model this using the simple map type `VariableRenaming`.

type
    VariableRenaming = Variable_Name $\twoheadrightarrow$ Variable_Name

The renaming for methods involves two parts. The first of these defines the correspondence between the names of the methods, while the second relates their parameters. Note that it is possible for several methods in the design to play the same *role* in the pattern, so we define the method renaming as the map type Method_and_Parameter_Renaming. This associates the names of methods in the design with instances of the type Method_Renaming, which consist of the method name in the pattern together with the variable renaming for the method's parameters. Note that the nested structure of the renaming is necessary because two different methods may have parameters with the same name.

type
  Method_Renaming ::
    method_name : Method_Name
    parameterRenaming : VariableRenaming,
  Method_and_Parameter_Renaming =
  Method_Name $\twoheadrightarrow$ Method_Renaming

The renaming of a class has a similarly nested structure, except that here we need to include both the map representing the renaming of the methods in the class and that representing the renaming of the state variables inside the record type ClassRenaming along with the name of the class in the pattern. The other difference is that in this case it is possible for a single class in the design to play several roles in the pattern (for instance, in the example illustrating the Command pattern in [55] the class Application in the design plays both the Client and the Receiver roles in the pattern). We therefore map each design class to a set of class renamings in the renaming map, and the full renaming map is represented by the type Renaming.

type
  ClassRenaming ::
    classname : Class_Name
    methodRenaming : Method_and_Parameter_Renaming
    varRenaming : VariableRenaming,
  Renaming = Class_Name $\twoheadrightarrow$ ClassRenaming-set

In order for the renaming map to be well-formed, no class in the design can have an empty set of renamings (we model the fact that a class in the design plays no role in the pattern by simply omitting it from the domain of the renaming map) and the renamings of any one design class must all refer to different pattern classes (otherwise a single design class can have two contradictory renamings).

We specify these two properties using the functions images_not_empty and different_images_class_name respectively, and these are combined in the function is_wf_Renaming, which then forms the defining predicate of the subtype Wf_Renaming.

value
  images_not_empty : Renaming → **Bool**
  images_not_empty(r) ≡ {} ∉ **rng** r,

  different_images_class_name : Renaming → **Bool**
  different_images_class_name(r) ≡
    (
      $\forall$ c : Class_Name, cr_1, cr_2 : ClassRenaming •
        c ∈ **dom** r ∧ cr_1 ≠ cr_2 ∧ cr_1 ∈ r(c) ∧ cr_2 ∈ r(c) ⇒
          classname(cr_1) ≠ classname(cr_2)
    ),

  is_wf_Renaming : Renaming → **Bool**
  is_wf_Renaming(r) ≡
    different_images_class_name(r) ∧ images_not_empty(r)

type
  Wf_Renaming = {| r : Renaming • is_wf_Renaming(r) |}

Then a design together with a renaming map which defines its correspondences to a given pattern is described by the simple Cartesian product type Design_Renaming.

type
  Design_Renaming = Wf_Design_Structure × Wf_Renaming

This combination must satisfy the following constraints:

is_correct_domain: every entity which has a renaming under the renaming map must be in the design;

equal_meth_ren_in_hierarchy: if a method plays some role in a superclass and also some role in a subclass then the two roles must be the same;

meth_ren_in_hierarchy: if a method plays some role in a superclass and the subclass inherits a different version of the method (i.e. the method is redefined locally or in an intermediate class) then the method must also play a role in the subclass;

card_images_of_parameters: no method has more than one parameter. (This constraint applies only to matching designs against GoF patterns and derives from the fact that no method in the GoF patterns has more than one parameter. It would be omitted if we wanted to generalise the matching to other forms of patterns.)

The function is_wf_design_renaming combines these constraints together, and this is then used to define the subtype Wf_Design_Renaming of Design_Renaming in the usual way.

value
  is_wf_design_renaming : Design_Renaming → **Bool**
  is_wf_design_renaming(dr) ≡
    card_images_of_parameters(dr) ∧
    is_correct_domain(dr) ∧
    equal_meth_ren_in_hierarchy(dr) ∧ meth_ren_in_hierarchy(dr)

type
  Wf_Design_Renaming =
    {| pr : Design_Renaming • is_wf_design_renaming(pr) |}

11.4 Specifying Properties of Patterns

The description of each particular pattern in [55] defines the properties of
the various components (classes, methods, and relations) in that pattern. We
can formally specify these properties for each individual pattern using our
model. We illustrate this process for the Command pattern, the structure of
which is shown in Figure 11.1. Corresponding specifications of most of the
other GoF patterns can be found in [100, 51, 118, 50, 6].

The structure essentially consists of a hierarchy of Command and ConcreteCommand classes which represent the commands, together with Invoker,
Receiver and Client classes. Each ConcreteCommand class has an Execute
method, which defines what the command does, and is associated with a particular Receiver class, which represents the objects on which the command
acts. The command stores an instance of its Receiver class in its receiver
state variable, and the command is executed by invoking a particular Action method from the Receiver class on this state variable as shown in the
annotation to the Execute method.

The interaction diagram in Figure 11.2 shows that the Client basically acts
as coordinator between the Invoker, Receiver and ConcreteCommand classes.
First, it creates a new concrete command and instantiates its receiver, then
it passes this concrete command to the invoker. However, the second of these
interactions, that is the interaction between the client and the invoker, is not
included in the pattern structure (Figure 11.1).

It is in fact quite common for information about different aspects of a
pattern to be given in different parts of its description in [55]. However, this
can make it difficult for a designer to be sure that a given design captures all
aspects of the pattern correctly. We therefore base our formal specification
on an extension of the pattern structure which is shown in Figure 11.5.

This includes the full invocation as shown in the interaction diagram in
Figure 11.2, and also introduces a new role, ClientMethod, into the Client
class to represent the method which invokes the StoreCommand method in
the Invoker, which we also show explicitly. However, we allow this invocation

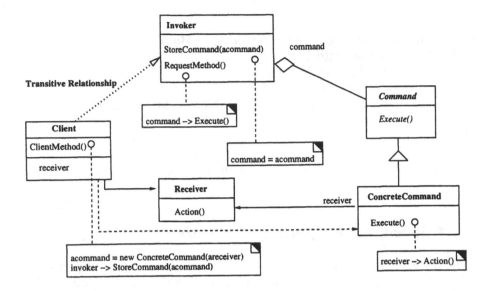

Fig. 11.5. The modified Command structure.

to be indirect, so that the relation between the Client and the Invoker may be transitive. We also explicitly define the body of the StoreCommand method based on its properties shown in the interaction diagram – it should have a single parameter which represents a command and it simply assigns this parameter to its command state variable.

Note that our modified pattern structure omits the state variable state from the ConcreteCommand class. This is because, according to the discussion of the Command pattern in [55], this variable is intended to support undo and redo operations and the pattern can in fact be used to design systems which do not have such operations[3].

The first step towards formally specifying the properties of the pattern is to introduce constants which represent the names of the classes, methods and variables appearing in the pattern and to use axioms to ensure that these values are all different[4]. These constants are:

value
 Invoker : Class_Name,
 Client : Class_Name,

---

[3] The state variable is in any case not sufficient to support undo and redo operations on its own. Additional methods would also be required in the Command and/or ConcreteCommand classes.

[4] These axioms are omitted here for brevity. They are entirely analogous to the similar axiom introduced in Section 11.2.2 to ensure that the two reserved variable names self and super are distinct.

Command : Class_Name,
ConcreteCommand : Class_Name,
Receiver : Class_Name,
command : Variable_Name,
receiver : Variable_Name,
command_param : Variable_Name,
Execute : Method_Name,
Action : Method_Name,
StoreCommand : Method_Name,
ClientMethod : Method_Name,
RequestMethod : Method_Name

Next we specify the properties of the various entities in the patterns.

Rather than specifying the properties of each pattern directly, however, we try to identify properties which are common to several patterns and specify these more generally (i.e. without explicit reference to any one pattern). This helps to make our specification not only shorter but also more general and easier to extend to new patterns – the generic functions we introduce encapsulate common properties in such a way that they only need to be specified once and, being generic, are more likely to be reusable if we later wish to extend our specification to new patterns.

Looking at the Command and ConcreteCommand classes in the Command pattern, we can see that these are related by an inheritance relation, the Command class being an abstract superclass of the ConcreteCommand class. Many patterns contain a pair of classes which have precisely these properties, so we introduce a generic function hierarchy which captures them and which has the names of the roles involved as parameters. Recall, however, that the pattern represents an idealised design and a concrete design may include other classes. In this particular instance this means first that there may be more than one subclass playing the ConcreteCommand role and second that there may be intermediate classes in the hierarchy (i.e. that the ConcreteCommand classes are not necessarily direct subclasses of the Command class. We incorporate this freedom into our specification of the hierarchy function, and the function thus checks that a hierarchy of classes in the design has as its root a class which plays a given role in the pattern and which is unique in the design (Command), has leaf classes which play any of a given set of roles in the pattern (ConcreteCommand), does not contain classes playing other roles in the pattern, and has roles which are consistent in superclasses and subclasses (i.e. if some subclass of the root class plays a particular role in the pattern and some subclass of that subclass also plays a role in the pattern then the two roles must be the same). The actual specification of the function hierarchy is quite long so we show only its signature here. The required property of the Command pattern is then embodied in the function Command_hierarchy which simply instantiates the function hierarchy with the appropriate roles.

value
  hierarchy : Class_Name × Class_Name-**set** ×
    Class_Name-**set** × Wf_Design_Renaming → **Bool**
  hierarchy(cp_1, cps_1, cps_2, ((dsc, dsr), r)) ≡ ... ,

  Command_hierarchy : Wf_Design_Renaming → **Bool**
  Command_hierarchy(dr) ≡
    hierarchy
      (
        Command,
        {ConcreteCommand},
        {Receiver, Invoker, Client},
        dr
)

Other properties of the classes, methods and relations in the Command pattern are specified in a similar way. Thus, for example, every class playing the ConcreteCommand role should contain exactly one state variable playing the receiver role, which is specified generically by the function store_unique_vble and for the Command pattern by the function store_receiver which is simply defined as the appropriate instantiation of this:

value
  store_receiver : Wf_Design_Renaming → **Bool**
  store_receiver(dr) ≡
    store_unique_vble(ConcreteCommand, receiver, dr)

Similarly, every class playing the Invoker role should contain at least one method playing the RequestMethod role, and every method playing this role in the class should be implemented and should contain an invocation to the command state variable of the method which plays the Execute role in the Command class. Furthermore, every class playing the Invoker role should have exactly one state variable which plays the command role and should be linked to the class playing the Command role by an aggregation relation representing the state variable playing the command role and there should be no other relations between classes of these two roles. For the properties of the methods playing the RequestMethod role, the function exists_method checks generally whether a class has some method playing a given role, while the function deleg_with_var checks that every method playing a particular role in a particular class is implemented and contains an invocation to a particular state variable in the same class of a given method in some other given class. For the properties of the state variable and the relations, the function store_unique_vble states that a class should have only one state variable playing a given role, the function has_unique_assoc_aggr checks that there is precisely one association or aggregation relation and no instantiation relations between two classes, and the function **has_assoc_aggr_var_ren** checks that the relation has given type and arity and corresponds to a state variable playing a particular role. These functions, appropriately instantiated, are combined in the functions **Invoker_invoke** and **Invoker_has_Command** which represent the required properties of the Command pattern.

value
   Invoker_invoke : Wf_Design_Renaming → **Bool**
   Invoker_invoke(ds, r) ≡
    exists_method(Invoker, RequestMethod, r) ∧
    deleg_with_var
     (Invoker, RequestMethod, command, Command, Execute, (ds, r)),

   Invoker_has_Command : Wf_Design_Renaming → **Bool**
   Invoker_has_Command(dr) ≡
    has_unique_assoc_aggr(Invoker, Command, dr) ∧
    has_assoc_aggr_var_ren
     (Invoker, Command, Aggregation, command, one, dr) ∧
    store_unique_vble(Invoker, command, dr)

The other properties of the Command pattern are specified analogously, and then combined together into the function **is_command_pattern** which then gives the complete specification of the properties of the pattern.

value
   is_command_pattern : Wf_Design_Renaming → **Bool**
   is_command_pattern(dr) ≡
    Command_hierarchy(dr) ∧
    store_receiver(dr) ∧
    Invoker_has_Command(dr) ∧
    Invoker_invoke(dr) ∧
    ...

Specifications like the above can be used to formally define whether a subset of a given design matches a given pattern – the renaming map introduced in Section 11.3 defines the correspondence between entities in the design and entities in the pattern (or which role in the pattern is played by a particular entity in the design), so the design matches the pattern if each entity in the renaming map at the design level satisfies the properties of the pattern level entity to which it renames. A concrete example of this process can be found in [52].

11.5 Extending to Multiple Patterns

The model of the renaming map presented in Section 11.3 above assumes that only a single instance of a single pattern is being linked to the design at any time. In reality, of course, a given design may involve many different patterns and also many different occurrences of the same pattern. In addition, the patterns may be overlapping, with a single class or method in a design playing one role in one pattern and another role in another pattern. In this section we extend the renaming map so that it can link a single design with a group of patterns simultaneously.

In order to do this, however, we need to know not just the role that a particular class plays but also the pattern in which it plays that role – this is because different GoF patterns contain the same role so in general it is impossible to deduce the pattern from the name of the role alone. In addition, we need to take account of the facts that one class can play different roles in different patterns and that many instances of the same pattern may occur in a single design.

We model each instance of each particular pattern using the same renaming map as we used in the matching of a design to a single pattern (the type Wf_Renaming defined in Section 11.3) and we introduce the abstract type RenId of *renaming identifiers* to distinguish the renamings associated with different occurrences of the same pattern in the design. The collection of renamings associated with one given pattern is then modelled using the map type Renaming_Map which associates renaming identifiers with well-formed renamings. Then the *multi-renaming*, which is the renaming for all instances of all patterns in the whole design, is represented as a map from *pattern names* to the collection of renamings corresponding to that pattern, where the pattern names are represented by the sort type Pattern_Name. This basically comprises the set of names of all the GoF patterns, but it is specified more abstractly to allow more patterns to be added to the specification if necessary. Thus we specify simply that the names Abstract_Factory, Adapter_Class, Adapter_Object, Bridge, and so on are all valid but different pattern names but we do not specify that these are the only such names[5].

type
    Pattern_Name,
    RenId,
    Renaming_Map = RenId $\overrightarrow{m}$ Wf_Renaming,
    Multi_Renaming = Pattern_Name $\overrightarrow{m}$ Renaming_Map

value
    Abstract_Factory, Adapter_Class, Adapter_Object, Bridge, Builder,

---

[5] Again we omit the axioms for brevity since they are once more entirely analogous to the similar axiom introduced in Section 11.2.2 to ensure that the two reserved variable names **self** and **super** are distinct.

Command, Composite, Decorator, Facade, Factory_Method, Flyweight,
Iterator, Mediator, Memento, Observer, Prototype, Proxy,
Singleton, State, Strategy, Template_Method, Visitor
  : Pattern_Name

Next, we associate each pattern name with the formal specification of
that pattern, in particular with the functions like is_command_pattern which
specify the complete set of properties of the patterns, in this case the Command
pattern. This is done using the *pattern table* which simply maps the
pattern name to the appropriate function.

type
  Pattern_Table = Pattern_Name $\overrightarrow{m}$ (Wf_Design_Renaming → **Bool**)

value
  pattern_table : Pattern_Table =
  [Command ↦ is_command_pattern,
      ...
  ]

If a particular pattern does not occur in a given design, we can indicate
this by simply omitting the pattern name from the domain of the multi-
renaming. We therefore rule out the possibility that a pattern has an empty
collection of renamings in the multi-renaming, which would basically also
amount to the pattern not occurring in the design, by imposing an appropriate well-formedness constraint. In addition, we require that only "known"
patterns, that is patterns whose names occur in the pattern table, may be
included in the multi-renaming. This is important because in order to check
whether a part of the design matches a pattern we need to know which function defines the properties of that pattern.

These two constraints are combined in the well-formedness function
is_wf_multi_renaming and this function is then used to construct the subtype Wf_Multi_Renaming of well-formed multi-renamings.

value
  is_wf_multi_renaming : Multi_Renaming → **Bool**
  is_wf_multi_renaming(mr) ≡
    [] $\not\in$ **rng** mr ∧ **dom** mr ⊆ **dom** pattern_table

type
  Wf_Multi_Renaming =
    {| p : Multi_Renaming • is_wf_multi_renaming(p) |}

A well-formed design together with a multi-renaming then forms the basis for checking whether a design matches a collection of patterns simultaneously. This is represented by the type Multi_Design_Pattern (cf. the definition of the type Design_Renaming in Section 11.3; we have simply replaced

the second component Wf_Renaming of the Cartesian product with the type Wf_Multi_Renaming).

type
    Multi_Design_Pattern = Wf_Design_Structure × Wf_Multi_Renaming

In the simple version of the model described in Section 11.3, we required that the renaming should be consistent with the design to which it is being applied (the function is_wf_design_renaming). In moving from a single renaming to a multi-renaming we have essentially replaced the single renaming map with a collection of renaming maps, so we similarly require that each of the renaming maps in this collection is consistent with the design, that is that the relationship between the design level and the pattern level that the multi-renaming defines is consistent. This means that each of the renaming maps in the multi-renaming must individually satisfy the well-formedness condition is_wf_design_renaming with respect to the design. This property is captured in the function each_renaming_is_wf:

value
    each_renaming_is_wf : Multi_Design_Pattern → **Bool**
    each_renaming_is_wf(ds, mr) ≡
        (
            ∀ p : Pattern_Name, r : Wf_Renaming •
                p ∈ **dom** mr ∧ r ∈ **rng** mr(p) ⇒ is_wf_design_renaming(ds, r)
)

We also require that each of the renamings associated with a single pattern in the multi-renaming must represent a different instance of the pattern, that is there cannot be two renamings for the same pattern in which every class plays the same role in both renamings. This property is embodied in the function each_instance_is_different, though its specification is made in terms of several auxiliary functions so is omitted here for brevity. The well-formedness constraint on the type Multi_Design_Pattern is then simply the conjunction of the two functions each_renaming_is_wf and each_instance_is_different. The function is_wf_multi_design_pattern combines these constraints and this is then used to define the subtype Wf_Multi_Design_Pattern of Multi_Design_Pattern:

type
    Wf_Multi_Design_Pattern =
        {| p : Multi_Design_Pattern • is_wf_multi_design_pattern(p) |}

value
    is_wf_multi_design_pattern : Multi_Design_Pattern → **Bool**
    is_wf_multi_design_pattern(mdp) ≡
        each_renaming_is_wf(mdp) ∧ each_instance_is_different(mdp)

With this extension, it is now possible to check whether a subset of a design matches a collection of patterns simultaneously. This is analogous to the method explained for a single pattern at the end of Section 11.4 except that in this case we require that for each renaming in the multi-renaming the design-level entities satisfy all the properties of the pattern-level entities to which they rename.

11.6 Conclusions

In this chapter we have described a formal model of a generic object-oriented design based on the extended OMT notation and we have shown how a design in this model can be linked to a GoF pattern using the renaming map. We have furthermore shown how the specific properties of individual GoF patterns can be specified in this model, and we have briefly indicated how such specifications can be used to determine whether or not a given design matches a given pattern. Finally, we have shown how it is possible with only slight modifications to extend the formal model from one which matches only a single design pattern against a subset of a design to one which matches a design against a set of patterns, possibly with overlapping roles and also allowing multiple instances of the same pattern.

The model allows designers to be sure, as well as to demonstrate to others, that they are using the patterns correctly and consistently. It can also help designers to understand the properties of the GoF patterns more clearly – indeed developing our specifications of the patterns such as that of the Command pattern discussed in Section 11.4 has identified a number of inconsistencies and incompletenesses in the informal descriptions of a number of patterns and has led us to propose similar modified or extended pattern structures for other patterns which resolve these problems.

Although we have limited our attention to GoF patterns in this work, we believe that the basic model of object-oriented design which we have presented in Section 11.2.2 is sufficiently general that it could be applied in a similar way to give formal descriptions of other design patterns based on the extended OMT notation. We also believe that the model could be modified relatively easily to give a similar model of object-oriented designs based on the UML notation (http://www.omg.org/uml).

Finally, we believe that the formality of our general model and of our specifications of the individual GoF patterns makes them a useful basis for tool support for GoF patterns and this is currently under investigation.

Background Information

This chapter is based on work undertaken by four members of the Facultad de Economía y Administración, Universidad Nacional de Comahue, Neuquén,

Argentina – Alejandra Cechich, Andres Flores, Luis Reynoso, and Gabriela Aranda – in collaboration with Richard Moore.

The first phase was carried out with Alejandra Cechich [21, 20] and concentrated on formally specifying the properties of some of the GoF patterns directly in RSL, concentrating particularly on the responsibilities and collaborations of the pattern participants. Here the structural aspects of the patterns were specified statically while the collaborations were specified in terms of sequences of interactions, thus closely mirroring the information presented in the interaction diagrams.

The generalisation of the model to a general object-oriented design and how to link a design with a single pattern using the renaming map was done with Andres Flores and Luis Reynoso [52, 53]. This model, which is the one presented here, represents both the structural properties and the collaborations statically, the collaborations being defined partly by the relations between the classes and partly by the requests the methods make to other classes through their bodies.

The specifications of the properties of the individual GoF patterns in the general model was done with Luis Reynoso (behavioural patterns; [100, 118]), Andres Flores (structural patterns; [51, 50]), and Gabriela Aranda (creational patterns; [6]).

Finally, the extension of the model to match a design against many patterns simultaneously, as well as work on specifying the properties of particular examples of so-called "compound patterns" (see for example [120, 141, 142, 143]) which is not presented here, was done with Gabriela Aranda [5].

12. Automated Result Verification with AWK

12.1 Introduction

The goal of implementation verification is to prove that a given program behaves correctly under all possible executions, for instance that it produces correct output for all legal inputs. There are several conditions on carrying out such verification in practice: (1) the implementation is available in a form suitable for analysis; (2) the implementation "size" is such that the proof remains feasible; (3) it is written in a language which supports specification and proof; and (4) there is enough human expertise to guide the proof.

Such conditions are often not satisfied in practice. Result verification is a possible alternative. It relies not on the implementation of the program but on its execution record. This record may be a sequence of inputs and the corresponding outputs from the program when it computes a certain function, or a sequence of values observed about the changing state of the program as it interacts with its environment, or perhaps such values augmented with time-stamps. Whatever the form, the goal is to decide if this record describes a correct execution of the program. A positive answer does not mean that the program is fault-free, only that this execution did not exhibit any errors. On the other hand, finding an error is like constructing a counter-example for claims of correctness about the program. Due to its modest goals, result verification has several advantages over implementation verification:

1. It can be carried out off-line, after the execution terminates, or on-line, as the execution unfolds.
2. Its application scope includes both off-the-shelf components (binary files) and remote service providers (distributed objects).
3. Due to the simple structure involved (a sequence of states), it is easier to automate.
4. Based solely on the execution record, its complexity is largely independent of the "size" of the implementation and the language used, which makes it particularly suitable for complex, heterogeneous systems.

In this chapter we propose a technical framework for carrying out automated result verification in practice. This framework is depicted in Figure 12.1. Its main features are as follows:

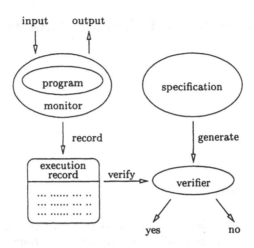

Fig. 12.1. Framework for result verification.

1. The execution record is a simple text file. Many programs produce such files during their normal operations, for administrative purposes. A general technique for recording exactly the information needed for verification, is to introduce a program monitor by wrapping.

2. The execution record is given as input to the verifier program, which does the actual verification. Given the execution record in a text file, we consider result verification as a text-processing task. Accordingly, the verifier is written in AWK, which is a special-purpose language for text processing [121]. Verification is done by the AWK interpreter, given the execution record and the verifier program as inputs.

3. The verifier program is not written by hand but specification-generated. The generator takes the property the verifier should check, called result specification, as input and produces the code of the verifier program as output. The specification-to-verifier generator is itself written in AWK.

4. A result specification is a first-order property built with two kinds of variables, state and record variables, using the functions and predicates over their respective types. A record variable refers to the contents of the record file. A state variable allows the calculation of the values that are not written in the record file but are derived from it. For each state variable we define its type, initial value and how this value changes for different operations invoked. We also allow specifications to be combined.

The rest of the chapter is as follows. Section 12.2 shows how to model the behaviour of a program. Section 12.3 describes how to wrap a program to record the relevant observations during its execution. Result verification, using a hand-written verifier program, is the subject of Section 12.4. Section 12.5 defines a result specification. Section 12.6 describes various ways such specifications can be combined. Section 12.7 describes the generator which produces the code of the verifier program given the specification. Section 12.8 contains an example and Section 12.9 presents some conclusions.

12.2 Modelling a Program

Suppose a program contains an internal state and provides several operations to access this state. The operations are readers, which return a value without modifying the state, or writers, which change the current state without returning any value. A reader can be a constant, whose result does not depend on the current state, or an observer. Likewise, a writer can be a generator, including the initial state init, or a modifier. The state does not change between invocations of generator/modifier operations (it is persistent) and the result of an operation is independent of other operations being executed concurrently (execution is atomic).

Suppose the type **State** represents the program's state-space and **Type** is any other type. We represent operations as constants or functions which take arguments and/or return values of certain types. The class of an operation depends on the presence of **State** among its arguments and/or results. In the simplest case we have:

value
    constant: Type,
    generator: State,
    observer: State $\rightarrow$ Type,
    modifier: State $\rightarrow$ State

In general, we assume that operations can take several arguments and return results of different types. **Type** includes **Bool**, **Nat**, the Cartesian product of two types, etc.

Type ::= **Bool** | **Nat** | Type $\times$ Type | ...

As a simple illustration consider an editor program for creating and modifying lists of elements. The elements are values of the abstract type Elem, which can be characters, words, records, etc. Editing is done relative to the position of a cursor which points at any element in the list or one position beyond the last element. We have one generator init which makes the list empty and sets the cursor position to one. We have two observers: pos returns the cursor position (natural number) and list returns the actual list. We also have four modifiers: left and right move the cursor one position backward or forward, insert inserts a given element at the current position and moves the cursor forward, and delete removes the element indicated by the cursor (if any). Here is the abstract specification for this editor:

type	value
Elem, State	init: State,
	pos: State → **Nat**,
	list: State → Elem*,
	insert: Elem × State → State,
	left, right, delete: State $\tilde{\to}$ State

The actual behaviour of the editor is captured by the axioms below. The following axioms constrain the state init to return position one and the empty list, and limit the current position to be always, for all states, in the range from one to one plus the length of the list.

axiom
  pos(init) = 1 ∧ list(init) = ⟨ ⟩,
  ∀ s: State •
    pos(s) ≥ 1 ∧ pos(s) ≤ 1 + **len**(list(s))

As the list has no upper limit, insert is a total function which can be applied to any value of its arguments. The axiom below describes the effect of insert: insert a given element at the current position; move the previous occupant and all its successors one position forward; increase by one the cursor position and the length of the list; and leave the rest unchanged.

axiom
  ∀ s: State, e: Elem •
    pos(insert(e, s)) = pos(s) + 1 ∧
    len(list(insert(e, s))) = **len**(list(s)) + 1 ∧
    (∀ i: **Nat** •
      i ≥ 1 ∧ i ≤ **len**(list(insert(e, s))) ⇒
      (i < pos(s) ⇒ list(insert(e, s))(i) = list(s)(i)) ∧
      (i = pos(s) ⇒ list(insert(e, s))(i) = e) ∧
      (i > pos(s) ⇒ list(insert(e, s))(i) = list(s)(i − 1))
)

Other modifiers are partial. For instance, the following axiom describes the effect of left: for all states where the cursor position is greater than one, left decreases the position and leaves the list unchanged. It says nothing about left when the cursor is already on the first position:

axiom
  ∀ s: State •
    pos(s) > 1 ⇒
    pos(left(s)) = pos(s) − 1 ∧ list(left(s)) = list(s)

Such axioms formalise the required effects of various operations of the program without saying how they should be implemented. They provide the basis for implementation verification. They can also help formulate properties to carry out result verification based on the program's execution record.

12.3 Program Execution Record

We consider that the main purpose of a program is to make available to its users the operations in its interface and to carry out such operations according to their intended meaning. In order to judge if the program indeed delivers this promised behaviour, we rely on its execution record. This section explains how the operations are executed, how to create the record of such executions, and how to use such records for error detection.

12.3.1 Operations and Execution

As an illustration consider again the editor program. Consider the type Operation which includes all state-changing operations with their parameters (if any). Operation is defined as the variant type below:

type
  Operation ==
    init | left |
    right | delete | insert(Elem)

In order to separate the names of the operations from their arguments, we introduce two more types: Name to represent operation names and Elem' to extend the type Elem (the only argument type) with the value none. We also define the functions name and argument which take an operation and return respectively its name and argument, if one exists, otherwise none.

type
  Elem' == none | put(get: Elem),
  Name == init | left | right | delete | insert

value
  name: Operation → Name
  name(opr) ≡
    case opr **of**
      init → init,
      left → left,
      right → right,
      delete → delete,
      insert(e) → insert
    end

value
  argument: Operation → Elem'
  argument(opr) ≡
    case opr **of**
      insert(e) → put(e),
      _ → none
    end

There are two more functions on the type Operation, to represent how and when the operations get executed. The function exec executes a given operation on the state according to the functions defined in Section 12.2. The function possible checks if the precondition for the corresponding operation is satisfied. It is used as the precondition to exec.

value
  exec: Operation × State $\xrightarrow{\sim}$ State
  exec(opr, s) ≡
    case opr **of**
      init → init,
      left → left(s),
      right → right(s),
      delete → delete(s),
      insert(e) → insert(e, s)
    end
    pre possible(opr, s)

value
  possible: Operation × State → **Bool**
  possible(opr, s) ≡
    case opr **of**
      left → pos(s) > 1,
      right → pos(s) ≤ **len**(list(s)),
      delete → pos(s) ≤ **len**(list(s)),
      _ → **true**
    end

12.3.2 Observations, Records and Wrapping

Many programs create execution records during their normal run, in the form of log or history files. However, because they are intended for administrative rather than verification purposes, such files may contain too little or too much information from the point of view of the properties we want to check. A general technique to create the execution record, according to different verification requirements, is wrapping. A wrapper does not modify the original program but rather includes this program to carry out certain activities vis-a-vis its usual behaviour. It takes over all communication between the program and the environment, but remains transparent itself. Here we only use the wrapper to record the interactions between the program and the environment and to make relevant observations about the resulting state.

Suppose the execution record is a sequence of observations, each produced by applying the function observe to an operation and a state on which that operation is invoked. Let the type Record contain all execution records and the type Observation represent observations. At this moment, Observation is defined as an abstract type. The function observe, without any axioms yet to constrain its behaviour, and both types are declared below.

type
  Observation,
  Record = Observation*
value
  observe: Operation × State → Observation

A wrapper is a function which takes an operation, a state and an execution record as arguments. It executes the operation on the state using the function **exec**, and creates the record of this execution using the function **observe**. The new observation is concatenated at the end of the execution record. The function assumes that the precondition for the operation is satisfied.

value
> wrapper: Operation × State × Record $\overset{\sim}{\to}$ State × Record
> wrapper(op, s, r) ≡
> (exec(op, s), r ⌢ ⟨observe(op, s)⟩)
> **pre** possible(op, s)

So far, the type **Observation** is defined as an abstract type and the **observe** function is unspecified. To make the definitions more concrete, suppose the observation consists of five fields: the operation name without arguments; the arguments to the operation, if any; the length of the list; the cursor position; and the current element, if any. The operation name is the value of the type **Name**. The operation argument as well as the current element are both values of the type **Elem'**. Here is how **Observation** is defined:

type
> Observation::
> op: Name arg: Elem'
> ln: **Nat** pos: **Nat** elem: Elem'

Below is the corresponding definition of the function **observe**. It applies the functions **name** to extract the operation name and **argument** to extract its arguments. Then it applies the **list** observer to record the length of the list, and **pos** to record the current cursor position. Finally, if the cursor is outside the list, **observe** writes the current element as **none**, otherwise it uses the element in the list indexed by the current position.

value
> observe: Operation × State → Observation
> observe(op, s) ≡
> mk_Observation
> (
>   name(op), argument(op),
>   **len** list(s), pos(s),
>   **if** pos(s) > **len** list(s)
>   **then** none **else** put(list(s)(pos(s))) **end**
>)

12.3.3 Record-Based Error Detection

Consider a concrete execution of the editor for editing strings of characters, as described below. The execution performs the task of creating a short string and then locating and correcting a character inside it. On the left is the execution record, on the right is the contents of the editor. Hyphen (-) means the absence of a value. Before invocation of init, the editor is not initialised so the values of the observers ln, pos and elem are not considered.

Table 12.1. One execution record of an editor.

name	arg	ln	pos	elem	editor
init	-				
insert	t	0	1	-	_
insert	e	1	2	-	t_
insert	s	2	3	-	te_
insert	t	3	4	-	tes_
left	-	4	5	-	test_
left	-	4	4	t	tes_t_
delete	-	4	3	s	te_st
insert	x	3	3	t	te_t
left	-	4	4	t	tey_t
		4	3	y	te_yt

In general, we can represent the execution record of a program as a text file with lines representing observations. Each line is a sequence of fields, part of the type Observation. The format is independent of the language used to implement the program and is suitable for automatic text-processing.

Without ever looking at the implementation, we can tell from the execution record if the program does not work as expected. Indeed, the record above shows that the fifth invocation of insert did not insert the character 'x', as required, but 'y'. This can be detected when the cursor is placed over the newly inserted character. Being able to find such errors is like constructing counter-examples for claims of correctness about the implementation which produced this execution record. On the other hand, verification which fails to discover any errors is inconclusive, similar to testing.

12.4 Result Verification

In this section we study how to write a verifier program, the program which carries out result verification. The verifier receives the execution record as input and carries out the computation to establish if this input is correct which respect to a given property. The property is part of the verifier. Before we discuss in general what is a possible structure for such programs and how to build them to fulfil their intended purpose, we present some examples based on the editor program. In the following sections, we consider how to specify different verifiers as total and then partial functions.

12.4.1 Verifiers as Total Functions

The range of properties we can verify depends on the contents of observations, part of the execution record. Suppose we only want to refer to operation names. Based on this we can check in particular if the editor allows movement of the cursor prior to the first position.

The verifier is described by the total function pre_first below. The auxiliary function pre_first' is defined recursively on the execution record, given the calculated position value pos as its argument: pos is initially one, and it is modified by different operations. The main property is that pos > 1 before the operation left. The two functions are defined as follows:

value
  pre_first: Record → **Bool**
  pre_first(rec) ≡ pre_first'(rec, 1),

  pre_first': Record × **Int** → **Bool**
  pre_first'(rec, pos) ≡
    rec = ⟨⟩ ∨
    (op(**hd** rec) = left ⇒ pos > 1) ∧
    case op(**hd** rec) **of**
      init → pre_first'(**tl** rec, 1),
      left → pre_first'(**tl** rec, pos − 1),
      delete → pre_first'(**tl** rec, pos),
      _ → pre_first'(**tl** rec, pos + 1)
    end

Similarly, checking whether the editor allows the cursor to move past the last position requires two variables: one for position (pos) and another one for length (ln). The main property is that pos ≤ ln before the operation right. The function post_last is defined as follows:

value
  post_last: Record → **Bool**
  post_last(rec) ≡ post_last'(rec, 0, 1),

  post_last': Record × **Int** × **Int** → **Bool**
  post_last'(rec, ln, pos) ≡
    rec = ⟨⟩ ∨
    (op(**hd** rec) = right ⇒ pos ≤ ln) ∧
    case op(**hd** rec) **of**

init → post_last'(tl rec, 0, 1),
    right → post_last'(tl rec, ln, pos + 1),
    left → post_last'(tl rec, ln, pos − 1),
    delete → post_last'(tl rec, ln − 1, pos),
    insert → post_last'(tl rec, ln + 1, pos + 1)
end

Consider checking if the execution record is consistent with respect to the values of ln and pos. As we examine the record, we calculate the values of ln and pos based on the operations invoked, and compare for every observation if the stored and the calculated values are the same. Here is the function:

value
    check_len_pos: Record → **Bool**
    check_len_pos(rec) ≡ check_len_pos'(rec, 0, 1),

    check_len_pos': Record × **Int** × **Int** → **Bool**
    check_len_pos'(rec, ln, pos) ≡
        rec = ⟨⟩ ∨
        ln = ln(**hd** rec) ∧ pos = pos(**hd** rec) ∧
        case op(**hd** rec) **of**
            init → check_len_pos'(tl rec, 0, 1),
            left → check_len_pos'(tl rec, ln, pos − 1),
            right → check_len_pos'(tl rec, ln, pos + 1),
            delete → check_len_pos'(tl rec, ln − 1, pos),
            insert → check_len_pos'(tl rec, ln + 1, pos + 1)
        end

The function **check_obs** checks if every observation in the execution record satisfies the following properties:

1. pos is greater than zero but less than or equal to ln + 1;
2. if op = left then pos is greater than one;
3. if op = right or op = delete then pos is not greater than ln;
4. if op = insert then arg is not equal to none; and
5. if elem ≠ none then pos is not greater than ln.

So, property (1) checks if pos is in the allowed range of values, properties (2) and (3) make sure if the operations are only invoked when their preconditions are satisfied, (4) checks if every invocation of insert takes an argument, and (5) makes sure that elem ≠ none implies the cursor is positioned at an element in the list. Unlike previous functions, check_obs does not need any auxiliary arguments. It is first defined on individual observations and then, recursively, on the whole execution record.

value
  check_obs: Observation → **Bool**
  check_obs(ob) ≡
    pos(ob) ≥ 1 ∧
    pos(ob) ≤ ln(ob) + 1 ∧
    (op(ob) = left ⇒ pos(ob) > 1) ∧
    (op(ob) = right ⇒ pos(ob) ≤ ln(ob)) ∧
    (op(ob) = delete ⇒ pos(ob) ≤ ln(ob)) ∧
    (op(ob) = insert ⇒ arg(ob) ≠ none) ∧
    (elem(ob) ≠ none ⇒ pos(ob) ≤ ln(ob)),

  check_obs: Record → **Bool**
  check_obs(rec) ≡
    rec = ⟨⟩ ∨
    check_obs(**hd** rec) ∧ check_obs(**tl** rec)

12.4.2 Verifiers as Partial Functions

Represented as total functions, all the verifiers presented so far were self-sufficient in checking the execution record. In contrast, the example in this section assumes that the record already satisfies certain properties. Those properties can in turn be checked using the existing verifiers.

Suppose we want to check if the elements in the list are inserted correctly by the operations of the editor. The idea is to recreate the contents of the list based on the operations in the execution record. To realise this idea we first introduce the auxiliary function `substr` which returns a sub-list of a given list of elements, determined by its first position and length:

value
  substr: Elem* × **Nat** × **Nat** $\overset{\sim}{\to}$ Elem*
  substr(s, n, k) ≡
    ⟨ s(i) | i **in** ⟨ n .. n + k − 1 ⟩ ⟩
    pre n > 0 ∧ n ≤ **len** s − k + 1

Verification is carried out by the function `check_el` which takes an execution record as an argument and returns `true` or `false`. It assumes about the record that: `pos` and `ln` are calculated correctly with respect to the operations performed; operations are only invoked when their preconditions are satisfied; every invocation of `insert` has an argument; and if elem ≠ none then the cursor is positioned at an element in the list. Such assumptions can be checked using the functions defined in Section 12.4.1: `check_len_pos` for the first assumption and `check_obs` for the rest. The function `check_el` applies the auxiliary `check_el'` which takes an empty list as its second argument.

value
 check_el: Record $\overset{\sim}{\to}$ **Bool**
 check_el(rec) $\equiv$
  check_el'(rec, $\langle\rangle$)
  pre check_obs(rec) $\wedge$ check_len_pos(rec)

 The function `check_el'` takes the current list of elements, `list`, as an argument. For each operation it modifies `list` as appropriate: for `init` it makes `list` empty; for `delete` it removes from `list` the element at the current position; for `insert` it inserts the new element at the current position; and for `left` and `right` it leaves `list` unchanged. The function `substr` is used to create two lists: bp contains the prefix of `list`, from the first position to one before the current position, and ap contains the suffix of `list`, from the current to the last position. The main property is: if `elem(r)` $\neq$ none where r is the current observation, then `elem(r)` equals the current element in the recreated list, i.e. the element in `list` at the position `pos(r)`. In order to check this property for the current observation we have to make sure that: the current position exists in the list; the function `substr` is applied within its precondition, in particular the sub-list does not extend beyond the last position in the list; the operation `delete` is not applied when the cursor is outside the list (otherwise the list ap is empty); and each invocation of `insert` has an argument. To ensure such properties the function has a number of preconditions. Here is the definition:

value
 check_el': Record $\times$ Elem* $\overset{\sim}{\to}$ **Bool**
 check_el'(rec, list) $\equiv$
  rec = $\langle\rangle$ $\vee$
  let
   r = **hd** rec,
   bp = substr(list, 1, pos(r) $-$ 1),
   ap = substr(list, pos(r), ln(r) $-$ pos(r) $+$ 1)
  in
   (elem(r) $\neq$ none $\Rightarrow$ elem(r) = put(list(pos(r)))) $\wedge$
   case op(r) **of**
    init $\to$ check_el'(**tl** rec, $\langle\rangle$),
    delete $\to$ check_el'(**tl** rec, bp $\frown$ **tl** ap),
    insert $\to$ check_el'(**tl** rec, bp $\frown$ $\langle$get(arg(r))$\rangle$ $\frown$ ap),
    _ $\to$ check_el'(**tl** rec, list)
   end
  end
  pre rec = $\langle\rangle$ $\vee$
    len(list) = ln(**hd** rec) $\wedge$
    check_obs(rec) $\wedge$
    check_len_pos'(rec, ln(**hd** rec), pos(**hd** rec))

12.4.3 Structure of a Verifier Program

Based on these examples we make some observations about the possible structure of the verifier program. The program takes the execution record **rec** as an argument and produces an ok/error answer (ok is represented by **true**, error by **false**) according to whether or not the record contains an error. The verifier may be either total – able to check any execution record without preconditions, or partial – requires the record to satisfy certain properties before it is checked. In the latter case, it will rely on one or more external verifiers, which may be also total or partial, to check the record beforehand. The program calculates the answer by recursively examining the execution record. Checking terminates on the first observation which contains an error, otherwise it continues until the record argument becomes empty. The program maintains a set of variables whose values are initialised and then modified depending on the operation invoked. These variables carry the state information from the first to the last observation, helping to decide if individual observations produced an error. The main property is a logical formula **main** which is expressed in terms of these variables and the contents of the current observation. The structure of the verifier program is shown below.

value
   check: Record $\overset{\sim}{\to}$ **Bool**
   check(rec) $\equiv$
     check'(rec, e_1, ... , e_n)
     pre $check_1(rec) \wedge ... \wedge check_k(rec)$,

   check': Record $\times$ T_1 $\times$ ... $\times$ T_n $\overset{\sim}{\to}$ **Bool**
   check'(rec, v_1, ... , v_n) $\equiv$
     rec $= \langle \rangle$ $\vee$
     main(**hd** rec, v_1, ..., v_n) $\wedge$
     case op(**hd** rec) **of**
       $op_1 \to$ check'(**tl** rec, $f_1^1(v_1)$, ..., $f_1^n(v_n)$),
       ...
       $op_m \to$ check'(**tl** rec, $f_m^1(v_1)$, ..., $f_m^n(v_n)$)
     end
     pre $check_1(rec) \wedge ... \wedge check_k(rec)$,

   main: Observation $\times$ T_1 $\times$ ... $\times$ T_n $\to$ **Bool**
   main(ob, v_1, ..., v_n) $\equiv$ ...

We can see that the main parameters to carry out checking are the formula which is calculated for each observation to detect an error (**main**) and the variables v_i used in this formula, together with their types T_i, initial values e_i and how the values change for different operations (functions f_j^i).

12.5 Result Specifications

The structure suggested for a verifier in Section 12.4 highlights what is essential for defining such programs: the property the program is supposed to check (logical part), not how it is checked (computational part). Later we show how to reuse the computational part, allowing the verifier to be generated from its property, not written by hand. Now we demonstrate how it is possible to define such properties, called result specifications.

12.5.1 Syntax of Result Specifications

Consider again the function pre_first from the editor example which checks if the cursor can be moved prior to the first position. The function calculates the current position, using the second argument to pre_first'. The argument is initialised to one and then modified according to the operations performed. For the verifier, this argument plays the role of a state variable. The function post_last requires an additional variable ln.

Suppose the relevant properties of each such variable are declared explicitly: their names; types; initial values; and how their values change for different operations. In order to describe how the variables change, we use a list of operation names with corresponding expressions to calculate the new value of the variable, perhaps involving its current value. If an operation is not mentioned in this list, the variable remains unchanged. Here is the syntax:

```
pos : Int = 1              ln : Int = 0
   init -> 1                  init -> 0
   left -> pos - 1           delete -> ln - 1
   right -> pos + 1          insert -> ln + 1
   insert -> pos + 1
```

Such variables provide the context for defining result specifications. In addition to the state variables we have also predefined variables to refer to the current observation. We call them record variables, and write \$$i$ where i is an integer between zero and NF, the number of fields in the observation: \$0 represents the whole observation as the sequence of values of its fields, \$1 is the value of the first field, \$2 is the value of the second field, etc. We introduce a convention that \$1 contains the name of the operation invoked and \$2 is the arguments of this operation, if any.

Consider the variable list, used by check_el to recreate the contents of the editor. It contains a list of elements which is initialised to the empty list and modified by the operations init, delete and insert. The expressions to re-calculate its value contain the calls to the auxiliary function substr and refer to the record variables. Here is the declaration, written in a form understandable by the target language (AWK). In particular, "" is the empty list and list concatenation is represented by juxtaposition (i.e. putting lists or elements of lists one after another).

```
list : Elem-list = ""
  init -> ""
  delete ->
    substr(list, 1, $4 - 1)
    substr(list, $4 + 1, $3 - $4 + 1)
  insert ->
    substr(list, 1, $4 - 1)
    $2 substr(list, $4, $3 - $4 + 1)
```

Consider such specifications in general. Being part of the verifier program, the specification must be concrete enough for its validity in a given state to be decided by calculation (automatically) rather than deduction (interactively). This in turn rules out the use of full first order logic, in particular quantifications over infinite domains, functions defined by pre/post conditions, etc. We define a specification to be a first-order predicate built from propositional connectives, relations over value terms, and a limited kind of quantification over a range of field variables. Terms are built from the state and record variables using the functions over their respective domains. Below, var represents a state variable, num is a natural number and nvar is a numerical state variable (one that can hold a number). We also use function to represent a function and relation to represent a relation. We define the syntax of specifications as follows:

```
term  ::=  var | $num | $nvar |
           function(term, ... , term)
spec  ::=  true | ! spec |
           spec && spec |
           relation(term, ... , term) |
           all nvar : num.num : spec
```

12.5.2 Examples of Result Specifications

The following are result specifications for some verifiers in Section 12.4. Again, we write them in a form understandable for AWK. In particular, == represents equality, != inequality, || disjunction and && conjunction. Also, implication must be written via negation and disjunction.

1. According to pre_first, if the operation is left then the cursor position must be greater than one.

   `$1 != "left" || pos > 1`

2. According to post_last, if the operation is right then the position value is not greater than the length.

   `$1 != "right" || pos <= ln`

3. According to check_len_pos, the stored and calculated values for position and length must be the same.

   `$3 == ln && $4 == pos`

4. According to check_el, if the recorded element is not '-' (none) then it equals the current element in the recreated list. In order to extract the current element from the list we use the function substr.

   `$5 == "-" || $5 == substr(list, $4, 1)`

12.5.3 Semantics of Result Specifications

Consider the formal semantics. We interpret spec against the execution record, record, and the contents of the state variables, state. record is a sequence of observations and each observation consists of a list of fields, the first being the operation name. We apply the usual head and tail functions to record and all its elements; in particular hd(hd(record)) is the most recent operation. Suppose init represents the initial value of all state variables and trans(state, op) returns their new values when the operation was op. Then record $\models$ spec means spec is true for the execution record. It is defined using the auxiliary relation record, state $\models$ spec as follows:

$$\text{record} \models \text{spec iff record, init} \models \text{spec}$$
$$\text{record, state} \models \text{spec iff}$$
$$\quad \text{record} = \langle\,\rangle \vee$$
$$\quad \text{hd(record), state} \models \text{spec} \wedge$$
$$\quad \text{tl(record), trans(state, hd(hd(record)))} \models \text{spec}$$

This definition takes into account the current observation in the execution record and the changes to the state variables caused by the operations. It relies on the evaluation of spec based on state and the contents of individual observations, using the auxiliary relation hd(record), state $\models$ spec. Let obs represent such an observation. Here is the definition of this relation, defined inductively on the structure of the specification:

$$\text{obs, state} \models \text{true}$$
$$\text{obs, state} \models \text{! spec iff not}$$
$$\quad\quad \text{obs, state} \models \text{spec}$$
$$\text{obs, state} \models \text{spec}_1 \text{ \&\& spec}_2 \text{ iff}$$
$$\quad\quad \text{obs, state} \models \text{spec}_i, i = 1, 2$$
$$\text{obs, state} \models \text{relation(term}_1, \text{term}_2) \text{ iff}$$
$$\quad\quad \text{relation}([\text{term}_1]_{\text{obs,state}}, [\text{term}_2]_{\text{obs,state}})$$
$$\text{obs, state} \models \text{all i} : n_1.n_2 : \text{spec iff}$$
$$\quad\quad \text{obs, state} \models \text{spec}[\text{obs}(i)/\$i], i = n_1, \dots, n_2$$

The last rule applies substitution within spec of the record variable $i with obs(i), the ith field of the observation. To evaluate a relation, we have to first calculate the values of its arguments, represented by the terms. Here is how we evaluate the terms, given the observation obs and the state state. In particular, we evaluate a state variable var by taking its value according to state (state(var)), a record variable $num by taking the value of the num-th field in obs (obs(num)), and $nvar where nvar is a numerical variable by taking the field in obs according to the value of nvar (obs(state(nvar))).

$$[\text{var}]_{\text{obs, state}} = \text{state(var)}$$
$$[\text{\$num}]_{\text{obs, state}} = \text{obs(num)}$$
$$[\text{\$nvar}]_{\text{obs, state}} = \text{obs(state(nvar))}$$
$$[\text{function(term}_1, \text{ term}_2)]_{\text{obs, state}}$$
$$= \text{function}([\text{term}_1]_{\text{obs, state}}, [\text{term}_2]_{\text{obs, state}})$$

12.6 Composition of Result Specifications

By specification composition we mean building a specification from simpler specifications according to some formation rules and intended semantics. The semantics of composition expresses how to calculate the result of checking a composite specification from the results of checking component specifications (on the same execution record). The following sections consider specification composition for binary checking, which returns a single answer for the whole record, and for observation-based checking, which returns an answer for every observation in the record. The latter is not formalised.

12.6.1 Binary Checking

Conjunction is a particularly useful composition method, allowing for one of several properties to detect an error. One example is check_len_pos which checks if both length and position are recorded correctly. The specification is really built from two specifications, one to check the length (len_ok) and another to check the position (pos_ok).

```
len_ok is ($3 == ln)
pos_ok is ($4 == pos)
check_len_pos is len_ok && pos_ok
```

Suppose pre_first is carried out on the record which has the position value written down. How useful is it then to know that the cursor moved prior to the first position if this position is wrongly recorded in the first place? We would rather like to check the conjunction below, stopping as soon as pos_ok is violated or the actual error detected:

```
pos_ok && pre_first
```

Conjunction is inappropriate if one specification defines relevant observations for another specification. For instance, only if the operation was `left` must `pos` be greater than one. In such cases we need to use implication.

```
$1 != "left" || pos > 1
```

We may also like to combine implication with conjunction, to check if pos_ok (correctness of the value of position) holds on all observations:

```
pos_ok && ($1 != "left" || pos > 1)
```

or if it holds on the relevant observations only:

```
$1 != "left" || (pos_ok && pos > 1)
```

So far we only referred to different fields of the observation by their numbers. Sometimes we may like to check properties which are shared between different fields. For instance the property which must be satisfied for the third and fourth fields of the observation record (length and position) is that their values are non-negative. This is where we can use numerical variables to refer to the range of fields and use quantification over them:

```
all i: 3.4 : $i >= 0
```

12.6.2 Observation-Based Checking

This treatment of composition is limited by the fact that checking produces a single answer for the whole record. Instead, suppose verification produces an answer for every observation in the record (if and where the error occurred). Let `error` represent the presence and `ok` the absence of an error. Consider some examples of unary operators for specification composition:

1. `stop(spec)` returns the same results as checking `spec` until and including the first `error`. From this moment, `stop(spec)` only returns errors.
2. `second(spec)` returns the same results as `spec` except it does not report the first `error`.
3. `twice(spec)` does not report on the isolated `error` when checking `spec` but only on two errors occurring consecutively.
4. `quarter(spec)` reports `error` when `spec` produces more than 25% of errors compared with the total number of observations so far.

Different methods can be combined, for instance `stop(second(spec))` returns the same results as checking `spec` except it does not report on the first `error` and after the second `error` it only returns errors. See Table 12.2.

Consider some examples of binary operators, combining specifications $spec_1$ and $spec_2$. Specification `or(`$spec_1$`, `$spec_2$`)` reports an `error` when at least one of $spec_1$ or $spec_2$ does. Specification `follow(`$spec_1$`, `$spec_2$`)` checks $spec_1$ until it detects an `error`, then from the next observation it

Table 12.2. Unary operators for specification composition.

s	stop(s)	second(s)	twice(s)	quarter(s)	stop(second(s))
ok	ok	ok	ok	ok	ok
ok	ok	ok	ok	ok	ok
error	error	ok	ok	error	ok
ok	error	ok	ok	ok	ok
ok	error	ok	ok	ok	ok
ok	error	ok	ok	ok	ok
ok	error	ok	ok	ok	ok
error	error	error	ok	ok	error
ok	error	ok	ok	ok	error
error	error	error	ok	error	error
error	error	error	error	error	error

starts to check spec$_2$. switch(spec$_1$, spec$_2$) checks spec$_1$ until it produces an error, then it starts checking spec$_2$ until spec$_2$ itself detects an error, then we resume checking spec$_1$, and so on. So checking switches back and forth between spec$_1$ and spec$_2$. See Table 12.3. One example of composition between unary and binary methods is follow(quarter(spec$_1$), spec$_2$): we start checking spec$_2$ when spec$_1$ reports more than 25% of errors.

Table 12.3. Binary operators for specification composition.

s$_1$	s$_2$	or(s$_1$, s$_2$)	follow(s$_1$, s$_2$)	switch(s$_1$, s$_2$)
ok	ok	ok	ok	ok
ok	ok	ok	ok	ok
error	ok	error	error	error
ok	ok	ok	ok	ok
error	error	error	error	error
ok	error	error	error	ok
ok	ok	ok	ok	ok
ok	ok	ok	ok	ok
error	ok	error	ok	error
ok	error	error	error	error
ok	ok	ok	ok	ok

All composition methods were presented based on their semantics: how to calculate the results of checking the specification based on the outcome of checking its components. We should also be able to show how such effects can be obtained by symbolic manipulation on component specifications and their declaration contexts (variables).

12.7 Specification-to-Verifier Generator

Instead of writing the verifier program by hand we decide to generate it from the specification it should check. Here we discuss the working of the generator by presenting its inputs and corresponding outputs (edited for presentation purposes) for three examples based on the editor program. The generated verifier programs are written in AWK. The language has been chosen for two main reasons: it allows such programs to be written conveniently by addressing directly their particular purpose, and it provides an execution environment for carrying out verification (the AWK interpreter).

12.7.1 Verifier Generator

The input to the generator program is the name of the declaration file and the specification the verifier is supposed to check. Below, we can see the generator program gen invoked from the command line. Its first argument is editor, the name of the file that contains declarations of all variables relevant for the editor example, like pos, ln and list. The second argument is `$1 != "left" || pos > 1`, the specification the verifier is supposed to check (the cursor cannot be moved prior to the first position), in quotes to prevent its interpretation by the command processor.

```
$ gen editor '$1 != "left" || pos > 1'
```

The output from the generator is the verifier program written in AWK which carries out checking of the specification. The program is shown below:

```
BEGIN {pos = 1}
!($1 != "left" || pos > 1) {exit(FNR)}
$1 == "init"   {pos = 1}
$1 == "right"  {pos = pos + 1}
$1 == "insert" {pos = pos + 1}
$1 == "left"   {pos = pos - 1}
```

As all AWK programs, it consists of several (here six) condition/action rules. Processing is done for every line of input: if the line satisfies a condition then the corresponding action gets executed; if the line satisfies several conditions then all corresponding actions get executed in the order in which they occur in the program. One special condition is BEGIN, which is only true before the first line of input. Here, the BEGIN condition causes the variable pos to be assigned the value one. The second condition is true on all lines which have left as the first field and the value of pos less than or equal to one. It is exactly the negation of the specification, describing when the line contains an error. If so, the action exit(FNR) causes the program to exit with the value FNR. FNR contains the current line number. There are four more actions which depend on the value of the first field: if it is init then pos is assigned the value one, if it is **right** or **insert** then pos is incremented; if it is **left** then pos is decremented. The absence of a condition involving **delete** means no action is executed in this case.

Consider the second property: the cursor cannot be moved past the last position (**post_last**). We initialise ln to zero and pos to one. The error condition checks if the operation is **right** and pos is greater than ln. Otherwise, **init** assigns ln to zero and pos to one, **right** increments and **left** decrements pos, **delete** decrements ln and **insert** increments both pos and ln. The generator is invoked as follows:

```
$ gen editor '$1 != "right" || pos <= ln'
```

It generates the following program:

```
BEGIN {ln = 0; pos = 1}
!($1 != "right" || pos <= ln) {exit(FNR)}
$1 == "init"   {ln = 0; pos = 1}
$1 == "right"  {pos = pos + 1}
$1 == "left"   {pos = pos - 1}
$1 == "delete" {ln = ln - 1}
$1 == "insert" {pos = pos + 1; ln = ln + 1}
```

Consider checking if the current element is recorded correctly; **check_el**. The following program checks this specification using the variable **list**. With this variable we recreate the contents of the editor based solely on the invoked operations. **list** is initialised to the empty string "" and then modified according to the operation invoked: **init** makes the list empty, **delete** removes the element at the current position, **insert** inserts its argument (value of the second field) at the current position. Operations **left** and **right** do not change **list**. The generator is invoked as follows:

```
$ gen editor '$5 == "-" || $5 == substr(list, $4, 1)'
```

It generates the program below.

```
BEGIN {list = ""}
!($5 == "-" || $5 == substr(list, $4, 1)) {exit(FNR)}
$1 == "init" {list = ""}
$1 == "delete" { list =
  substr(list, 1, $4 - 1)
  substr(list, $4 + 1, $3 -$4 + 1)}
$1 == "insert" { list =
  substr(list, 1, $4 - 1)
  $2 substr(list, $4, $3 - $4 + 1)}
```

12.7.2 Verification with Generated Verifiers

To carry out verification we give the verifier program as input to the AWK interpreter, together with the file containing the execution record. Below we execute the verifier generated above (file check_el) on the execution record for the editor program (file **record**) as in Table 12.1. We use the **Bash** shell to execute two operations. The first operation is **gawk**, the invocation of the GNU interpreter for AWK; the -f option informs the interpreter that check_el is the AWK program. The second operation displays the contents of the environment variable '?' which holds the exit code of the last invoked operation (according to the **Bash** shell). Here it displays the value 11, which indicates that line 11 of the execution record contains an error:

```
bash-2.01$ gawk -f check_el record
bash-2.01$ echo $?
11
```

One comment is in place. As indicated in Section 12.4, the function check_el has to assume that the record contains correctly calculated values of pos and ln, that the operations are only invoked within their preconditions, that every **insert** has an argument, etc. The same applies to the verifier check_el which has to rely on: the variable $3 to represent the length of the list; $4 to represent the current position; and the expressions involving $3 and $4 to represent the range of indexes inside the list. Otherwise, the invocation of **substr** could produce arbitrary results. Therefore, before running check_el on the record, one would like to first generate and run check_len_pos and check_obs to make sure the preconditions are satisfied.

The generator is itself written in AWK. It works as follows:

1. When invoked, it first looks into the specification, given as the second argument in the command line. From this specification it creates the array of all variables used.
2. It examines the contents of the declaration file, given as the first argument in the input line, to find the declarations for all variables in the array.
3. It prints on the screen the BEGIN condition with the semicolon-separated list of initialisations of all variables in the array.
4. It prints the negated contents of the specification with the exit action immediately following.
5. Finally, for each operation which modifies at least one variable in the array it prints the condition $1=="operation" and then the semicolon-separated list of assignment expressions, one for each variable modified by the operation, according to its declared effect on that variable.

12.8 Application: WWW Access Log

Consider an example from real-life computing: the WWW access log created and maintained by a WWW server. According to the HTTP protocol [48] the file contains a separate line for each request, composed of several tokens separated by spaces: the client's IP address; the client's identity and password information; date and time of the request; the request itself; the response returned to the client; and the message-body. Figure 12.4 shows an example. Programs like Analog [137] read this file and give summaries of its contents, e.g. how many times the server was accessed each day, which files were requested, and so on. Our approach is similar, but we look into the file to check if the applications which create and modify the file behaved correctly.

Table 12.4. Fragment of the WWW access log file.

```
195.92.198.83 - - [07/Mar/2000:00:25:35 +0800] "GET cornish.html HTTP/1.1" 200 1407
208.219.77.29 - - [07/Mar/2000:00:33:50 +0800] "HEAD lyme.html HTTP/1.1" 200 0
194.128.161.132 - - [07/Mar/2000:01:08:25 +0800] "GET favicon.ico HTTP/1.1" 404 317
216.35.116.96 - - [07/Mar/2000:01:12:19 +0800] "GET robots.txt HTTP/1.0" 404 276
199.172.149.143 - - [07/Mar/2000:11:26:21 +0800] "GET raise HTTP/1.0" 301 306
131.114.9.246 - - [07/Mar/2000:21:28:15 +0800] "GET tj1.gif HTTP/1.1" 304 -
192.203.232.241 - - [07/Mar/2000:23:59:22 +0800] "GET backgrd.jpg HTTP/1.0" 206 0
```

The HTTP protocol presents many properties a well-formed access log should possess, all described informally. For example: "All responses to the HEAD request and all $1xx$, 204 and 304 responses must not include a message-body. All other responses do, although it may be of zero length." (Section 4.3 of [48]). Such a property can serve as a specification for checking the log file. The specification is presented below. Field number six ($6) contains the name of a method, $(NF-1) contains the status code, and the last field ($NF) contains the length of a message. Hyphen (-) means the absence of a value.

```
! (
    $6 == "\"HEAD ||
    $(NF-1) < 200 ||
    $(NF-1) == 204 ||
    $(NF-1) == 304
) || $NF == '-'
```

Note that $(NF-1) applies an arithmetic expression to identify a field in the execution record, which is an extension to the language. The hand-written AWK program to check this property is below. The program examines every line of the log file and exits with the current line number as soon as the property is violated:

```
! (
  !($6 == "\"HEAD ||
    $(NF-1) < 200 ||
    $(NF-1) == 204 ||
    $(NF-1) == 304
  ) || $NF == '-'
) {exit(FNR)}
```

Another property: "Response status codes beginning with the digit '5' indicate cases in which the server is aware that it has erred or is incapable of performing the request." (Section 10.5 of [48]). Here we may like to check if a server-side error occurs more than a certain number of times within a given time interval. Such a check could help to monitor the performance of the server. The verifier needs four variables: count to calculate the number of error occurrences; from and to to represent the bounds of the time interval; and max for the maximum number of errors allowed. count is initialised to zero and is incremented with every error, i.e. on all lines where the status code is at least 500 and whose time-stamp is between the bounds. This, however, requires extending the use of the plain operation names in variable declarations into logical properties. The specification is simply count <= max. The (hand-written) verifier program requires the function before to decide about chronological ordering between two time-stamps. The program is below.

```
BEGIN {count = 0}
!(count <= max) {exit(FNR)}
( before(from, $4) && before($4, to) &&
  $(NF - 1) > 500
) {count = count + 1}
```

The final property, not enforced by the HTTP protocol, is that successive entries in the log file have strictly increasing time stamps: before(time, $4). time is a time variable which holds the time value of the previous access, initially the origin of time. Here is the program:

```
BEGIN {time = origin}
! before(time, $4) {exit(FNR)}
true {time = $4}
```

12.9 Conclusions

In this chapter we discussed result verification as an alternative to implementation verification, its limitations, advantages and the technical context to make this technique usable in practice. The main limitation is the fact that result verification reasons about a single execution run of a program, whereas implementation verification considers all possible runs. Advantages are: result verification has fewer preconditions for its applications in practice, gives more opportunities for automation and, being based on the execution record not the implementation details, is particularly suitable for complex systems. The technical context includes the following issues:

1. How to obtain the execution record? The record is a text file containing observations made at different points of the execution, line by line: the operation invoked and the values observed about the state. It is either obtained as the usual log file produced by a program, or by specially designed wrapping software.
2. How to specify the properties we want to check about the record? The specification is a first-order predicate built from the variables, functions, relations and limited kind of quantification. The variables allow reference to individual fields within the lines of the record, as well as how their values change for different invoked operations. We introduced the syntax and formal semantics for such specifications.
3. How to build such properties from the existing properties? We put forward several methods for specification composition, depending on whether checking produces an ok/error answer for the whole record or an ok/error answer for every observation within the record.
4. How to carry out verification for a given record and specification? Verification is carried out automatically and the verifier program is generated from the specification (not written by hand). The generated program is written in AWK [121]. The AWK interpreter is applied both to generate this program and to carry out the actual verification.

We showed two examples: the editor program (created by us) and the WWW access log [48] (created by the WWW server).

Result verification receives growing interest in the technical literature. The concept of a program correctness checker, an algorithm for checking the output of a computation was introduced in [11] and studied for a range of numerical, sorting and matrix problems. Efficient checkers and correctors were introduced in [147]. Both papers concern the algorithmic foundations, for functional problems and correctness expressed in probabilistic terms. In this chapter we focus more on the design of verifiers and define correctness in deterministic terms. In the applied stream, [56] demonstrates how program-checking can reduce the amount of verification work using compiler back-ends (generated by unverified construction tools) and [136] presents an industrial application of mechanised result verification for an automatic train protection system. In [86] a language is proposed which supports on-line automatic result verification of imperative implementations based on their complete functional specifications. In this chapter, specifications can be partial, they are expressed logically and have their semantics defined formally.

The ideas in this chapter evolved from earlier work described in Chapter 13 which introduced logic-based regular expressions to specify the behaviour of software components, suitable for their checking at run-time. The aim was to achieve the fail-stop property [126] of the components affected by errors. Compared with result specifications, patterns are more expressive but also more expensive to verify, both in terms of time and memory requirements. Result verification can be also used as a tool to carry out specification-based testing [119]. The background for formalisation of software components in this chapter is the co-algebraic approach to semantics [70] and its application to object-oriented classes [67]. The idea of software monitoring as a complement to formal techniques to increase application dependability is reviewed in [128]. AWK is one in the growing family of scripting languages for rapid application development [110]. The language presented here to describe result specifications is an example of a domain-specific language [151].

Background Information

This chapter is based on work [7] done by Balkhis Abu Bakar of the School of Information Technology, University of Northern Malaysia, and Tomasz Janowski.

13. Fail-Stop Components by Pattern Matching

13.1 Introduction

Object-based distributed systems challenge the traditional ways of applying formal methods via specification and proof. One of the problems is the large number of the components involved, partly decided at compile-time (static invocation) and partly at run-time (dynamic invocation). Another problem is having to rely on the vendor's claims about correctness of individual components, without being able (lacking implementation details) to verify such claims ourselves. Yet another is expressing component specifications in interface definition languages, which describe how to communicate with a component (syntax), but not the expected results of such communication (semantics). Such problems make static verification difficult, at best.

On the other hand, the structuring of the whole system in terms of the independent, distributed components, is particularly suitable for making such a system fault-tolerant [85]. The goal is to ensure that failures of individual components (violation of their specifications) will not cause the whole system to fail (violation of the system's specification). The latter specification can be used at design-time to prove if the system is indeed fault-tolerant. The former specifications can be used at run-time to detect if components have failed. This chapter describes an approach to formally specify software components in order to make such error detection possible.

Defining such specifications is not without problems. Specifications may contain infinite constructs like quantifiers (for all values of a type), liveness properties (for all states in a sequence) or modal properties of branching time (for all transitions from a state). Such constructs are generally non-executable and non-checkable. This means we cannot execute them directly on the machine and we cannot check effectively at run-time that they indeed hold. On the other hand, specifications based on propositional logic which can be checked at run-time, are insufficiently expressive in practice. Also, checking specifications which use equality of states is not possible when the state can be only accessed via defined operations; the best we can do is checking observational equivalence [97]. Such problems require a different kind of specification to carry out effective run-time checking from those to support static verification.

In this chapter we propose an approach to define and check such specifications at run-time. Technically, the approach is as follows:

1. Specifications are formally-based. They are defined as logic-based regular expressions built from the propositions about the states or pairs of states of a component, via its observer operations.
2. Specifications are checkable at run-time, based on the recorded history of the component's execution. This history is a sequence of values observed about individual states and the operations, with arguments, whose invocation caused state-changes.
3. Checking is carried out by a wrapper which is generated from the component and its specification. The wrapper takes over all communication between the component and its environment. It remains transparent to the clients except being able to detect (as it carries out run-time checking after every state-change) and announce (via the additional boolean observer **error**) the occurrence of an error.
4. The required effect of run-time checking is described formally as the failstop property. The wrapper generator is to transform a given component, which may fail in an arbitrary way, into a component which only fails by refusing to operate, which fact is also announced by the observer **error**.

Figure 13.1 illustrates the approach. It describes the intended result of the wrapper generator for specifications given as state invariants. The component comp may or may not satisfy the invariant **spec** but its transformed version wrap(comp,spec) satisfies the fail-stop version of **spec**: **spec** holds if and only if error is false; by comp $\models$ **spec** we mean that **spec** is satisfied for all reachable states of comp. Importantly, this property is not verified for each component and its specification but proved about the wrapper generator in general, then applied to all components and specifications. The property is formalised using RAISE, in order to make possible the proof of correctness of the wrapper generator (that every wrapped component is fail-stop). The proof itself is not presented.

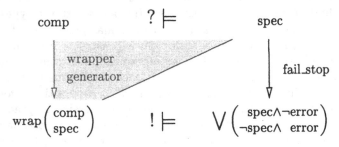

Fig. 13.1. Fault-free versus fail-stop software components.

The rest of this chapter is as follows. Section 13.2 explains and illustrates the concept of a 'component'. Section 13.3 discusses and compares 'fault-free' and 'fail-stop' behaviours of components. Section 13.4 shows how to ensure fail-stop behaviour by pattern matching. Section 13.5 presents an example, a line editor. Sections 13.6 and 13.7 describe how pattern matching can become part of an automatically generated wrapper. Section 13.6 specifies the wrapper generator and Section 13.7 describes a prototype implementation. Section 13.8 provides some conclusions.

13.2 Components

We treat a component as an entity with its own state and the operations defined on it. The state is persistent – it maintains its value between operation invocations, and the operations are atomic – to execute them concurrently is the same as executing them in an arbitrary order.

We represent the state-space of a component as State and its operations by the functions on State. Depending on the type of access we divide the operations into 'readers' which return a value without modifying the state and 'writers' which change the current state without returning any value. Readers are further divided into 'constants' which return some value independent from the current state and 'observers' which return a value based on the current state. Writers are divided into 'generators' which return a new state, independent from the current one, and 'modifiers' which modify the current state. We use Type to represent a collection of values used as arguments to the operations or as results returned by them. Type does not include states. The class of an operation depends on the 'position' of State in its signature:

value
    constant: Type $\rightarrow$ Type,
    generator: Type $\rightarrow$ State,
    observer: Type $\times$ State $\rightarrow$ Type,
    modifier: Type $\times$ State $\rightarrow$ State

We assume that the generator init represents the initial state. In the simplest case the only type is **Bool**, with constants and observers as propositional variables. The first-order model adopts one more type, say **Nat**, and allows operations to take several arguments and return results of this type. In the higher-order model operations take several arguments and return results of different types. In this case Type represents **Bool**, **Nat**, the Cartesian product of two types in Type, etc.

As a simple illustration consider a component representing a bounded stack. Elem is the type of elements inserted on the stack. The component comes with six operations: bnd is a constant of type **Nat**, it represents the maximum number of elements allowed on the stack; init is a generator which represents the state of the empty stack; push and pop are modifiers, push adds the new top element to the stack and pop removes the top element; and top and ln are observers, top returns the top element and ln returns the number of elements in the stack. The axioms define the actual behaviour of the operations, except when pop is applied to the empty stack or push when the stack is full. Their behaviour is not constrained in such cases. The stack is implemented as a list of elements, with corresponding concrete definitions for the operations init, push, pop, top and ln. They apply the standard list functions ⌢ (concatenation), **hd** (head), **tl** (tail) and **len** (length). The component is represented by the RSL class expression STACK$_1$ which contains the definitions of types, values and axioms, as below.

scheme STACK$_1$ = **class**
  type
    Elem,
    State = Elem*
  value
    bnd: **Nat**,
    init: State,
    ln: State → **Nat**,
    top: State $\overset{\sim}{\to}$ Elem,
    pop: State $\overset{\sim}{\to}$ State,
    push: Elem × State $\overset{\sim}{\to}$ State
  axiom
    init = ⟨ ⟩,
    ∀ s: State • ln(s) = **len** s,
    ∀ s: State, e: Elem • ln(s) < bnd ⇒ push(e, s) = ⟨e⟩ ⌢ s,
    ∀ s: State • ln(s) > 0 ⇒ pop(s) = **tl** s ∧ top(s) = **hd** s
end

For the purpose of this chapter we consider such components in isolation, as individual objects. On the other hand, to build an application we may need a richer component including a collection of objects [114]. This would be also the right level to introduce fault-tolerance (system level), based on the error detection on the lower level (individual objects).

13.3 Fault-Free versus Fail-Stop Components

A generator is a typical algebraic operation to construct state values [124]. An observer is a co-algebraic operation for making observations about the state [70]. A modifier is both an algebraic operation and co-algebraic. This casting of components into an algebra (a carrier set with functions into this set) or a co-algebra (a carrier set with functions from this set) provides the means to describe how the concrete execution of a component unfolds. Here we are interested in the opposite: how to abstract away from such concrete executions in order to describe how the component should behave.

For instance, for the stack component we put forward five axioms: the length of init is zero, pop decrements and push increments the length, top returns the element which was recently pushed onto the stack and pop modifies the state back before the last push. All axioms except the last compare the reader operations, involving equality over **Nat** or **Elem**. The last axiom compares two writers and involves equality over **State**.

scheme STACK$_0$ = **class**
  type
    Elem, State
  value
    bnd: **Nat**,
    ...
  axiom
    ln(init) = 0,
    $\forall$ s: State • ln(s) > 0 $\Rightarrow$ ln(pop(s)) = ln(s) − 1,
    $\forall$ s: State, e: Elem •
      ln(s) < bnd $\Rightarrow$
      ln(push(e, s)) = ln(s) + 1 $\wedge$
      top(push(e, s)) = e $\wedge$ pop(push(e, s)) = s
end

Once we have described the component on the abstract and concrete levels, we should be able to verify that the concrete component is fault-free. The proof has to demonstrate that concrete definitions in STACK$_1$ satisfy the axioms in STACK$_0$, which boils down to proving first-order properties about concrete value domains. This fact is stated as the following theorem:

theory STACK_THEORY :
axiom
  in STACK$_1$ $\vdash$
    $\forall$ s : State, e : Elem •
      ln(init) = 0 $\wedge$
      (ln(s) > 0 $\Rightarrow$ ln(pop(s)) = ln(s) − 1) $\wedge$
      (ln(s) < bnd $\Rightarrow$ ln(push(e, s)) = ln(s) + 1) $\wedge$
      (ln(s) < bnd $\Rightarrow$ top(push(e, s)) = e $\wedge$ pop(push(e, s)) = s)
end

However, this static verification is very often impossible, given the requirements for the availability of an implementation and a specification, and the feasibility to carry out the proof. The stack example was chosen to provide a demonstration with a minimum of the technical details, however such details would certainly complicate any more realistic proof.

Suppose instead of proving that the component is fault-free, we want to make sure that faults, after they occur, do not spread out uncontrollably, i.e. that we detect the errors as soon as they occur, and then make this fact known to the environment by the boolean observer **error**.

value
    error: State $\to$ **Bool**

We call such a component 'fail-stop'. A fail-stop component need not be fault-free but a fault-free component is certainly fail-stop, only its **error** indicator is permanently set to **false**. We can verify that the component is fail-stop with respect to a given specification by proving that it is fault-free with respect to the weaker "fail-stop specification". We obtain such a specification by syntactic transformation from the original specification, adding **error** to its signatures and modifying the axioms to include the possibility of them being violated. We require that the value of **error** is **true** in a given state iff at least one of the original axioms is violated in this state. When the axioms involve more than one state then we only require this property about the last state, provided none of the prior states have set **error** to **true**. $STACK_2$ below describes such a fail-stop version of $STACK_0$.

scheme $STACK_2 = $ **class**
  type
    Elem, State
  value
    error: State $\to$ **Bool**
    ...
  axiom
    $\sim error(init) = (ln(init) = 0),$
    $\forall$ s: State, e: Elem •
      $\sim error(s) \wedge ln(s) < bnd \Rightarrow$
      $\sim error(push(e, s)) =$
      $(ln(push(e, s)) = ln(s) + 1 \wedge top(push(e, s)) = e),$
    $\forall$ s: State, e: Elem •
      $\sim error(s) \wedge ln(s) < bnd \wedge \sim error(push(e, s)) \Rightarrow$
      $\sim error(pop(push(e, s))) =$
      $(pop(push(e, s)) = s \wedge ln(pop(push(e, s))) = ln(push(e, s)) - 1)$
end

Although we could try proving directly that a component satisfies the fail-stop specification, this would not solve our problems, nor utilize the special form of such specifications. Instead, we would like to guarantee the satisfaction of the fail-stop specification by run-time checking. We now describe a specification method to make such checking possible.

13.4 Fail-Stop Components by Pattern Matching

Run-time checking is only possible if the specification method allows it to be automated – checking automatically if a given behaviour complies with the specification. However, specification methods are normally designed in order to be expressive, to enable abstraction and support effective reasoning, not to allow automatic behaviour-checking. In particular, we cannot check specifications which contain quantifiers (over infinite types) and we cannot check equality between states (pop(push(e, s)) = s).

In the sequel we discuss and illustrate five methods, with increasing expressive power, to specify software components. All allow run-time checking, based on the component's execution history.

13.4.1 Invariants

The first specification is a simple propositional formula built from the constant/observer operations, playing the role of propositional variables. Let con represent a constant, obs an observer and inv an invariant. Invariants are defined according to the BNF syntax below.

$$inv ::= con \mid obs \mid \neg inv \mid inv \vee inv \mid \ldots$$

The specification is required to hold invariantly for every state in the execution sequence, represented by the symbol s. Note the difference between constants and observers and how they depend on the state.

$$
\begin{aligned}
s &\models con & \text{iff}\quad & con \\
s &\models obs & \text{iff}\quad & obs(s) \\
s &\models \neg inv & \text{iff}\quad & \text{not } s \models inv \\
s &\models inv_1 \vee inv_2 & \text{iff}\quad & s \models inv_1 \text{ or } s \models inv_2 \\
&\quad\vdots
\end{aligned}
$$

Consider two example invariants for the stack component: the length of the stack never exceeds the bound and if the last operation was push then the value of top equals the argument to push:

$$ln \leq bnd$$
$$\mathbf{op} = push \Rightarrow top = \mathbf{arg}$$

The first is the first-order formula, written with a relation over **Nat**. The second is the higher-order formula where **op** returns the name of the last state-changing operation, i.e. the operation which produced the current state, and **arg** gives the arguments to this operation. The first and higher orders are explained later in this section.

13.4.2 Actions

Invariants allow us only to formulate properties about individual states, to hold statically over the whole execution. In contrast, an action is a propositional formula over pairs of states. It is built from constants and two kinds of observer operations: evaluated in the first state (a pre-state) and in the second state (a post-state), the latter written with a prime. A pre-state is the state before the execution of a generator/modifier operation, a post-state is the state after the execution. Let act represent an action. Then:

$$act ::= con \mid obs \mid obs' \mid \neg act \mid act \vee act \mid \ldots$$

The action is required to hold over any pair of adjacent states in the execution sequence, here represented by the symbols s_1 and s_2. Note that observers without prime refer to s_1 and observers with prime to s_2; constants refer to none. The semantics of actions is defined as follows:

$$
\begin{array}{lll}
s_1, s_2 \models con & \text{iff} & con \\
s_1, s_2 \models obs & \text{iff} & obs(s_1) \\
s_1, s_2 \models obs' & \text{iff} & obs(s_2) \\
s_1, s_2 \models \neg act & \text{iff} & \text{not } s_1, s_2 \models act \\
s_1, s_2 \models act_1 \vee act_2 & \text{iff} & s_1, s_2 \models act_1 \text{ or } s_1, s_2 \models act_2 \\
\end{array}
$$

$$\vdots$$

Consider two example actions for the stack component: pop decrements the length, provided the stack is not empty; and push increments the length, provided the stack is not full. Suppose s_1 is the state before the execution of pop and s_2 is the state after the execution. Then, since op' contains the name of the operation which produced s_2 (unlike op which produced s_1), op' = pop, and $ln' = ln - 1$ represents the fact that the length of the stack in s_2 (after the execution of pop) is one less than the length in s_1 (before the execution). Both properties are written as higher-order actions:

$$(ln > 0 \wedge \mathbf{op'} = pop) \Rightarrow ln' = ln - 1$$
$$(ln < bnd \wedge \mathbf{op'} = push) \Rightarrow ln' = ln + 1$$

13.4.3 Patterns

Actions will not suffice for specifying those components for which correct behaviour depends not only on the current state and the state immediately before, but the whole execution history. For instance, suppose we want to decide if the value returned by top, after performing the pop operation, is correct. This requires finding the most recent state in the execution history which contains the same number of elements as the current state, and then checking that the values of top in this and the current state are the same. Here the length of the search depends on the value of an observer ln.

The idea is to use regular expressions, similar to specifying words over an alphabet, but the alphabet contains vectors of observer values and words are sequences of such records (histories). A pattern is a regular expression built with usual operators + (sum), · (concatenation), * (Kleene's star) and λ (empty sequence), for which basic components are invariants and actions. Inside a pattern, we surround invariants with angle brackets and actions with square brackets, to be able to distinguish what is an invariant and what is an action. Let pat represent a pattern, and inv and act represent invariants and actions, as before. Patterns are defined as follows:

$$pat ::= \lambda \mid \langle inv \rangle \mid [act] \mid pat + pat \mid pat \cdot pat \mid pat^*$$

The operators have the usual interpretation over sequences of states. Such a sequence represents the execution history – the first state is generated by init and subsequent states are obtained by repeated invocations of the generator and modifier operations.

Suppose t represents an execution history and s represents a state, as before. Consider a pattern pat and the question if pat is satisfied by t, written $t \models pat$. If t is empty then pat is only satisfied if it is equal to λ. Otherwise, we use the head and the tail of t, written hd(t) and tl(t), to carry out the evaluation $hd(t), tl(t) \models pat$. The first element of t plays a special role, as it is used to evaluate all primed observers in the action components of the pattern. Here is the definition:

$$t \models pat \quad \text{iff} \quad \begin{cases} pat = \lambda & \text{if} \quad ln(t) = 0 \\ hd(t), tl(t) \models pat & \text{if} \quad ln(t) > 0 \end{cases}$$

Consider the evaluation $s, t \models pat$ where s is a state, t is a sequence of states and pat is a pattern. It is defined on the structure of pat:

1. pat = λ
   Then t must be empty.
2. pat = $\langle inv \rangle$
   Then t must consist of only one state which satisfies the invariant inv, as in Section 13.4.1.
3. pat = [act]
   Then t must consist of only one state, such that s and this state satisfy the action act, as in Section 13.4.2. Primed observers always refer to s and unprimed to hd(t).
4. pat = pat_1 + pat_2
   Then s and t must either satisfy pat_1 or pat_2, or both.
5. pat = pat_1 · pat_2
   Then it should be possible to split t into some t_1 and t_2 such that s and t_1 satisfy pat_1 and s and t_2 satisfy pat_2. s provides the same interpretation for the primed observers in both patterns.

6. pat = pat$_1^*$

   Then either t is empty or it can be split into t$_1$ and t$_2$ such that: t$_1$ is non-empty; s and t$_1$ satisfy pat$_1$; and s and t$_2$ again satisfy pat$_1^*$. Like concatenation, s remains the same for both expressions.

Formally, we define the relation s,t $\models$ pat below. The definition makes use of ln(t) to represent the length of the sequence t, and t$_1$: t$_2$ to represent concatenation of the sequences t$_1$ and t$_2$.

$$s, t \models \lambda \qquad \text{only if } ln(t) = 0$$

$$s, t \models \langle inv \rangle \qquad \text{iff} \qquad ln(t) = 1 \text{ and } hd(t) \models inv$$

$$s, t \models [act] \qquad \text{iff} \qquad ln(t) = 1 \text{ and } s, hd(t) \models act$$

$$s, t \models pat_1 + pat_2 \text{ iff} \qquad s, t \models pat_1 \text{ or } s, t \models pat_2$$

$$s, t \models pat_1 \cdot pat_2 \text{ iff} \qquad \text{there exist } t_1 \text{ and } t_2 \text{ such that}$$
$$t = t_1 : t_2 \text{ and } s, t_1 \models pat_1 \text{ and } s, t_2 \models pat_2$$

$$s, t \models pat_1^* \qquad \text{only if } ln(t) = 0 \text{ or}$$
$$\text{there exist } t_1 \text{ and } t_2 \text{ such that}$$
$$t = t_1 : t_2 \text{ and } ln(t_1) > 0 \text{ and}$$
$$s, t_1 \models pat_1 \text{ and } s, t_2 \models pat_1^*$$

We carry out pattern matching with every modification of the history, i.e. after invocation of every modifier/generator operation, from the most recent state towards the initial state. If we can run successful pattern matching with every modification of the component's execution history then it means that up till now the component behaved in a proper way. In other words, every non-empty suffix of the execution history must satisfy the pattern to regard the component as behaving correctly. Consider an example below.

$$\langle a \vee b \rangle + \langle a \vee b \rangle \cdot \langle a \Leftrightarrow \neg b \rangle^* \cdot [c' \Leftrightarrow a \vee b]$$

By convention, we let * bind stronger than ·, and · stronger than +, so the pattern could be also written as:

$$\langle a \vee b \rangle + (\langle a \vee b \rangle \cdot (\langle a \Leftrightarrow \neg b \rangle^*) \cdot [c' \Leftrightarrow a \vee b])$$

The pattern says the following: either the history contains only one state such that a ∨ b holds, or at least two states such that a ∨ b holds in the last state, a ∨ b in the first state equals c in the last, and a ⟺ ¬b holds for all intermediate states (if any). Matching this pattern against a given execution history is shown below. The history records the values of the observers a, b and c for eight consecutive states, the first state recorded in the rightmost column, the current (number 8) in the leftmost column. We can see that the pattern is satisfied for all non-empty suffixes until state three. However, the value of a ∨ b in the first state is different than c in the fourth state, thus the pattern is violated by the history suffix containing the states one to four.

$\langle a \vee b\rangle + \langle a \vee b\rangle \cdot \langle a \Leftrightarrow \neg b\rangle^* \cdot [c' \Leftrightarrow a \vee b]$								
check						×	√	√	√
states	8	7	6	5	4	3	2	1

	a	false	true	true	true	true	false	true	false
	b	false	true	false	false	true	true	false	true
	c	true	true	false	true	false	true	true	false

13.4.4 First Order Patterns

We now demonstrate how to extend such specifications into first- and higher-order patterns. Suppose first-order patterns allow for observers which return integer values. This change will not directly affect patterns but their elements – invariants and actions. Both will be built from integer expressions involving integer literals, arithmetic operators and observer names with or without primes, combined with integer relations and propositional connectives. Such first order patterns will be matched against an execution history which contains integer values as entries in the history table.

As a simple illustration, consider the first-order extensions to concrete invariants, actions and patterns, as below. Here is how they are matched against the execution history: a+b≥c+2 is matched successfully for every state until it fails in state eleven; a'+b'≥c'+2 ∧ a'>b is matched successfully for every pair of states until it fails for states eight and nine; $\langle a+b\geq c+2\rangle \cdot (\lambda+[a'>b] \cdot (\lambda+\langle true\rangle^* \cdot [a'+a=b'+b]))$ is matched for every non-empty suffix until and including state five, but it fails in state six.

$a + b \geq c + 2$										
check	×	√	√	√	√	√	√	√	√	√	√

$a' + b' \geq c' + 2 \wedge a' > b$										
check			×	√	√	√	√	√	√	√

$\langle a + b \geq c + 2 \rangle \cdot$ $(\lambda + [a' > b] \cdot (\lambda + \langle true \rangle^* \cdot [a' + a = b' + b]))$										
check						×	√	√	√	√	√
states	11	10	9	8	7	6	5	4	3	2	1

	a	5	6	5	9	2	4	5	3	2	4	1
	b	3	4	3	7	0	1	3	1	0	1	3
	c	7	8	5	6	0	1	6	2	0	1	2

13.4.5 Higher Order Patterns

With higher order patterns we allow observers of any type. Each type comes with its own set of functions and relations. We also assume two special observers: **op** returns the name of the generator/modifier invoked to obtain the current state (initially **op** = *init*) and **arg** returns the set of arguments this generator/modifier was invoked with (if any). From now on, we will also assume a ⟨true⟩* trailer for any pattern used: any prefix of the execution history can be used to satisfy the pattern, not just the whole history.

As an example, consider a higher-order pattern for specifying the stack. We have the usual observers top and ln which come with the definition of the stack and two generic observers **op** and **arg**. **op** returns the name of one of three possible modifier/generator operations: init, push or pop. **arg** returns the argument used for the invocation of push. By × we represent that the observer value is not available.

$$\textbf{op} : State \rightarrow \{init, push, pop\}$$
$$\textbf{arg} : State \rightarrow Elem \cup \{\times\}$$

The pattern includes three possibilities: if the state was produced by init then ln must be zero; if it was produced by push then top equals the argument of push and the value of ln is increased by one; and if it was produced by pop then the value of ln is decreased by one, and the values of top in the current state and the most recent state with the same ln value are the same.

$$\langle \textbf{op} = init \wedge ln = 0 \rangle +$$
$$\langle \textbf{op} = push \wedge top = \textbf{arg} \rangle \cdot [ln' = ln + 1] +$$
$$\langle \textbf{op} = pop \rangle \cdot [ln' = ln - 1] \cdot [ln > ln']^* \cdot [ln = ln' \wedge top = top']$$

Below we describe how this pattern can be matched against a concrete history where values put on the stack are real numbers. If the entry contains × then it means that the value of a given observer was not available, for instance **arg** = × when the operation **op** does not take any arguments or top = × when the stack is empty. The pattern is satisfied until and including state nine but is violated for state ten: the value of top is 2.14 and of ln is 1, but the most recent state with the same value of ln has top = 1.0.

check	×	✓	✓	✓	✓	✓	✓	✓	✓	✓
states	10	9	8	7	6	5	4	3	2	1

$$\underbrace{op=pop,\ ln=ln'+1}\quad \underbrace{ln>ln'}\quad \underbrace{ln=ln'\ \wedge\ top\neq top'}\quad \underbrace{true}$$

op	pop	pop	pop	push	push	push	pop	push	push	init
arg	×	×	×	3.5	5.9	0.2	×	2.14	1.0	×
top	2.14	0.2	5.9	3.5	5.9	0.2	1.0	2.14	1.0	×
ln	1	2	3	4	3	2	1	2	1	0

13.5 Example: Line Editor

As an illustration of patterns, consider the example of a line editor. The editor provides some basic operations to modify the list of elements depending on the position of a caret. The caret can be positioned at an element in the list or after the list. We have one generator init which makes the list empty and sets the caret position at one (after the empty list). We have four modifiers:

1. right moves the caret forward, if possible.
2. left moves the caret backward, if possible.
3. If there is a current element, insert inserts an element before it, and retains the same current element. Otherwise, insert appends an element to the list and makes it current. In either case, insert moves the caret one place forward.
4. If there is a current element, delete deletes it and then, if there is a following element, makes it current. It leaves the caret position unchanged.

We also have three observers: ln returns the length of the list; ps returns the current position of the caret (a natural number); and el returns the current element, if there is such an element. Here are the signatures in RSL:

type
    State, Elem
value
    init: State,
    el: State $\overset{\sim}{\to}$ Elem,
    ln, ps: State $\to$ **Nat**,
    insert: Elem $\times$ State $\to$ State,
    delete, left, right: State $\overset{\sim}{\to}$ State

The pattern defining the behaviour of the editor is the sum of five patterns. Each of these patterns indicates which modifier/generator operation was executed:

   pat-init + pat-insert + pat-delete + pat-right + pat-left

The pattern **pat-init** requires that ps is one and ln is zero in the state resulting from the execution of init.

   pat-init $=_{def}$ $\langle$**op** $=$ init $\land$ ps $= 1 \land$ ln $= 0\rangle$

The pattern **pat-insert** requires that the values of ps and ln are both increased by one by the execution of the operation insert, and the current element (if any) remains the same.

   pat-insert $=_{def}$ $\langle$**op** $=$ insert$\rangle \cdot$
        $[ln' = ln + 1 \land ps' = ps + 1 \land (ps \leq ln \Rightarrow el' = el)]$

pat-delete divides into three cases, depending if ps, after the execution of delete, is greater than, equal to, or less than ln. If greater, then we only require that ps and ln remain unchanged. If equal, then ps must be the same and ln must decrease by one; this is when we just deleted the last element in the list. In both cases, the resulting position is after the list, so we are not interested in the value of el. If less, then ps must not change and ln must decrease, as before, but we also search the history to find the current element. We look for the state where the caret position equals the current one, but counting from the end of the list. This is because prior to delete, the caret was on the left of the new current element. We look for the most recent state in which the caret position is the same distance from the end of the list as the current position, ln - ps = ln'- ps', and we check that the current element in that state is the same as in the state following the delete.

$$
\textit{pat-delete} =_{def} \langle \textbf{op} = \textit{delete} \rangle \cdot \\
\left(
\begin{array}{l}
[ps' > \textit{ln}' \wedge ps' = ps \wedge \textit{ln}' = \textit{ln}]+ \\
[ps' = \textit{ln}' \wedge ps' = ps \wedge \textit{ln}' = \textit{ln} - 1]+ \\
[ps' < \textit{ln}' \wedge ps' = ps \wedge \textit{ln}' = \textit{ln} - 1] \cdot \\
\quad [\textit{ln} - ps > \textit{ln}' - ps']^* [\textit{ln} - ps = \textit{ln}' - ps' \wedge el' = el]
\end{array}
\right)
$$

pat-right is similar to pat-delete. It divides into three cases for the value of ps being greater than, equal to, or less than ln. The position must increase, provided it is at an element in the list, and ln must remain the same. We also check the value of the current element, as we did for pat-delete, counting the distance from the caret position to the end of the list.

$$
\textit{pat-right} =_{def} \langle \textbf{op} = \textit{right} \rangle \cdot \\
\left(
\begin{array}{l}
[ps' > \textit{ln}' \wedge ps' = ps \wedge \textit{ln}' = \textit{ln}]+ \\
[ps' = \textit{ln}' \wedge ps' = ps + 1 \wedge \textit{ln}' = \textit{ln}]+ \\
[ps' < \textit{ln}' \wedge ps' = ps + 1 \wedge \textit{ln}' = \textit{ln}] \cdot \\
\quad [\textit{ln} - ps > \textit{ln}' - ps']^* [\textit{ln} - ps = \textit{ln}' - ps' \wedge el' = el]
\end{array}
\right)
$$

pat-left also has three cases. If the caret is already at the first position, then ln, ps and el (provided the current element exists) must stay the same. Otherwise, ln remains unchanged and ps must decrease. Moreover, if the previous operation was insert then its argument must be the current element. Otherwise we look for the most recent state when either: (1) the caret position was the same as now, in which case the current element then must be the same as the current element now; or (2) the caret position was one greater than now and insert was the last operation, in which case the argument to that insert and the current element now must be equal. The complication in this case is due to the fact that insert both inserts an element and moves the caret forward.

$$pat\text{-}left =_{def} \langle \mathbf{op} = left \rangle \cdot$$

$$\begin{pmatrix} [ps' = 1 \land ps' = ps \land ln' = ln \land (ln' > 0 \Rightarrow el' = el)] + \\ [ps' > 1 \land \mathbf{op} = insert \land \\ \quad ps' = ps - 1 \land ln' = ln \land el = \mathbf{arg}] + \\ [ps' > 1 \land \mathbf{op} \neq insert \land ps' = ps - 1 \land ln' = ln] \cdot \\ [ps > ps' \land (ps = ps' + 1 \Rightarrow \mathbf{op} \neq insert)]^{*} \cdot \\ [ps = ps' \land el' = el \lor \\ \quad ps = ps' + 1 \land \mathbf{op} = insert \land el' = \mathbf{arg}] \end{pmatrix}$$

One comment is in place. This pattern appears complicated, given a rather simple component it is supposed to check. There are two reasons to explain this. The first is the fact that we specified the component in a complete way, when normally one would like to specify and check selected properties. Second, the pattern has been defined directly in terms of observers, without the intermediate level of auxiliary definitions, specially designed to capture recurring properties. On the other hand, the pattern above is composed of five independent patterns which, one can argue, are simple on their own. Whatever point of view we adopt, the scalability of the whole approach is no doubt an important practical concern, which we plan to address in our future work, along with other issues discussed in the conclusions.

13.6 Specifying the Wrapper Generator

One way to make sure that a given component is fail-stop is to prove that it satisfies the fail-stop specification. But this method ignores the special form of the fail-stop property, and typically requires a fair amount of human assistance. Instead, we want to guarantee this property at run-time, where a specification is given in the form of a pattern and run-time checking is carried out by a specification generated wrapper. The aim of this section is to formalise the goals of the wrapper generator using RSL. The model consists of four parts: components, invariants and actions, patterns, and wrapping.

13.6.1 Components

Each component consists of an interface, which is based on the type **Name** of operation names, and semantics, based on **State**.

The abstract type **Name**, values **init** and **error**, and the variant type **Role** with four values **con**, **gen**, **obs** and **mod**, are defined in the module **NAME**.

scheme NAME = **class**
  type
    Name,
    Role ==
      con | gen | obs | mod

value
   init, error: Name
end

An interface is defined in the module INTR which takes NAME as a parameter. It is represented as an abstract type Intr with two functions defined on it: names returns the set of operation names and role assigns such names one of the four roles: constant, generator, observer or modifier. The axiom requires that any interface contains the generator init.

scheme INTR(N: NAME) = **class**
  type
    Intr
  value
    names : Intr $\to$ N.Name-set,
    role : Intr $\times$ N.Name $\to$ N.Role
  axiom
    $\forall$ i : Intr • N.init $\in$ names(i) $\land$ role(i, N.init) = N.gen
end

Let us turn to semantics. The type State represents the state space of a component. It is defined as an abstract type in the module STATE.

scheme STATE =
class
  type
    State
end

The semantics defines the meanings for all the operations of a component: a boolean value for a constant, a state value for a generator, a function from State to Bool for an observer and a function from State to State for a modifier. This assignment is defined according to the type Sem, defined in the module SEM. The module takes STATE as a parameter.

scheme SEM(S: STATE) = **class**
  type
    Sem ==
      con(**Bool**) |
      gen(S.State) |
      obs(S.State $\to$ **Bool**) |
      mod(S.State $\to$ S.State)
end

A component is represented according to the type Comp and has its interface and semantics defined via the functions intr and sem. We require that the roles of the operations in the interface and their semantics are consistent. Comp is defined in the module COMP which extends the modules INTR and SEM, and takes the modules NAME and STATE as parameters.

scheme COMP(N: NAME, S: STATE) =
  extend INTR(N) **with**
  extend SEM(S) **with class**
  type
    Comp
  value
    intr: Comp $\rightarrow$ Intr,
    sem: Comp $\times$ N.Name $\overset{\sim}{\rightarrow}$ Sem
  axiom
    ($\forall$ c: Comp, n: N.Name •
      n $\in$ names(intr(c)) $\Rightarrow$
      case sem(c, n) **of**
        con(_) $\rightarrow$ role(intr(c), n) = N.con,
        obs(_) $\rightarrow$ role(intr(c), n) = N.obs,
        gen(_) $\rightarrow$ role(intr(c), n) = N.gen,
        mod(_) $\rightarrow$ role(intr(c), n) = N.mod
      end
)
end

COMP also contains the boolean functions isreader and iswriter, which decide if a given name exists in the interface and is associated with a reader or a writer operation, respectively.

value
  isreader: Comp $\times$ N.Name $\rightarrow$ **Bool**
  isreader(c, n) $\equiv$
    n $\in$ names(intr(c)) $\wedge$
    (role(intr(c), n) = N.con $\vee$
      role(intr(c), n) = N.obs),
  iswriter: Comp $\times$ N.Name $\rightarrow$ **Bool**
  iswriter(c, n) $\equiv$
    n $\in$ names(intr(c)) $\wedge$
    (role(intr(c), n) = N.gen $\vee$
      role(intr(c), n) = N.mod)

Given a reader (constant or observer) operation which exists in the interface, the operation can be evaluated on a given state of the component to obtain a boolean value. This is done by the function **eval**. Similarly, given a writer (generator or modifier) operation, the operation can be executed on the state to obtain a new state. This is described by the function **exec**. Both functions are defined below.

value
  eval : Comp × S.State × N.Name $\tilde{\to}$ **Bool**
  eval(c, s, n) ≡
    case sem(c, n) **of**
      con(c) → c, obs(o) → o(s)
    end
    pre isreader(c, n),
  exec : Comp × S.State × N.Name $\tilde{\to}$ S.State
  exec(c, s, n) ≡
    case sem(c, n) **of**
      gen(g) → g, mod(m) → m(s)
    end
    pre iswriter(c, n)

13.6.2 Invariants and Actions

Consider the types Inv and Act to represent invariants and actions, respectively. Inv is a variant type which applies op as the constructor for operation names, and neg and or as constructors for negation and disjunction respectively. Act applies one more constructor, op' to represent post-names, while op represents pre-names. The types are defined in the modules INV and ACT. Both apply the modules NAME, STATE and COMP as parameters.

scheme INV(N: NAME, S: STATE, C: COMP(N,S)) =
class
  type
    Inv == op(N.Name) | neg(Inv) | or(Inv, Inv) | ...
end

scheme ACT(N: NAME, S: STATE, C: COMP(N, S)) =
class
  type
    Act == op(N.Name) | op'(N.Name) | neg(Act) | or(Act, Act) | ...
end

We continue with the declarations related to actions. The function **names** returns the set of operation names used by an action.

value
  names: Act → N.Name-**set**
  names(a) ≡
    case a **of**
      op(n) → {n}, op'(n) → {n},
      neg(a) → names(a), or(a_1, a_2) → names(a_1) ∪ names(a_2)
    end

An action is well-formed with respect to a component if and only if all its names exist in the component's interface as reader operations.

value
  iswf: Act × C.Comp → **Bool**
  iswf(a, c) ≡
    (∀ n: N.Name •
      n ∈ names(a) ⇒ C.isreader(c, n)
)

Function **eval** is used to evaluate an action on a pair of states. The function is defined by recursion. It requires that the action argument is well-formed with respect to the component. We define **eval** as follows:

value
  eval: Act × S.State × S.State × C.Comp $\xrightarrow{\sim}$ **Bool**
  eval(a, s_1, s_2, c) ≡
    case a **of**
      op(n) → C.eval(c, s_1, n),
      op'(n) → C.eval(c, s_2, n),
      neg(b) → ~eval(b, s_1, s_2, c),
      or(a_1, a_2) → eval(a_1, s_1, s_2, c) ∨ eval(a_2, s_1, s_2, c)
    end
    pre iswf(a, c)

13.6.3 Patterns

Patterns are represented as the variant type **Pat**. The type is built with six variants, one for each constructor of patterns, following the definition in Section 13.4.3. The type is defined in the module **PAT** which extends the modules INV and ACT, and takes the modules NAME, STATE and COMP as parameters.

scheme PAT(N: NAME, S: STATE, C: COMP(N, S)) =
  extend INV(N, S, C) **with**
  extend ACT(N, S, C) **with**
class
  type
    Pat ==
      lambda |
      inv(Inv) | act(Act) |
      sum(Pat, Pat) | con(Pat, Pat) | star(Pat)
    ...
end

We continue by extending the module **PAT** with more declarations. The function **names** returns the set of names used in a pattern.

value
  names : Pat → N.Name-set
  names(p) ≡
    case p **of**
      lambda → {},
      inv(i) → names(i),
      act(a) → names(a),
      sum(q, q') → names(q) ∪ names(q'),
      con(q, q') → names(q) ∪ names(q'),
      star(q) → names(q)
    end

A pattern is well-formed with respect to a component if and only if all its invariants and actions are well-formed with respect to this component; they use only the names of the component's reader operations.

value
  iswf: Pat × C.Comp → **Bool**
  iswf(p, c) ≡
  (∀ n: N.Name •
    n ∈ names(p) ⇒ C.isreader(c, n)
)

Consider a pattern p, a state-sequence t and a component c, such that p is well-formed with respect to c. The function **eval** evaluates p on t according to c. There are two cases in the definition: if t is empty then p must be equal to lambda, otherwise the evaluation applies the auxiliary function **eval** which considers separately the head and the tail of t, as in Section 13.4.3.

value
  eval: Pat × S.State* × C.Comp $\overset{\sim}{\to}$ **Bool**
  eval(p, t, c) ≡
    if t = ⟨⟩
    then p = lambda
    else eval(p, **hd** t, **tl** t, c)
    end pre iswf(p, c)

This auxiliary **eval** function is defined below. It takes a pattern p, a state s, a state sequence t, and a component c as its arguments, such that p is well-formed with respect to c. The function is defined by recursion on the structure of p, following the definition in Section 13.4.3. In particular, if p is inv(i) where i is an invariant, then i must be satisfied on the first state of t, and if p is act(a) where a is an action, then a must be satisfied on s and the first element of t. In these cases, evaluation is carried out according to the **eval** functions defined for invariants and actions in Section 13.6.2.

value
    eval: Pat × S.State × S.State* × C.Comp $\overset{\sim}{\to}$ **Bool**
    eval(p, s, t, c) ≡
      case p **of**
        lambda → t = $\langle\rangle$,
        inv(i) → **len** t = 1 ∧ eval(i, **hd** t, c),
        act(a) → **len** t = 1 ∧ eval(a, s, **hd** t, c),
        sum(p_1, p_2) → eval(p_1, s, t, c) ∨ eval(p_2, s, t, c),
        con(p_1, p_2) →
          ($\exists$ t_1, t_2: S.State* •
            t = t_1 $\frown$ t_2 ∧
            eval(p_1, s, t_1, c) ∧ eval(p_2, s, t_2, c)
          ),
        star(p_1) →
          t = $\langle\rangle$ ∨
          ($\exists$ t_1, t_2: S.State* •
            t = t_1 $\frown$ t_2 ∧ t_1 ≠ $\langle\rangle$ ∧
            eval(p_1, s, t_1, c) ∧ eval(p, s, t_2, c)
)
      end pre iswf(p, c)

13.6.4 Wrapping

Consider the declarations of objects: N for NAME, S for STATE, C for COMP(N,S), and P for PAT(N,S,C). In particular, N.Name represents the type of operation names, S.State represents the states, C.Comp contains the components with operation names in N.Name and semantics based on S.State, and P.Pat contains the patterns expressing the properties of components in C.Comp. The declarations are as follows:

object
    N: NAME,
    S: STATE,
    C: COMP(N, S),
    P: PAT(N, S, C)

A wrapper will take a component c in C.Comp and a pattern p in P.Pat, and produce a new component which is able to check the behaviour of c according to p. In order for this to be possible, the generated component must be based on a larger state-space than S.State. In addition to the current state, it must remember the execution history, i.e. the list of states that led to this state, and a boolean value to indicate the presence or absence of an error. We represent this enriched state as the record type State, defined in the module $STATE_1$. The module takes STATE as a parameter.

scheme STATE$_1$(S: STATE) =
class
  type
    State::
      present: S.State
      past: S.State*
      error: **Bool**
end

The wrapped components are represented by the type D.Comp, where the object D instantiates the module COMP for N as the name-space and T (i.e. STATE$_1$ applied to S), as the state-space. Therefore the names of the components in D.Comp are shared with the component in C.Comp, but their semantics is based on a richer state-space. Here is the declaration:

object
  T: STATE$_1$(S),
  D: COMP(N, T)

The wrapper generator is specified as the function **wrap** which takes a pattern p in P.Pat and a component c in C.Comp, and returns a new component d in D.Comp. The function is defined implicitly, using a pre-condition and a post-condition. The pre-condition requires that p is well-formed with respect to c and c does not contain the operation **error** in its interface. The post-condition involves four auxiliary functions: extends_interface to check if d properly maintains and extends the interface of c; preserves_semantics to check if the corresponding operations in c and d have the same semantics; records_history to check if every state-changing operation in d updates the history record; and detects_errors to check if d detects errors with respect to the pattern p. The function **wrap** is defined as follows:

value
  wrap: P.Pat × C.Comp $\overset{\sim}{\to}$ D.Comp
  wrap(p, c) **as** d
    post
    extends_interface(c, d) ∧
    (∀ n: N.Name •
      n ∈ C.names(C.intr(c)) ⇒
      preserves_semantics(c, d, n) ∧
      (
        D.iswriter(d, n) ⇒
        records_history(d, n) ∧ detects_errors(c, d, n, p)
)
)
    pre P.iswf(p, c) ∧ N.error ∉ C.names(C.intr(c))

Function extends_interface requires that the generated component contains all the operations of the original component and assigns them the same roles. However, if an operation is a generator then its role will change into a modifier, as wrapping requires recording all state-changes caused by the writer operations. An exception to this is init, which is required by the axioms to be present in any interface, and be assigned the role of a generator. The function extends_interface also requires that the generated component contains error as an observer. It is defined as follows:

value
    extends_interface: C.Comp × D.Comp → **Bool**
    extends_interface(c, d) ≡
      D.names(D.intr(d)) = C.names(C.intr(c)) ∪ {N.error} ∧
      D.role(D.intr(d), N.error) = N.obs ∧
      (∀ n: N.Name •
        n ∈ C.names(C.intr(c)) ⇒
        if C.role(C.intr(c), n) = N.gen ∧ n ≠ N.init
        then D.role(D.intr(d), n) = N.mod
        else D.role(D.intr(d), n) = C.role(C.intr(c), n) **end**
)

The function preserves_semantics compares the operations in the components c and d which are identified by the same name n, and checks if those operations have the same semantics. The pre-condition requires that the component d extends the interface of c, and the operation n exists in both the components c and d. Having the same semantics means:

1. Two constants return equal values.
2. Two observers return equal values when applied to "equal" states.
3. Two generators (only possible if n = init) return "equal" states.
4. A generator and a corresponding modifier return "equal" states.
5. Two modifiers return "equal" states when applied to "equal" states.

Unlike comparing the values of constants or observers, which all return the type **Bool**, the modifiers return the states of c and d which have unequal types: S.State and T.State. Saying that s of type S.State is "equal" to t of type T.State means s equals the present part of t: s = present(t). Moreover, preserves_semantics does not require "equal" semantics when the state of d already indicates the presence of an error. In such states, the meaning of the operations in the generated component is left unspecified. An exception to this is the generator init, whose role is to initialise the state regardless of any error in the previous state. The function preserves_semantics is defined as follows:

value
    preserves_semantics: C.Comp × D.Comp × N.Name $\xrightarrow{\sim}$ **Bool**

preserves_semantics(c, d, n) ≡
   case (C.sem(c, n), D.sem(d, n)) **of**
     (C.con(cs), D.con(ds)) → cs = ds,
     (C.gen(cs), D.gen(ds)) → cs = T.present(ds),
     (C.gen(cs), D.mod(ds)) →
       ($\forall$ s: T.State • $\sim$T.error(s) $\Rightarrow$ cs = T.present(ds(s))),
     (C.obs(cs), D.obs(ds)) →
       ($\forall$ s: T.State • $\sim$T.error(s) $\Rightarrow$ cs(T.present(s)) = ds(s)),
     (C.mod(cs), D.mod(ds)) →
       ($\forall$ s: T.State • $\sim$T.error(s) $\Rightarrow$ cs(T.present(s)) = T.present(ds(s)))
   end
   pre extends_interface(c, d) $\land$
     n $\in$ C.names(C.intr(c)) $\cap$ D.names(D.intr(d))

The function `records_history` decides if the generated component properly updates the execution history with every writer operation. If the operation is `init`, the only generator left, it checks if the execution history is empty. In other words, `init` is required to clear the execution history. The remaining operations are all modifiers. The function takes the semantics of such an operation, which is a function ds from `T.State` to `T.State`, and checks if for every state s: ds inserted the `present` part of ds(s) at the head of the execution record, `hd(T.past(ds(s))) = T.present(ds(s))`, and also maintains the record created so far, `tl(T.past(ds(s))) = T.past(s)`. `T.past(s)` is the execution history before the operation and `T.past(ds(s))` is the history after the operation. This requirement applies to all states, whether or not the `error` observer is `true`. Here is the definition:

value
   records_history: D.Comp $\times$ N.Name $\overset{\sim}{\to}$ **Bool**
   records_history(d, n) ≡
     case D.sem(d, n) **of**
       D.gen(ds) → T.past(ds) = $\langle\rangle$,
       D.mod(ds) →
         ($\forall$ s: T.State • T.past(ds(s)) = $\langle$T.present(ds(s))$\rangle$ $^\frown$ T.past(s))
     end pre D.iswriter(d, n)

The last function is `detects_errors`. It takes two components, the original c and the generated d, the name n of the writer operation and the pattern p, and decides if d detects errors in the execution of n, with respect to the pattern p. When n = `init`, which is the only generator left in d, the role of n is to initialise `error` to `false`. Suppose n is a modifier operation, ds is the semantics of n, a function from `T.State` to `T.State`, and s is a state in `T.State`. If `error` is `true` on s then it is also `true` on ds(s); no operation except `init` can reset an error. If `error` is `false` on s then `error(ds(s))` depends if the pattern p is satisfied when evaluated on the updated execution history `past(ds(s))`, considering the semantics of all operations in

the component c (the same as the semantics of d, according to the function
preserves_semantics). The function is defined as follows:

value
   detects_errors: C.Comp × D.Comp × N.Name × P.Pat $\overset{\sim}{\to}$ **Bool**
   detects_errors(c, d, n, p) ≡
     case D.sem(d, n) **of**
       D.gen(ds) → T.error(ds) = **false**,
       D.mod(ds) →
        (∀ s: T.State •
         T.error(ds(s)) = (T.error(s) ∨ ~P.eval(p, T.past(ds(s)), c))
)
     end pre P.iswf(p, c) ∧ D.iswriter(d, n)

13.7 Implementing the Wrapper Generator

In this section we discuss the implementation of the wrapper generator. There
is currently no formal relation between the specification in Section 13.6 and
the implementation. Indeed, the implementation has not been formalised.
However, the specification helped implementation by clarifying a number of
design issues and affecting design decisions. The challenge to formally prove
correctness of the wrapper generator is one direction of our future work.

Consider the structure of the wrapped component. The signature is the
same as that of the original component plus the observer **error**. The state
includes some part of the execution history (as necessary for checking) and
the error indicator. The wrapper takes over all communication between the
original component and its users:

- Invocation of a constant/observer is passed to the component and obtained
  results directly returned to the user, no checking is done in this case.
- Invocation of a generator/modifier is carried out on the original component,
  observations about the new state and operation itself are recorded. Then
  we carry out pattern matching with respect to this modified history and
  set the error flag accordingly.

The wrapper may conduct more activities, in particular maintain the
history record, remove the observations with no effect on future checking,
etc. Figure 13.2 depicts this structure.

We would like this component to be generated automatically for a given
pattern. We designed a prototype wrapper generator for components written
in a small subset of Java. The generator is intended as a tool for writing
case studies on the use of patterns for specifying components, and pattern
matching for checking their behaviour at run-time. At this moment, there
are several constraints we impose on the input Java class: the only data type

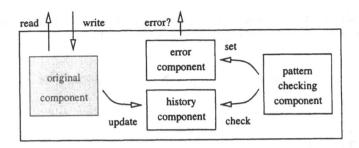

Fig. 13.2. Structure of the wrapped component.

is natural numbers; modifiers take zero or one argument; class constructors take no arguments; and exceptions are not allowed. The wrapper generator Wrap is itself written in Java, using the JavaCC tool to support parsing. The input is the specification file that contains the name of the class to be wrapped, its signature in a simplified form, and the pattern specifying the correct behaviour of the class. Here is the specification file for the stack:

#Classname	#Actions	#Pattern
NatStack	q0 = {op = init /\ ln = 0}	q0 +
#Modifiers	q1 = {op = push /\ top = arg}	q1.q2 +
push();	q2 = {ln = ln' - 1}	q3.q4.q5*.q6
pop;	q3 = {op = pop}	
#Observers	q4 = {ln = ln' + 1}	
top;	q5 = {ln > ln'}	
ln;	q6 = {ln = ln' /\ top = top'}	

Wrap produces the source code for the wrapper class, which is a subclass of the class specified in the input file. The class contains some additional variables to store the execution history, the automaton representing the regular expression, an error indicator, methods to update and check the history, etc. All observers are inherited from the parent class and all modifiers and generators are overridden: they call the parent method, update the history record, carry out pattern matching, and set the error indicator accordingly. Wrap also creates an applet to test the execution of the wrapped class. The applet allows one to invoke the modifiers individually or in a sequence, and to display the execution history and the values of the observers (including error). It also compares the execution times of the two classes.

We make a few comments on the implementation and the use of wrappers. As our main purpose is error detection, we do not consider how the wrapped component should be used to build reliable distributed systems. This belongs to the next level – implementation of fault-tolerance. One idea would be to integrate patterns with a component framework like CORBA: make them part of the IDL description of a component; generate the code for run-time checking along with the usual stub code; and build applications which actively inspect the error status for the components they are built from. Another idea is to use the wrapper in a remote way, as a smart proxy for its component, or as a CORBA interceptor to become part of the growing class of objects providing infrastructure services for other objects. Whatever method is used, wrappers represent the knowledge (reflection) of how their components should behave. They cannot change how the components behave, but rather the behaviour of applications built from such components.

13.8 Conclusions

We demonstrated how regular expressions can be used to formally specify software components, in order to be able to check their behaviour at run-time. We built such expressions from the propositions about pairs of states of a component, one of which is the current state, another is some previous state determined by the checking process. Checking is carried out by a specification-generated wrapper which produces a fail-stop component [126] from the component which may fail in an arbitrary way. We also presented a formal specification of the wrapper generator and its implementation for components written as Java classes.

We argue that run-time checking is particularly suitable for open, object-based distributed systems. Distribution makes testing such systems difficult in general, given the large number of components and many possible ways for them to interact. Openness means such systems are relatively easy to modify but also hard to verify. In particular, deciding at run-time which components should be used makes it hard to approach an a priori verification. Openness also means the components may come from many origins, lacking proper certification or not allowing, because of their proprietary format, independent inspection of their quality. Moreover, decisions to include components are often based on their IDL descriptions, which typically lack the semantic information or describe this semantics in a natural language. Run-time checks often provide the only method of protection for the whole system from its unsound, unreliable components. The chapter showed how to introduce such checks in a systematic way, generated from formal specifications.

Related work on software specification with regular expressions include [39], but there the focus is symbolic reasoning, not run-time behaviour checking. Specification-based testing [119] is another related area whose purpose is mainly analysis (off-line), unlike here where we try to improve reliability (on-line). Run-time checks are implemented practically in the Java Assert class (of java.lang.object) but only to check invariants. The background for formalisation of software components in this chapter is the co-algebraic approach to semantics [70] and its application to object-oriented classes [67]. One more related area is fault-tolerance. Formalisation of fault-tolerance has been carried out in many papers (see [91] for an overview), but mostly to specify and verify an existing system. Here, in contrast, we provide a constructive approach to actually build such systems, the wrapper generator, although for now we focus only on error detection.

The disadvantage of patterns as formal specifications of software components is the fact that they are relatively concrete, expressed in terms of execution histories, states, observations about states, state-changes and the operations causing them. The amount of detail they have to contain makes them probably unsuitable for doing proofs of correctness – that components behave correctly for all possible executions, to capture requirements – what kind of functionality is needed from a component, or to document steps of development – from abstract towards more concrete descriptions of components. On the other hand, our purpose was allowing automatic behaviour-checking based on execution histories, not to support analysis, requirements or development. This task can be difficult to achieve for many more abstract specifications, so it is really the purpose of a specification to decide how abstract or how concrete it should be.

Defining refinement of patterns according to their strengths, and relating patterns to more abstract algebraic or co-algebraic specifications, is a possible direction for future work in this area. Another direction is application of patterns to build and verify fault-tolerant systems: how to verify fault-tolerance on the system level based on run-time checking on the component level. This could provide a demonstration of how symbolic and run-time techniques can work together. Then there are real-time and memory requirements for the whole scheme to work in practice. In particular, it must be possible to analyse patterns to see which parts of the history we have to remember for future checking and which we can discard.

Background Information

This chapter is based on work [72] done by Wojciech Mostowski, originally from the Institute of Mathematics, University of Gdańsk, Poland, currently a PhD student in Computer Science at Chalmers University of Technology, Gothenburg, Sweden, and Tomasz Janowski.

14. An Infrastructure for Software Reuse

14.1 Introduction

It has long been recognised that it is quite common for parts of different software systems to have the same or at least very similar functionality, even when the systems have widely different application domains. It should thus be possible to reduce the cost of developing new software systems, as well as improving their reliability and quality, by identifying and reusing appropriate, already existing components. However, although much work has been done on software reuse and many different solutions have been proposed for making reuse practical, efficient reuse remains problematic. Indeed in many cases a software developer may actually take longer to develop a new system by attempting to reuse existing components than by starting from scratch.

One reason for this [94] is that software components are typically very information-rich, which makes it difficult to characterise and classify them in such a way that their relevant properties are captured and to match existing components against current requirements. Other reasons include:

1. that proposed or already available reuse libraries (repositories) generally contain just one type of software component, which is usually code although software development projects involve much more than just source code;
2. that software component descriptions are often incomplete. In particular they generally lack important information such as guidelines on how to reuse components and information about relationships between different components;
3. that different libraries usually have their own individual retrieval systems, which generally depend on the type of components stored there, and there is no single interface through which a whole collection of libraries can be accessed;
4. that to use a library efficiently and effectively usually requires a detailed understanding of the structure of the library and how its information is organised: in many cases the user's knowledge regarding the form in which information is stored and the format in which queries should be presented must be on a par with that of the maintainer of the library; and

5. that libraries usually characterise the properties of components either functionally (using, for example, algebraic or relational specifications; see e.g. [31, 49, 66, 74, 75, 155]) or structurally (using for example, keywords or natural language; see e.g. [19]) but not both, although being able to formulate queries based on both kinds of properties can be very useful when searching for a particular component.

In this chapter we describe a generalised reuse infrastructure which takes these points into account and which can thus, we believe, improve both the ease and efficiency of reusing software components. We begin by discussing and specifying the data storage system in Section 14.2, then in Section 14.3 we discuss and specify the query system. Finally, Section 14.4 summarises the work and outlines some possible future developments of it.

14.2 The Reuse Infrastructure

Software support for reuse is usually based around a basic library of reusable components to which some sort of query system has been added, and, as indicated in points 3 and 4 above, different libraries usually have their own query systems and using this efficiently often requires good knowledge about how information is stored in the library. In order to be able to support many libraries and to avoid the problem of them having disparate interfaces, we introduce an intermediate interface between the libraries and the query system, which we call the *meta-library*. This offers abstract descriptions of the individual components stored in the libraries, together with information about relationships between different components (thus addressing point 2). In addition, to take account of point 5, the abstract description encapsulates both semantic (functional) and structural properties of the components.

We further extend the basic architecture by including a *lexicon*, which records relationships between query terms and similar terms which actually occur in the reuse meta-library. Thus, for example, the lexicon might record that the terms *software* and *program* are essentially synonymous, that the term *computer system* is a generalisation of the term *software*, and that the term *routine* is a specialisation of the term *software*. Such relationships can then be used as a basis for estimating the precision with which a particular component matches a given query: if the query uses the same or an equivalent term to the one found in the component then the match is effectively exact; if the query uses a term which is more general or more specialised, then the match is not so good and the number of levels of generalisation or specialisation can be used as a quantitative measure of the accuracy of the match – the more levels the worse the match; and if the query term and the component term are unrelated then they do not match. The lexicon thus offers the user better control of the search process because the minimum ac-

ceptable precision of the match can be specified as part of the query. The
whole infrastructure is illustrated in Figure 14.1.

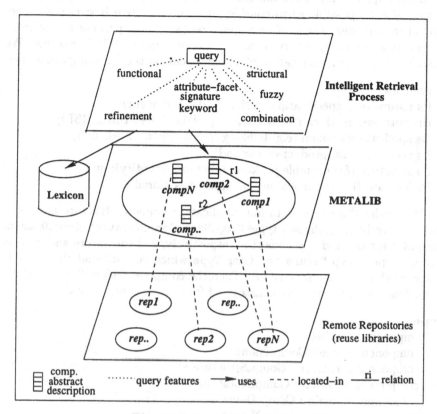

Fig. 14.1. Reuse infrastructure.

We consider a reusable component to be any element of the software
design process as well as actual code, so a component could be, for example,
a specification in RSL, a design in UML, code in C++, etc. etc. In order
to be able to distinguish different components, we introduce the notion of
a *component identifier*. However, instead of specifying this abstractly as one
would normally do, we wish here to give a more concrete definition which
takes account of the information that we know is going to be used to uniquely
identify components in the search process.

In each individual repository, components are likely to be identified by
some form of name (for example the name of the function that they perform). However, this is in general not sufficient if we want a system which
encompasses components from the various stages of the software lifecycle
because we would probably like to use the same name for all development
stages of a particular component. In addition, it may be possible that we

have several essentially equivalent instances of "the same" component, for example we may have a single abstract design of a component in UML and RSL but implementations of this design in different programming languages. It may also be possible when considering a reuse system based on a collection of repositories instead of on a single repository for parts of a repository or indeed a whole repository to be duplicated ("mirrored") in another. We therefore base our identification of a component on the following attributes:

- its name;
- its nature (e.g. specification, design, code, document);
- the notation in which it is written (e.g. Ada, C++, UML, RSL);
- its application domain (e.g. banking, management, medicine);
- its type (process, product or method);
- its structure (for example package, function, or entity); and
- its location (i.e. the repository in which it is stored).

We model the name, notation, application domain, structure and location abstractly using the sort types Comp_Name, Comp_Notation, Comp_Domain, Comp_Structure and Rep_Location respectively, and the nature and type as variant types Comp_Nature and Comp_Type which comprise all the possible values of that particular attribute. Then the component identifier as a whole is modelled as a record type constructed from these components.

type
  Component_Identifier ::
    component_name : Comp_Name
    component_structure : Comp_Structure
    component_notation : Comp_Notation
    component_domain : Comp_Domain
    component_nature : Comp_Nature
    component_type : Comp_Type
    component_location : Rep_Location,

  Comp_Type == process | product | method,

  Comp_Nature ==
    req_specification | design | code | document | test_cases | _

The remainder of the description of a particular component is structured as a set of *attributes*. The following information is recorded in this way:

- a set of keywords associated with the component;
- an indication of the level of reuse of the component (e.g. the number of times it has been retrieved);
- some measure of the size of the component;
- the date on which the component was created;

- who created the component;
- information about the objectives of the component;
- an example of the use of the component;
- some comments on the component; and
- guidelines which indicate how to reuse the component (for example, information about the platform/operating system required to use it).

We again model the units of each of these kinds of information abstractly using sort types. Of course a particular component may have been created by more than one person and may have more than one associated keyword so these attributes are modelled as sets of values of the appropriate type. These various attributes are combined into a record type again, with the less important attributes (the last four) being factored out into the separate record type Other_Attributes.

type
   Attributes ::
      component_author : Comp_Authors
      component_keywords : Comp_Keywords ↔ change_keyword
      component_reuse_frequency : Comp_Frequency
      component_size : Comp_Size
      component_creation_date : Comp_Date
      other_attributes : Other_Attributes,

   Comp_Authors = Comp_Author-set,

   Comp_Keywords = Comp_Keyword-set,

   Other_Attributes ::
      objectif : Comp_Objective
      example : Comp_Example
      comments : Comp_Comments
      comp_guidelines : Comp_Guidelines

The above attributes characterise "black box" components, that is components which must be reused exactly as they are provided. In some cases, however, components may be supplied as "white box" components instead. White box components can, at least to some extent, be customised by the user, so in this case additional information regarding this customisation needs to be recorded.

Two forms of customisation are in fact possible [95]. First, if the component has actually been designed so as to be generic or abstract [95, 80] then the customisation guidelines may offer possible specialisations and/or instantiations of the component as foreseen by the author of the component (this is called *selection* in [83]) and/or restrictions associated with instantiating the component in case the user wishes to use a different instantiation (i.e. one not documented by the author). To be specific, we model this first form as a collection of possible specialisations or instantiations of generic or abstract objects in the component definition (we use a map from the type Object to itself to model this), together with sets of restrictions associated with the generic functions which the user must observe when customising the component (which we model as a map from function names to sets of restrictions).

The second form of customisation relates to components for which changes have not been anticipated or have been poorly planned by the author of the component. In this case the customisation guidelines are likely to be simply textual advice to the user on how to modify the component, perhaps appearing in the comments associated with the component.

We define the attributes of a white box component using the record type Adaptable_Attributes, which comprises the basic attributes defined earlier together with customisation guidelines and some (unspecified) measure of component modification. The attributes of a black box component are described by the type Basic_Attributes. Then the union type C_Attributes of these two describes the attributes of either kind of component.

type
   Basic_Attributes :: attributes : Attributes,

   Adaptable_Attributes ::
     attributes : Attributes $\leftrightarrow$ change_attributes
     component_adaptation_guidelines : Comp_Adaptation_Guidelines
                   $\leftrightarrow$ change_guideline
     component_modification_percentage : Comp_Modification_Percentage
                   $\leftrightarrow$ change_percentage,

   Comp_Adaptation_Guideline ::
     object_type : Object $\twoheadrightarrow$ Object
     function_typ : Function_Name $\twoheadrightarrow$ Restriction-**set**,

   Comp_Adaptation_Guidelines = Comp_Adaptation_Guideline-**set**,

   C_Attributes = Basic_Attributes | Adaptable_Attributes

In order to include the functional properties of a component as well as its structural properties, we include information about the *services* provided by the component. These services are characterised by:

- a *function name*, usually a verb describing the service (e.g. add, remove, define, describe).
- a *function type*, which may be *observer* or *generator*. The function type is *observer* if the function simply gives information about the objects to which it is applied without changing their state. For example, a function

providing the service "check whether a book is in a library" is an observer because it does not change the state of the library or the book. On the other hand, the function type is *generator* if the function does modify one or more of the objects to which it is applied. For example, a function providing the service "add a new e-mail message to an inbox" is a generator because it changes the state of the inbox.

- *situation objects*, which is the set of objects that should be available for the component service to be executed (e.g. class, model, stack, type).
- *result objects*, which is the result of executing a service represented as a set of objects.
- a *signature*, which represents the input and output types of a function (service).
- *pre-conditions*, which are the conditions which the input parameters of the function must satisfy before it is executed.
- *post-conditions*, which give a logical representation of the result of executing the function assuming its pre-conditions are all satisfied.
- a *function description*, which describes the service (generally text but may also include figures or other graphical representations).

The signature is modelled as a record type consisting of two lists of types (represented by the abstract type Type_T), one for the types of the inputs to the function and one for the types of its result. The other components are modelled abstractly, except for the function type which is a variant type comprising just the two values observer and generator. The record type Service then combines these to give a description of a service.

type
   Service ::
      function_name : Function_Verb
      function_type : Function_Type
      situation_objects : Situation_Objects ↔ change_situation_objects
      result_objects : Result_Objects ↔ change_result_objects
      signature : Signature
      pre_conditions : Pre_Conditions ↔ change_pre_conditions
      post_conditions : Post_Conditions ↔ change_post_conditions
      function_description : Function_Description,

   Function_Type == observer | generator,

   Signature ::
      input_types : Type_T*
      output_types : Type_T*

A component may of course provide more than one service, so we introduce the type Services to represent sets of services (we are assuming that a set is sufficient here on the grounds that it is enough to know whether or not a particular service is provided). Then the entire description of a component, including both its structural and its functional properties, is represented by the record type Comp_Atts:

type
Services = $\{| \; s : \text{Service-set} \cdot s \neq \{\} \; |\}$,

Comp_Atts ::
  c_attributes : C_Attributes
  comp_services : Services ↔ change_service

The last aspect of the description of a component that we wish to take into account is that a given component may exist in several different versions (for example a textual document may need to be updated to be compatible with new versions of word processing systems). A new version of the component does not necessarily have the same attributes as an older version – at the very least the date of creation is likely to be different, and the authors, keywords, comments, etc. may well be different too – though each particular version of course has a fixed set of attributes. We therefore use a map from versions to attributes to represent the attributes of all the versions of a given component, and another map from component identifiers to this first map to record the information about all versions of all components. Note that this structure models the physical structure we are trying to describe exactly – one component exists in many versions (given by the domain of the second map) and each version of a component has a particular fixed set of attributes.

This map forms one field of the record type Component_Model, which represents a combination of the meta-library with the reuse libraries, which we call *repositories*. The other two components represent the set of relations between components that are recorded in the meta-library, and the repositories themselves.

type
Component_Model ::
  relations : Relation_0-set ↔ change_relation
  components :
    Component_Identifier $\xrightarrow{m}$ (Comp_Version $\xrightarrow{m}$ Comp_Atts) ↔
                                          change_component
  repositories : Repository ↔ change_repository

A relation records some relationship between a pair of components, for example that one is the documentation of the other, that one is an implementation of the other, or that the two are equivalent. However, it is not sufficient to represent the related components simply by their identifiers because different versions of the components may not necessarily have the same relations. We therefore define the type Comp_Id as a record type comprising both a component identifier and a version, and define the two related components in terms of this type. Then a relation is a pair of related components together with the relation type as represented by the record type **Relation**.

type
  Relation ::
    related_comp : Related_Components
    relation_type : Relation_Type,

  Related_Components ::
    source_component : Comp_Id
    target_component : Comp_Id,

  Comp_Id::
    identifier : Component_Identifier
    version : Comp_Version

Of course there must be some restrictions on the type of relations that can link two components. For example, it does not make sense for there to be a relationship of type "implementation" between a specification and a user manual. In general, the type of the relation is restricted by the kinds (nature) of the components, but we do not want to specify exactly what these restrictions are, just that they exist. We therefore define the function **valid_relation** abstractly, giving just its signature, and interpret the function as defining all the types of relations that can exist between two given components. We can then use this function to define the predicate **is_valid_relation** which checks whether a given relation is valid – the type of the relation must be one of those allowed between the two components that the relation links. The type **Relation$_0$** which represents the collection of all relations in the system is then defined as a subtype of the type **Relation** with this function as its defining predicate. Note that the functions **source_identifier** and **target_identifier** which are used in the definition of **is_valid_relation** simply extract the component identifier of the source and the target of the relation respectively.

type
  Relation$_0$ = {| r : Relation • is_valid_relation(r) |}
value
  is_valid_relation : Relation $\rightarrow$ **Bool**
  is_valid_relation(r) $\equiv$
    let i$_1$ = source_identifier(r), i$_2$ = target_identifier(r),
      n$_1$ = component_nature(i$_1$), n$_2$ = component_nature(i$_2$),
      t = relation_type(r)
    in t $\in$ valid_relation(n$_1$, n$_2$) **end**,

  valid_relation : Comp_Nature $\times$ Comp_Nature $\rightarrow$ Relation_Type-**set**

A repository is simply modelled as a record type comprising the name of the repository, its portability and its creator, and the repositories themselves are then represented as a map type which maps repository locations (which could be Internet addresses) to repository attributes.

type
  Repository = Rep_Location $\overrightarrow{m}$ Rep_Attributes,

  Rep_Attributes ::
    repository_name : Rep_Name
    repository_portability : Rep_Portability
    repository_creator : Rep_Creator

Returning now to the definition of the type `Component_Model`, we need to impose various consistency constraints on the fields of the record type, specifically to ensure that the component identifiers and versions mentioned in relations must all belong to the meta-library and that the repositories cited in the meta-library as sources of components are all real repositories. These properties are captured by the function `is_wf_cm`, and this is then used to define the subtype `Component_Model`$_0$ of `Component_Model`. The auxiliary function `exist_id_version` simply checks that a component with the given identifier and the given version actually exists in the meta-library.

value
  is_wf_cm : Component_Model $\rightarrow$ **Bool**
  is_wf_cm(m) $\equiv$
    ($\forall$ r : Relation$_0$ • r $\in$ relations(m) $\Rightarrow$
       exist_id_version(source_identifier(r), source_version(r), m) $\wedge$
       exist_id_version(target_identifier(r), target_version(r), m)
) $\wedge$
    ($\forall$ i : Component_Identifier • i $\in$ **dom** components(m)
       $\Rightarrow$ component_location(i) $\in$ **dom** repositories(m)),

  exist_id_version :
    Component_Identifier $\times$ Comp_Version $\times$ Component_Model $\rightarrow$ **Bool**
  exist_id_version(i, v, m) $\equiv$
    let cm = components(m) **in**
      i $\in$ **dom** cm $\wedge$ v $\in$ **dom** cm(i) **end**

type
  Component_Model$_0$ = {| cm : Component_Model • is_wf_cm(cm) |}

The remaining component of the data storage parts of the system is the lexicon. This contains different terms representing values (standard and non-standard) of the attributes structure, notation, domain, type and function_name, together with semantic relations between pairs of such terms. The lexicon thus has a structure like a thesaurus and can be used to resolve the problem of ambiguous use of terms. The basic structure of the lexicon is given by the record type Lexicon, where the types Str_Terms_0, Not_Terms_0, etc. represent the sets of possible values of each of the attributes and the relations between values.

type
  Lexicon ::
    structure : Str_Terms_0
    notation : Not_Terms_0
    domain   : Dom_Terms_0
    typ   : Typ_Terms_0
    function : $Func\_Terms_0$

Consider the component Str_Terms_0 which represents the structure attribute. (The other components are analogous and are formalised similarly.) This records all the possible values of the structure attribute, including values appearing as attributes of components in the repositories as well as values which the user may use in queries. In addition, it records relationships between these values (for example equivalence, specialisation, and generalisation as mentioned in the discusion about the lexicon at the beginning of this section). The values must all be of type Comp_Structure, of course, since they represent posssible values of the structure, and the semantic relations must link pairs of values from this set. The typing information is recorded in the definition of the record type Str_Terms, and the constraint on the relations forms the defining predicate of the subtype Str_Terms_0.

type
  $Str\_Terms_0 = \{|\ s : Str\_Terms \bullet \forall\, r : Semantic\_Relation \bullet$
    $r \in str\_relations(s) \Rightarrow$
      $source\_val(r) \in str\_vals(s) \land sink\_val(r) \in str\_vals(s)\ |\},$

  Str_Terms ::
    str_vals : Comp_Structure-**set**
    str_relations : Semantic_Relation-**set**,

  Semantic_Relation ::
    source_val : Facet
    sink_val : Facet
    relation_t : S_Relation,

  Facet = Comp_Structure | Comp_Notation | Comp_Domain |
          Comp_Type | Function_Verb | _

The entire data storage part of the system (the repositories, the meta-library and the lexicon) is then represented by the record type **System**, which comprises two fields: model, which represents the repositories and the meta-library and which is of type Component_Model$_0$; and lexicon, which represents the lexicon (the type Lexicon). In order for these two fields to be consistent the actual values of the structure, notation, domain, type and function name attributes of any component in the meta-library must also be in the lexicon. This is specified by the predicate is_wf_s and this is used in the standard way to define the subtype System$_0$ of System.

type

> System ::
>   model : Component_Model$_0$
>   lexicon : Lexicon,
>
> System$_0$ = {| s : System • is_wf_s(s) |}

value

> is_wf_s : System → **Bool**
> is_wf_s(s) ≡
>   **let** mk_System(m, l) = s **in**
>   (∀ i : Component_Identifier • i ∈ **dom** components(m) ⇒
>   component_structure(i) ∈ str_vals(structure(l)) ∧
>   component_notation(i) ∈ not_vals(notation(l)) ∧
>   component_domain(i) ∈ dom_vals(domain(l)) ∧
>   component_type(i) ∈ typ_vals(typ(l)) ∧
>   (∀ v: Comp_Version • v ∈ **dom** components(m)(i) ⇒
>   **let** c = components(m)(i)(v), se = comp_services(c) **in**
>   ∀ serv : Service • serv ∈ se ⇒
>   function_name(serv) ∈ func_vals(function(l)) **end**)) **end**

14.3 The Query System

The query/retrieval process uses the information recorded in the meta-library and the lexicon to provide flexible search facilities based on both the functional and structural attributes of components. We distinguish four basic types of query:

1. structural keyword query;
2. structural attribute query;
3. functional facet query; and
4. signature matching.

We deal with each of these separately below.

14.3.1 Structural Keyword Queries

The structural keyword query is the simplest form of query and involves matching a set of user input values against the keywords of actual components stored in the meta-library. The user input is thus just a set of values representing possible keywords, which we specify using the type KeyWord_Query, and processing a keyword query involves simply checking the intersection between the keywords of the components (the attribute *KeyWords*) and these query keywords – a component satisfies the query if and only if this intersection is not empty. This is specified by the function satisfy_keyword.

type
  KeyWord_Query = Comp_Keywords

value
  satisfy_keyword :
    Component_Model$_0$ × Component_Identifier × Comp_Version ×
    KeyWord_Query → **Bool**
  satisfy_keyword(m, i, v, k) ≡
    exist_id_version(i, v, m) ∧
    let cm = components(m), c = cm(i)(v), ca = c_attributes(c) **in**
      case ca **of**
        mk_Basic_Attributes(c_1) → k ∩ component_keywords(c_1) ≠ {},
        mk_Adaptable_Attributes(c_1, g, p) →
          k ∩ component_keywords(c_1) ≠ {}
      end
    end

14.3.2 Structural Attribute Queries

The structural attribute query is based on a number of the basic attributes of a component: its name, authors, reuse frequency, location, size, type, domain, structure, notation, and nature. For each of these attributes the user can give a set of possible matching values for which to search and can additionally specify *preferences* for the attributes. These preferences are expressed as *importance* values which give some indication of the relative importance to be attached to particular attributes (for example *very important*, *important*, *can_be_neglected*). They can be used to refine the results of an initial search if the number of potentially matching components is too large – a refining query may, for instance, neglect the least important attributes or retain only the attributes with the highest importance in order to try to find a more suitable result.

Some flexibility can also be incorporated into the query in the form of approximate matching which is based on relationships between terms as defined in the lexicon. For the size and reuse frequency attributes, it is unlikely to be useful to input actual values since the user has no way of determining appropriate values. We therefore define them as *linguistic variables* which are variables whose values are words or sentences in a natural or synthetic language [154]. Each linguistic variable (LV) is characterised by a set of possible *linguistic values* that correspond to common human understanding and concepts related to that variable. Thus, for example, we might associate the linguistic values *high*, *medium* and *low* with the attributes size and reuse frequency.

For the domain, structure, notation and type attributes the user can give precise values for the search as well as choosing linguistic values to qualify the specification of these values. The particular linguistic values we use for these attributes are *substantially*, *almost* and *related-to*. Thus, the user can formulate a query such as "find the software components that deal with **almost** the *domain bank management*, having **substantially** the *type source code* and with a **low** *size*", where the terms in bold face type are linguistic values and the terms in italics are linguistic variables.

We associate a different degree of closeness with each linguistic value so that the three values given above are considered to be ordered, with the value *substantially* representing the values which are closest to the actual value given and the value *related-to* the values which are furthest away. Thus, two terms which are related by the fuzzy relation *substantially* are closer than two others related by the fuzzy relation *almost*.

Each linguistic value defines a *fuzzy set* that is characterised by a membership function whose values are real numbers in the interval [0,1], as illustrated in Figure 14.2. To each component we have to assign a degree of membership in the fuzzy set *medium* associated with the linguistic variable *reuse frequency*. For example, if a component C_1 has a reuse frequency equal to 30 then the statement "the reuse frequency of C_1 is medium" is 0.5 true.

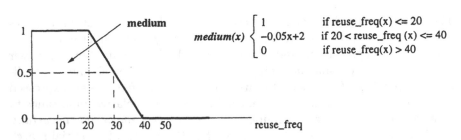

$$medium(x) \begin{cases} 1 & \text{if reuse\_freq}(x) <= 20 \\ -0{,}05x+2 & \text{if } 20 < \text{reuse\_freq}(x) <= 40 \\ 0 & \text{if reuse\_freq}(x) > 40 \end{cases}$$

Fig. 14.2. Interpretation of medium reuse frequency as a linguistic value.

The value of this membership function for a given linguistic value and a given actual value of the appropriate attribute then defines the extent to which the actual value belongs to the fuzzy set associated with the given linguistic value. If the degree of membership is zero then the element does not belong to the fuzzy set, and if the degree is 1 the element completely belongs to the set. In fact our reuse infrastructure allows the user to specify this degree of membership as well as the basic fuzzy linguistic values within a query, thus making the query more precise. Thus, for example, the query can specify that the size of the component should be high with a degree of at least 0.9.

We introduce the record type **Attribute_Input** to represent the query input values for a single attribute in a structural attribute query, the four fields representing respectively the set of precise values, the preferences, the degree of membership for the approximate matching, and the linguistic search values. The first of these is defined as a union type composed of the type of each of the possible attributes (**Comp_Name**, **Comp_Author**, **Comp_Frequency**, etc.), while the others are defined only abstractly as sorts.

type
    Attribute_Input ::
      val : Value_att-set
      importance : Importance
      theta   : Theta
      ling_val : Ling_Value,

    Value_att = Comp_Name | Comp_Author | Comp_Frequency | ...

Then a structural attribute query involving several attributes can be represented using a map type which associates the names of the attributes included in the search with the corresponding query input values for that attribute. In fact we split the query into two parts, the first representing structural attributes which are not defined in the lexicon (name, authors, reuse frequency, location, size, and nature) and the second representing attributes which are (domain, structure, notation, and type). We define union types Attribute_Name$_1$ and Attribute_Name$_2$ to represent these two sets of attributes, and we define two map types Attribute_Query$_1$ and Attribute_Query$_2$ which respectively map these types to the type Attribute_Input which represents query input values. An attribute query as a whole is then represented by the record type Attribute_Query which contains one field of type Attribute_Query$_1$ for the part of the query relating to the attributes which are not in the lexicon and one field of type Attribute_Query$_2$ for the part of the query relating to the attributes which are in the lexicon.

type
    Attribute_Query$_1$ = Attribute_Name$_1$ $\xrightarrow{m}$ Attribute_Input,

    Attribute_Query$_2$ = Attribute_Name$_2$ $\xrightarrow{m}$ Attribute_Input,

Attribute_Query ::
   att_1 : Attribute_Query$_1$
   att_2 : Attribute_Query$_2$

Processing a structural attribute query involves approximate matching of a query input value (of type Value_att) against the value of the attribute of the actual component. This matching process in general depends on the kind of attribute, and for attributes whose possible values are stored in the lexicon it can additionally involve using the lexicon to transform the query input values to actual component values. We introduce the two functions closea$_1$ and closea$_2$ to represent this matching process, the second using the lexicon. However, at this level of abstraction we do not specify the bodies of these functions, just their signatures, which are:

value
   closea$_1$: Attribute_Name$_1$ × Value_att × Value_att → **Bool**,
   closea$_2$: Lexicon × Attribute_Name$_2$ × Value_att × Value_att → **Bool**

Then a particular version of a particular component in the repository satisfies a structural attribute query if at least one of the query input values for each attribute in the query is sufficiently close (as defined by the above functions) to the value of that attribute for the component. This is specified by the function **satisfy_attribute**. The functions comp_attribute_value$_1$ and comp_attribute_value$_2$ used in the body of this function do the actual comparison between query values (either the actual values given in the query or the corresponding values obtained from the lexicon) and the attributes of the components in the repositories. The functions q_attribute_values$_1$ and q_attribute_values$_2$ extract just the query input values for each attribute from the two parts of the attribute query.

Note that the function **satisfy_attribute** is actually underspecified. We do not take the condition explained above as the exact definition of when a component matches a structural attribute query. Rather, we use an implicit specification with an implication in the postcondition to indicate that if the component matches the query then this condition must be true but there may be other properties, as yet unspecified, which need to be taken into account as well. This specification is thus flexible – it specifies the basic properties of the matching but allows for additional properties to be added later in a refinement step.

value
  satisfy_attribute :
    System$_0$ × Component_Identifier × Comp_Version ×
    Attribute_Query → **Bool**
  satisfy_attribute(sy, i, v, aq) **as** r
  post r ⇒ exist_id_version(i, v, model(sy)) ∧
    let mk_System(m, l) = sy,

$q\_attributes_1 = q\_attribute\_values_1(att_1(aq))$,
$q\_attributes_2 = q\_attribute\_values_2(att_2(aq))$

in

$(\forall\ q_1 : Attribute\_Name_1 \bullet q_1 \in \textbf{dom}\ q\_attributes_1 \Rightarrow$
$(\exists\ v : Value\_att \bullet v \in q\_attributes_1(q_1)\ \wedge$
$\quad closea_1(q_1, v,$
$\qquad\qquad comp\_attribute\_value_1(i, components(m)(i)(v), q_1))))$
$\wedge$
$(\forall\ q_2 : Attribute\_Name_2 \bullet q_2 \in \textbf{dom}\ q\_attributes_2 \Rightarrow$
$(\exists\ v : Value\_att \bullet v \in q\_attributes_2(q_2)\ \wedge$
$\quad closea_2(l, q_2, v,$
$\qquad\qquad comp\_attribute\_value_2(i, q_2))))$

end,

$q\_attribute\_values_1$:
  $Attribute\_Query_1 \rightarrow (Attribute\_Name_1 \overrightarrow{m} Value\_att\textbf{-set})$
$q\_attribute\_values_1(aq) \equiv$
  $[\ n \mapsto val(aq(n))\ |\ n : Attribute\_Name_1 \bullet a \in \textbf{dom}\ aq\ ]$,

$q\_attribute\_values_2$:
  $Attribute\_Query_2 \rightarrow (Attribute\_Name_2 \overrightarrow{m} Value\_att\textbf{-set})$
$q\_attribute\_values_2(aq) \equiv$
  $[\ n \mapsto val(aq(n))\ |\ n : Attribute\_Name_2 \bullet a \in \textbf{dom}\ aq\ ]$

14.3.3 Functional Facet Queries

The functional facet query represents searching for components based on their functional properties as defined in Section 14.2, in particular on four of these functional properties, which are termed *facets*: the function name; the function type; the situation objects; and the result objects. Using facets to search for components by their functional properties is a good strategy for novice users because it requires little or no knowledge of the "semantics" of the components. The result can then be refined by applying signature matching (see Section 14.3.4).

In fact we treat facets and attributes uniformly and allow facets to be used in a query just like other attributes. Thus, the user can qualify facet search values with linguistic values and a membership degree as described above for attribute search values, the lexicon being used again as the basis for calculating the similarity between terms. The specification of the query input values for a single attribute in a facet query is therefore represented by the record type `Facet_Input` which is exactly analogous to the record type `Attribute_Input` introduced in Section 14.3.2 to represent the query input values for a single attribute in a structural attribute query. Similarly, a facet query involving several facets is represented using the map type

Facet_Query which is entirely analogous to the map types Attribute_Query$_1$ and Attribute_Query$_2$ except that it associates the names of the facets included in the search with the corresponding query input values for each facet. The type Facet_Name is just a variant type composed of four values representing the four different facets.

type
    Facet_Query = Facet_Name $\overrightarrow{m}$ Facet_Input,

    Facet_Input ::
      term : Term-**set**
      importance : Importance
      theta : Theta
      ling_val : Ling_Value,

    Facet_Name ==
      function_verb | situation_objects | result_objects | function_type

Processing a facet query is also similar to processing an attribute query, involving approximate matching. This is based around the lexicon in the case of the function verb facet, but not for the other facets since their values are not stored in the lexicon. So we once again introduce two functions, this time closef$_1$ and closef$_2$, which represent the approximate matching, the second using the lexicon, and again we leave these unspecified at this level of abstraction. Their signatures are:

value
    closef$_1$: Facet_Name $\times$ Term $\times$ Term-**set** $\rightarrow$ **Bool**,
    closef$_2$: Lexicon $\times$ Term $\times$ Term-**set** $\rightarrow$ **Bool**

Then a particular version of a particular component in the repository satisfies a facet query if at least one of the query input values for each facet in the query is sufficiently close (as defined by the above functions) to the value of that facet for the component. This is specified by the function satisfy_f_facet which is similar to the corresponding function for structural attribute queries (satisfy_attribute) except that the distinction between whether or not to include the lexicon in the approximate matching is determined by the type of the facet and so is specified using a case expression. Note that this function is underspecified in exactly the same way as the function satisfy_attribute, specifying only the basic properties of the matching and allowing for additional properties to be added later in a refinement step. The function q_facet_term used below simply extracts the query input values from the facet query, and the function comp_facet_term performs the comparison between query values and the facets of the components in the repositories (i.e. it is analogous to the functions comp_attribute_value$_1$ and comp_attribute_value$_2$ introduced in Section 14.3.2 above).

value
    satisfy_facet : System$_0$ × Component_Identifier ×
        Comp_Version × Facet_Query → **Bool**
    satisfy_facet(sy, i, v, fq) **as** r
    post r ⇒
        exist_id_version(i, v, model(sy)) ∧
        let mk_System(m, l) = sy, q_facets = q_facet_term(fq) **in**
            (∀ f$_1$: Facet_Name • f$_1$ ∈ **dom** q_facets ⇒
            (∃ t : Term • t ∈ q_facets(f$_1$) ∧
                case f$_1$ **of**
                    function_verb →
                        closef$_2$(l, t, comp_facet_term(components(m)(i)(v), f$_1$)),
                        _ → closef$_1$(f$_1$, t, comp_facet_term(components(m)(i)(v), f$_1$))
                end
)
)
    end,

    q_facet_term : Facet_Query → (Facet_Name $\twoheadrightarrow$ Term-set)
    q_facet_term(f) ≡
        [fn ↦ term(f(fn)) | fn : Facet_Name • fn ∈ **dom** f],

comp_facet_term : Comp_Atts × Facet_Name → Term-set
comp_facet_term(a, f) ≡
    let se = comp_services(a) **in**
        case f **of**
        function_verb →
            {Term_from_Function_Verb(v) | v : Function_Verb •
                ∀ s : Service • s ∈ se ⇒ v = function_name(s)},
        situation_objects →
            {Term_from_Situation_Objects(v) | v : Situation_Objects •
                ∀ s : Service • s ∈ se ⇒ v = situation_objects(s)},
        result_objects →
            {Term_from_Result_Objects(v) | v : Result_Objects •
                ∀ s : Service • s ∈ se ⇒ v = result_objects(s)},
        function_type →
            {Term_from_Function_Type(v) | v : Function_Type •
                ∀ s : Service • s ∈ se ⇒ v = function_type(s)}
        end end

14.3.4 Signature Matching

Signature matching involves queries based around the types of a function's
input parameters and result (called its *signature*) [155]. In addition to trying

to match these types exactly, we allow relaxed matching based on semantic relationships between types, including equivalence, specialisation, generalisation, composition, and reordering.

Our semantic relationships are based on the semantics of RSL types [116]. Thus, for example, we consider the types **Char*** and **Text** to be equivalent because they are equivalent (in fact synonymous) in RSL. We also consider two sort types to be equivalent because they can be refined to the same type. Two signatures are equivalent if both their input types and their result types are equivalent and in the same order.

We consider a type t_2 to be a specialisation of a type t_1 if the set of all possible elements of t_2 is a subset of the set of all possible elements of t_1. Thus, for example, the integer type **Int** is a specialisation of the type **Real** of real numbers. Similarly, the type **Int-set** is a specialisation of the type **Real-set**. We also consider any type to be a specialisation of a sort type. Then one signature is a specialisation of another if its input types and result types are either equivalent to or specialisations of the other's.

Generalisation is the inverse of specialisation, so that a type t_2 is a generalisation of a type t_1 if t_1 is a specialisation of t_2. Similarly, a signature s_2 is a generalisation of a signature s_1 if s_1 is a specialisation of s_2.

A type t_2 is a composition of another type t_1 if t_1 is somehow a "part" of t_2. Thus, for example, the type **Int-set** is a composition of the type **Int** because it is constructed from the type **Int**. A signature s_2 is a composition of a signature s_1 if the input types and result types of s_2 are either equivalent to or compositions of the corresponding input types and result types of s_1.

In addition to the above relations, which insist that the input types and result types defined in the query and the actual component should be in the same order, we allow relaxation in which the order of these types can be changed. Two signatures are equivalent under such a reordering if both the input types and the output types are equivalent but possibly in a different order.

Of course several relaxations can be permitted simultaneously, so in general signature matching involves a query signature and a set of possible relaxations. However, we want to fix the order in which to apply the relaxations in order to improve the search efficiency – with an arbitrary ordering the combinatorics can rapidly increase the complexity of the search if we want to allow several simultaneous relaxations. We therefore allow the user to associate a *priority* with each relaxation. A signature matching query is thus represented by the record type `Signature_Query`, which comprises a signature and a map from relation types to priorities. Relation types are represented by the variant type `Relation_T` whose values are all the possible kinds of relaxation, and priorities are specified abstractly using the sort type `Priority_val`. Comparison between different priorities is also specified abstractly via the function `leq`.

type
  Signature_Query ::
    signature : Signature
    relations_t : Relation_T $\overrightarrow{m}$ Priority_val,

  Relation_T ==
    equivalence | generalization | specialization | composition | reorder | _

value
  leq : Priority_val × Priority_val → **Bool**

The function **matchx** then defines whether or not a given signature matches a given signature query. First the highest priority relaxation, which will usually be equivalence in practice, is chosen (using the function **priority_relation**) and the match is attempted. Alternatively, the result of this first match may fail but include a signature which matches the required signature under the next most important relaxation, and so on recursively. The actual matching under a single relaxation is specified abstractly using the function **matches**. Note that the function **priority_relation** is also under-specified – if two relaxations have the same priority it does not specify the order in which they should be applied but just chooses one of them arbitrarily.

value
  matchx : Signature_Query × Signature → **Bool**
  matchx(q, c) ≡
    let mk_Signature_Query(s, rs) = q **in**
      rs ≠ [ ] ∧
      let r = priority_relation(rs) **in**
        matches(r, s, c) ∨
        (∃ q' : Signature •
          matches(r, s, q') ∧ matchx(mk_Signature_Query(q', rs \ {r}), c))
      end
    end,

  matches : Relation_T × Signature × Signature → **Bool**,

  priority_relation : (Relation_T $\overrightarrow{m}$ Priority_val) $\overset{\sim}{\to}$ Relation_T
  priority_relation(rm) **as** r
    post r ∈ **dom** rm ∧
      (∀ r' : Relation_T • r' ∈ **dom** rm ⇒ leq(rm(r), rm(r')))
    pre rm ≠ [ ]

14.3.5 Processing and Refining Queries

We can use the functions defined above which determine whether or not a given component matches a given query to specify "search" functions. In general, these search functions simply return the set of components in the whole collection of repositories which satisfy the given query. However, we also need to take component versions into account because not every version of a component necessarily satisfies the query, so the result of a search is actually a map from component identifiers to sets of versions, indicating that the particular set of versions of that component satisfy the query. Thus, for example, we can specify a search function for a keyword query as follows:

value
  keyword_search :
    Component_Model$_0$ × KeyWord_Query →
    (Component_Identifier $\twoheadrightarrow$ Comp_Version-**set**)
  keyword_search(m, k) ≡
    let cm = components(m) **in**
      [i ↦ vs | i : Component_Identifier, vs : Comp_Version-**set** •
        i ∈ **dom** cm ∧ vs ≠ {} ∧ (∀ v : Comp_Version •
          v ∈ vs ⇒ satisfy_keyword(m, i, v, k))]
    end

Note that in the above expression the condition that the set of variants **vs** is not empty is crucial – without it we could simply return a map containing all the components in the repository, each with an empty set of versions.

We can define similar functions for the attribute and facet queries. The one for the attribute query, for example, is as follows:

value
  result_att_query :
    System$_0$ × Attribute_Query →
    (Component_Identifier $\twoheadrightarrow$ Comp_Version-**set**)
  result_att_query(sy, aq) ≡
    let m = model(sy), cm = components(m) **in**
      [i ↦ v | i : Component_Identifier, v : Comp_Version-**set** •
        i ∈ **dom** cm ∧
        (∀ iv : Comp_Version •
          iv ∈ v ⇒ satisfy_attribute(sy, i, iv, aq))]
    end

However, although this function is specified exactly, the fact that the function satisfy_attribute is under-specified means that this function is also implicitly under-specified. More specifically, at this level of abstraction the function satisfy_attribute can always return **false** because it is specified implicitly with an implication, which means that the corresponding search function can always return the empty map. However, when the specification of the function `satisfy_attribute` is completed the result of the search function also becomes well-defined.

We can also specify refinements of searches, where the results returned by a particular search are filtered in order to reduce the number of potentially matching components. Such refinements could be done simply by directly applying another basic search function to the current result. Alternatively, we can specify refinements based on the notion of importance of attributes and facets as introduced in Sections 14.3.2 and 14.3.3 above.

As an example of this, the function `ign_least_imp_repeat_search` performs an attribute query as defined in Section 14.3.2 (i.e. using the function `result_att_query`) but if this returns an empty result (i.e. if there are no components in the repositories which match the query) then it discards all the least important attributes from the query and tries again, and so on recursively until a non-empty result is obtained or until the query is empty.

The functions `least_imp`$_1$ and `least_imp`$_2$, which find the attributes with the least importance in the two parts of the query, are specified implicitly by requiring that the resulting set of attributes all have the same importance, which is less than the importance of all other attributes (the unspecified function `limp`). We give only the specification of `least_imp`$_1$ below because the two functions are almost identical.

value
  ign_least_imp_repeat_search :
    System$_0$ × Attribute_Query →
      (Component_Identifier $\overrightarrow{m}$ Comp_Version-set)
  ign_least_imp_repeat_search(m, aq) ≡
    let r = result_att_query(m, aq) **in**
      if r = [ ]
      then let a_1 = least_imp$_1$(aq), a_2 = least_imp$_2$(aq),
            q'' = att$_1$(aq) \ a_1, q' = att$_2$(aq) \ a_2,
            q_3 = mk_Attribute_Query(q'', q')
         in if q'' = [ ] ∧ q' = [ ] **then** [ ]
              else ign_least_imp_repeat_search(m, q_3) **end end**
      else r **end end**,

least_imp$_1$: Attribute_Query → Attribute_Name$_1$-set
least_imp$_1$(aq) **as** a
  post a ⊆ **dom** att$_1$(aq) ∧
    (∀ a_1, a_2 : Attribute_Name$_1$ • a_1 ∈ a ⇒
      (a_2 ∈ a ⇒ importance(att$_1$(aq)(a_1)) = importance(att$_1$(aq)(a_2))) ∧
      (a_2 ∈ **dom** att$_1$(aq) \ a ⇒
         limp(importance(att$_1$(aq)(a_1)), importance(att$_1$(aq)(a_2))))),

limp : Importance × Importance → **Bool**

Other functions for refining searches can be specified similarly.

14.4 Conclusions

In this chapter we have described a reuse infrastructure which, although not offering a new solution for storage and retrieval in the context of application engineering, does, we believe, offer a way of improving reuse in practice. It combines many of the important features of reuse systems identified in the existing literature, and also offers additional features such as reuse guidelines and the ability to search uniformly for different kinds of components.

We have also presented a flexible query/search process based on this infrastructure which supports a wide range of different forms of query, including queries involving both structural and functional attributes of components. It also allows fuzziness in the queries which can be used to perform approximate instead of exact matching, and allows the user to freely choose the input values for the queries, matching these to values actually used in the repositories with the help of the lexicon.

Finally, we have described how queries can be refined, for example by repeatedly ignoring the least important attributes until a non-empty result is obtained.

The work has in fact been extended beyond the abstract specification presented here to a more concrete specification. This will form the basis for the implementation of a working prototype of our infrastructure.

Background Information

This chapter is based on work [8] undertaken by Raoudha Beltaifa from the National School of Computer Science (ENSI), Tunis, Tunisia, and Richard Moore.

About the Editors

Hung Dang Van obtained a PhD (equivalent) in Computer Science from the Computer and Automation Research Institute (SZTAKI), Hungarian Academy of Sciences, Budapest, Hungary in 1988. He was a member of the parallel programming group at the Institute of Information Technology, Hanoi, Vietnam between 1989 and 1994. He has been a Research Fellow at UNU/IIST since 1995. His research interests include: concurrent and distributed computing, and formal design techniques for real-time systems.

Chris George worked on the original RAISE project and managed the successor LaCoS project where RAISE was used by a number of European industrial companies. He wrote the major part of the RAISE method book. Since joining UNU/IIST in 1994 as Senior Research Fellow he has written the type-checking part of the RAISE tool rsltc and supervised UNU/IIST fellows who have produced various extensions to that tool. His current research interests are in extending RAISE to include real time and in making links between RAISE and UML. He wrote Chapter 2 of this book and prepared the book's web site.

Tomasz Janowski has a PhD in Computer Science from the University of Warwick, England, and an MSc in Mathematics from the University of Gdańsk, Poland. He has been a Research Fellow at UNU/IIST since 1995. His research interests include: formal design and verification of fault-tolerant systems, and formal modelling of mission-critical enterprise systems. He wrote Chapter 1 of this book.

Richard Moore has a BA and MA in Mathematics from the University of Cambridge, and a PhD in Theoretical Physics from the University of Manchester. He was a member of the formal methods research group at Manchester University between 1985 and 1994, and from 1995 to 2001 he was a Research Fellow at UNU/IIST. He is now Senior Consultant in the area of Formal Methods and Tools at IFAD in Denmark.

About the Web Site

An internet site http://www.iist.unu.edu/RAISE_Case_Studies has been set up to provide additional material for this book. It contains the complete specifications from the case studies and the RAISE tool. It is organised into the following sections:

case_studies Each case study has its own directory in here, named as the case study is in the thematic introduction, Chapter 1. Each of the case study directories has a gzipped tar file and a zip file containing a readme file with comments on the structure of the RSL modules and the modules themselves: each module is in a file of the same name as the module with extension .rsl.

rsltc This is the main directory for the RAISE tool, called *rsltc*. There are two emacs-lisp files that may be used with emacs to provide a convenient user interface for rsltc, and a number of sub-directories:

user_guide The rsltc user and installation guide in gzipped postscript, pdf and html formats. There is also a syntax document in postscript and pdf formats containing a BNF grammar for RSL, a list of ASCII equivalents for symbols, and a list of keywords.

windows rsltc for Windows. There is also a minimal version of emacs copied from the DJGPP port of the GNU tools (http://www.delorie.com).

linux rsltc binary for linux.

solaris rsltc binary for Sun Solaris.

dos rsltc binary for DOS.

cpp C++ libraries for the translator to C++.

sml SML libraries for the translator to SML. The code produced by the translator is intended for use with SML/NJ (SML of New Jersey), which is based on SML'97 [98]. The run-time system for SML/NJ is freely available for a variety of platforms from http://cm.bell-labs.com/cm/cs/what/smlnj/.

vcg The Visualisation of Computer Graphs tool for Windows and Unix (used with rsltc to draw module dependency graphs). Also obtainable from ftp://ftp.cs.uni-sb.de/pub/graphics/vcg/.

source The source files for rsltc.

method_book The RAISE method book [117] in gzipped postscript and zipped pdf formats, together with possible solutions to the exercises in it.

chinese A tutorial on RSL translated into Chinese by Ms He Hua and Prof Zhang Naixiao of Peking University, Beijing. It is included as gzipped postscript and zipped pdf.

New versions of the RAISE tool are announced to the news group comp. specification.misc.

References

1. Jean-Raymond Abrial. *The B-Book*. Cambridge University Press, 1996.
2. Univan Ahn and Chris George. C++ Translator for RAISE Specification Language. Technical Report 220, UNU/IIST, P.O. Box 3058, Macau, November 2000.
3. Bernhard K. Aichernig. Test-design through abstraction, a systematic approach based on the refinement calculus. *Journal of Universal Computer Science (J.UCS)*, 7(8), 2001.
4. Brad Appleton. Patterns and Software: Essential Concepts and Terminology. http://www.enteract.com/~bradapp, November 1997.
5. Gabriela Aranda and Richard Moore. Formally Modelling Compound Design Patterns. Technical Report 225, UNU/IIST, P.O. Box 3058, Macau, December 2000.
6. Gabriela Aranda and Richard Moore. GoF Creational Patterns: A Formal Specification. Technical Report 224, UNU/IIST, P.O. Box 3058, Macau, December 2000.
7. Balkhis Abu Bakar and Tomasz Janowski. Automated Result Verification with AWK. Technical Report 205, UNU/IIST, P.O. Box 3058, Macau, June 2000. Presented at and published in the proceedings of the 6th IEEE International Conference on Engineering of Complex Computer Systems, Tokyo, Japan, September 2000, IEEE Computer Society Press.
8. Raoudha Beltaifa and Richard Moore. A Software Reuse Infrastructure for an Efficient Reuse Practice. Research Report 233, UNU/IIST, P.O. Box 3058, Macau, May 2001.
9. Joseph K. Berry. *Beyond Mapping - Concepts, Algorithms, and Issues in GIS*. GIS World, Inc., Fort Collins, Colorado, USA, 1993.
10. Joseph K. Berry. *Spatial Reasoning for Effective GIS*. GIS World, Inc., Fort Collins, Colorado, USA, 1995.
11. Manuel Blum and Sampath Kannan. Designing Programs that Check their Work. *Journal of the ACM*, 42(1):269–291, 1995.
12. D. Bolignano and M. Debabi. A Denotational Model for the Integration of Concurrent, Functional, and Imperative Programming. In *Proceedings of the NAPAW'93 Workshop*. Cornell University, August 1993.
13. D. Bolignano and M. Debabi. On the Semantic Foundations of RSL: a Concurrent, Functional and Imperative Specification Language. In *Proceedings of FORTE '93*. Boston University, 1993.
14. Dominique Bolignano. Towards a Mechanization of Cryptographic Protocol Verification. In *Computer Aided Verification*, volume 1254 of *LNCS*. Springer-Verlag, 1997.
15. Dominique Bolignano. Integrating Proof-Based and Model-Checking Techniques for the Formal Verification of Cryptographic Protocols. In *Computer Aided Verification*, volume 1427 of *LNCS*. Springer-Verlag, 1998.

16. Henri Brouchoud, Ciara Byrne, et al. Experiences in the use of FIPA Agent Technologies for the Development of a Personal Travel Application. In *International Conference on Autonomous Agents*. ACM, June 2000.

17. M. Burrows, M. Abadi, and R. Needham. A Logic of Authentication. *ACM Transactions on Computer Systems*, 8(1):18–36, 1990.

18. Michael Butler. Using Refinement to Analyse the Safety of an Authentication Protocol. Technical Report DSSE-TR-98-8, Declarative Systems and Software Engineering Group, Department of Electronics and Computer Science, University of Southampton, July 1998.

19. S. Castano and V. De Antonellis. Reusing Process Specifications. In *Proc. International IFIP Conference on Information System Development Process*, 1993.

20. Alejandra Cechich and Richard Moore. A Formal Specification of GoF Design Patterns. Technical Report 151, UNU/IIST, P.O.Box 3058, Macau, January 1999. Presented at and published in the proceedings of 6th Asia-Pacific Software Engineering Conference (APSEC'99) Takamatsu, Japan, December 7-10, 1999, IEEE Computer Society Press, pp. 284–291.

21. S. Alejandra Cechich and Richard Moore. A Formal Specification of GoF Design Patterns. In *Proceedings of the Asia Pacific Software Engineering Conference: APSEC'99*, Takamatsu, Japan, December 1999.

22. D.L. Chalmers, B. Dandanell, J. Gørtz, J. Storbank Pedersen, and E. Zierau. Using RAISE — First Impressions From a LaCoS User Trial. In *Proceedings of VDM '91*, volume 551 of *LNCS*. Springer-Verlag, 1991.

23. Zhou ChaoChen, C. A. R. Hoare, and A. P. Ravn. A Calculus of Durations. *Information Proc. Letters*, 40(5), 1992.

24. J.H. Cheng and C.B. Jones. On the usability of logics which handle partial functions. In C. Morgan and J. Woodcock, editors, *Proceedings of the Third Refinement Workshop*. Springer-Verlag, 1990.

25. Kim Yong Chun and Dang Van Hung. Specification and Verification of Spatial Data Types with B-Toolkit. Technical Report 242, UNU/IIST, P.O. Box 3058, Macau, October 2001.

26. The Unicode Consortium. *The Unicode Standard, Version 3.0*. Addison Wesley, 2000.

27. WWW Consortium. Extensible Markup Language (XML) 1.0 (Second Edition). http://www.w3c.org/TR/2000/REC-xml-20001006, October 2000. W3C Recommendation.

28. Than Quoc Dang and Richard Moore. Formal Modelling of Future Demand Forecasting and Frequent Flyer Programs. Technical Report 156, UNU/IIST, P.O.Box 3058, Macau, February 1999.

29. Peter T. Daniels and William Bright, editors. *The World's Writing Systems*. Oxford University Press, 1996.

30. T.H. Davenport. *Mission Critical, Realising the Promise of Enterprise Systems*. Harvard Business School Press, 2000.

31. María del Rosario Girardi Gutierrez. *Classification and Retrieval of Software Through their Descriptions in Natural Language*. Thèse de doctorat en informatique, Université de Genève, 1995.

32. A.A. Desrochers and R.Y. Al-Jaar. *Applications of Petri Nets in Manufacturing Systems*. IEEE Press, 1995.

33. D. Dolev, S. Even, and R. M. Karp. On the Security of Ping-Pong Protocols. *Information and Control*, 55:57–68, 1982.

34. Do Tien Dung, Le Linh Chi, Nguyen Le Thu, Phung Phuong Nam, Tran Mai Lien, and Chris George. Developing a Financial Information System. Technical Report 81, UNU/IIST, P.O.Box 3058, Macau, September 1996.

35. Do Tien Dung, Chris George, Hoang Xuan Huan, and Phung Phuong Nam. A Financial Information System. Technical Report 115, UNU/IIST, P.O.Box 3058, Macau, July 1997. Partly published in *Requirements Targeting Software and Systems Engineering*, LNCS 1526, Springer-Verlag, 1998.

36. R. Durmiendo and J. Ong. *Protocol Specification for a Digital Multiplexed Radio Telephone System*. ASTI, Philippines, May 1995. This Document gives a narrative technical specification of the DiMulTS protocol.

37. Roderick Durmiendo and Chris George. Formal Development of a Digital Mutiplexed Radio-Telephone System. Research Report 67, UNU/IIST, P.O.Box 3058, Macau, Feb 1996.

38. Bruno Dutertre and Steve Schneider. Using a PVS Embedding of CSP to Verify Authentication Protocols. In *Theorem Proving in Higher Order Logics*, volume 1275 of *LNCS*. Springer-Verlag, 1997.

39. M. Dwyer, G. Avrunin, and J. Corbett. Patterns in Property Specifications for Finite-State Verification. In *International Conference on Software Engineering*, 1999.

40. Myatav Erdenechimeg and Richard Moore. Multi-directional Multi-lingual Script Processing. Technical Report 75, UNU/IIST, P.O.Box 3058, Macau, June 1996. Published in Proceedings of the Seventeenth International Conference on the Computer Processing of Oriental Languages, Hong Kong, April 2 - 4, 1997, under the title *Multi-directional Multi-lingual Script Processing*.

41. Myatav Erdenechimeg and Richard Moore. Multi-directional Multi-lingual Script Processing. In *Proceedings of the Seventeenth International Conference on the Computer Processing of Oriental Languages, Vol. 1*, pages 29 – 34, 1997.

42. Myatav Erdenechimeg and Richard Moore. MultiScript III: Creating and Editing Multi-lingual Documents. Technical Report 113, UNU/IIST, P.O.Box 3058, Macau, September 1997. Revised June 1998.

43. Myatav Erdenechimeg, Richard Moore, and Yumbayar Namsrai. MultiScript I: The Basic Model of Multi-lingual Documents. Technical Report 105, UNU/IIST, P.O.Box 3058, Macau, June 1997. A part of the work has been presented at and published in the proceedings of the Workshop on the *Principles of Digital Document Processing*, March 1998, St. Malo, France, Ethan V. Munson, Charles Nicholas and Derick Wood (Eds), volume 1481 of *LNCS*, pages 70–81. Springer Verlag, 1998.

44. Myatav Erdenechimeg, Richard Moore, and Yumbayar Namsrai. On the Specification of the Display of Documents in Multi-lingual Computing. In Ethan V. Munson, Charles Nicholas, and Derick Wood, editors, *Principles of Digital Document Processing*, volume 1481 of *LNCS*, pages 70–81. Springer Verlag, 1998.

45. Myatav Erdenechimeg, Richard Moore, and Yumbayar Namsrai. Traditional Mongolian Script in the ISO/IEC 10646 and Unicode Standards. Technical Report 170, UNU/IIST, P.O.Box 3058, Macau, August 1999. Presented by Myatav Erdenechimeg at the 16th International Unicode Conference, Amsterdam, The Netherlands, 27-30 March 2000, and published in the proceedings, Part 1, Section B2, under the title "Encoding and Implementation Issues in Standardising Traditional Mongolian Script". The Unicode Consortium, March 2000.

46. H. Eertink et al. A Business Process Design Language. In *Formal Methods Congress*, volume 1708 of *LNCS*, pages 76–95. Springer Verlag, 1999.

47. R. Anupindi et al. *Managing Business Process Flows*. Prentice Hall, 1999.

48. R. Fielding, J. Gettys, et al. Hypertext Transfer Protocol 1.1. http://www.w3.org/Protocols/rfc2616/rfc2616.html, 1999.

49. Bernd Fischer. Specification-Based Browsing of Software Component Libraries. In *Automated Software Engineering*, October 1998.

50. Andres Flores and Richard Moore. GoF Structural Patterns: A Formal Specification. Technical Report 207, UNU/IIST, P.O. Box 3058, Macau, August 2000. Presented at and published in the proceedings of the IASTED International Conference on Applied Informatics (AI 2001), Innsbruck, Austria, 19-22 February 2001, pp. 625–630.

51. Andres Flores and Richard Moore. Analysis and Specification of GoF Structural Patterns. In *Proceedings of the IASTED International Symposia: Applied Informatics*, pages 625–630, Innsbruck, Austria, February 2001.

52. Andres Flores, Richard Moore, and Luis Reynoso. A Formal Model of Object-Oriented Design and GoF Design Patterns. In José Nuno Oliveira and Pamela Zave, editors, *FME2001: Formal Methods for Increasing Software Productivity*, volume 2021 of *LNCS*, pages 223–241. Springer Verlag, 2001.

53. Andres Flores, Luis Reynoso, and Richard Moore. A Formal Model of Object-Oriented Design and GoF Design Patterns. Technical Report 200, UNU/IIST, P.O. Box 3058, Macau, July 2000. Presented at and published in the proceedings of FME 2001, Berlin, Germany, 12-16 March 2001, LNCS 2021, Springer Verlag 2001, pp. 223–241.

54. Alan O. Freier, Philip Karlton, and Paul C. Kocher. The SSL Protocol Version 3.0. On the internet at `http://home.netscape.com/eng/ssl3/ssl-toc.html`, 1996.

55. Erich Gamma, Richard Helm, Ralph Johnson, and John Vlissides. *Design Patterns: Elements of Reusable Object-Oriented Software*. Addison Wesley, 1995.

56. Thilo Gaul et al. Construction of Verified Software Systems with Program-Checking: An Application To Compiler Back-Ends. In *Workshop on Run-Time Result Verification, Federated Logic Conference, Trento, Italy*, 1999.

57. Chris George. Proving Safety of Authentication Protocols: a Minimal Approach. Technical Report 154, UNU/IIST, P.O.Box 3058, Macau, February 1999. Presented at and published in the proceedings of the *International Conference on Software: Theory and Practice* (ICS2000), Yulin Feng, David Notkin and Marie-Claude Gaudel (eds), Beijing, August 21-24, 2000, pp. 492–499.

58. Chris George and S. Prehn. The RAISE Tools Users Guide. LaCoS Report DOC/7, Computer Resources International A/S, 1992.

59. Chris George and Xia Yong. An Operational Semantics for Timed RAISE. Technical Report 149, UNU/IIST, P.O.Box 3058, Macau, November 1998. Presented at and published in the proceedings of FM'99, Toulouse, France, 20–24 September 1999, LNCS 1709, Springer-Verlag, 1999, pp. 1008–1027.

60. J. Goossenaerts, M. Gruninger, J.G. Nell, M. Petit, and F. Vernadat. Formal Semantics of Enterprise Models. In K. Kosanke, editor, *Proceedings of ICEIMT'97, Berlin*. Springer Verlag, 1997.

61. Hartmut Güting, Ralf, Schneider, and Markus. Realm: A Foundation for Spatial Data Types in Database Systems. In David Abel and Beng Chin Ooi, editors, *Advances in Spatial Database, Third International Symposium, SSD'93 Singapore, June 23-25, 1993 Proceedings*. Springer-Verlag, June 1993.

62. John V. Guttag and James J. Horning, editors. *Larch: Languages and Tools for Formal Specification*. Texts and Monographs in Computer Science. Springer-Verlag, 1993. With Stephen J. Garland, Kevin D. Jones, Andrés Modet, and Jeannette M. Wing.

63. Tri T. Ha. *Digital Satellite Communications*. Electronic Engineering Series. McGraw Hill, Singapore, 1990.

64. G.A. Hansen. *Automating Business Process Reengineering*. Prentice Hall, 1997.

65. Elliotte Rusty Harold. *XML Bible.* IDG Books, 1999.

66. D. Hemer and P. Lindsay. Specification-Based Retrieval Strategies for Module Reuse. Technical Report 99–11, University of Queensland, July 1999.

67. Ulrich Hensel et al. Reasoning about Classes in Object-Oriented Languages: Logical Models and Tools. In *European Symposium on Programming*, LNCS. Springer Verlag, 1998.

68. Johann Hörl and Bernhard K. Aichernig. Validating voice communication requirements using lightweight formal methods. *IEEE Software*, pages 21–27, May/June 2000.

69. International Organization for Standardization. *ISO 10646-1: Information Technology – Universal Multiple-Octet Coded Character Set (UCS) – Part 1: Architecture and Basic Multilingual Plane.*

70. Bart Jacobs and Jan Rutten. A Tutorial on (Co)Algebras and (Co)Induction. *Bulletin of the European Association for Theoretical Computer Science*, 62:222–259, 1997.

71. Tomasz Janowski. Distributed Production with Specification-Generated Processes. In *4th IEEE/IFIP International Conference on Information Technology for Balanced Automation Systems in Production and Transportation (BASYS00)*. Kluwer Academic Publishers, 2000.

72. Tomasz Janowski and Wojciech Mostowski. Fail-Stop Software Components by Pattern Matching. Technical Report 164, UNU/IIST, P.O.Box 3058, Macau, May 1999. Presented at the Workshop on Run-Time Result Verification, part of the Federated Logic Conference, Trento, Italy, July 1999. Presented at and published at the IFIP 4th International Conference on Formal Methods for Open Object-Based Distributed Systems, Stanford University, USA, September 2000, Kluwer.

73. W. Janssen, H. Jonkers, and J.P.C. Verhoosel. What Makes Business Processes Special? An Evaluation Framework for Modelling Languages and Tools in Business Process Redesign. In *2nd IFIP Workshop on Evaluation of Modelling Methods in Systems Analysis and Design, Barcelona*, 1997.

74. Jun-Jang Jeng and Betty.H.C. Cheng. Using Formal Methods to Construct a Software Component Library. In *Proceedings of the 4th European Software Engineering Conference*, volume 717, pages 397–417, September 1993.

75. L. Labed Jilani. *Preuve Automatiques de Théorèmes Relationels: Axiomatisation et Applications.* Thèse de doctorat en informatique, Faculté des Sciences, Tunis, December 1998.

76. C.B. Jones and R.C.F. Shaw. *Case Studies in Systematic Software Development.* Prentice Hall International, 1990.

77. Cliff B. Jones and Kees Middelburg. A typed logic of partial functions reconstructed classically. *Acta Informatica*, 31(5):399–430, 1994.

78. A. Kay and J.N. Reed. A Rely and Guarantee Method for Timed CSP: A Specification and Design of a Telephone Exchange. *IEEE Trans. on Software Engineering*, Vol. 19, No. 6:625–639, June 1993.

79. L. Kempe. A Modular Specification of a Telephone System. Technical Report DoCS 94/51, Uppsala University, October 1994.

80. J. C. Knight and M. F. Dunn. Software Quality Through Domain-Driven Certification. *Annals of Software Engineering*, 5:293–315, September 1998.

81. K. Kosanke. *CIMOSA: Open System Architecture for CIM.* Springer Verlag, 1993.

82. A. Kotok. Open Travel Alliance Message Specifications, July 2000. http://www.opentravel.org.

83. C. W. Krueger. Software Reuse. *ACM Computing Surveys*, 24(2):131–183, June 1992.

84. Hoang Thi Tung Lam and Richard Moore. Specification of a Switching Communications System. Technical Report 106, UNU/IIST, P.O.Box 3058, Macau, May 1997.

85. J.C. Laprie. Dependability: Basic Concepts and Associated Terminology. Technical report, PDCS, 1990.

86. E.F.A. Lederer and R.A. Dumitrescu. Automatic Result Verification by Complete Run-Time Checking of Computations. www.ifi.unibas.ch, 2000.

87. F. Lessing, M. Haltod, J.G. Hangin, and S. Kassatkin. *Mongolian-English Dictionary*. University of California Press, 1960.

88. Li Li and He Jifeng. A Denotational Semantics of Timed RSL using Duration Calculus. Technical Report 168, UNU/IIST, P.O.Box 3058, Macau, July 1999. Presented at and published in the proceedings of The Sixth International Conference on Real-Time Computing Systems and Applications (RTCSA'99), part of the federated 1999 International Computer Congress, December 13 - 15, Hong Kong, IEEE Computer Society Press, 1999, pp. 492–503.

89. Li Li and He Jifeng. Towards a Denotational Semantics of Timed RSL using Duration Calculus. Technical Report 161, UNU/IIST, P.O.Box 3058, Macau, April 1999. Publication by Chinese Journal of Advanced Software Research in 2000.

90. Bing Liu. Intelligent Air Travel and Tourist Information Systems. In *8th International Conference on Industrial and Engineering Applications of Artificial Intelligence and Expert Systems*. ACM, 1995.

91. Z. Liu and M. Joseph. Specification and Verification of Fault-Tolerance, Timing, and Scheduling. *ACM Transactions on Programming Languages and Systems*, 21(1), 1999.

92. G. Lowe. Breaking and fixing the Needham-Schroeder public-key protocol using FDR. *Software Concepts and Tools*, 17:93–102, 1996.

93. M.Alexis, M.Nick, and G.George. Intelligent Software Agents in Travel Reservation Systems. Technical report, Imperial College of Science Technology and Medicine Departments of Computing and Electronic Engineering, 1997.

94. A. Mili, Sherif Yacoub, E. Addy, and H. Mili. Towards an Engineering Discipline of Software Reuse. *IEEE Software*, October 1999.

95. H. Mili, F. Mili, and A. Mili. Reusing Software: Issues and Research Directions. *IEEE Transactions on Software Engineering*, 21(6):528–561, June 1995.

96. R.E. Milne. The Formal Basis for the RAISE Specification Language. In *Semantics of Specification Languages*, Workshops in Computing. Springer-Verlag, 1993.

97. R. Milner. *Communication and Concurrency*. Prentice Hall, 1989.

98. Robin Milner, Mads Tofte, Robert Harper, and David MacQueen. *The Definition of Standard ML — Revised*. MIT Press, 1997.

99. Richard Moore. The MultiScript Project: Multi-directional, Multilingual Script Processing. In *Proceedings: 16th International Unicode Conference*, Amsterdam, Netherlands, March 27–30 2000.

100. Richard Moore and Luis Reynoso. A Precise Specification of GoF Behavioural Patterns. In *Proceedings of the ACIS 2nd International Conference on Software Engineering, Artificial Intelligence, Networking & Parallel/Distributed Computing: SNPD'01*, pages 262–270, Nagoya, Japan, August 2001.

101. Peter D. Mosses. CASL: A Guided Tour of its Design. In J. L. Fiadeiro, editor, *Recent Trends in Algebraic Development Techniques, Proc. 13th International Workshop, WADT '98, Lisbon, 1998, Selected Papers*, volume 1589 of *LNCS*, pages 216–240. Springer-Verlag, 1999.

102. Erdenechimeg Myatav and Richard Moore. Encoding and Implementation Issues in Standardising Traditional Mongolian Script. In *Sixteenth International Unicode Conference, Amsterdam, The Netherlands: Conference Proceedings Part 1*, page Section B2. The Unicode Consortium, 2000.

103. Yumbayar Namsrai and Richard Moore. MultiScript II: Displaying and Printing Multi-lingual Documents. Technical Report 112, UNU/IIST, P.O.Box 3058, Macau, June 1997. A part of the work has been presented at and published in the proceedings of the Workshop on the *Principles of Digital Document Processing*, March 1998, St. Malo, France, Ethan V. Munson, Charles Nicholas and Derick Wood (Eds), volume 1481 of *LNCS*. Springer Verlag, 1998, pages 70 - 81.

104. Yumbayar Namsrai, Richard Moore, and Myatav Erdenechimeg. On the Use of Control Symbols in the Mongolian Script Encoding. Technical report, UNU/IIST, January 1997. Presented at Meeting No. 32 of ISO/IEC JTC1 SC2 WG2 (Universal Multiple-Octet Coded Character Set), Singapore, 20–24 January, 1997.

105. Shirnen Nyambaa, Ishdorj Tseren-Onolt, and Richard Moore. A Management System for University Teaching. Technical Report 177, UNU/IIST, P.O. Box 3058, Macau, September 1999.

106. Swiss Society of Cartography. *Cartographic generalisation*. Number 2 in Cartographic Publications. SGK-Publikationen, Zurich, 1987.

107. Adegboyega Ojo and Tomasz Janowski. Formalising Distributed Business Processes. Technical Report 240, UNU/IIST, P.O. Box 3058, Macau, August 2001. Presented at and published in the proceedings of the 2nd International Workshop on Conceptual Modeling Approaches for e-Business (ECOMO2001), Yokohama, Japan, November 2001, Springer Verlag.

108. Pak Jong Ok, Ri Hyon Sul, and Chris George. A Management System for a University Library. Technical Report 186, UNU/IIST, P.O. Box 3058, Macau, February 2000.

109. Pak Jong Ok, Ri Hyon Sul, and Chris George. Translating RSL on Unix and porting to a PC. Technical Report UNESCO/1, UNU/IIST, February 2000.

110. John K. Ousterhout. Scripting: Higher-Level Programming for the 21st Century. *IEEE*, pages 23–30, March 1998.

111. Sam Owre, John Rushby, Natarajan Shankar, and Friedrich von Henke. Formal verification for fault-tolerant architectures: Prologomena to the design of PVS. *IEEE Transactions on Software Engineering*, 21(2):107–125, February 1995.

112. L.C. Paulsen. Inductive Analysis of the Internet Protocol TLS. Technical Report 440, Computer Laboratory, University of Cambridge, England, December 1997.

113. Lawrence C. Paulson. The Inductive Approach to Verifying Cryptographic Protocols. *J. Computer Security*, 1998.

114. C. Pfister and C. Szyperski. Why Objects are not Enough. In *Int. Component Users Conference, Munich, Germany*, 1996.

115. G.D. Plotkin. A structured approach to operational semantics. Technical report, University of Edinburgh, 1981.

116. The RAISE Language Group. *The RAISE Specification Language*. BCS Practitioner Series. Prentice Hall, 1992. Available from Terma A/S. Contact jnp@terma.com.

117. The RAISE Method Group. *The RAISE Development Method*. BCS Practitioner Series. Prentice Hall, 1995. Available by ftp from `ftp://ftp.iist.unu.edu/pub/RAISE/method_book`.

118. Luis Reynoso and Richard Moore. GoF Behavioural Patterns: A Formal Specification. Technical Report 201, UNU/IIST, P.O. Box 3058, Macau, May 2000. Presented at and published in the proceedings of the ACIS 2nd International Conference on Software Engineering, Artificial Intelligence, Networking & Parallel/Distributed Computing (SNPD'01), Nagoya, Japan, August 2001, pp. 262–270.

119. D. Richardson, O. O'Malley, and C. Tittle. Approaches to Specification-Based Testing. In *ACM Symposium on Software Testing, Analysis and Verification*, 1989.

120. Dirk Riehle. Composite Design Patterns. In *Object-Oriented Programming Systems, Languages, and Applications (OOPSLA'97) Conference Proceedings*, volume 32, pages 218–228, October 1997. ACM Sigplan Notices.

121. A.D. Robbins. *Efective AWK Programming*. Free Software Foundation, 1989.

122. A. W. Roscoe. Modelling and verifying key-exchange protocols using CSP and FDR. In *Proceedings of 8th IEEE Computer Security Foundations Workshop*. IEEE Computer Society Press, 1995.

123. J. Rumbaugh. *Object-Oriented Modeling and Design*. Prentice Hall, 1991.

124. Donald Sannella and Andrzej Tarlecki. Essential Concepts of Algebraic Specification and Program Development. *Formal Aspects of Computing*, 9:229–269, 1997.

125. A.W. Scheer. *ARIS – Business Process Frameworks*. Springer Verlag, 1998.

126. R.D. Schlichting and F.B. Schneider. Fail Stop Processors: An Approach to Designing Fault-Tolerant Computing Systems. *ACM Transactions on Computer Systems*, 1(3):222–238, 1983.

127. I. J. Schmidt. *Grammatik der mongolischen Sprache*. 1831.

128. Beth Schroeder. On-Line Monitoring: A Tutorial. *IEEE Computer*, pages 72–78, June 1995.

129. Friedrich Wilhelm Schroër. *The GENTLE Compiler Construction System*. R. Oldenbourg, 1997. Available from http://www.first.gmd.de/gentle/.

130. Nitesh Shrestha and Tomasz Janowski. Model-Based Travel Planning. Technical Report 219, UNU/IIST, P.O. Box 3058, Macau, November 2000.

131. J. M. Spivey. *The Z Notation: A Reference Manual*. Prentice Hall International Series in Computer Science, 2nd edition, 1992.

132. Anthony Steed et al. The London Travel Demonstrator. In *Virtual Reality Software and Technology*. ACM, December 1999.

133. Toshiyuki Tanaka and Chris George. Proving Properties of a Security Protocol Specified in RSL. Technical Report 143, UNU/IIST, P.O.Box 3058, Macau, August 1998. A paper in Japanese based on this work is being published by IPSJ-SIGMPS (Information Processing Society of Japan - SIG in Mathematical modeling and Problem Solving).

134. Ngo Quoc Tao. A Formal Specification of Realm – Spatial Data Type. Research Report 71, UNU/IIST, P.O.Box 3058, Macau, April 1996.

135. M. Torrens and B. Faltings. SmartClients: Constraint Satisfaction as a Paradigm for Scaleable Intelligent Information System. In *Workshop: Artificial Intelligence for Electronic Commerce (AAAI-00)*. AAAI Press, 1999.

136. Paolo Traverso and Piergiorgio Bertoli. Mechanized Result Verification: an Industrial Application. In *Workshop on Run-Time Result Verification, Federated Logic Conference, Trento, Italy*, 1999.

137. Stephen Turner. Analog. http://www.statslab.cam.ac.uk, Nov. 1999.

138. W.M.P. van der Aalst. Workflow Verification: Finding Control-Flow Errors using Petri-net-based Techniques. In *Business Process Management: Models, Techniques, and Empirical Studies*, volume 1806 of *LNCS*, pages 161–183. Springer Verlag, 2000.

139. F.B. Vernadat. *Enterprise Modeling and Integration*. Chapman and Hall, 1996.

140. J. L. Vivas. Design of Telephony Services in Lotos. Technical Report T94/03, SICS, March 22, 1994.

141. John Vlissides. Composite Design Patterns (They Aren't What You Think). C++ Report, June 1998. http://www.research.ibm.com/people/v/vlis/pubs.html.

142. John Vlissides. Pluggable Factory, Part I. C++ Report, November-December 1998. http://www.research.ibm.com/people/v/vlis/pubs.html.

143. John Vlissides. Pluggable Factory, Part II. C++ Report, February 1999. http://www.research.ibm.com/people/v/vlis/pubs.html.

144. T.E. Vollmann. *Manufacturing, Planning and Control Systems*. Irwin, 1992.

145. M. Voorhoeve. Compositional Modeling and Verification of Workflow Processes. In *Business Process Management: Models, Techniques, and Empirical Studies*, volume 1806 of *LNCS*, pages 184–200. Springer Verlag, 2000.

146. David Wagner and Bruce Schneier. Analysis of the SSL 3.0 protocol. On the internet at http://www.cs.berkeley.edu/~daw/ssl3.0.ps, 1996.

147. Hal Wasserman and Manuel Blum. Software Reliability via Run-Time Result-Checking. *Journal of the ACM*, 44(6):826–849, 1997.

148. Ke Wei and Chris George. An RSL to SML Translator. Technical Report 208, UNU/IIST, P.O. Box 3058, Macau, August 2000.

149. H. Werthner and R. Carter, editors. *Open Issues and Challenges in IT and Tourism, IFITT White Paper*. International Federation for Information Technology and Tourism, September 1998. http://www.ifitt.org/.

150. WFMC. Terminology and Glossary. Technical Report WFMC-TC-1011, Workflow Management Coalition, 1999.

151. David Wile and Christopher Ramming. Domain-Specific Languages, Special Issue. *IEEE TSE*, 25(3), 1999.

152. J.C.P. Woodcock and M. Loomes. *Software Engineering Mathematics*. Pitman Publishing, London, 1988.

153. Wu Xiaojun and Richard Moore. Specification of a University Personnel Management System. Technical Report 193, UNU/IIST, P.O. Box 3058, Macau, April 2000.

154. L. Zadeh. Soft Computing and Fuzzy Logic. *IEEE Software*, 11(6):48–56, November 1994.

155. Amy M. Zaremski. *Signature and Specification Matching*. Phd thesis in computer science, School of Computer Science, Carnegie Mellon University, 1996.

156. Jin Zhendong and Richard Moore. Specification of Software Systems for Managing Student Accommodation and a Research Laboratory Network. Technical Report 194, UNU/IIST, P.O. Box 3058, Macau, April 2000.